# Lecture Notes in Computer Science    11333

*Commenced Publication in 1973*
Founding and Former Series Editors:
Gerhard Goos, Juris Hartmanis, and Jan van Leeuwen

More information about this series at http://www.springer.com/series/7407

Hermes Senger · Osni Marques ·
Rogerio Garcia · Tatiana Pinheiro de Brito ·
Rogério Iope · Silvio Stanzani ·
Veronica Gil-Costa (Eds.)

# High Performance Computing for Computational Science – VECPAR 2018

13th International Conference
São Pedro, Brazil, September 17–19, 2018
Revised Selected Papers

 Springer

*Editors*
Hermes Senger (iD)
Federal University of São Carlos
São Carlos, São Paulo, Brazil

Rogerio Garcia (iD)
Universidade Estadual Paulista Júlio
de Mesquita Filho
Presidente Prudente, São Paulo, Brazil

Rogério Iope
Universidade Estadual Paulista Júlio
de Mesquita Filho
São Paulo, São Paulo, Brazil

Veronica Gil-Costa
Universidad Nacional de San Luis
San Luis, Argentina

Osni Marques
Lawrence Berkeley National Laboratory
Berkeley, CA, USA

Tatiana Pinheiro de Brito
Universidade Estadual Paulista Júlio
de Mesquita Filho
São Paulo, São Paulo, Brazil

Silvio Stanzani
Universidade Estadual Paulista Júlio
de Mesquita Filho
São Paulo, São Paulo, Brazil

ISSN 0302-9743          ISSN 1611-3349  (electronic)
Lecture Notes in Computer Science
ISBN 978-3-030-15995-5       ISBN 978-3-030-15996-2   (eBook)
https://doi.org/10.1007/978-3-030-15996-2

Library of Congress Control Number: 2019934743

LNCS Sublibrary: SL1 – Theoretical Computer Science and General Issues

This Springer imprint is published by the registered company Springer Nature Switzerland AG
The registered company address is: Gewerbestrasse 11, 6330 Cham, Switzerland

# Preface

The International Meeting on High-Performance Computing for Computational Science (VECPAR) is a biannual conference and a major venue for the presentation and discussion of the latest research and practice in high-end computer modeling and complex systems. The audience and participants of VECPAR are researchers and students in academic departments, government laboratories, and industrial organizations. There is a permanent website for the conference series at http://vecpar.fe.up.pt, maintained by the Faculty of Engineering of the University of Porto.

The 13th edition of VECPAR was organized in São Pedro, Brazil, during September 17–19, 2018. Previous editions of VECPAR were held in Porto (Portugal, 2016), Oregon (USA, 2014), Kobe (Japan, 2012), Berkeley (USA, 2010), Toulose (France, 2008), Rio de Janeiro (Brazil, 2006), Valencia (Spain, 2004), and Porto (Portugal, 2002, 2000, 1998, 1996 and 1993).

This edition of VECPAR had a very exciting program with 17 full papers accepted, one short paper, and two posters, contributed by authors from 15 different countries. The acceptance rate was 53%, repeating the pattern of previous editions.

We had a varied selection of papers, with major themes covering heterogeneous systems, shared memory systems and GPUs, and techniques including domain decomposition, scheduling and load balancing, with a strong focus on computational science applications.

To enrich the conference, we had five keynote presentations:

- Gabriel Wainer (Carleton University), "Simulation Everywhere"
- Richard Vuduc (Georgia Institute of Technology), "An Algorithm, a Data Structure, and a Machine That All (Try to) Move or Store Fewer Bits"
- Kentaro Sano (R-CCS, RIKEN), "FPGA-Based Data-Flow Computing for High-Performance Numerical Simulation"
- Tal Ben-Num (ETH Zurich), "Demystifying Parallel and Distributed Deep Learning"
- Gerard Gorman (Imperial College), "Code Generation for Finite Difference and Data Inversion – Where Angles Fear to Thread"

VECPAR 2018 also held a panel discussion focused on the convergence of HPC and AI in the context of science and industry. The invited panelists were: Dr. Pedro Cruz (NVIDIA, Brazil), Dra. Carla Oshtoff (LNCC, Brazil), Dr. Edson Borin (Unicamp, Brazil), Dr. Eduardo Michelis (LNLS, Brazil), and Dr. Gerard Gorman (Imperial College, UK). The panel was moderated by Dr. Osni Marques (LBNL, USA).

The social program of the conference included a welcome reception party with local specialties in the evening of the first day, and a fantastic gala dinner with live music at the end of the second day.

The most significant contributions to VECPAR 2018 are made available in the present book, edited after the conference and after a second review of all accepted papers that were presented. The paper submission and selection were managed via the EasyChair conference management system.

The success of the VECPAR conference and its long life are a result of the collaboration of many people. In particular, for their contribution to the present book, we would like to thank all the authors for their work and for meeting the tight deadlines, and all members of the Scientific Committee for their commitment and invaluable contribution in the selection of papers.

January 2019

Hermes Senger
Osni Marques
Rogerio Garcia
Tatiana Pinheiro
Rogério Iope
Silvio Stanzani
Veronica Gil-Costa

# Organization

VECPAR 2018, the 13th edition of the VECPAR series of conferences, was organized by Universidade Estadual Paulista Júlio de Mesquita Filho, UNESP (Brazil), Universidade Federal de São Carlos, UFSCar (Brazil), Universidade do Porto (Portugal), and Universidad Nacional de San Luis (Argentina).

## Executive Committee

| | |
|---|---|
| Hermes Senger | Federal University of São Carlos, Brazil |
| Inês Dutra | University of Porto, Portugal |
| Osni Marques | LBL, USA |
| Rogerio Garcia | UNESP, Brazil |
| Tatiana Pinheiro | UNESP, Brazil |
| Rogério Iope | UNESP, Brazil |
| Silvio Stanzani | UNESP, Brazil |
| Veronica Gil-Costa | UNSL, Argentina |

## Steering Committee

| | |
|---|---|
| Osni Marques (Chair) | Lawrence Berkeley National Laboratory, USA |
| Alvaro Coutinho | COPPE/UFRJ, Brazil |
| Michel Daydé | ENSEEIHT, France |
| Jack Dongarra | University of Tennessee, USA |
| Inês Dutra | University of Porto, Portugal |
| Kengo Nakajima | University of Tokyo, Japan |
| Sameer Shende | University of Oregon, USA |

## Scientific Committee

A. Augusto Sousa, Portugal
Abdelkader Hameurlain, France
Akihiro Ida, Japan
Akihiro Fujii, Japan
Alberto Proenca, Portugal
Aleardo Manacero, Brazil
Alex Breuer, USA
Alexandre Sena, Brazil
Alexey Lastovetsky. Ireland
Alfredo Goldman, Brazil
Alonso Inostrosa Psijas, Chile
Alvaro Coutinho, Brazil

Antonio J.Tomeu-Hardasmal, Spain
Calebe Bianchini, Brazil
Carla Osthoff Barros, Brazil
Carlos Alvarez, Colombia
Claudio Amorim, Brazil
Claudio Geyer, Brazil
Cristina Boeres, Brazil
Daniel Cordeiro, Brazil
Daniel Kressner, Switzerland
Doallo Ramón, Spain
Dolores Rexachs, Spain
Edson Borin, Brazil

## Sponsoring Institutions

The São Paulo Funding Agency - FAPESP
Springer International Publishing
Huawei do Brasil Telecomunicações and Vivo Open Cloud
Hewlett Packard Enterprise and Intel Semicondutores do Brasil
Agência UNESP de Inovação and Santander Universidades
Research Centre for Gas Innovation, The University of São Paulo (USP)

## Platinum Sponsors

## Gold Sponsors

## Bronze Sponsor

## Funding Agency

## Supporters

**Organized by**

# Contents

**Regular Papers**

Communication–Free Parallel Mesh Multiplication for Large
Scale Simulations ........................................... 3
*Rômulo M. Silva, Benaia S. J. Lima, José J. Camata, Renato N. Elias,*
*and Alvaro L. G. A. Coutinho*

Dynamic Configuration of CUDA Runtime Variables for CDP-Based
Divide-and-Conquer Algorithms ................................. 16
*Tiago Carneiro, Jan Gmys, Nouredine Melab,*
*Francisco Heron de Carvalho Junior, Pedro Pedrosa Rebouças Filho,*
*and Daniel Tuyttens*

Design, Implementation and Performance Analysis of a CFD Task-Based
Application for Heterogeneous CPU/GPU Resources .................. 31
*Lucas Leandro Nesi, Lucas Mello Schnorr,*
*and Philippe Olivier Alexandre Navaux*

Optimizing Packed String Matching on AVX2 Platform............... 45
*Mehmet Akif Aydoğmuş and M. Oğuzhan Külekci*

A GPU-Based Metaheuristic for Workflow Scheduling on Clouds........ 62
*Elliod Cieza, Luan Teylo, Yuri Frota, Cristiana Bentes,*
*and Lúcia M. A. Drummond*

A Systematic Mapping on High-Performance Computing for Protein
Structure Prediction.......................................... 77
*Gesiel Rios Lopes, Paulo Sergio Lopes de Souza,*
*and Alexandre C. B. Delbem*

Performance Evaluation of Deep Learning Frameworks over
Different Architectures....................................... 92
*Rafael Gauna Trindade, João Vicente Ferreira Lima,*
*and Andrea Schwerner Charão*

Non-uniform Domain Decomposition for Heterogeneous Accelerated
Processing Units............................................. 105
*Gabriel Freytag, Philippe Olivier Alexandre Navaux,*
*João Vicente Ferreira Lima, Lucas Mello Schnorr, and Paolo Rech*

Performance Evaluation of Two Load Balancing Algorithms
for Hybrid Clusters . . . . . . . . . . . . . . . . . . . . . . . . . . . . . . . . . . . . . . . .    119
    *Tiago Marques do Nascimento, Rodrigo Weber dos Santos,
    and Marcelo Lobosco*

An Improved OpenMP Implementation of the TVD–Hopmoc Method
Based on a Cluster of Points . . . . . . . . . . . . . . . . . . . . . . . . . . . . . . . . . .    132
    *Frederico Cabral, Carla Osthoff, Roberto Pinto Souto,
    Gabriel P. Costa, Sanderson L. Gonzaga de Oliveira,
    Diego N. Brandão, and Mauricio Kischinhevsky*

A Scheduling Theory Framework for GPU Tasks Efficient Execution . . . . . .    146
    *Antonio-Jose Lázaro-Muñoz, Bernabé López-Albelda,
    Jose María González-Linares, and Nicolás Guil*

A Timer-Augmented Cost Function for Load Balanced DSMC . . . . . . . . . . .    160
    *William McDoniel and Paolo Bientinesi*

Accelerating Scientific Applications on Heterogeneous Systems
with HybridOMP . . . . . . . . . . . . . . . . . . . . . . . . . . . . . . . . . . . . . . . . . . .    174
    *Matthias Diener, Daniel J. Bodony, and Laxmikant Kale*

A New Parallel Benchmark for Performance Evaluation
and Energy Consumption . . . . . . . . . . . . . . . . . . . . . . . . . . . . . . . . . . . . . .    188
    *Adriano Marques Garcia, Claudio Schepke,
    Alessandro Gonçalves Girardi, and Sherlon Almeida da Silva*

Bigger Buffer k-d Trees on Multi-Many-Core Systems. . . . . . . . . . . . . . . .    202
    *Fabian Gieseke, Cosmin Eugen Oancea, Ashish Mahabal,
    Christian Igel, and Tom Heskes*

A Parallel Generator of Non-Hermitian Matrices Computed
from Given Spectra . . . . . . . . . . . . . . . . . . . . . . . . . . . . . . . . . . . . . . . . . .    215
    *Xinzhe Wu, Serge G. Petiton, and Yutong Lu*

LRMalloc: A Modern and Competitive Lock-Free Dynamic
Memory Allocator. . . . . . . . . . . . . . . . . . . . . . . . . . . . . . . . . . . . . . . . . . .    230
    *Ricardo Leite and Ricardo Rocha*

**Short Paper**

Towards a Strategy for Performance Prediction
on Heterogeneous Architectures . . . . . . . . . . . . . . . . . . . . . . . . . . . . . . . .    247
    *Silvio Stanzani, Raphael Cóbe, Jefferson Fialho, Rogério Iope,
    Marco Gomes, Artur Baruchi, and Júlio Amaral*

**Posters**[*]

HPC for Predictive Models in Healthcare . . . . . . . . . . . . . . . . . . . . . . . .   257
  *Luiz Fernando Capretz*

A Methodology for Batching Matrix Kernels in HPC Applications . . . . . . . .   259
  *Hans  Johansen and Osni Marques*

**Author Index** . . . . . . . . . . . . . . . . . . . . . . . . . . . . . . . . . . . . . . . . . . .   263

---

[*] The posters are not visible as papers in the online version of the proceedings, they are included in the back matter.

# Regular Papers

# Communication–Free Parallel Mesh Multiplication for Large Scale Simulations

Rômulo M. Silva[1], Benaia S. J. Lima[1], José J. Camata[2], Renato N. Elias[1], and Alvaro L. G. A. Coutinho[1(✉)]

[1] High Performance Computing Center and Civil Engineering Department, COPPE/Federal University of Rio de Janeiro, Rio de Janeiro, Brazil
{romulo.silva,benaia,renato,alvaro}@nacad.ufrj.br
[2] Department of Computer Science, Federal University of Juiz de Fora, Juiz de Fora, Brazil
camata@ice.ufjf.br

**Abstract.** Often unstructured grid methods, such as finite elements, are used in high fidelity simulations. In these methods, solution accuracy is associated to the interpolation order and to the grid size. Unstructured parallel mesh refinement is computationally expensive due to subdomains interface communication. In the present work we develop a uniform edge-based parallel tetrahedral mesh refinement scheme completely free of communication, fast, simple to implement and highly scalable. This is achieved by an index generation for subdomain interface grid points based on special pairing functions.

**Keywords:** Parallel mesh refinement · Edge-based data structures · Pairing functions

## 1 Introduction

Computational power has been growing in the last decades, and scientists have now the ability to run simulations on unstructured meshes with billions of elements. However, building such large meshes is still a cumbersome task even in today's largest computers and parallel mesh generation represents an open and active research topic. During adaptive mesh refinement, a base mesh is refined according to some metric which guides in what regions elements must be refined or coarsened [7]. In a parallel environment, this process usually leads to unbalanced mesh partitions. Elements and nodes must be exchanged among processes to recover a nearly uniform mesh distribution per processor. This operation relies on message passing, often at a high computational cost. Mesri *et al.* [20], for instance, proposes to keep parallel interfaces unchanged, during local re-meshing, and leave interface refinements for a later phase to reduce communication costs. Another common issue in parallel adaptive mesh refinement is keeping track of mesh entities shared among processes. These entities are responsible for synchronizing the solution for the whole mesh, making it consistent, and

H. Senger et al. (Eds.): VECPAR 2018, LNCS 11333, pp. 3–15, 2019.
https://doi.org/10.1007/978-3-030-15996-2_1

are also used during the solution phase in point–to–point (usually non-blocking) message passing [9].

Bauman and Stogner in [3] present a review of parallel adaptive software libraries. In particular they discuss MOOSE [11], FEniCS [19], deal.II [2] and libMesh [15]. In their paper, they propose GRINS, a framework built on top of libMesh to support multiphysics applications. In particular, libMesh does mesh partitioning through interfaces to several packages, including Hilbert space-filling curves and graph-based algorithms such as Metis and ParMetis [10]. GRINS and MOOSE also share the same mesh partitioning and adaptive strategies of libMesh. Currently libMesh scales to hundreds of thousands of cores [3]. Bangerth *et al.* in [1] extended the open source deal.II library functionality, offering the ability to solve finite element problems on fully adaptive meshes with billions of cells and several billion unknowns. *p4est* [6] library is used to efficiently generate and partition hierarchically refined meshes on several thousands of cores. It also provides information on the distributed nature of the mesh through a well-defined set of queries and executes directives to coarsen, refine, and re-partition the mesh. *P4est* is based on avoiding global communication wherever possible in favor of gather/scatter and point–to–point operations.

A different approach for quickly building large-scale parallel meshes is based on uniform element subdivision, a technique usually called mesh multiplication [12,27,28]. In this method, each element of the original coarse mesh is subdivided into smaller elements following a common pattern for the entire mesh. Figure 1 shows how this process applies to a single tetrahedron being divided into eight smaller ones. By applying the same subdivision for all mesh elements, a new and finer mesh, eight times larger is created. The process can be applied hierarchically creating different refinement levels and could also be extended to other elements. The benefit of such approach is that element creation is known a priori and follows a constant pattern. Therefore, distributed parallel processes may apply the same algorithm independently. However, as the interface among processes is also subdivided, new shared mesh entities (nodes, edges, and element faces for instance) are created and must be accounted for in the refinement process. It is well known that the main computational cost from parallel adaptive mesh refinement comes from keeping this shared entities consistent [2,15,19]. These operations are usually performed with the help of a dual or nodal graph, storing the neighborhood structure of each parallel process and mesh partitions [22], and must be updated as new nodes and elements are created due to the refinement process. Moreover, in the mesh multiplication method, the finer mesh preserves the original element distribution and, consequently, the refinement pattern of the original coarser mesh.

Mesh multiplication methods found in the literature still relies on communication when the parallel interface is modified due to element refinements. In [12], the array holding nodes, that must be communicated during the solution phase, is updated to take into account new nodes created at the parallel interface. In [28], a linked list holding information about parallel edges, local and global indexes is built and communicated using specialized routines developed by the authors. Kabelikova *et al.* in [13], also reports the need for communicating data across parallel interfaces to re-index global nodes.

In this work, we propose a fast tetrahedral mesh multiplication technique. Although general, it can be used as a standalone procedure or incorporated into an unstructured grid multiphysics solver [21]. The proposed method is based on a uniform tetrahedral mesh refinement scheme applying recursively edge bisection (also called Bey's refinement [4]). The method is very fast and does not require any communication among processes. This is achieved by applying a particular pairing function to create unique indexes for globally shared mesh entities. The method is tested and produces unstructured meshes with billions of elements very quickly. The remainder of this paper is organized as follows. In the next section, we describe the mesh multiplication scheme. Test cases are shown in the sequel, and the paper ends with a summary of our main conclusions.

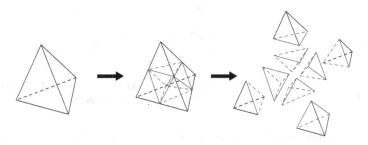

**Fig. 1.** Tetrahedral splitting  (Bey's refinement [4])

## 2    Mesh Multiplication Method

The process of applying uniform mesh refinement is straightforward and based on the element splitting pattern shown in Fig. 1 for linear tetrahedra. This scheme was introduced in Bey [4]. New nodal coordinates are created by applying edges bisection. Each edge will give rise to a new node with local *id* computed as $edge_i + nn_p$, where $edge_i$ is the *id* of the edge and $nn_p$ is the number of nodes in partition $p$.

### 2.1    Communication Map

Based on how the communication map is built, now, we must find a way to keep it updated and consistent while creating new nodes, due to the refinement process. Moreover, it is desirable that the proposed method can avoid communication. Indeed, as we shall see, the proposed method does not require any communication at all. The problem is illustrated in Fig. 2 where new nodes are created after bisection of the parallel edge shared by three partitions. New *lids* are freely created by each process, as previously explained. However, as these nodes are the same in the global problem, a unique *gid* must be computed by the different processes. Therefore, we must find a way to create new global *ids* that are unique across shared partitions, ideally, without having to exchange information among processors. To create these new *gids*, we propose the application of *pairing functions*. By definition, a pairing function is a bijection $f : \mathbb{N} \times \mathbb{N} \to \mathbb{N}$ where $f$ is strictly monotone in each argument such that: $\forall i, j \in \mathbb{N} \Rightarrow f(i,j) < f(i+1,j)$ and $f(i,j) < f(i,j+1)$ are true [23].

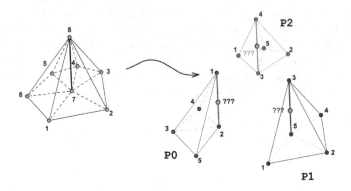

**Fig. 2.** Problem definition: creating new global ids. Original mesh with global numbering on left and mesh split in three parts with local numbering

Pairing bijection functions have the property to map two natural numbers onto a single one. Its inverse, $f^{-1}$, is called *unpairing functions*. They were made popular after Cantor's work in the second half of the 19th century on set theory [26] and are used in the theory of recursive functions, multidimensional dynamic arrays, network mapping, indexing and proximity search using space-filling curves [16,17], computational systems, among many other applications. Pairing bijection functions may be constructed to fulfill specific requirements. In Rosenberg [23] and Tarau [26] the authors discuss different methods for creating these functions. However, consider the classical Cantor pairing function, defined by: $f(i,j) = (i+j)(i+j+1)/2+i$, which assigns consecutive numbers to points along diagonals in the plane, as shown in Fig. 3(a), this function can be applied for building new global *ids* during the refinement process. For this purpose, global *ids* for nodes $i$ and $j$ of parallel edges, are paired to create a new global *id*. Note that, since Cantor's function is a bijection, the inverse operation is possible and nodes $i$ and $j$ could be recovered at any time by solving:

$$k = f(i,j)$$
$$w = \left\lfloor \frac{\sqrt{8k+1}-1}{2} \right\rfloor$$
$$t = \frac{w^2 + w}{2} \tag{1}$$
$$j = k - t$$
$$i = w - j$$

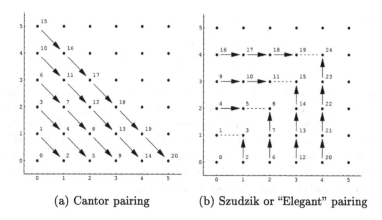

(a) Cantor pairing          (b) Szudzik or "Elegant" pairing

**Fig. 3.** Pairing bijection functions for mapping two natural numbers into a single one (from [25])

Although Cantor's pairing function supplies a straightforward way for building new global *ids*, we shall discuss its limitations when used in a computer program. Note that, if we take two 16-bits integer numbers, ranging from 0 to $2^{16} - 1$, there will be $2^{16} \times 2^{16} - 1$ possible combinations and, from the Pigeonhole principle, an output of size $2^{16} \times (2^{16} - 1)$ which equals to $2^{32} \times 2^{16}$ will be necessary. In other words, a successful pairing function from two 16-bits integer would require, at least, a 32-bits integer as output[1]. Therefore, for practical purposes in large-scale simulations, a good pairing function should be capable of mapping the largest index values possible within the range of the output number representation. Now, we check this assumption for Cantor's pairing function. For this purpose, consider the pair $\langle 65535; 65535 \rangle$, of the largest unsigned 16-bit integers. It returns 8589803520 when paired by Cantor's function, which is a number greater than the largest unsigned 32-bits integer ($2^{32}$) and, consequently, limits its use for our purposes. To overcome this limitation, we have adopted the Szudzik's or "Elegant" pairing bijection presented in [25] and expressed by

$$f(i,j) = \begin{cases} j^2 + i & i \neq \max(i,j) \\ i^2 + i + j & i = \max(i,j) \end{cases} \tag{2}$$

This function assigns consecutive numbers to points along the edges of squares as shown in Fig. 3(b). With Szudzik's function, mapping $\langle 65535; 65535 \rangle$ results in 4294967295 which is smaller than the largest 32-bits unsigned integer. Therefore, Szudzik's function is more space efficient than Cantor's function. Indeed, if we take the sequence corresponding to the paired values along the diagonal $(i = j)$ (Fig. 3) we find out:

$$\text{Cantor}: 0, 4, 12, 40, ..., n \Rightarrow a_n^C = 2(n+1)n \tag{3}$$

$$\text{Szudzik}: 0, 3, 8, 15, ..., n \Rightarrow a_n^S = n^2 - 1 \tag{4}$$

---

[1] Discussion originally initiated at http://stackoverflow.com/questions/919612/mapping-two-integers-to-one-in-a-unique-and-deterministic-way.

and if we take

$$\lim_{x \to \infty} \frac{a_n^C}{a_n^S} = \frac{2}{n-1} + 2 \to 2 \tag{5}$$

thus, the mapping produced by Cantor's function grows twice as fast as Szudzik's, justifying our choice. Applying Szudzik's pairing function to *gids* 7 and 8 in Fig. 4 will return 71 in all processors and the new *gid* can be inserted in the updated communication map consistently. It is important to clarify that *gids*, in our implementation, have two main purposes: (a) to preserve parallel nodes uniqueness and (b) to provide a way to sort them in the communication map so as data transfer might happen consistently.

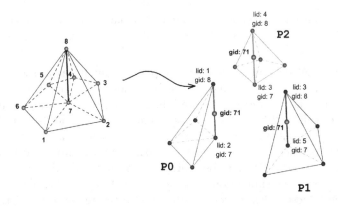

**Fig. 4.** Communication map: inserting new global ids

Another critical aspect in mesh multiplication is how elements quality is affected across refinement levels. For investigating mesh quality, we adopt the quality metric presented in [18] and expressed by:

$$Q_0 = \frac{72\sqrt{3}V^e}{\left(\sum_{i=1}^{6} l_i^2\right)^{2/3}} \tag{6}$$

where $V^e$ is the element volume, $l_i$ is the length of the local edge $i$ and $Q_0 \in ]0,1]$. Consider a regular tetrahedron, with $Q_0 = 1$, and formed by joining the opposite diagonals of a unity cube as shown in Fig. 5. In this figure, the "father" tetrahedron is formed by vertexes $n_1 = (1,0,0), n_2 = (0,1,0), n_3 = (0,0,1), n_4 = (1,1,1)$. After applying the subdivision pattern shown in Fig. 1, eight new tetrahedra will be formed. Four of them, formed by the corner vertexes, will preserve the father's quality, while the other four, formed by joining the newly created vertexes, will loose 23.64% of quality, resulting in $Q_0 = 0.7935$. This indicates that mesh multiplication degrades element quality across mesh refinement levels.

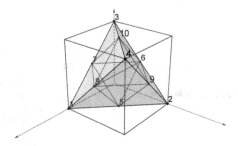

**Fig. 5.** Regular tetrahedron quality metric. $tet1234 \Rightarrow Q_0 = 1.0$

## 2.2 Assigning Processes to New Communication Nodes

The following question expresses another common issue that may appear in mesh multiplication methods: *how to correctly assign parallel partitions to nodes created at the communication interface?* As illustrated in Fig. 6, where a new node is created after bisection of edge $AB$. It is shown that nodes A and B are shared by partitions 0 (blue), 1 (red) and 2 (green), however, the new node created will only be part of partitions 1 and 2. It proves that this information can not be obtained from the intersection of the sets of processes shared by nodes $i$ and $j$ of an edge. Moreover, the sets of processes shared by edges would also lead to erroneous results since, in 3D, edges can be shared by an unknown number of elements. In other words, this information should not be built from mesh entities with a varying number of sharing processes such as nodes and edges. Therefore, we propose to assign processes to new communication nodes with the help of ghost (or halo) elements. A ghost elements for a partition $i$ is defined by the set of elements from other partitions that share information with $i$ and is illustrated in Fig. 7. Note that, for the problem of assigning processes to new parallel nodes, only elements sharing at least one edge with partition $i$ are required. This information is held by a data structure which is updated during the refinement process. Thus, ghost elements must also be refined following the same method described for regular elements.

## 2.3 Boundary Smoothing

The uniform refinement performed by the Mesh Multiplication method improves the approximation of the physical fields but keeps the boundary geometry the same as the coarse mesh. Thus, it is necessary to do a repositioning of the boundary nodes using a refined surface mesh (which is less expensive to generate than the volumetric mesh). The file format used to store the refined geometry is the VTK (**V**isualization **T**ool**K**it), which represents a mesh by using a set of nodal coordinates and incidences. To re-positioning the nodes, we need to look for the nearest neighbor node that lies in the refined geometry and project its distance vector on the normal direction of the node. However, without a domain partitioning technique, the search for nearest neighbors will cause overhead. We reduce the search overhead by using a data structure well known as KD-Tree [14].

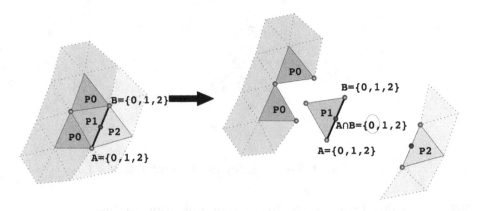

**Fig. 6.** Problem to assign processes to new communication nodes (left) New partition assigned from nodes A and B (right) $A \cap B$ returns wrong partition assignment, suggesting this information should not be inherited from edges (Color figure online)

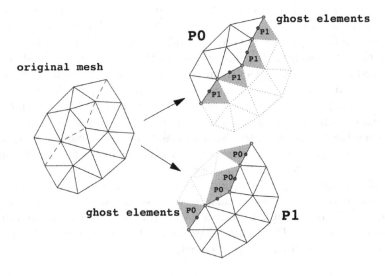

**Fig. 7.** Ghost elements for partitions 0 and 1

## 3 Test Case

### 3.1 YF-17 Mesh Multiplication

To evaluate the performance of the proposed method of parallel mesh multiplication, we consider the YF-17 aircraft model [8] shown in Fig. 8. The original mesh, (level 1) or "base mesh", formed by 528,915 elements, 639,846 edges, and 97,104 nodes is refined up to 2.2 billions of elements in 512 cores on Stampede. It was necessary 5 min (wall time) to perform four multiplication levels and reach

2.2 billion elements as shown in Table 1, where NElem is the number of elements (tetrahedra), NNodes the number of nodes (vertices) and NEdges the number of edges. A detail of the obtained surface mesh can be seen in Fig. 9. For the sake of simplicity of this scalability study, we discarded any improvements on the geometry as the mesh is refined. The lack of surface refinement also allows us to investigate element quality as we refine the mesh. The important issue in this scalability study is the index generation for the sub-domain boundaries and not the insertion of new points and faces to improve the object shape as we refine the mesh.

A strong scalability evaluation is performed considering 128, 256 and 512 cores and the results are listed in Table 2. As we may note, a superlinear speedup is achieved when using two and four times more processors for the same computational effort – to perform four parallel mesh multiplication sweeps and reach 2.2 billion elements. It turns out that this may be explained by (a) cache effects (b) unnecessary communication. Thus, as the processors do not require communication, if we distribute the mesh in a larger number of cores, the partitions will be smaller and more feasible to fit in lower and faster memory cache levels.

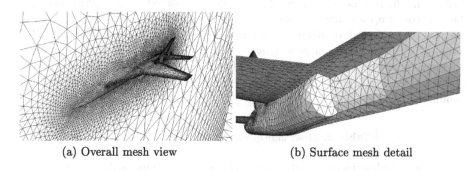

(a) Overall mesh view                    (b) Surface mesh detail

**Fig. 8.** YF17 ("Cobra") aircraft: original mesh, level 1

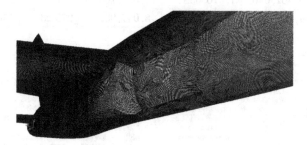

**Fig. 9.** Detail of the surface mesh for the 4th refinement level. Mesh with 2.2 billion of tetrahedra

**Table 1.** Time spent by refinement level (512 cores)

| Levels | NElem | NNodes | NEdges | Time (sec) |
|---|---|---|---|---|
| 1 | $528,915$ | $97,104$ | $719,744$ | 0.0 |
| 2 | $4,231,320$ | $3,579,392$ | $5,370,398$ | 2.99 |
| 3 | $33,850,560$ | $8,949,760$ | $41,470,464$ | 7.07 |
| 4 | $270,804,480$ | $50,420,224$ | $325,909,504$ | 21.44 |
| 5 | $2,166,535,840$ | $376,329,728$ | $2,584,090,624$ | 275.23 |

In Fig. 10 we evaluate the hot spots for the proposed method when running on 512 cores. For this purpose, the mesh multiplication scheme is instrumented by TAU (Tuning Analysis Utility) tool [24]. In this figure, routines are listed by inclusive time. The top consuming time routines are GetGlobalID and AddNode, both from ParallelNodesModule, a Fortran90 module responsible to manage the list of parallel nodes, storing the corresponding local ids of nodes and neighboring information. AddNode is called every time a new *lid* and corresponding *gid* is created. The new node is inserted in a linked list sorted by *gid*, which justifies the time consumption due to linked list traversal. GetGlobalID is called when, in the final stage of mesh multiplication, a new communication map is created. The kernel of this routine consists in traverse the list of global ids shared by each neighboring processor. Note that no MPI calls exist within MeshSubdivision module, what confirms that the proposed method is completely parallel and communication-free.

**Table 2.** Mesh multiplication strong scalability.

| Cores | NElem/Core | NNodes/Core | NEdges/Core | Time (sec) | Speedup |
|---|---|---|---|---|---|
| 128 | $16,925,280$ | $2,940,076$ | $20,188,208$ | 1237.74 | 1.00 |
| 256 | $8,462,640$ | $1,470,038$ | $10,094,104$ | 567.72 | 2.18 |
| 512 | $4,231,320$ | $735,019$ | $5,047,052$ | 275.23 | 4.50 |

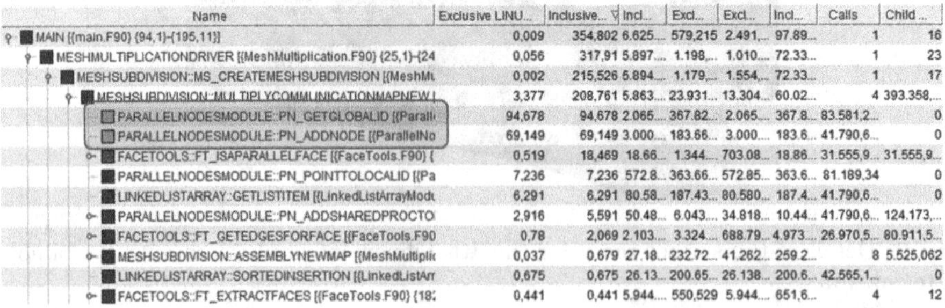

**Fig. 10.** Mesh multiplication hotspots for 512 cores and 4 refinement levels

Next, we examine the mesh quality at each refinement level. In Table 3, we show the element quality histogram computed using the metric given by Eq. 6. We may observe that most of the elements have $0.4 < Q_0 \leq 0.8$ and around 10% of them have low quality and 20% high quality. The element quality degradation between two levels of refinement with respect to the reference tetrahedron of Fig. 5 is shown in Table 4. We may see that the element quality deteriorates more than 25% in the worst case. Of course, mesh quality can be improved by using techniques presented, for instance, in the software package MESQUITE [5].

**Table 3.** Element quality histogram

| Level | $0.4 < Q_0$ | $0.4 < Q_0 \leq 0.8$ | $Q_0 > 0.8$ | NElem |
|---|---|---|---|---|
| 1 | $5,497$ | $251,392$ | $272,026$ | $528,915$ |
| 2 | $158,974$ | $2,572,928$ | $1,499,418$ | $4,231,320$ |
| 3 | $1,649,466$ | $21,871,860$ | $10,329,234$ | $33,850,560$ |
| 4 | $21,286,830$ | $178,223,742$ | $71,293,908$ | $270,804,480$ |
| 5 | $234,455,754$ | $1,433,010,008$ | $498,970,078$ | $2,166,435,840$ |

**Table 4.** Element quality degradation for one level refinement of the reference tetrahedron

| Level/Tet | $Q_0$ | Relative $Q_0$ |
|---|---|---|
| 1/1 | 0.7698 | |
| 2/1 | 0.7698 | 0% |
| 2/2 | 0.7698 | 0% |
| 2/3 | 0.7698 | 0% |
| 2/4 | 0.7698 | 0% |
| 2/5 | 0.6572 | −15% |
| 2/6 | 0.5697 | −26% |
| 2/7 | 0.5697 | −26% |
| 2/8 | 0.6572 | −15% |

## 4   Conclusions

In this paper, we have introduced a new parallel mesh multiplication scheme for unstructured grids composed by tetrahedra. The scheme involves no communication thanks to the index generation in each processor, which is based on the elegant pairing technique. Experimental results show the strong scalability of the scheme on generating an unstructured grid with 2 billion of tetrahedra. A hot spot analysis on 512 cores demonstrates that the whole process is communication-free.

**Acknowledgments.** This work is partially supported by CNPq and FAPERJ. Computer time is provided by the Texas Advanced Computer Center (TACC) at University of Texas at Austin. We acknowledge also the support of the European Commission (HPC4E H2020 project) and the Brazilian Ministry of Science, Technology, Innovation and Communications through Rede Nacional de Pesquisa (RNP) grant agreement no 689772.

# References

1. Bangerth, W., Burstedde, C., Heister, T., Kronbichler, M.: Algorithms and data structures for massively parallel generic adaptive finite element codes. ACM Trans. Math. Softw. (TOMS) **38**(2), 14 (2011)
2. Bangerth, W., Hartmann, R., Kanschat, G.: deal.II-a general-purpose object-oriented finite element library. ACM Trans. Math. Softw. (TOMS) **33**(4), 24 (2007)
3. Bauman, P.T., Stogner, R.H.: GRINS: a multiphysics framework based on the libmesh finite element library. SIAM J. Sci. Comput. **38**(5), S78–S100 (2016)
4. Bey, J.: Simplicial grid refinement: on Fredenthal's algorithm and the optimal number of congruence classes. Numer. Math **85**, 1–29 (2000)
5. Brewer, M., Diachin, L., Knupp, P., Leurent, T., Melander, D.: The mesquite mesh quality improvement toolkit. In: Proceedings of the 12th International Meshing Roundtable, pp. 239–250 (2003)
6. Burstedde, C., Wilcox, L.C., Ghattas, O.: p4est: scalable algorithms for parallel adaptive mesh refinement on forests of octrees. SIAM J. Sci. Comput. **3**(33), 1103–1133 (2011)
7. Carey, G.F., Generation, C.G.: Adaptation and Solution Strategies. Series in Computational and Physical Processes in Mechanics and Thermal Sciences. Taylor & Francis, Milton Park (1997)
8. CGNS: Unstructured mesh for yf-17. https://cgns.github.io/CGNSFiles.html. Accessed 22 Aug 2018
9. Elias, R.N., Camata, J.J., Aveleda, A., Coutinho, A.L.G.A.: Evaluation of message passing communication patterns in finite element solution of coupled problems. In: Palma, J.M.L.M., Daydé, M., Marques, O., Lopes, J.C. (eds.) VECPAR 2010. LNCS, vol. 6449, pp. 306–313. Springer, Heidelberg (2011). https://doi.org/10.1007/978-3-642-19328-6_29
10. Karypis, G., Kumar, V.M.: Unstructured graph partitioning and sparse matrix ordering system (1998). Technical report. Department of Computer Science, University of Minnesota, Mineapolis, EUA. http://glaros.dtc.umn.edu/gkhome/views/metis
11. Gaston, D.R., et al.: Physics- based multiscale coupling for full core nuclear reactor simulation. Ann. Nuclear Energy **84**, 45–54 (2015). https://doi.org/10.1016/j.anucene.2014.09.060. Special Issue on Multi-Physics Modelling of LWR Static and Transient Behaviour
12. Houzeaux, G., la Cruz, R., Owen, H., Vazquez, M.: Parallel uniform mesh multiplication applied to a navier-stokes solver. Comput. Fluids **80**, 142–151 (2013)
13. Kabelikova, P., Ronovsky, A., Vondraka, V.: Parallel Mesh Multiplication for Code_Saturne. Partnership for Advanced Computing in Europe, Prace white paper available online at, PRACE. http://www.prace-ri.eu/meshing/
14. Kennel, M.B.: KDTREE 2: Fortran 95 and C++ software to efficiently search for near neighbors in a multi-dimensional Euclidean space, August 2004. http://arxiv.org/abs/physics/0408067

15. Kirk, B.S., Peterson, J.W., Stogner, R.H., Carey, G.F.: libMesh: a C++ library for parallel adaptive mesh refinement/coarsening simulations. Eng. Comput. **22**, 237–254 (2006)
16. Lawder, J.K., King, P.J.H.: Using space-filling curves for multi-dimensional indexing. In: Lings, B., Jeffery, K. (eds.) BNCOD 2000. LNCS, vol. 1832, pp. 20–35. Springer, Heidelberg (2000). https://doi.org/10.1007/3-540-45033-5_3
17. Lawder, J.K., King, P.J.H.: Querying multi-dimensional data indexed using the hilbert space-filling curve. SIGMOD Rec. **30**, 19–24 (2001)
18. Liu, A., Joe, B.: Quality local refinement of tetrahedral meshes based on 8-subtetrahedron subdivision. Math. Comput. **65**(215), 1183–1200 (1996)
19. Logg, A., Mardal, K.A., Wells, G. (eds.): Automated Solution of Differential Equations by the Finite Element Method. LNCSE, vol. 84. Springer, Heidelberg (2012). https://doi.org/10.1007/978-3-642-23099-8
20. Mesri, Y., Zerguine, W., Digonnet, H., Silva, L., Coupez, T.: Dynamic parallel adaptation for three dimensional unstructured meshes: application to interface tracking. In: Garimella, R.V. (ed.) Proceedings of the 17th International Meshing Roundtable, pp. 195–212. Springer, Heidelberg (2008). https://doi.org/10.1007/978-3-540-87921-3_12
21. Miras, T., Camata, J.J., Elias, R.N., Alves, J.L., Rochinha, F.A., Coutinho, A.L.: A staggered procedure for fluid-object interaction with free surfaces, large rotations and driven by adaptive time stepping. J. Braz. Soc. Mech. Sci. Eng. **40**(4), 239 (2018)
22. Ovcharenko, A., et al.: Neighborhood communication paradigm to increase scalability in large-scale dynamic scientific applications. Parallel Comput. **38**, 140–156 (2012). https://doi.org/10.1016/j.parco.2011.10.013
23. Rosenberg, A.L.: Efficient pairing functions - and why you should care. Int. J. Found. Comput. Sci. **14**(1), 3–17 (2003)
24. Shende, S.S., Malony, A.D.: The tau parallel performance system. Int. J. High Perform. Comput. Appl. **20**(2), 287–311 (2006)
25. Szudzik, M.: An elegant pairing function. In: NKS 2006 Wolfram Science Conference (2006)
26. Tarau, P.: On Two Infinite Families of Pairing Bijections. [cs.MS]
27. Vazquez, M., et al.: Alya: multiphysics engineering simulation toward exascale. J. Comput. Sci. **14**, 15–27 (2016)
28. Yilmaz, E., Aliabadi, S.: Surface conformed linear mesh and data subdivision technique for large-scale flow simulation and visualization in variable intensity computational environment. Comput. Fluids **80**, 388–402 (2013)

# Dynamic Configuration of CUDA Runtime Variables for CDP-Based Divide-and-Conquer Algorithms

Tiago Carneiro[1,4](✉), Jan Gmys[2,4], Nouredine Melab[4],
Francisco Heron de Carvalho Junior[3], Pedro Pedrosa Rebouças Filho[1],
and Daniel Tuyttens[2]

[1] Instituto Federal de Educação, Ciência e Tecnologia do Ceará, Fortaleza, Brazil
{tiago.carneiro,pedrosa}@ppgcc.ifce.edu.br
[2] Mathematics and Operational Research Department (MARO),
University of Mons, Mons, Belgium
{jan.gmys,daniel.tuyttens}@umons.ac.be
[3] Programa de Mestrado e Doutorado em Ciência da Computação,
Universidade Federal do Ceará, Fortaleza, Brazil
heron@lia.ufc.br
[4] Inria Lille Nord Europe, Université Lille 1, CNRS/CRIStAL,
Villeneuve-d'Ascq, France
Nouredine.Melab@univ-lille1.fr

**Abstract.** CUDA Dynamic Parallelism (CDP) is an extension of the GPGPU programming model proposed to better address irregular applications and recursive patterns of computation. However, processing memory demanding problems by using CDP is not straightforward, because of its particular memory organization. This work presents an algorithm to deal with such an issue. It dynamically calculates and configures the CDP runtime variables and the GPU heap on the basis of an analysis of the partial backtracking tree. The proposed algorithm was implemented for solving permutation combinatorial problems and experimented on two test-cases: N-Queens and the Asymmetric Travelling Salesman Problem. The proposed algorithm allows different CDP-based backtracking from the literature to solve memory demanding problems, adaptively with respect to the number of recursive kernel generations and the presence of dynamic allocations on GPU.

**Keywords:** CUDA dynamic parallelism · Backtracking ·
Divide-and-conquer

## 1 Introduction

Irregular applications are present in different research fields, such as combinatorial optimization, data mining, and simulations [1]. The difficulty of parallelizing an application is closely related to its degree of irregularity [2]. Applications that

© Springer Nature Switzerland AG 2019
H. Senger et al. (Eds.): VECPAR 2018, LNCS 11333, pp. 16–30, 2019.
https://doi.org/10.1007/978-3-030-15996-2_2

present irregular control structure, irregular data structures, and an irregular pattern of communication are notably difficult to parallelize [3]. Unstructured tree search methods for solving combinatorial problems, such as *backtracking* and *branch-and-bound*, are examples of such applications. These problem solver paradigms are present in many different areas, e.g., combinatorial optimization, artificial intelligence, and operations research [4]. The program model usually applied to parallelize backtracking algorithms for GPUs, allied to characteristics of the problems commonly solved, results in fine-grained and irregular workloads, which is detrimental to the performance of the GPU.

Although GPUs suffer from performance degradation while processing irregular applications, they are still attractive accelerators. They are ubiquitous, energy efficient, and deliver a high price/GFLOP rate [5]. Furthermore, GPU programming interfaces and tools have become more flexible and expressive. Recent extensions to the general-purpose graphics processing unit (GPGPU) programming model, such as CUDA dynamic parallelism (CDP), can raise the expressiveness of the GPGPU programming model, making it possible to better address irregular applications and recursive patterns of computation [6], such as divide-and-conquer, used by backtracking algorithms.

Despite CDP's purpose of better coping with recursive computations, it is not straightforward to use this technology for processing memory demanding problems [7]. CDP presents several hardware limitations and a different memory organization [6,8]: it is required to configure the CUDA runtime to reserve memory for synchronization between kernel generations. Moreover, in the case of dynamic allocations on GPU, it is also necessary to set the GPU heap size. Both GPU heap and memory for synchronization are not available for use. The related work on CDP does not address these issues.

This work presents an algorithm that dynamically calculates and configures the CDP runtime requirements and the GPU heap size. This calculus is based on an analysis of the partial backtracking tree. The proposed algorithm was implemented for solving permutation combinatorial problems, experimented on two test-cases: N-Queens and the Asymmetric Travelling Salesman Problem. The proposed algorithm allows different CDP-based backtracking from the literature to solve memory demanding problems, autonomously with respect to the number of recursive kernel generations and the presence of dynamic allocations on GPU.

The remainder of this paper is structured as follows. Section 2 brings background information and related works. Section 3 presents the proposed algorithm, and Sect. 4 brings the performance evaluation. Finally, conclusions and directions for further investigations are outlined in Sect. 5.

## 2    Background and Related Works

### 2.1    N-Queens and ATSP

The Traveling Salesman Problem (TSP) consists in finding the shortest Hamiltonian cycle(s) through a given number of cities in such a way that each city is visited exactly once. For each pair of cities $(i, j)$ a cost $c_{ij}$ is given by a cost matrix $C_{N \times N}$. The TSP is called *symmetric* if the cost matrix is symmetric ($\forall i, j : c_{ij} = c_{ji}$), and *asymmetric* otherwise (ATSP). Due to its relevance, the TSP is often used as a benchmark for novel problem-solving strategies [9].

The ATSP instances used in this work come from a generator that creates instances based on real-world situations [10]. Three classes of instances have been selected: *crane*, modeling stacker crane operations; *coin*, modeling a person collecting money from pay phones in a grid-like city; and *tsmat*, consisting of asymmetric instances where the triangle inequality holds. Each class of instances has its own characteristics. Hence, two instances of the same size $N$ may result in a different behavior for the same algorithm.

The N-Queens problem consists in placing $N$ non-attacking queens on a $N \times N$ chessboard. It is also often used as a benchmark for new GPU-based backtracking strategies [11,12]. We consider the version of N-Queens that consists in finding *all* feasible board configurations. N-Queens can be modeled as a permutation problem: position $r$ of a permutation of size $N$ designates the column in which a queen is placed in row $r$.

## 2.2  CUDA Dynamic Parallelism Programming Model

In the CDP terminology, the thread that launches a new kernel is called *parent*. The grid, kernel, and block to which this thread belongs are also called parents. The launched grid is called *child*. The launch of a child grid is non-blocking, but the parent grid only finishes its execution after the termination of all child grids. Inside a block, different kernel launches are serialized. To avoid serialization of kernel launches, the programmer must link each kernel launch to a different stream [8]. Concerning the memory model, blocks of a child grid also have shared memory, and child threads also have local and register memories. A Child grid is not aware of its parent context data, and a parent thread should not pass to child threads pointers to its local or shared memories. Thus, the communication between parent and child is performed through global memory.

### 2.2.1  Related Works on CUDA Dynamic Parallelism

The parallelization of irregular applications using CDP has received little attention in the literature. Particularly, CDP has been used for processing graphs, clustering, simulations, and backtracking algorithms [1,7,11,13,14]. According to related works, CDP is beneficial for processing applications whose data are hierarchically arranged. In such situations, the use of CDP results in performance gains and a code closer to the high-level description of the algorithm [13,14]. However, when these requirements are not met, using CDP may result in significant overheads and makes the code much more complex [7,11].

## 2.3  GPU-Accelerated Backtracking

Backtracking algorithms explore the solution space by dynamically building a tree in a depth-first order [15]. The algorithm iteratively generates and evaluates new nodes, where each child node is more restricted than its father node. If a child node leads to a feasible and valid solution, it is branched, and its child nodes are stored in the *Active Set*. Otherwise, the node in question is discarded, and the algorithm backtracks to an unbranched node in the Active Set. The search generates and evaluates nodes until the Active Set is empty.

GPU-based backtracking algorithms usually consist of two stages: backtracking on CPU until a cutoff depth $d_{cpu}$ and parallel backtracking on GPU [7,11,12, 16,17]. Algorithm 1 presents a pseudocode for the GPU-accelerated backtracking in question.

Initially, the algorithm gets the problem to be solved (*line* 1) and the properties of the GPU (*line* 2). Next, the variable $d_{cpu}$ receives the initial cutoff depth (*line* 3). The cutoff depth $d_{cpu}$ is a problem-dependent parameter, usually determined by manual tuning. For the ATSP, the cutoff depth $d_{cpu}$ corresponds to all feasible and valid permutations with $d_{cpu}$ cities. The initial backtracking on CPU (*line* 4) fills the active set $A_{cpu}$ with all objective nodes found at $d_{cpu}$, as illustrated in Fig. 1. In the present context, an objective node is a valid, feasible and incomplete solution (permutation) at $d_{cpu}$.

Before launching the backtracking on GPU, a subset $S \subseteq A_{cpu}$ of size $chunk \leq |A_{cpu}|$ is chosen (*line* 7). Next, the CPU updates $A_{cpu}$ and transfers $S$ to GPU's global memory (*lines* 8–11). Then, the host configures and launches the kernel (*lines* 12–14). In the kernel, each node in $S$ represents a concurrent backtracking root $R_i$, $i \in \{0, ..., chunk - 1\}$. Therefore, each thread $Th_i$ explores a subset $S_i$ of the solution space $S$ concurrently. The kernel ends when all threads have finished the exploration of $S$. The kernel may be called several times until $A_{cpu}$ is empty (*lines* 6–16).

---

**Algorithm 1.** CPU-GPU parallel backtracking algorithm.

```
1   I ← get_problem()
2   p ← get_gpu_properties()
3   d_cpu ← get_cpu_cutoff_depth()
4   A_cpu ← generate_initial_active_set(d_cpu, I)
5   S ← ∅
6   while  A_cpu is not empty do
7   |    S ← select_subset(A_cpu, p)
8   |    chunk ← |S|
9   |    A_cpu ← A_cpu \ S
10  |    allocate_data_on_gpu(chunk)
11  |    transfer_data_to_gpu(S, chunk)
12  |    nt ← get_block_size()
13  |    nb ← ⌈chunk/nt⌉
14  |    parallel_backtracking <<< nb, nt >>> (I, S, chunk, d_cpu)
15  |    synchronize_gpu_cpu_data()
16  end
```

---

### 2.3.1   CDP-Based Backtracking Algorithms

Plaut *et al.* [11] propose two CDP-based backtracking for enumerating all feasible and unique solutions of the N-Queens, called DP2 and DP3. Both approaches

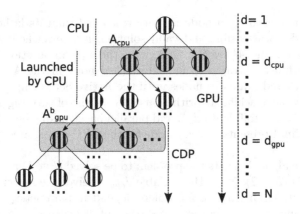

**Fig. 1.** Illustration of the DP2 strategy.

launch recursively Algorithm 1 by using CDP. The strategy called DP2 is based on two depths: $d_{cpu}$ and $d_{gpu}$. Each node in $A_{cpu}$ (at depth $d_{cpu}$) is a root of a backtracking that searches for objective nodes at depth $d_{gpu}$. To store the objective nodes, the first thread of block $b$ that finds an objective node allocates memory for the maximum number of objective nodes block $b$ can find. This block-based active set will be further referred to as $A^b_{gpu}$. Then, a recursive new generation of kernels is launched by using CDP, searching from $d_{gpu}$ to $N$, as illustrated in Fig. 1. In turn, DP3 doubles $d_{gpu}$ at each new recursive kernel launch, until the search reaches the base depth of the recursion.

Results show that the overhead caused by dynamic allocations and dynamic kernel launches outweighs the benefits of the improved load balance yielded by CDP. Moreover, the performance of both algorithms strongly depends on the tuning of several parameters, such as block size and cutoff depth.

Applications that perform dynamic allocations on GPU and/or launch more than two kernel generations that synchronize require the configuration of the CUDA runtime, which is not straightforward [6,8]. Under this scope, Carneiro Pessoa *et al.* [7] propose CDP-BP: a CDP-based backtracking that performs no dynamic allocations on GPU and avoids the need for dynamic setup of CUDA runtime variables. CDP-BP is also based on two depths, like DP2. The memory requirements of the application are dynamically calculated on the host, taking into account an analysis of the partial backtracking tree. The *host* allocates memory for further kernel generations and launches the search on GPU. Each GPU thread identifies its portion of the device-side active set based on thread-to-data mappings. Results show that CDP-BP has much better worst-case execution times and smaller dependence on parameters tuning than its non-CDP counterpart. Additionally, the authors also reported a difficulty in comparing CDP-BP to DP2 and DP3 using memory demanding instances, due to the complexity of dynamically calculating the upper bound on the required CUDA heap size.

# 3    The Proposed Algorithm

As previously pointed out, it is not straightforward to calculate an upper bound on the GPU heap size a CDP-based application needs. It is necessary to take into account the memory requirements of several CDP kernel generation until the search reaches the base depth. If the programmer does not configure the CUDA heap size before launching the first kernel generation, the GPU reserves a default memory space of 8 MB, which may be insufficient to store the objective nodes found by several kernel generations. However, it is not possible to configure the GPU heap size equal to the GPU's global memory size, as the CDP runtime reserves memory for other purposes.

Up to 150 MB of global memory are reserved for each kernel generation that performs parent-child synchronization. This memory is used to keep track of the state of the parent grid and cannot be used by the programmer. Additionally, in case the application launches more than two kernel generations that perform synchronization, a CUDA runtime variable must be explicitly configured with such a number of generations to avoid runtime errors [8].

This section presents a new algorithm to calculate the memory requirements of the search, independently of the number of launched kernel generations. The proposed algorithm works on the host. The upper bound on the GPU heap size is dynamically calculated according to an analysis of the partial backtracking tree, by applying for different kernel generations the memory requirement analysis of [7]. Additionally, the proposed algorithm also configures the CUDA runtime accordingly, before the first kernel generation is launched.

The following sections provide a detailed description of the proposed algorithm. It consists of two main parts: *memory requirement analysis* and *launching the first kernel generation*. For the sake of greater simplicity, only the algorithm for solving instances of the ATSP to optimality is presented, which can be adapted for solving other permutation combinatorial problems with straightforward modifications.

## 3.1    Memory Requirement Analysis

As pointed out in Sect. 2.3, GPU-based backtracking performs an initial search on CPU to generate $A^h_{cpu}$. Before launching the first kernel generation, it is necessary to find a subset $S \subseteq A^h_{cpu}$ of size *chunk* for which its memory requirement fits the device limitations. The *Device* (GPU) and *Host* (CPU) data structures will be further distinguished by the superscripts $d$ and $h$, respectively.

Backtracking algorithms that dynamically allocate memory on GPU's heap, such as DP3, need to store in global memory $A^d_{cpu}$, the cost matrix $C_{N \times N}$, and control data for the subsequent kernel generations. Moreover, it is necessary to reserve memory for parent-child synchronization and the heap. The memory requirement analysis consists of three steps: getting the number of kernel generations, heap size calculation, and calculation of the required global memory. These steps are detailed in the following sections.

### 3.1.1  Calculating the Number of Kernel Generations

It is necessary to know the number of kernel generations before launching the first one. This value is used to configure the runtime and to calculate the memory reserved by the GPU to keep track of context data of the parent grid.

---

**Algorithm 2.** Calculating the number of kernel generations.

---

**Input:** The size $N$ of the problem, and the initial cutoff depth $initial\_depth$.
**Output:** Number of kernel generations that perform synchronization. Also including the one launched by the host.

1  $base \leftarrow get\_base\_depth(N)$
2  $current\_depth \leftarrow initial\_depth$
3  $kernel\_gen \leftarrow 1$
4  **while** $current\_depth \leq base\_depth$ **do**
5  $\quad\mid\quad current\_depth \leftarrow get\_next\_depth(current\_depth, N)$
6  $\quad\mid\quad kernel\_gen \leftarrow kernel\_gen + 1$
7  **end**

---

One can see in Algorithm 2 the function that returns the number of kernel generations. Initially, the function receives the *intial_depth* of the search and the size $N$ of the problem. Next, it gets the base of the recursion (*line* 1). Then, the number of generations that perform parent-child synchronization is calculated in lines 4–6. The programmer must provide two functions: *get_base_depth()* and *get_next_depth()*. The first one is responsible for calculating the base of the recursion (*line* 1). In turn, the second one is responsible for returning the next depth of the recursion (*line* 5), which works like an iterator.

### 3.1.2  Upper Bound on the Required GPU Heap Size

The heap size calculation is the main step of the memory requirement analysis. The strategy employed in this step takes into account the maximum number of children nodes that a node at *current* depth can have at *next* depth, which is:

$$expected\_children_{next} = \frac{max_{next}}{max_{current}}$$

where the maximum number of nodes of a given depth $d$ is:

$$max_d = \frac{(N-1)!}{(N-d)!}$$

Algorithm 3 presents a function that estimates an upper bound on the required GPU heap size. This function receives as parameters *chunk*, which is the size of a subset $S \subseteq A_{cpu}^h$, and the size $N$ of the problem. Then, it calculates, for each recursive kernel call until the search reaches the base depth, the memory required to store the upper bound on the number of objective nodes at depth *next* (*lines* 4–11). After getting the heap requirements for *chunk* nodes, it is possible to determine the amount of global memory required by the application.

---

**Algorithm 3.** Upper bound on the GPU heap size.

**Input:** The size *chunk* of $S \subseteq A_{cpu}^h$, and the size $N$ of the problem.
**Output:** Upper bound on the requested GPU heap size (in bytes).

1  $ub\_requested\_heap \leftarrow sizeof(Node) \times chunk$
2  $base \leftarrow get\_base\_depth(N)$
3  $current\_depth \leftarrow get\_initial\_depth()$

4  **while** $current < base$ **do**
5     $next\_depth \leftarrow get\_next\_depth(current\_depth)$
6     $max_{current} \leftarrow \frac{(N-1)!}{(N-current)!}$
7     $max_{next} \leftarrow \frac{(N-1)!}{(N-next)!}$
8     $expected\_children_{next} \leftarrow \frac{max_{next}}{max_{current}}$
9     $ub\_requested\_heap \leftarrow ub\_requested\_heap \times expected\_children_{next}$
10    $current\_depth \leftarrow next\_depth$
11 **end**

---

### 3.1.3  Global Memory Required by the Application

Algorithm 4 returns the amount of global memory required by the application based on a subset $S \subseteq A_{cpu}^h$ of size *chunk*. Initially, the memory reserved for synchronization is calculated in line 1. As previously pointed out, a memory space of 150 MB is reserved for each kernel generation that performs parent-child synchronization. The amount of global memory required to store the control data, $A_{cpu}^d$, and the heap is calculated in lines 3–4. Finally, in line 6, the required global memory is calculated by adding the values got in lines 2–5.

All algorithms presented in this section take into consideration a subset $S \subseteq A_{cpu}^h$ of size *chunk*. The next section shows how to choose $S$, to set up the CUDA runtime variables, and to launch the first kernel generation.

### 3.2  Launching the First Kernel Generation

Before launching the first kernel generation from the host, the application must find a subset $S \subseteq A_{cpu}^h$ of size *chunk* such that an upper bound on its requirements fit into the global memory. Algorithm 5 shows how to get such a subset. Initially, the upper bound on the requirements of $S$ is calculated in line 1, using Algorithm 4. If the memory required by $S$ is bigger than the available global

---

**Algorithm 4.** Global memory required by the application.

**Input:** The size *chunk* of $S \subseteq A_{cpu}^h$, the size $N$ of the problem, and the number $k$ of kernel generations that perform parent-child synchronization.
**Output:** The total of global memory required by the application (in bytes).

1  $required\_memory \leftarrow 0$
2  $nesting\_memory \leftarrow k \times 150MB$
3  $activeSet\_memory \leftarrow chunk \times sizeof(Node)$
4  $control\_memory \leftarrow chunk \times sizeof(ControlData)$
5  $required\_heap \leftarrow get\_heap(chunk, N)$
6  $required\_memory \leftarrow$
    $required\_heap + nesting\_memory + activeSet\_memory + control\_memory$

---

**Algorithm 5.** Calculating a suitable chunk size.

---

**Input:** $chunk$, the size $N$ of the problem, and the number $k$ of kernel generations.
**Output:** A suitable chunk size.

```
1  total_required ← required_memory(chunk, N, k)
2  available_memory ← get_GPU_properties(global_memory)
3  while total_required > available_memory do
4  │   chunk ← decrease_chunk(chunk)
5  │   total_required ← required_memory(chunk, N, k)
6  │   if chunk < 1 then
7  │   │   return error
8  │   end
9  end
```

---

memory, $chunk$ is decreased until its requirements fit into the available global memory (*lines* 3–5). If there is no $S$ such that its requirement fits into the available global memory, the program returns an error (*lines* 6–8).

Algorithm 6 presents the launching of the first kernel generation on GPU. After determining a suitable $S$ (*line* 1), the CUDA runtime variables of heap size and number of kernel generations are set in line 2. All allocations on device memory are performed in line 3. There is no host allocation for other active sets than $A_{cpu}^d$ because threads on device dynamically allocate memory on GPU's heap. Finally, lines 7 – 18 process $S \subseteq A_{cpu}^h$ of size $chunk$ until $A_{cpu}^h$ is empty. After each kernel call, control data is retrieved (*line* 12) and the variables *counter* and *remaining* are updated (*lines* 13–17). The variable *counter* is used to make $A_{cpu}^d$ point to unexplored nodes (*line* 10) and as termination criteria (*line* 7).

---

**Algorithm 6.** Launching the first kernel generation on GPU.

---

**Input:** Cost matrix $C_{N \times N}^d, A_{cpu}^h$, the global upper bound, and the size $N$ of the problem.

```
1  chunk ← get_suitable_chunk(survivors_d_cpu, N)
2  set_CDP_variables(get_heap(chunk, N), get_num_gen(N, d_cpu))
3  device_memory_allocation(A_{cpu}^d, chunk, sizeof(Node), control_data^d)
4  survivors_d_cpu ← |A_{cpu}^h|
5  counter ← 0
6  remaining ← survivors_d_cpu
7  while counter < survivors_d_cpu do
8  │   nt ← get_block_size()
9  │   nb ← ⌈chunk/nt⌉
10 │   cudaMemCpy(A_{cpu}^d, (A_{cpu}^h + counter), chunk × sizeof(Node), H2D)
11 │   GPU_search <<< nb, nt >>> (C^d, chunk, A_{cpu}^d, control_data^d, upper_bound, N)
12 │   syncDataD2H(control_data^h, control_data^d, chunk)
13 │   counter ← counter + chunk
14 │   remaining ← remaining − chunk
15 │   if remaining < chunk then
16 │   │   chunk ← remaining
17 │   end
18 end
```

---

# 4    Performance Evaluation

The proposed algorithm was implemented to manage three recursive CDP-based backtracking from the literature:

- **DP2** and **DP3**: CDP-based algorithms introduced in Sect. 2.3.1.
- **CDP-DP3**: hybridization between CDP-BP and DP3 proposed by [7]. Compared to DP3, CDP-DP3 also doubles $d_{cpu}$ until the search reaches the base depth. However, CDP-DP3 launches less CDP kernels than DP3, and dynamic allocations start on the second CDP kernel generation.

These GPU-based searches are launched in line 11 of Algorithm 6. For comparison, the following backtracking strategies are also considered.

- **BP-DFS**: non-CDP implementation of Algorithm 1 proposed by [17].
- **CDP-BP**: CDP-based algorithm introduced in Sect. 2.3.1 that makes no dynamic allocations on GPU and launches two kernel generations.
- **Multicore**: multi-threaded version of BP-DFS that applies a pool scheme for load balancing.
- **Serial**: serial control implementation optimized for single-core execution.

All implementations (but the serial one) use the data structures, the algorithm for consistency of the incumbent solution, and the kernel code of BP-DFS. For more details, refer to [7].

## 4.1    Experimental Protocol and Parameters Settings

All CUDA programs were parallelized using CUDA C 8.0 and compiled with GCC 5.4. The testbed, operating under CentOS 7.1 64 bits, is composed of *two* Intel Xeon E5-2650v3 @ 2.30 GHz with 20 cores, 40 threads, and 32 GB RAM. It is equipped with an NVIDIA Tesla K40m (GK110B), 12 GB RAM, and 2880 CUDA cores @ 745 MHz.

In the experiments, ATSP instances of sizes (N) ranging from 10 to 19 are solved to optimality. In turn, N-Queens problems of sizes (N) ranging from 10 to 18 are also considered. The memory requirement of the test-cases ranges from few KB to several GB.

To compare the performance of two parallel backtracking algorithms, both should explore the *same* search space [18]. Therefore, for all ATSP instances, the initial upper bound is set to the optimal value. This initialization ensures that all implementations above outlined explore the same feasible region, which is always the case for the N-Queens problem.

The performance of GPU-accelerated backtracking algorithms strongly depends on the tuning of several parameters [7,11]. Preliminary experiments were carried out to find out a suitable block size, $d_{cpu}$ and $d_{gpu}$ for all GPU-based implementations. Table 1 summarizes the best parameter configurations of all parallel implementations. The chosen parameters are the best for most of the instances, but not for all of them.

**Table 1.** List of best parameters found experimentally for all parallel implementations. The superscript $Q$ and $A$ indicate that the settings are for the N-Queens or, respectively, the ATSP implementation.

| Implementation | Parameters settings | | | |
|---|---|---|---|---|
| | Block size | Bl. size-CDP | $d_{cpu}$ | $d_{gpu}$ |
| BP-DFS[a] | 128 | - | 7 | - |
| CDP-BP$_A$ | 128 | 64 | 6 | 8 |
| CDP-BP$_Q$ | 128 | 64 | 5 | 7 |
| CDP-DP3[a] | 128 | 64 | - | - |
| DP2$^A$ | 128 | 64 | 4 | 7 |
| DP2$^Q$ | 128 | 32 | 4 | 7 |
| $DP3^A$ | 128 | 64 | - | - |
| DP3$^Q$ | 128 | 32 | - | - |
| Multicore[a] | - | - | 4 | - |

[a]Parameter are the same for ATSP and N-Queens.

Both DP3 and CDP-DP3 have no cutoff depth tuning because they follow the strategy proposed by [11], which doubles $d_{cpu}$. For the N-Queens, there are $N$ possibilities of starting node at depth $d_{cpu}$. This way, four kernel generations can be launched: at $d_{cpu} = 1$, $d_{gpu} = 2, 4$ and 8 (base). For the ATSP, there is only one possible starting city. This way, three kernel generations are launched.

## 4.2   Results

First of all, it is important to point out that the proposed algorithm is necessary to make DP2, DP3, and CDP-DP3 solve all test-cases without runtime errors. According to preliminary experiments, these implementations that make dynamic allocations on GPU cannot solve instances of size $N > 12$ using the default GPU heap size of 8 MB. The CUDA runtime returns an *"illegal memory*

**Table 2.** Average speedup reached by all parallel implementations for different ranges of sizes compared to the serial baseline.

| Implementation | Average speedup | | | |
|---|---|---|---|---|
| | 10–12 | 13–15 | 16–19(18) | All sizes |
| DP2 | 1.3× | 3.26× | 5.11× | 2.99× |
| DP3 | 1.08× | 5.20× | 6.68× | 4.20× |
| CDP-DP3 | 2.10× | 7.89× | 7.12× | 5.72× |
| CDP-BP | 5.24× | 8.38× | 7.72× | 7.10× |
| BP-DFS | 5.82× | 15.86× | 15.70× | 12.37× |
| Multicore | 4.63× | 14.71× | 16.00× | 11.41× |

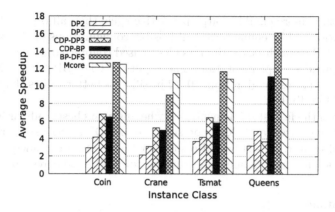

**Fig. 2.** Average speedup reached by all parallel implementations compared to the serial baseline.

*access*" error in situations where the GPU heap requirement of the application is bigger than the configured one.

Table 2 reports the average speedup achieved by all parallel implementations for different ranges of problem sizes compared to the serial baseline. In turn, Fig. 2 presents the average speedup reached by all parallel implementations compared to the serial baseline.

The lowest values of average speedup in Table 2 are observed for DP2, DP3, and CDP-DP3. These applications perform dynamic allocations/deallocations on GPU and launch a new kernel per GPU thread. The overhead of dynamic allocations, multiple streams creation/destruction, and several kernel launches amount negatively for small sizes. However, as the solution space grows, this overhead becomes less significant, and the benefits of a more regular load yielded by the DP3 algorithm are observed: as can be seen in Fig. 2, CDP-DP3 is the CDP-based implementation with the best overall results for the ATSP.

The benefits of using the DP3 strategy would not be realized without the proposed algorithm. As previously said, DP2, DP3, and CDP-DP3 can only solve instances of size up to $N = 12$ without GPU heap configuration. According to Table 2, CDP-BP is 2.5× faster than CDP-DP3 and 4.8× faster than DP3 for sizes ranging from 10 to 12. These values change considerably for bigger problems, and CDP-DP3 becomes superior to CDP-BP for solving the ATSP, as previously pointed out. However, it is not the case for the N-Queens, as one can see in Fig. 2.

Launching one new kernel for each GPU thread is not a good strategy for the N-Queens problem. The load processed by a child kernel is much smaller than the one launched when solving the ATSP [7]. This way, DP2, DP3, CDP-DP3 produce a significant overhead for processing small loads. In turn, CDP-BP launches a new kernel generation based on the load of the whole block, instead of the load of a single thread. According to NVIDIA Visual Profiler, by using the block-based kernel launch, CDP-BP can archive *twice* more occupancy and *three times* more eligible warps per active cycle than all other CDP-based implementations while enumerating all feasible configurations of the N-Queens. Thus, CDP-BP is much faster than its CDP-based counterparts and as faster as the multi-threaded implementation. The results of CDP-BP for the N-Queens and instances of sizes ranging from 10–12 justifies its better values than the ones of CDP-DP3 in Table 2.

BP-DFS is the fastest implementation when using its best configuration since it is highly optimized and does not suffer from CDP's intrinsic performance penalties. Moreover, BP-DFS is also superior to the multi-threaded implementation that applies load balance and runs on *two* CPUs, 20 cores/40 threads.

### 4.3    Discussion

One of CDP's purposes is to better cope with divide-and-conquer applications. This is in part true for our implementations of both CDP-DP3 and DP3. The use of dynamic allocations removes the need for complex thread-to-data mapping. Furthermore, the strategy of doubling $d_{gpu}$ makes almost the whole search to be executed on GPU, which avoids $d_{cpu}/d_{gpu}$ tuning. However, solving memory demanding problems requires extra programming efforts.

Using a different value than the default one makes it necessary to configure the CUDA heap beforehand, which brings complexity to the code. The heap size calculation takes into account a subtree rooted at $d_{cpu}$ that goes down to the *base* depth. The definition of a recursion base is also challenging: for an ATSP instance of size $N = 18$, 4 generations of kernels would be launched. Furthermore, it would require an enormous amount of memory to store the possible children nodes at $d_{cpu} = 16$ (refer to Sect. 3.1.2). However, the last kernel generation would perform no search at all. For example, consider instance *tsmat*18. The fourth kernel generation of DP3 would evaluate less than 3% of the solution space.

Moreover, the initial $d_{cpu}$ for both DP3 and CDP-DP3 is 2. Taking into account the ATSP, it is unlikely that pruning of unfeasible nodes happens in such a shallow depth. As a consequence, the memory requirement analysis of both DP3 and CDP-DP3 would return a heap requirement close to the maximum possible size, which wastes memory. This is not the case for DP2: both $d_{cpu}$ and $d_{gpu}$ need tuning, and the number of objective nodes at deeper depths is much smaller than the maximum one. This way, DP2 can solve instance *crane*15 in a configuration with the default heap and a deep $d_{cpu}$. However, this configuration is slower than the one of Table 1 that needs GPU heap setup.

Finally, the memory for parent-child synchronization cannot be ignored, and it can be a limitation for more modest hardware: there may be a situation where the memory reserved for depth synchronization takes almost the whole global memory, leaving nearly no memory space for the search procedure on GPU.

# 5    Conclusion and Future Works

This work has presented an algorithm to calculate the memory requirements of CDP-based divide-and-conquer algorithms and configure the CUDA runtime accordingly. The proposed algorithm was implemented to manage different CDP-based backtracking from the literature and experimented on two test-cases: N-Queens and ATSP.

Using CDP may be a good choice for programmers that intent to parallelize recursive divide-and-conquer application for solving nondemanding problems. The use of recursion removes much of the complexity in programming and parameters tuning. Moreover, despite the intrinsic overhead of CDP, speedups are observed for all CDP-based implementations. However, using CDP for processing memory demanding recursive applications brings extra complexity on configuring the runtime before launching the first kernel generation.

A future research direction is on investigating different ways of calculating the next $d_{gpu}$ and a rule for determining the base depth. Another future work is to investigate the limitations of modest gamer hardware while processing memory demanding CDP-based recursive applications.

# References

1. Wang, J., Yalamanchili, S.: Characterization and analysis of dynamic parallelismin unstructured GPU applications. In: 2014 IEEE International Symposium on Workload Characterization (IISWC), pp. 51–60. IEEE (2014)
2. Mukherjee, S.S., Sharma, S.D., Hill, M.D., Larus, J.R., Rogers, A., Saltz, J.: Efficient support for irregular applications on distributed-memory machines. In: ACM SIGPLAN Notices, vol. 30, pp. 68–79. ACM (1995)
3. Yelick, K.A.: Programming models for irregular applications. ACM SIGPLAN Not. **28**(1), 28–31 (1993)
4. Gendron, B., Crainic, T.G.: Parallel branch-and-bound algorithms: survey and synthesis. Oper. Res. **42**(6), 1042–1066 (1994)
5. Brodtkorb, A., Dyken, C., Hagen, T., Hjelmervik, J., Storaasli, O.: State-of-the-art in heterogeneous computing. Sci. Program. **18**(1), 1–33 (2010)
6. Adinetz, A.: CUDA dynamic parallelism: API and principles (2014). Accessed 10 May 2018
7. Carneiro Pessoa, T., Gmys, J., de Carvalho Junior, F.H., Melab, N., Tuyttens, D.: GPU-accelerated backtracking using CUDA dynamic parallelism. Concurr. Comput.: Pract. Exp. **30**(9), e4374 (2017)
8. NVIDIA: CUDA C programming guide (version 9.1) (2018)
9. Cook, W.: In Pursuit of the Traveling Salesman: Mathematics at the Limits of Computation. Princeton University Press, Princeton (2012)
10. Cirasella, J., Johnson, D.S., McGeoch, L.A., Zhang, W.: The asymmetric traveling salesman problem: algorithms, instance generators, and tests. In: Buchsbaum, A.L., Snoeyink, J. (eds.) ALENEX 2001. LNCS, vol. 2153, pp. 32–59. Springer, Heidelberg (2001). https://doi.org/10.1007/3-540-44808-X_3
11. Plauth, M., Feinbube, F., Schlegel, F., Polze, A.: A performance evaluation of dynamic parallelism for fine-grained, irregular workloads. Int. J. Netw. Comput. **6**(2), 212–229 (2016)

12. Zhang, T., Shu, W., Wu, M.-Y.: Optimization of $N$-queens solvers on graphics processors. In: Temam, O., Yew, P.-C., Zang, B. (eds.) APPT 2011. LNCS, vol. 6965, pp. 142–156. Springer, Heidelberg (2011). https://doi.org/10.1007/978-3-642-24151-2_11

13. Zhang, P., et al.: Dynamic parallelism for simple and efficient GPU graph algorithms. In: Proceedings of the 5th Workshop on Irregular Applications: Architectures and Algorithms, p. 11. ACM (2015)

14. DiMarco, J., Taufer, M.: Performance impact of dynamic parallelism on different clustering algorithms and the new GPU architecture. In: Proceedings of SPIE Defense, Security, and Sensing Symposium (2013)

15. Zhang, W.: Branch-and-bound search algorithms and their computational complexity. Technical report, DTIC Document (1996)

16. Feinbube, F., Rabe, B., von Löwis, M., Polze, A.: NQueens on CUDA: optimization issues. In: Ninth International Symposium on Parallel and Distributed Computing (ISPDC), pp. 63–70. IEEE (2010)

17. Carneiro, T., Muritiba, A., Negreiros, M., de Campos, G.: A new parallel schema for branch-and-bound algorithms using GPGPU. In: 23rd International Symposium on Computer Architecture and High Performance Computing (SBAC-PAD), pp. 41–47 (2011)

18. Karypis, G., Kumar, V.: Unstructured tree search on SIMD parallel computers. IEEE Trans. Parallel Distrib. Syst. 5(10), 1057–1072 (1994)

# Design, Implementation and Performance Analysis of a CFD Task-Based Application for Heterogeneous CPU/GPU Resources

Lucas Leandro Nesi, Lucas Mello Schnorr$^{(\boxtimes)}$,
and Philippe Olivier Alexandre Navaux

Institute of Informatics/PPGC/UFRGS, Porto Alegre, Brazil
{llnesi,schnorr,navaux}@inf.ufrgs.br

**Abstract.** The development of parallel solutions over contemporary heterogeneous supercomputers is complex and challenging, especially for coding, performance analysis, and behavioral characterization. The task-based programming model is a possible alternative to adequately reduce the burden on the programmer. Such model consists of dividing the application into tasks with dependencies through a directed acyclic graph (DAG), and subject the DAG to a runtime scheduler that will map tasks to resources. In this paper, we present the design, development, and performance analysis of a task-based heterogeneous (CPU and GPU) application of a Computational Fluid Dynamics (CFD) problem that simulates the flow of an incompressible Newtonian fluid with constant viscosity. We implement our solution based on the StarPU runtime and use the StarVZ toolkit to conduct a comprehensive performance analysis. Results indicate that our solution provides a 6.5× speedup compared to the serial version on the target machine using 7 CPU workers and a 60× speedup using 5 CPU and 2 GPU workers.

**Keywords:** Task-based model · Performance analysis ·
Computational Fluid Dynamics

## 1 Introduction

The increasing size of the supercomputers, with the adoption of many heterogeneous accelerators, provides remarkable parallelism exploited by many applications. Computational Fluid Dynamic (CFD) applications have been made parallel using the most common programming methods, based on MPI [12] (for multi-nodes), OpenMP [10] (for many-core processors), CUDA [16] (for GPG-PUs), and OpenCL [20] (for hybrid platforms). If correctly used, these APIs may provide the best possible performance from a machine. Yet, the complexity of programming such hybrid environments using these APIs is significant because

© Springer Nature Switzerland AG 2019
H. Senger et al. (Eds.): VECPAR 2018, LNCS 11333, pp. 31–44, 2019.
https://doi.org/10.1007/978-3-030-15996-2_3

data partitioning, process mapping, and load balancing are usually done manu-
ally. This scenario creates a problem between code productivity versus application performance [9]. Despite the noticeable majority of HPC code be developed
with these APIs, alternative and mature parallel programming models are developed to reduce the complexity involved in coding parallel applications.

The task-based programming model is an example of an alternative way
of coding parallel applications. It consists in organizing the application as a
directed acyclic graph (DAG), with sequential tasks (nodes) with data dependencies (edges) among them. Tasks are submitted sequentially to a runtime
equipped with scheduling heuristics capable of mapping tasks to workers bound
to the heterogeneous computing resources (CPU or GPU). Among alternatives
[5,11,19], StarPU [4] is a runtime that monitors ready tasks, schedules them to
heterogeneous resources, and handles data dependencies automatically. This significantly reduces the burden of the programmer. Although such programming
paradigm has been extensively used with good performance in linear algebra
(examples include the set of subroutines of the Chameleon framework [2] and
the qr_mumps solver [7]), the use of the task-based programming model in the
CFD area remains vastly unexplored.

In this article, we describe the steps to design a task-based and heterogeneous
(CPU and GPU) parallel application of a simple fluid flow simulation using some
recurrent CFD methods (Jacobi relaxation, MacCormack, and general Finite
Difference Methods) along with a detailed analysis of its computational behavior.
Our implementation breaks each simulation method into tasks of different types,
and relies on the StarPU memory manager to provide temporary data between
them. We have tried to use as many StarPU features as possible, in a way it can
control most of the parallel behavior. We analyze the use of different schedulers,
granularity of the domain decomposition, and the use of naive GPU codelets.
The main contributions of this article are:

- The novel task-based implementation in StarPU of a 2D fluid flow simulation
  using established CFD methods as detailed by Pletcher [18] and Xie [21];
- A characterization of its parallel and heterogeneous behavior in conjunction
  with a list of possible optimizations and parameters tuning;
- A performance analysis using the StarVZ framework [17] (a workflow written
  in the R language) to pin-point the limitations of the approach.

The rest of this paper is organized as follows. Section 2 presents the basic
concepts on computational fluid dynamics and the task-based programming
paradigm, including information about the StarPU runtime. Section 3 presents
related work about other implementations of CFD parallel applications, the
adoption of task-based in CFD and how others have conducted performance
analysis using this paradigm. Section 4 introduce our implementation of CFD
application, the sequential implementation and the design and implementation of our parallel task-based version. Section 5 presents the experiment design
used and the comprehensive performance analysis of the application. Section 6

concludes the paper illustrating the main contributions and future work. The companion material of this work is publicly available at https://doi.org/10.5281/zenodo.1298665.

# 2  Basic Concepts

We present some basic concepts behind CFD, focusing on our simulation, and the general concepts about task-based programming over StarPU.

## 2.1  Computational Fluid Dynamics (CFD)

The CFD can be applied to simulate several fluid behaviors, and are usually described by governing equations. In our case, as shown in Eq. 1, we simulate the flow of an incompressible Newtonian fluid with constant viscosity that is modeled with the simplified form of the Navier-Stokes equation [18, 21], where $\mathbf{v}$ is the velocity vector, $t$ is time, $\alpha$ is the kinematic viscosity, $\rho$ is the density, $P$ is the pressure, and $\mathbf{f}$ are external body forces. The equation is divided in two steps: diffusion $(\alpha\nabla^2\mathbf{v} - \frac{1}{\rho}\nabla P + \mathbf{f})$ and advection $(-(\mathbf{v} \cdot \nabla)\mathbf{v})$ steps [21]. Also, to consider the nature conservation laws in fluid mechanics, the Eq. 2 is applied to ensure the conservation of mass [18, 21].

$$\frac{\partial \mathbf{v}}{\partial t} = \alpha\nabla^2\mathbf{v} - \frac{1}{\rho}\nabla P + \mathbf{f} - (\mathbf{v} \cdot \nabla)\mathbf{v} \tag{1}$$

$$\nabla \cdot \mathbf{v} = 0 \tag{2}$$

The numerical solution of these equations can be achieved using different methods to compute each step. A common way is the Finite Difference Method, where the simulation space/time is discretized to a grid with horizontal and vertical number of cells given by $Nx$ and $Ny$. Each cell assumes one value for each variable at one time-step. Iterative methods are executed to compute the fluid's variables over a finite number of time steps where the computation of a new cell time state depends only on its neighbors' variables of the last computed time step. In our 2D simulation, each cell has a horizontal and vertical real size representation given by $\Delta x$ and $\Delta y$ in meters. The time difference between time steps is given by $\Delta t$ in seconds.

## 2.2  Task-Based Parallel Programming Paradigm

The structure of a program following the task-based programming paradigm consists of a collection of tasks (a sequential code region) that have a specific purpose over a collection of data regions. In that way, the interaction between tasks occurs primarily by the use of identical memory regions in different tasks, causing implicit dependencies among them to guarantee computation coherence. Usually, a task-based application is represented by a Directed Acyclic Graph (DAG), where nodes are tasks, edges are dependencies. Such dependencies can be inherently induced by data reuse or explicitly inserted by the programmer.

One of the benefits of adopting the task-based model is that the programming of HPC applications is much more abstract, far from the details of the heterogeneous execution platform. So, instead of an explicit mapping of tasks to resources by the programmer, the parallelism is obtained by letting a middleware take such decisions. This can be achieved using the Sequential Task Flow (STF), where tasks are submitted sequentially to the middleware interface, and the runtime decides where tasks execute [3]. Because of the inevitable random and irregular state of the system environment, the tasks' execution order is stochastic. Many runtimes act like this middleware, for example, PaRSEC [6], XKaapi [11], and StarPU [4]. Although there are similarities among them, we detail only the StarPU runtime over which this work is conducted.

StarPU is a runtime system designed to operate as an interface layer between a task-based application and a multi-core system with different accelerators such as the Nvidia CUDA/OpenCL GPGPUs [4]. To use StarPU, the programmer needs to provide the implementation of each task on any desirable resource (CPU, CUDA, OpenCL), and declare the used memory regions as handles. The submission of tasks can be achieved using the provided API, declaring the data used for each task. To decide where tasks should be allocated in the resources, StarPU employs different scheduling heuristics. The ones used in our work are LWS (local work stealing) and heft-based heuristics [4]: DM (deque model), DMDA (deque model data aware), and DMDAS (deque model data aware sorted). Because different accelerators and nodes usually require manual memory transfers among them, StarPU uses information from the scheduler decisions to automatically transfer data between resources when required by a task, trying to minimize total transfers and keep resources busy [4].

## 3   Related Work and Motivation

CFD simulations require massive computational power to be concluded in feasible time. The adoption of parallel processing is natural and has been extensively used to accelerate such programs. Many parallel versions of CFD simulations are described by a survey [1]. We can verify that most of the parallel implementations employ OpenMP, MPI, CUDA, and combinations. In these programming paradigms, the programmer is responsible for a series of low-level software decisions. Yet, there are no significant task-based strategies reported. One example of heterogeneous architectures usage is presented by [13]. They have implemented a parallel solver using MPI+CUDA of the Navier-Stokes equations to simulate buoyancy-driven incompressible fluid flows on multi-GPU clusters. The reported results show a speedup of 130× over a pthread version using 128 GPU on four nodes. The CFD simulation implements static domain decomposition across nodes and GPUs, something that may lead to unbalanced conditions among computing elements. In our work, we show that StarPU can handle most of this work automatically.

The use of task-based programming paradigm in some sections of CFD is already present in the state-of-the-art as a recent topic. In [14] the authors implemented a gradient reconstruction of a CFD software called Code_Saturne over

StarPU and PaRSEC, conducting CPU-only experiments with multiple nodes. Their results show a potential use of StarPU on these algorithms when compared with the OpenMP, Pure MPI and MPI+OpenMP versions. Their performance analysis is conducted by comparing the execution time of different implemented versions; a secondary analysis presents statistics of cores in one rank using a space/time view, concluding that StarPU has some instability when tasks are submitted. Also, they argue that the performance analysis of applications running over StarPU is extremely difficult to conduct, especially by the lack of dedicated tools. Another use of task-based paradigm in CFD was presented by [8], where the authors use StarPU in some Finite Volume Methods of their software FLUSEPA, an aerodynamic solver. They concentrate their analyses on parameter tuning, focusing the study in one time-step program. Compared with [14], they present richer performance analysis.

In our work, we present a novel task-based CFD simulation on top of StarPU with support for multiple GPUs. Our goal is to verify the feasibility of the task-programming model for CFD applications. Although we also employ makespan (execution time) and traditional space/time views in the first steps of the performance analysis, the adoption of StarVZ framework enables a more refined visualization of the execution behavior. Some features explored are the resources states, StarPU states, and memory utilization [17]. The next section presents our task-based parallel implementation of a CFD for a heterogeneous platform.

## 4   Design of a Parallel Heterogeneous CFD Application

We design and implement a CFD application to be executed in a heterogeneous platform with CPUs and GPUs. For the sake of comparison, we have implemented also a sequential version to serve as reference for speedup and simulation error verification. The physics comes from the methods and mathematical equations described and formulated by Pletcher [18] and Xie [21]. In what follows, we describe all steps with the adopted numerical methods. The parallel task-based version uses the same methods but implemented as a DAG with block partitioning where the steps are divided into tasks with CPU and GPU versions.

### 4.1   Serial CFD Application Design and Implementation

We developed a 2D fluid flow simulation following the guidelines explained by Pletcher [18] and Xie [21]. The main goal of using this simulation was to generate computational load to analyze the task-based approach implemented in StarPU and, at the same time, implement some real and widely used numerical methods. The base simulation execution consists of a fan inside a closed room. This scenario can be seen on Fig. 1(a), where there is a fan vertically centered in the left side of a room, it moves the air from left to right, and in all sides there is a wall that perfectly reflects the air. An example of the simulation on this scenario can be viewed on Fig. 1(b), generated by an in-house real-time visualization tool, where the color represents the total velocity of the fluid.

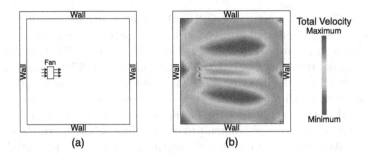

**Fig. 1.** (a) Schematic of the proposed simulation. (b) Simulation visualization. (Color figure online)

First we use a Finite Difference Method decomposing the problem domain in a perfect square grid so the number of horizontal and vertical cells are equal ($Nx = Ny$) and the discrete steps are fixed, and summarized in $\Delta d$ ($\Delta x = \Delta y = \Delta d$). Each cell has the total velocity in the horizontal ($u$) and vertical axis ($v$). Some external forces are added to the initial fluid state. To calculate the next time step in an arbitrary cell $C$, it only requires to access the variables of its northern $N$, east $E$, southern $S$ and west $W$ cells. The simulation consists of solving the Diffusion and Advection components of Eq. 1, then the Conservation component given by Eq. 2. Also, some other functions are applied to satisfy the rest of the simulation requirements, like boundary conditions, and the addition of external forces at each time step.

The numerical methods used to compute the simulation in the serial application are divided in four steps: Start, Diffuse, Advection, and Conserve steps. The Conserve step is required after the Diffuse and the Advection step to ensure the conservation of mass on the final result of both methods. In that way, the order of the simulation for one time step is Start, Diffuse, Conserve, Advection, and Conserve. Detailed information about each step is given as follows. For a given cell $C$, the **Start** step takes as input the previous time step data $C^{t-1}$, adds external forces, such as fans, and saves the computed result in $C^t$. The **Diffuse** step solves its component of the Eq. 1 using the Jacobi relaxation method. For a number of relaxation iterations $nk$, it computes the $u$ and $v$ components for each iteration $k$ using the Eq. 3. We depict only the calculus for $u$, as an example. The input data is provided by the Start step, $C^t$. Different spaces of memory are used to respect the independence of each iteration data and the Jacobi method. In the end, the results are used by the Conserve step.

$$C_u^{t,k+1} = \frac{1}{1 + 4\frac{\alpha\Delta t}{\Delta d^2}}\left(C_u^{t,k} + \frac{\alpha\Delta t}{\Delta d^2}(N_u^{t,k} + S_u^{t,k} + E_u^{t,k} + W_u^{t,k})\right) \qquad (3)$$

The **Advection** step uses the MacCormack method [18] to solve the Advection component. The MacCormack is divided into two sub-steps, the Predictor Step, given by Eq. 4 and the Corrector Step, given by Eq. 5, using $u$ as example. The input is given by the Conserved Diffused data $C^t$, where the $C'^t$ is the temporary data for the predictor step and $C''^t$ is the temporary data used for the corrector step that will be again passed to the conserve step.

$$C'^t_u = C^t_u - \frac{\alpha \Delta t}{\Delta d^2}(N^t_u N^t_v - S^t_u S^t_v) - \frac{\alpha \Delta t}{\Delta d^2}(L^t_u L^t_u - W^t_u W^t_u) \tag{4}$$

$$C''^t_u = \frac{1}{2}(C^t_u + C'^{t+1}_u) - \frac{\alpha \Delta t}{2\Delta d^2}(C'_v(N'^{t+1}_u - S'^{t+1}_u) + C^t_u(L'^{t+1}_u - W'^{t+1}_u)) \tag{5}$$

The **Conserve** step can be divided into three sub-steps. The first one is given by Eq. 6, where a temporary component $p$ is computed. The second sub-step, given by Eq. 7, is also solved with a relaxation method and the result is saved in the temporary component $d$. The third and final sub-step is to commit the changes on components $u$ and $v$ following the Eq. 8. The input for the Conserve part is either the last iteration of the Diffuse step $C^{t,nk}$ or the corrector step of the Advection step $C''^t$. After running the conserve over the Advection step, $C^t$ is the simulated flow for the time step $t$.

$$C^t_p = \frac{1}{\Delta x + \Delta y}(L^t_u - W^t_u) + \frac{1}{\Delta x + \Delta y}(N^t_v - S^t_v) \tag{6}$$

$$C^{t,k+1}_d = \frac{1}{4\Delta d^2}(\frac{1}{\Delta d^2}(N^{t,k}_d + S^{t,k}_d) + \frac{1}{\Delta d^2}(L^{t,k}_d + W^{t,k}_d) - C^t_p) \tag{7}$$

$$C^t_u = C^t_u - \frac{1}{\Delta x + \Delta y}(L^{t,nk}_d - W^{t,nk}_d) \tag{8}$$

The serial implementation solves all these equations one-by-one for each cell $C$ and timestamp $t$. After the final iteration, we have the simulated fluid flow for a given period of time. In the following section, we explain how we adapted the serial steps to the Task-Based programming method using StarPU.

## 4.2   Task-Based Heterogeneous Parallel Version

The design of a task-based parallel version starts with the definition of tasks. Since the numerical methods are already divided into very specific and modular steps (and sub-steps), we define each task to solve each step or sub-step of the method. In the Advection phase, we split it into two tasks: the Predictor (MacCormack$_1$) and the Corrector sub-step (MacCormack$_2$). Also, the Conserve step is split into three sub-steps, each one solving one of the earlier conserve equations, the first task (Conserve$_1$), the relaxation task (Conserve$_{relax}$) and the commit task (Conserve$_{commit}$).

To exploit enough parallelism without incurring too much overhead, cells (the smallest compute-bound grain) are grouped into blocks. Each task then operate with a block granularity. An example of domain partitioning is presented in Fig. 2(a), using 3 as partition width division, resulting in nine blocks. Each block has a coordinate related to its X and Y position. The number of blocks determines the total number of tasks, and by consequence the size of the DAG. The implementation supports different block sizes to validate the best configuration. Using this layout, one task being applied to a block will require some data in the edges. We implement two different approaches to express this data dependency: full block and ghost cells [15] dependency. The full block version uses the entire neighbors' blocks as dependency, simplifying the implementation, it is presented on Fig. 2(a). Where the task diffuse_relax for the block (1, 1), in purple, depends from the Start task from its neighbors in orange. The second version uses ghost cells for each block, where the dependencies are just the rows or columns used. This version replicates the data, as each task needs to update not only the used block, but each ghost row/column structure that will be used by his neighbors. This representation can be seen on Fig. 2(b), where the data dependencies of the task diffuse_relax for block (1, 1), in purple, are only the ghost cells, in orange, of its neighbors. In both versions the application DAG is the same and presented on Fig. 2(c). Each circle is a task related to a block, with its coordinate inside; each color a task type; and each arrow a dependency.

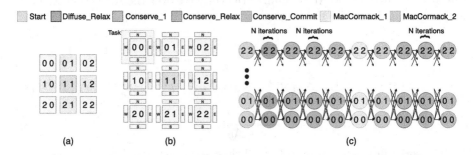

(a)     (b)     (c)

**Fig. 2.** With a 9 blocks (width 3) partition: (a) Full block dependency version. (b) Ghost cells version. (c) Application DAG. (Color figure online)

All the tasks are coded for both CPU and GPU. The GPU version uses the CUDA specification. Even if implementations can be considered naive, they permit an extensive analysis of StarPU using different number of resources and application blocks. We force the execution of the first task on GPU. In the initial implementation, we used two temporary buffers to compute each method, but because it causes an implicit synchronization we opt to use the StarPU mechanism to keep temporary data, and pass all the responsibility to StarPU's memory manager. The tasks' submission order follows the STF paradigm, where for each time step method, we submit the correspondent task for each block, hence, all tasks of a given method have a submission order id smaller than the next method's tasks for that time step. This is important for some schedulers because the submission order is used as priority.

## 5   Performance Analysis

The conducted performance analysis relies on experiments over a heterogeneous single node machine, with controlled HW/SW environments. First we present our experiment design, following a performance overview evaluation using speedup analysis, and finally a more comprehensive trace-based analysis.

## 5.1   Experimental Design

The experiments relies on the simulation of the previously described scenario (Sect. 4). Only three time-steps are executed to check how the different tasks behave inside a time step, to limit the trace size, and to have a reasonable execution time. Also, three iterations enable the observation of the first time-step, a middle one (which would repeat many times), and the last one. This characterizes all possible interactions among time-steps. All experiments are executed on a host equipped with 1x CPU Intel E5-2620v4 2.10 GHz with 8 cores, 2× GPUs Nvidia GTX 1080Ti, and 64 GB of main memory.

Our experimental design involves the problem domain size, the number of blocks, the runtime scheduler adopted, the use or not of GPUs in the application, and the dependency version (full block or ghost cells). Four input mesh sizes are evaluated: a mesh width of 5000 (5K) cells with 25 million cells; 10K with 100 million cells; 20K with 400 million cells, and 30K with 900 million cells. Different partition widths are employed to evaluate the task granularity with respect to other factors. We varied the partition width from 3 to 10, where a width of 3 generates $3^2$ blocks. The LWS, DM, DMDA, and DMDAR StarPU schedulers are used (see [4] for details). Finally, the application is divided in three versions: CPU-only, hybrid CPU/GPU with full block dependencies, and the CPU/GPU with optimized dependencies using ghost cells. All execution times for speedup measurements are collected with the trace generation feature disable, to reduce intrusion.

## 5.2   Speedup Analysis: CPU, CPU/GPU, and Ghost Cells

The first metric presented is the speedup of the implemented versions against the serial execution. We use 25 as number of blocks (width 5) for these experiments to generate enough parallelism. Each configuration is executed at least 10 times, and speedups are calculated using the mean of the configuration and of serial times. The speedup is plotted in the Y axis of Fig. 3a as a function of the mesh size. In this plot, each color represents a scheduler, the facets show three scenarios: CPU-only (left), CPU/GPU, and CPU/GPU with the ghost cells implementation.

The results show that the best speedup achieved (≈60×) is the one with CPU/GPU and ghost cells using the DMDAR scheduler with 20K as input. The StarPU CPU-only version have stable speedups independent of the scheduler and input size; while in CPU/GPU, LWS achieves lower performance because it is unaware of the cost of copying data to/from the GPUs. For the input size 30K, the CPU/GPU full block version has a very low speedup (even lower than the CPU counterpart). Such strange behavior disappears when we use our implementation based on ghost cells. This behavior is further investigated with traces in the following sections. Additionally, we also provide another overview based on the number of blocks. Figure 3b depicts the speedup (on Y) as a function of the block width (on X) for the three scenarios. These results are obtained with an input size width fixed to 20K (the best result in the left).

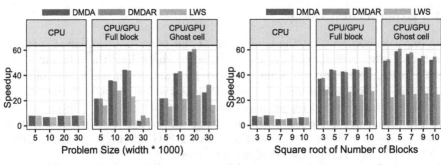

(a) Using 25 blocks (width 5) and com-  (b) Using a problem size of 20000 and
paring simulation size widths.             comparing many number of blocks.

**Fig. 3.** Speedup for different schedulers, input size, blocks, application versions.

The Fig. 3b shows that the best overall speedup is obtained with a partition width of five. Such parameter influences the total number of tasks that can potentially be executed in parallel. A smaller width leads to less tasks, so the application becomes incapable to generate enough tasks to occupy all the resources. A bigger width leads to too much tasks, imposing scheduler overheads. Such results also shows that the behavior of the schedulers on different partitions widths are similar, favoring DMDA-based schedulers. Next section details such behavior using StarPU execution traces.

### 5.3   Block Size Comparison and Application Iteration Overlapping

We provide a more detailed performance analysis based on traces and an analysis on the StarVZ toolkit. We demonstrate how the number of blocks impacts the speedup and also the application behavior with different schedulers. We compare the DM scheduler with the 20K problem size for cases with nine blocks (partition width of 3), shown in Fig. 4 (left), against the use of 16 (partition width 4), shown in Fig. 4 (center) and using the LWS scheduler with 36 blocks (partition width 6) in Fig. 4 (right). Each of these figures consists of three panels, from top to bottom: the **Iteration** plot where the colored rectangles representing tasks of the application time-steps (on the Y axis) are depicted as a function of time (on X); the **Applications** plot, where tasks for each resource (on Y), along with the idle time percentages (left) and the makespan (right), are represented along time; finally, the **Ready** plot shows the number of ready tasks (on Y) along time. Ready tasks are tasks that have all dependencies satisfied, so they are ready to be executed.

The first notable difference in the comparison of Fig. 4 is the makespan. The version using 9 blocks is 10% slower than the 16 blocks one. We can check that the overall idle time of the resources are higher on that version, presenting idle times from 6% to 13%. The cause for this is answered in the Ready plot. It shows the total amount of Ready Tasks: in the 9 blocks version, many time steps have

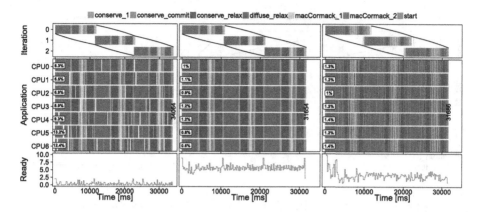

**Fig. 4.** CPU-only performance with 20K size, DM scheduler with 9 blocks (left) and with 16 blocks (center), and the LWS scheduler and 36 blocks (right).

the total amount of ready tasks reaching zero. This indicates that StarPU was unable to schedule any task on any resource because tasks were unavailable. In the 16-block version (center), we can see that the minimum ready tasks during the whole execution is three.

Besides the number of blocks, the scheduler also affects the performance. Figure 4 (right) shows a case with the LWS scheduler and 36 blocks. Comparing this case with the other ones we can see that the Iteration panel (top) shows that the LWS heuristic prefer to execute tasks of different methods together (respecting dependencies) leading to the execution of different time-steps simultaneously. In the DM, the submission order is used as priority if none other value is specified. Since all tasks of one method are submitted before the next one, the heuristic attempts to finish the former method first. For the LWS, tasks are schedule when they are ready, no matter for which iteration or method they belong to. Some submitted tasks from future iterations or methods can then be executed in advance, causing the overlap. This serves as an application signature to differentiate schedulers. Yet, in this case, no difference in the makespan is seen as only the tasks execution order changes while all workers are kept busy.

## 5.4   Behavior Characterization of the StarPU GPU Version

The performance overview (Fig. 3) depicts a performance drop with the GPU versions for the 30K simulation size. The full block dependency version became worse than the CPU-only version. However, even with a drop, the ghost cells version is still the best for that input size. To understand the reason behind such behavior, Fig. 5 (left) depicts the case when using the full blocks dependency version, while Fig. 5 (right) shows the case when using ghost cells. Both are enriched with new plots: (a) the **StarPU** plot shows the runtime states for each resource; (b) the **Used Memory** plot shows how much memory (on Y) is used for each memory manager (color) along time; (c) the **Bandwidth** plot shows the

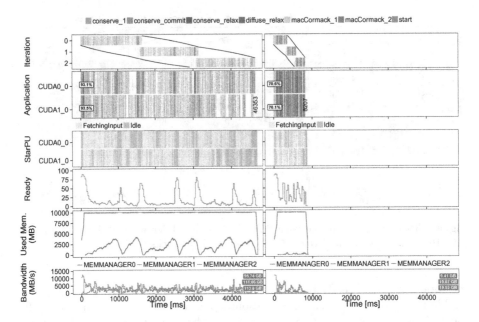

**Fig. 5.** Performance using GPUs with the DM scheduler, 100 blocks, input size of 30K with the total block dependency version (left) and ghost cells (right).

out transfers bandwidth for each memory manager, where the numbers in the right indicate the total amount of memory transferred. The MEMMANAGER0 is the memory ram, and the MEMMANAGER1 and 2 were for GPUs 1 and 2 respectively.

The overall data visualization shows that these executions have a different behavior as seen in the only CPU version. Here the CPUs don't appear because were not used, and the accelerators have high idle times, 90%+ on the total block dependency and 70%+ on the ghost cell version. To compare and understand the difference between makespan (46353 ms × 8207 ms), we can use the new memory related plots. In both versions, the total memory used on GPUs is the same, that is actually the total physical memory available and used by StarPU. However, the different of used memory RAM is huge. Also some related information can be checked in the Bandwidth plot, where the total amounts of data transferred are significant higher in the total block dependency version compared to the ghost cells version. This fact is explained because the accelerators need to transfer more portions of data between them (the entire block versus only the row or column used) causing high idle times waiting for data. In the StarPU plot is possible to check the states of Fetching Input, meaning that the tasks were waiting data of another device to execute. The combination of these observations (too much data transfers, high RAM memory usage) makes the ghost cell implementation much more scalable.

# 6    Conclusion

This article presents the implementation and the performance analysis of a CFD application using the task-based programming model over the StarPU runtime system. We present the numerical methods used, how they are organized into tasks to formulate a DAG required by the runtime, and the needed steps to build the parallel version (domain decomposition) of the program. The experiments conducted registered a 6.5× speedup compared to the serial version on the target machine using 7 CPU workers and a 60× speedup using 5 CPU and 2 GPU workers. Traces are used to check extra information about the execution, explaining why certain configurations for domain decomposition are inappropriate. Larger granularities, like partition width 3, were insufficient to provide enough tasks to the workers. Also, the behavior comparison between different StarPU schedulers showed that DM based schedulers prefer to compute all tasks' method first before advancing, while the LWS scheduler overlapped different tasks and iterations. The use of detailed execution traces has enabled us to explain why the ghost cells versions achieve better results compared with the total block dependency version. This article shows that the adopted numerical methods can be modeled using the task-based programming model, yet, careful attention should be taken to the definition of tasks, the DAG design, and the data dependency among tasks, as they are the primary structure to express the parallelism and data movement conducted by the runtime.

The future work of this investigation includes the use of new methods, tasks definition, and DAG structure to reduce data transfers among resources, to overcome the problem causing idle times while tasks could not start because of data dependencies still being transferred to the GPU. Finally, we also intend to implement of a multi-node version with StarPU-MPI. Besides enabling larger simulations that require more memory, we intend to verify the scalability of the static partitioning for our CFD setup.

**Acknowledgements.** This study was financed by the National Council for Scientific and Technological Development (CNPq). We thank these projects for supporting this investigation: FAPERGS GreenCloud (16/488-9), the FAPERGS MultiGPU (16/354-8), the CNPq 447311/2014-0, the CAPES/Brafitec EcoSud 182/15, and the CAPES/Cofecub 899/18. The companion material is hosted by CERN's Zenodo for which we are also grateful.

# References

1. Afzal, A., Ansari, Z., Faizabadi, A.R., Ramis, M.K.: Parallelization strategies for computational fluid dynamics software: state of the art review. Arch. Comput. Methods Eng. **24**(2), 337–363 (2017)
2. Agullo, E., et al.: Faster, cheaper, better-a hybridization methodology to develop linear algebra software for GPUS (2010)
3. Agullo, E., Buttari, A., Guermouche, A., Lopez, F.: Implementing multifrontal sparse solvers for multicore architectures with sequential task flow runtime systems. ACM Trans. Math. Softw. **43**(2), 13:1–13:22 (2016)

4. Augonnet, C., Thibault, S., Namyst, R., Wacrenier, P.A.: StarPU: a unified plat-formfor task scheduling on heterogeneous multicore architectures. Concurr. Comput.: Pract. Exp. **23**, 187–198 (2011). SI: Euro-Par 2009

5. Blumofe, R.D., Joerg, C.F., Kuszmaul, B.C., Leiserson, C.E., Randall, K.H., Zhou, Y.: Cilk: an efficient multithreaded runtime system. J. Parallel Distrib. Comput. **37**(1), 55–69 (1996)

6. Bosilca, G., Bouteiller, A., Danalis, A., Herault, T., Lemarinier, P., Dongarra, J.: DAGuE: a generic distributed dag engine for high performance computing. Parallel Comput. **38**(1–2), 37–51 (2012)

7. Buttari, A.: Fine granularity sparse $QR$ factorization for multicore based systems. In: Jónasson, K. (ed.) PARA 2010. LNCS, vol. 7134, pp. 226–236. Springer, Heidelberg (2012). https://doi.org/10.1007/978-3-642-28145-7_23

8. Carpaye, J.M.C., Roman, J., Brenner, P.: Design and analysis of a task-basedparallelization over a runtime system of an explicit finite-volume CFD code withadaptive time stepping. J. Comput. Sci. **28**, 439–454 (2017)

9. Chafi, H., Sujeeth, A.K., Brown, K.J., Lee, H., Atreya, A.R., Olukotun, K.: A domain-specific approach to heterogeneous parallelism. SIGPLAN Not. **46**(8), 35–46 (2011)

10. Dagum, L., Menon, R.: OpenMP: an industry standard api for shared-memory programming. IEEE Comput. Sci. Eng. **5**(1), 46–55 (1998)

11. Gautier, T., Lima, J.V.F., Maillard, N., Raffin, B.: XKaapi: a runtime system for data-flow task programming on heterogeneous architectures. In: IEEE International Symposium on Parallel and Distributed Processing, pp. 1299–1308 (2013)

12. Gropp, W., Lusk, E., Skjellum, A.: Using MPI: Portable Parallel Programming with the Message-Passing Interface, vol. 1. MIT Press, Cambridge (1999)

13. Jacobsen, D., Thibault, J., Senocak, I.: An MPI-CUDA implementation for massively parallel incompressible flow computations on multi-GPU clusters. In: 48th AIAA Aerospace Sciences Meeting Including the New Horizons Forum and Aerospace Exposition, p. 522 (2010)

14. Jeannot, E., Fournier, Y., Lorendeau, B.: Experimenting task-based runtimes on a legacy computational fluid dynamics code with unstructured meshes. Comput. Fluids **173**, 51–58 (2018)

15. Kjolstad, F.B., Snir, M.: Ghost cell pattern. In: Proceedings of the 2010 Workshop on Parallel Programming Patterns, p. 4. ACM (2010)

16. NVIDIA: CUDA Toolkit Documentation v9.2.88. NVIDIA Corporation, Santa Clara, CA, USA (2018)

17. Pinto, V.G., Schnorr, L.M., Stanisic, L., Legrand, A., Thibault, S., Danjean, V.: A visual performance analysis framework for task-based parallel applications running on hybrid clusters. Pract. Exp. Concurr. Comput. **30**(18), e4472 (2018). https://onlinelibrary.wiley.com/doi/abs/10.1002/cpe.4472

18. Pletcher, R.H., Tannehill, J.C., Anderson, D.: Computational Fluid Mechanics and Heat Transfer. CRC Press, Boca Raton (2012)

19. Robison, A.D.: Intel® threading building blocks (TBB). In: Padua, D. (ed.) Encyclopedia of Parallel Computing, pp. 955–964. Springer, Boston (2011). https://doi.org/10.1007/978-0-387-09766-4_51

20. Stone, J.E., Gohara, D., Shi, G.: OpenCL: a parallel programming standard for heterogeneous computing systems. Comput. Sci. Eng. **12**(3), 66–73 (2010)

21. Xie, C.: Interactive heat transfer simulations for everyone. Phys. Teach. **50**(4), 237 (2012)

# Optimizing Packed String Matching on AVX2 Platform

Mehmet Akif Aydoğmuş[1,2(✉)] and M. Oğuzhan Külekci[1]

[1] Informatics Institute, Istanbul Technical University, Istanbul, Turkey
{aydogmusm,kulekci}@itu.edu.tr
[2] TUBITAK, The Scientific and Technological Research Council of Turkey, Kocaeli, Turkey

**Abstract.** Exact string matching, searching for all occurrences of given pattern $P$ on a text $T$, is a fundamental issue in computer science with many applications in natural language processing, speech processing, computational biology, information retrieval, intrusion detection systems, data compression, and etc. Speeding up the pattern matching operations benefiting from the SIMD parallelism has received attention in the recent literature, where the empirical results on previous studies revealed that SIMD parallelism significantly helps, while the performance may even be expected to get automatically enhanced with the ever increasing size of the SIMD registers. In this paper, we provide variants of the previously proposed EPSM and SSEF algorithms, which are originally implemented on Intel SSE4.2 (Streaming SIMD Extensions 4.2 version with 128-bit registers). We tune the new algorithms according to Intel AVX2 platform (Advanced Vector Extensions 2 with 256-bit registers) and analyze the gain in performance with respect to the increasing length of the SIMD registers. Profiling the new algorithms by using the Intel Vtune Amplifier for detecting performance bottlenecks led us to consider the cache friendliness and shared-memory access issues in the AVX2 platform. We applied cache optimization techniques to overcome the problems particularly addressing the search algorithms based on filtering.

Experimental comparison of the new solutions with the previously known-to-be-fast algorithms on small, medium, and large alphabet text files with diverse pattern lengths showed that the algorithms on AVX2 platform optimized cache obliviously outperforms the previous solutions.

**Keywords:** String matching · AVX2 SIMD · Cache optimization · Intel Vtune Amplifier

© Springer Nature Switzerland AG 2019
H. Senger et al. (Eds.): VECPAR 2018, LNCS 11333, pp. 45–61, 2019.
https://doi.org/10.1007/978-3-030-15996-2_4

# 1   Introduction

Finding all occurrences of given pattern on a text, named as exact string matching is one of the basic tasks in computer science. It has many applications in diverse fields such as natural language processing, speech processing, computational biology, information retrieval, intrusion detection systems, data compression etc. Nowadays most applications requiring string matching works with large datasets thus the speed of string matching is gaining importance. The exact string matching problem is described as counting all the occurrences of a pattern $P$ of length m in a text $T$ of length n assuming m $\ll$ n, over a finite alphabet $\Sigma$. Numerous string matching algorithms have been presented since the 1970s with the various theoretical point of view. Even so, new methods are still being developed to achieve better searching times. Knuth-Morris-Pratt algorithm is based on finite automata with $\mathscr{O}(m)$ and $\mathscr{O}(n)$ time complexity [6]. Boyer-Moore algorithm is a combination of heuristic approaches which are "bad character heuristic" and "good suffix heuristic" with $\mathscr{O}(mn)$ worst-case time complexity (best case time $\mathscr{O}(n/m)$) [13]. Backward-DAWG-Matching algorithm [8] (BDM) is based on the suffix automaton for the reversed pattern and it has asymptotic optimum average time complexity $\mathscr{O}(n(\log_\sigma m)/m)$ especially for the long pattern.

Shift Or (SO) and Backward Nondeterministic DAWG Matching (BNDM) algorithms are based on the bit-parallelism technique. BNDM algorithm uses bit parallel simulation of the suffix automaton and its efficient variants are presented later like BNDMq [1], BSDM [20], FSBDNMq [2], SBNDMq [3], UFNDMq [1], EBOM [21].

Filter based solutions have been also developed for string matching, Karp-Rabin algorithm [12] is the first filtering algorithm using a hashing function with $\mathscr{O}(mn)$ time complexity but $\mathscr{O}(n + m)$ expected running time. Another filtering algorithm is Q-Gram (QF) which is based on consecutive q-grams in the text with $\mathscr{O}(mn)$ worst case complexity and $\mathscr{O}(nq/(m - q))$ best case complexity. String matching algorithms are classified into 4 classes by Faro and Lecroq [17]; comparison, automata type, bit-parallelism and packed type. An extensive review of the string matching algorithms between 2000–2010 and comprehensive experimental evaluation of 85 exact string matching algorithms are presented by Faro and Lecroq, [18,19] respectively.

The usage of SIMD (Single Instruction Multiple Data) in string matching algorithms is appeared in recent years [11,15,22,24,25]. Tarhio et al. [10] newly proposed the algorithm compares 16 or 32 characters in parallel by applying SSE2 and AVX2 instructions besides they use the increasing order for comparisons of pattern symbols for better results. In this paper, we present Intel-AVX2 (Advanced Vector Extensions 2) based variations of the EPSM [22] and SSEF [11] algorithms with a different point of view. Especially we concentrate on the practical efficiency of new algorithms and so optimize the algorithms in this manner according to the profiling results.

## 2   Notions and Basics

String p of length $m > 0$ can be defined as character array $p[0...m-1]$ over the finite alphabet $\Sigma$ of size $\sigma$ and $p[i]$ corresponds the $(i+1)$-st character for $0 \le i < m$. Substring of p between indexes $(i+1)$-st and the $(j+1)$-st characters is represented by $p[i...j]$ while $0 \le i \le j < m$. Also it can be expressed as $p_i = p[i]$ and $p = p_0p_1...p_{m-1}$. Using notations above, exact string matching is searching of condition as $p_0p_1...p_{m-1} = t_it_{i+1}...t_{i+m-1}$ where the text is $T = t_0t_1...t_n$. We make use of bitwise operators on computer words in the algorithms such as bitwise AND "&", bitwise OR "|" and left shift "≪" where computer word size is denoted by $w$.

A string can be represented as $S = s_0s_1...s_{k-1}$ where k is the number of the characters and each character corresponds to the single byte. The bits of single byte $s_i$ can be defined as bit array like $s_i = b_0^i b_1^i b_2^i b_3^i b_4^i b_5^i b_6^i b_7^i$ where $b_0^i$ is the msb bit. The chunk of 32-byte is represented as $C^i = s_{32 \cdot i}s_{32 \cdot i+1}s_{32 \cdot i+2}...s_{32 \cdot i+31}$ hereby string is described in terms of 32-byte chunks as $S = C^0C^1C^2...C^z$ where $z = \lfloor (k-1)/32 \rfloor$ and $0 \le i \le z$. If k value is not divisible by 32, the last chunk $C^z$ is incomplete and zero padding is applied for the rightmost empty part as $s_l = 0$ where $k-1 < l$. The number of 32-byte chunks of text $(T)$ and pattern $(P)$ are shown as $N = \lceil n/32 \rceil$ and $M = \lceil m/32 \rceil$. The chunk and byte symbols of text $(T)$ and pattern $(P)$ are presented such as:

Text Representation: single byte $t_i$, $0 \le i < n$; 32-byte chunks: $Y^i$, $0 \le i < N$

| $Y^0$ | $Y^1$ | ... | $Y^{N-1}$ |
|---|---|---|---|
| $t_0t_1...t_{31}$ | $t_{32}t_{33}...t_{63}$ | ... | $t_{32 \cdot (N-1)}t_{32 \cdot (N-1)+1}...t_{n-1}$ |

Pattern Representation: single byte $p_i$, $0 \le i < m$; 32-byte chunks: $R^i$, $0 \le i < M$

| $R^0$ | $R^1$ | ... | $R^{M-1}$ |
|---|---|---|---|
| $p_0p_1...p_{31}$ | $p_{32}p_{33}...p_{63}$ | ... | $p_{32 \cdot (M-1)}p_{32 \cdot (M-1)+1}...p_{m-1}$ |

## 3   Algorithms

Firstly we will give descriptions of word-size instructions which are composed of AVX2 intrinsics, our newly presented matching algorithms are based on this instructions operating with 256 bits on Intel Broadwell architecture.

**wscmp_a(a; b) (word-size compare instruction on AVX2).** In the EPSM algorithm, wscmp instruction is defined as $a = a_0a_1...a_{\alpha-1}$ and $b = b_0b_1...b_{k-1}$, wscmp returns an $\alpha$ bit value, $r = r_0r_1...r_{\alpha-1}$ where $r_i = 1$ if and only if $a_i = b_i$ and $r_i = 0$ otherwise. We emulate this operation with 256-bit SIMD instructions named as wscmp_a instead of using 128-bit instructions like in EPSM.

$h \leftarrow$ _mm256_cmpeq_epi8$(a, b)$

$r \leftarrow$ _mm256_movemask_epi8$(h)$

_mm256_cmpeq_epi8 (latency $= 1$) compares packed 8-bit integers in 256-bit a and b for equality, and returns the result as 256-bit data. _mm256_movemask_epi8 instruction creates mask using the most significant bit of each 8-bit element in 256-bit $h$ and returns the 32-bit result. The Fig. 1 shows an example of the operation of wscmp_a(a; b) when working with characters in ASCII code on 256-bit registers, assuming a:"*tcgac...atg*" and b:"*cagtc...cta*" which are composed of 32 characters.

| Char: | 1 | 2 | 3 | 4 | 5 | ...... | 30 | 31 | 32 |
|---|---|---|---|---|---|---|---|---|---|
| a: | 01110100 | 01100011 | 01100111 | 01100001 | 01100011 | | 01100001 | 01110100 | 01100111 |
| b: | 01100011 | 01100001 | 01100111 | 01110100 | 01100011 | | 01100011 | 01110100 | 01100001 |
| | ⇓ | | wscmp_a(a, b) | | | ⇓ | | | |
| r: | 0 | 0 | 1 | 0 | 1 | | 0 | 1 | 0 |

Fig. 1. An example of the operation of wscmp_a(a; b) instruction

**wsmatch_a(a; b) (word-size matching instruction on AVX2).** wsmatch instruction is defined as in the EPSM; $a = a_0a_1...a_{\alpha-1}$ and $b = b_0b_1...b_{\alpha-1}$, wsmatch returns an $\alpha$ bit integer value, $r = r_0r_1...r_{\alpha-1}$ where $r_i = 1$ if and only if $a_{i+j} = b_j$ for $j = 0...k - 1$. Also, let z be a 256-bit register with all elements are set to zero by _mm256_setzero_si256 intrinsic. We emulate this operation with 256-bit SIMD instructions named as wsmatch_a instead of using 128-bit instructions.

$h \leftarrow$ _mm256_mpsadbw_epu8$(a, b, imm8)$

$h \leftarrow$ _mm256_cmpeq_epi8$(h, z)$

$r \leftarrow$ _mm256_movemask_epi8$(l)$

_mm256_mpsadbw_epu8 (latency $= 6$) calculates 16 SADs, however, operates on 128-bit lanes separately instead of the whole 256-bit data. This condition requires additional shuffling of input data to properly store data compatible with instruction. wspermute_a instruction is used to make this shuffling. The Fig. 2 shows an example of the wsmatch_a(a; b) operating with characters in ASCII code on 256-bit registers, assuming a:"*gatcatgct...*" (32 characters) and b:"*tcat*" (4 characters).

| Char: | 1 | 2 | 3 | 4 | 5 | 6 | 7 | 8 | ... | 32 |
|---|---|---|---|---|---|---|---|---|---|---|
| a: | 01100111 | 01100001 | 01110100 | 01100011 | 01100001 | 01110100 | 01100111 | 01100011 | ... | ... |
| b: | 01110100 | 01100011 | 01100001 | 01110100 | | | | | | |
| | ⇓ | | | wsmatch_a(a, b) | | ⇓ | | | | |
| r: | 0 | 0 | 1 | 0 | 0 | 0 | 0 | 0 | ... | ... |

**Fig. 2.** An example of the operation of wsmatch_a(a, b) instruction

### wspermute_a($a, b$) (word-size permute instruction on AVX2)

wspermute_a corresponds to the wsblend instruction of EPSM algorithm and it arranges the 256-bit input data for the right order required while SADs operation.

```
h = _mm256_permute2f128_si256 (a, b, imm8);
permute = _mm256_setr_epi32(0, 1, 2, 0, 2, 3, 4, 0);
r = _mm256_permutevar8x32_epi32(h, permute);
```

_mm256_permute2f128_si256 (latency = 3) instruction shuffles 128-bits data selected by $imm8$ from $a$ and $b$, and returns data in 256-bit type. _mm256_setr_epi32 instruction assigns eight input data with the packed 32-bit integer to 256-bit data in reverse order and returns the arranged 256-bit data. _mm256_permutevar8x32_epi32 shuffles 32-bit integers between across lanes using the input permute variable and returns the 256-bit result (latency = 6). Also, vpermd (_mm256_permutevar8x32_epi32) instruction is used to shuffle the text chunk while second level filtering as shown in the EPSMA-2 algorithm pseudo code.

### popcnt($a$) instruction

popcnt instruction corresponds to the _mm_popcnt_u32(a) (latency = 3) instruction which counts the number of bits set to 1 in input $a$ which is unsigned 32-bit integer and returns the count value.

### wsfilter_a(C; K) (word-size filter computing instruction on AVX2)

wsfilter_a specialized word-size packed instruction calculates the filter values using shift value K on 32-byte chunks C. This instruction can be emulated in constant time by the following AVX2 intrinsics function (Latency of _mm256_slli_epi64=1).

$$D \leftarrow \text{_mm256_slli_epi64}(C, K)$$

$$f \leftarrow \text{_mm256_movemask_epi8}(D)$$

## 3.1  EPSMA

EPSM (Exact Packed String Matching) algorithm is implemented using SSE instructions operated on 128-bit registers called XMM [22]. In the EPSMA (new version of EPSM) we will use AVX2 instructions which operate on 256-bit registers called YMM.

**EPSMA-1 Algorithm:** The EPSMA-1 algorithm is developed for short patterns so it is used for pattern lengths which are smaller than 8. The algorithm is based on wscmp_a instruction described above. It has two main phase; the preprocessing of the algorithm (lines 2–5) and the searching phase (lines 6–13) as shown in EPSMA-1 pseudo code 1. It can be said that by taking into account descriptions of wscmp_a, $p[0...m-1]$ has occurrence starting at position $j$ of $T_i$ if and only if $r_j = 1$. Occurrence count is calculated by popcnt instruction (line 10) and carry bits are stored (line 11) for comparison of next loop.

---

**Algorithm 1.** EPSMA-1 Algorithm Pseudo Code

---

1: **procedure** EPSMA1( $p,m,t,n$ )
2:     $n' \leftarrow 32 *( n /32 )$  // last index divisible by 32
3:     **for** $i \leftarrow 0$ to ( $m$ -1 )  **do**
4:         **for** $j \leftarrow 0$ to (32-1)  **do**
5:             $B_i[j] \leftarrow p[i]$
6:     **for** $i \leftarrow 0$ to ( $n'/32$ )- 1  **do**
7:         **for** $j \leftarrow 0$ to ( $m$ - 1 )  **do**
8:             $s_j \leftarrow$ wscmp_a( $T_i, B_j$ )
9:             $r \leftarrow ( s_j \ll j ) - ( carry_j \gg ( 32\text{-}j ) )$
10:            $count \leftarrow count +$ popcnt($r$ ) , $carry_j \leftarrow s_j$ & $mask_j$
11:    **for** $j \leftarrow n' - 32$ to $n$ **do**
12:        check position at($j - m$ )  // for last remaining part

---

**EPSMA-2 Algorithm:** The EPSMA-2 algorithm is designed by taking advantage of wsmatch_a instruction which implements the SADs operation. It is applied for pattern lengths from 8 to 32, while it could be used for greater pattern lengths performance of algorithm decreases experimentally. This algorithm is a type of filtering technique, 2-stage filtering is applied using 8 characters $(4+4)$ of pattern assigned in preprocessing phase (lines 2–3). At the initial stage wsmatch_a instruction is applied to first 4 characters $p'_1$ (lines 6) and if this stage is passed successfully then wsmatch_a is applied again to second 4 characters $p'_2$ (lines 9). When this 2-stage filtering is passed, if m = 8 the algorithm reports pattern occurrence easily otherwise the naive check is applied to positions starting at $i*32$ regarding $r$ (lines 11–13). For the arrangement of text data required while applying wsmatch_a instruction to second 16-byte chunk, wspermute_a instruction described above is used (lines 14). Then the same operations are performed again for second part of each loop (lines 15–22). Additionally when pattern length $m$ is between 16 and 32, 4 characters of the pattern are skipped while assigning characters in preprocessing (line 2–3) in order to filter more effectively. So, second assignment (line 3) is like that $p'_2 \leftarrow p[8..11]$ for $16 \leq m < 32$.

**EPSMA-3 Algorithm:** The EPSMA-3 algorithm uses a filtering approach based on SSEF algorithm [11]. 16-bit filters are calculated for filtering stage as in SSEF algorithm but the calculation of EPSMA-3 filters are made on 256-bit data chunks, unlike SSEF. This algorithm benefits wsfilter_a instruction which composed of shifting and masking operations as depicted above. Filter computing is performed on 256-bit chunks and separate filters $f_1$ and $f_2$ are extracted from 32-bit filter $f$ (line 9 and 15). In the preprocessing phase (line 2–10) all possible filters of the pattern are computed and then stored as an array of filters. If filters $f_1$ and $f_2$ computed in searching phase (line 11–19) exist in $FilterArray_{1,2}$, naive check operation will be applied separately whether there is an exact occurrence of the pattern. Furthermore, the loop of searching phase is unrolled by a factor of 2 in order to achieve optimal performance. EPSMA-3 algorithm is used for pattern length between 32 and 64 ($32 \leq m < 64$).

| **Algorithm 2.** EPSMA-2 Pseudo Code | **Algorithm 3.** EPSMA-3 Pseudo Code |
|---|---|
| 1: **procedure** EPSMA2( $p,m,t,n$ ) | 1: **procedure** EPSMA3 ( $p,m,t,n$ ) |
| 2:    $p'_1 \leftarrow p[0..3]$, $p'_2 \leftarrow p[4..7]$ | 2:    $L \leftarrow \lceil m/16 \rceil - 1$ |
| 3:    $idx \leftarrow$ _mm256_setr(1,2,3,0,3,4,5,0) | 3:    $FilterArray_{1,2} \leftarrow \emptyset$ |
| 4:    **for** $i \leftarrow 0$ to ( $n/32$ )- 1  **do** | 4:    $mask \leftarrow$ 0x3FFF |
| 5:        $r \leftarrow$ wsmatch_a( $T_i, p'_1$ ) | 5:    $K \leftarrow$ a, $0 \leq a < 8$, according to the alphabet; |
| 6:        **if** $r > 0$ **then** | 6:    **for** $i \leftarrow 0$ to ( $16 \cdot L + 1$ ) **do** |
| 7:            $S \leftarrow$ vpermd($T_i$, idx) | 7:        $d \leftarrow$ _mm256_set_epi8 ( $p_i + 31, ..., p_i$ ) |
| 8:            $r \leftarrow$ wsmatch_a($S, p'_2$ ) | 8:        $f \leftarrow$ wsfilter_a(($d,K$)) , $ftemp \leftarrow$ f $\gg 2$ |
| 9:            **if** $r > 0$ **then** | 9:        $f_1 \leftarrow ftemp\&$ (mask) ; $f_2 \leftarrow ftemp \gg$ (16) |
| 10:                **if** $m = 8$ **then** | 10:        $FilterArray_{1,2}[ f_{1,2}] \leftarrow Filter[ f_{1,2}] \cup i_{1,2}$ |
| 11:                    report match at ($i$*32 + $r$) | 11:    **while** $i < N$ **do** |
| 12:                **else** check match at ($i$*32 + $r$) | 12:        **if** $L = 2$ **then** |
| 13:            $S \leftarrow$ wspermute_a( $T_i, T_{i+1}$ ) | 13:            $T_i \leftarrow$ vperm2f128 _a( $T_i, T_{i+1}, 32$ ) |
| 14:            $r \leftarrow$ wsmatch_a( $S, p'_1$ ) | 14:        $f \leftarrow$ wsfilter_a(($T_i,K$)) , $ftemp \leftarrow$ f $\gg 2$ |
| 15:            **if** $r > 0$ **then** | 15:        $f_1 \leftarrow ftemp\&$ (mask) ; $f_2 \leftarrow ftemp \gg$ (16) |
| 16:                $S \leftarrow$ vpermd($S$, idx) | 16:        **for all** $j \in FilterArray_1 [ f_1]$ **do** |
| 17:                $r \leftarrow$ wsmatch_a( $S, p'_2$ ) | 17:            check occurrence at( $t_{32 \cdot (i)-j}$ ) |
| 18:                **if** $r > 0$ **then** | 18:        **for all** $j \in FilterArray_2 [ f_2]$ **do** |
| 19:                    **if** $m = 8$ **then** | 19:            check occurrence at( $t_{32 \cdot (i+L)-j}$ ) |
| 20:                        report match at ($i$*32+16 + $r$) | 20:        $i \leftarrow i + L$ |
| 21:                    **else** check match at ($i$*32+16 + $r$) | |

## 3.2   SSEFA

SSEFA is a new variation of SSEF algorithm which is filter based algorithm composed of filtering and the verification parts. SSEFA is designed for long patterns such as greater sizes than 64 ($64 \leq$ m). The zero-based address of the last 32-byte chunk of pattern not including zero padding is represented by L symbol as $L = \lfloor m/32 \rfloor - 1$. For instance, let's assume m $= 120$, in this case, 32-byte chunks of the pattern are like that $R = R^0 R^1 R^2 R^3$. Last chunk $R^3$ has 24 bytes of the pattern so remaining 8 bytes are padded with zero and L value becomes $L = \lfloor 120/32 \rfloor - 1 = 2$. If we define $0 \leq h < \lfloor N/L \rfloor$, the filter computing is applied on chunk $Y^{h \cdot L + L}$. If there is a proper alignment of pattern part between the $Y^{h\cdot L}$ and $Y^{h\cdot L+(L-1)}$ according to the filter value, naive checking on remaining part of the text will be applied for this matching candidates. Possible alignments of pattern bytes are given in the following figure when we compute the filters on 32-byte chunks from $Y^{i+L}$ where $i = h \cdot L$ and all bytes representing with $Y^{i+L}$ chunks are filled with patterns.

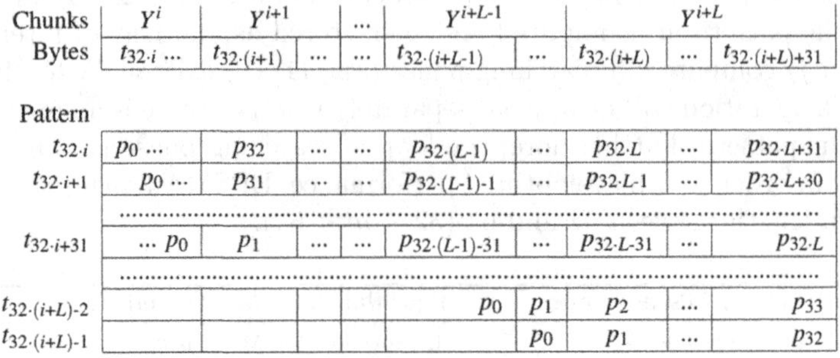

| Chunks | $Y^i$ | $Y^{i+1}$ | ... | $Y^{i+L-1}$ | | $Y^{i+L}$ | |
|---|---|---|---|---|---|---|---|
| Bytes | $t_{32\cdot i}$ ... | $t_{32\cdot(i+1)}$ | ... | ... $t_{32\cdot(i+L-1)}$ | ... | $t_{32\cdot(i+L)}$ | ... $t_{32\cdot(i+L)+31}$ |

Pattern

| | | | | | | | |
|---|---|---|---|---|---|---|---|
| $t_{32\cdot i}$ | $p_0$ ... | $p_{32}$ | ... | ... $p_{32\cdot(L-1)}$ | ... | $p_{32\cdot L}$ | ... $p_{32\cdot L+31}$ |
| $t_{32\cdot i+1}$ | $p_0$ ... | $p_{31}$ | ... | ... $p_{32\cdot(L-1)-1}$ | ... | $p_{32\cdot L-1}$ | ... $p_{32\cdot L+30}$ |
| ... | | | | | | | |
| $t_{32\cdot i+31}$ | ... $p_0$ | $p_1$ | ... | ... $p_{32\cdot(L-1)-31}$ | ... | $p_{32\cdot L-31}$ | ... |
| ... | | | | | | | |
| $t_{32\cdot(i+L)-2}$ | | | | $p_0$ | $p_1$ | $p_2$ | ... $p_{33}$ |
| $t_{32\cdot(i+L)-1}$ | | | | | $p_0$ | $p_1$ | ... $p_{32}$ |

**Fig. 3.** Appropriate pattern alignments

SSEFA algorithm has two part as preprocessing (line 2–10) and searching phase (line 11–19) as depicted in pseudo-code 2. The preprocessing part includes the initializations of data variables and the calculation of filter values over given pattern. All possible filter alignments illustrated in Fig. 3 are calculated and then stored in an array named as *FilterArray*. We use wsfilter_a instruction to calculate filter values over 256-bit data chunks. Filter calculation has two main operations as shifting and masking of 32-byte blocks. Shifting operation is required to make the filter more distinguishable. If text characters are inside in the first 128 of ASCII table, msb of each character is 0 so all filters will become zero without shifting. The most informative bit of text characters should be determined to create distinguishing filters. A convenient method is taking into account only the alphabet ($|\Sigma|$ bytes) with assuming the text characters have a uniform distribution.

Preprocessing procedure corresponds to the lines 2–11 of pseudo-code in Algorithm 4 which represents the skeleton of the SSEFA. Distinguishing bit position is assigned to K as shift value and shifting operation is applied as shown in line 8 and 13 of Algorithm 4. Shifting operation is performed by _mm256_slli_epi64(a,i) instruction which left shifts 256-bit data by input $i$ while padding zeros and masking operation is performed by _mm256_movemask_epi8(a) instruction which creates 32-bit mask from msb of each 32 bytes stored as 256-bit register. The following diagram sketches the operation of filter computing using AVX2 intrinsics on 32-byte chunks $C^j$ of pattern and text. Filter computing over 256-bit chunk (32 char) bit with representation is sketched in the Fig. 4. An example operation of wsfilter_a instruction is given in the Fig. 4 where shifting value K is 7 and sample text is composed of 32 characters given as "*abcdefghijklmnopqrstuvwxyz 01234*".

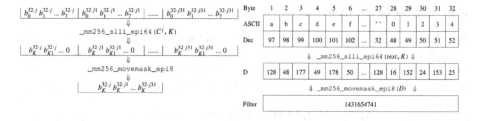

**Fig. 4.** Sketch and example operation of the filter instruction

In the searching phase, the main loop operates on 32-byte chunks $Y^i$ of text T in steps of L where $i = h \cdot L + L$ and $0 \leq h < \lfloor N/L \rfloor$. After masking operation filter is composed of 32-bit data, therefore, filter decimal value can be between 0 and $2^{32}$ (4294967295:4 GB). We use filter values as indexes while creating filters vector and the size of filter vector is determined by the maximum value of filters can get. If we use 32-bit filters, vector size becomes extremely larger as 4GB and latencies of memory access in searching phase will become the performance bottleneck. Filters vector could not fit in lower level caches and memory access time becomes dominant in overall searching performance. We apply memory access analysis using hardware event metrics on Intel Vtune Amplifier to detect memory issues and find optimal filter length. Detailed descriptions of memory analysis and optimization are given in the next section named as Cache Optimization.

---

**Algorithm 4.** SSEFA Algorithm Pseudo Code

---

1: **procedure** SSEFA ( $p,m,t,n$ )
2:     $L \leftarrow \lceil m/32 \rceil$ - 1
3:     $FilterArray_{1,2} \leftarrow \emptyset$
4:     $shift \leftarrow 18$ ; $mask \leftarrow$ 0x3FFF
5:     $K \leftarrow$ a, $0 \leq a < 8$, according to the alphabet;
6:     **for** $i \leftarrow 0$ to $(32 \cdot L + 1)$ **do**
7:         $d \leftarrow$ _mm256_set_epi8 $(p_i + 31, .., p_i)$
8:         $f \leftarrow$ wsfilter_a$((d,K))$
9:         $f_1 \leftarrow f \gg (shift)$ ; $f_2 \leftarrow f$ & $(mask)$
10:        $FilterArray_{1,2}[ f_{1,2}] \leftarrow FilterArray_{1,2}[ f_{1,2}] \cup i_{1,2}$
11:    **while** $i < N$ **do**
12:        $f \leftarrow$ wsfilter_a$((T_i,K))$
13:        $f_1 \leftarrow f \gg (shift)$
14:        **for all** $j \in FilterArray_1 [ f_1]$ **do**
15:            $f_2 \leftarrow f$ & $(mask)$
16:            **for all** $j \in FilterArray_2 [ f_2]$ **do**
17:                **if** $P = [t_{32 \cdot (i-L)+j} ... t_{32 \cdot (i-L)+j+m-1}]$ **then**
18:                    pattern occurrence at$( t_{32 \cdot (i-L)+j} )$
19:        $i \leftarrow i + L$

---

## 3.3    Cache Optimization

Intel Vtune Amplifier, performance analyzer tool for HPC applications, is used to identify memory-related issues especially memory access time when data can not fit in the L1 or L2 caches. Hardware Event-Based Sampling Analysis is selected for collecting event metrics values related to caches from microarchitecture.

$$L_i MissRate \equiv \frac{MEM\_LOAD\_UOPS\_RETIRED.L_i\_MISS}{INST\_RETIRED.ANY} \qquad i:1,2,3 \quad (1)$$

High miss rate implies that the advantage of the cache memory cannot be utilized exactly. The processor waste more time accessing the requested data if processing data don't exist in lower cache level. Hardware Event Metrics values over 100 test samples on SSEFA algorithm are shown in the following table:

**Table 1.** Intel microarchitecture hardware events

| Hardware event | Definition |
|---|---|
| MEM_LOAD_UOPS_RETIRED.L1_HIT | Counts retired load uops which data sources were hits in the nearest-level (L1) cache |
| MEM_LOAD_UOPS_RETIRED.L1_MISS | Counts retired load uops which data sources were misses in the nearest-level (L1) cache |
| MEM_LOAD_UOPS_RETIRED.L2_HIT | Counts retired load uops which data sources were hits in the mid-level (L2) cache |
| MEM_LOAD_UOPS_RETIRED.L2_MISS | Counts retired load uops which data sources were misses in the mid-level (L2) cache |
| MEM_LOAD_UOPS_RETIRED.L3_HIT | Counts retired load uops which data sources were data hits in the last-level (L3) cache |
| MEM_LOAD_UOPS_RETIRED.L3_MISS | Count misses in last-level (L3) cache |
| INST_RETIRED.ANY | Counts the number of instructions retired from execution |
| CPU_CLK_UNHALTED.THREAD | Counts the number of core cycles while the thread is not in a halt state |

**Table 2.** Values of hardware event metrics

| List Size | 4KB | 16KB | 64KB | 256KB | 1MB | 4MB | 16MB | 64MB | 256MB | 1GB | 4GB |
|---|---|---|---|---|---|---|---|---|---|---|---|
| CPU_CLK_UNHALTED.THREAD | 612,000,918 | 610,00,915 | 612,000,918 | 612,000,918 | 622,000,933 | 652,000,978 | 732,001,098 | 844,001,266 | 2,222,003,333 | 6,928,010,392 | 25,738,038,607 |
| INST_RETIRED.ANY | | 1,352,002,028 | 1,354,002,025 | 1,350,002,025 | 1,354,002,031 | 1,356,002,034 | 1,358,002,037 | 1,368,002,052 | 1,426,002,139 | 1,640,002,460 | 2,500,003,750 | 5,942,008,913 |
| MEM_LOAD_-RETIRED.L1_HIT | 1,004,001,506 | 992,001,488 | 1,000,001,500 | 1,000,001,500 | 1,004,001,506 | 996,001,494 | 992,001,488 | 1,012,001,518 | 1,020,001,530 | 1,052,00,578 | 1,220,001,830 |
| MEM_LOAD_RETIRED.L1_MISS | 2,400,072 | 2,300,072 | 2,600,078 | 2,600,078 | 2,640,078 | 2,675,260 | 2,800,078 | 3,200,096 | 4,400,132 | 8,600,258 | 25,400,762 |
| MEM_LOAD_RETIRED.L2_HIT | 1,200,036 | 1,600,048 | 1,000,030 | 800,024 | 600,018 | 600,018 | 600,018 | 1,000,030 | 1,200,036 | 3,000,090 | 9,000,270 |
| MEM_LOAD_RETIRED.L2_MISS | 0 | 0 | 0 | 0 | 0 | 0 | 0 | 0 | 0 | 0 | 0 |

**CPI Rate:** CPI (Cycles per Instruction), is a master performance metric for the analysis with hardware event-based sampling collections on Intel Vtune Amplifier. It indicates how many cycles have been executed to complete related instruction. Modern processor architectures can execute four instructions per cycle therefore theoretical best CPI value is 0.25. In general, high CPI value shows that performance decrease of the application which could be caused by issues such as memory stalls, long latency instructions, branch misprediction or instruction starvation. CPI value can be reduced as a result of optimizations using hardware-related metrics which identifies what is causing high CPI.

**Table 3.** Time and rate values for various list sizes

| List size | 4 KB | 16 KB | 64 KB | 256 KB | 1 MB | 4 MB | 16 MB | 64 MB | 256 MB | 1 GB | 4 GB |
|---|---|---|---|---|---|---|---|---|---|---|---|
| Elapsed time [ms] | 0.218 | 0.210 | 0.224 | 0.215 | 0.222 | 0.234 | 0.264 | 0.360 | 0.782 | 2.413 | 8.927 |
| CPI-Rate | 0.453 | **0.450** | 0.454 | 0.452 | 0.459 | 0.480 | 0.535 | 0.718 | 1.355 | 2.771 | 4.532 |
| L1 miss rate % | 1.775 | **1.698** | 1.925 | 1.920 | 1.946 | 1.969 | 2.046 | 2.244 | 2.683 | 3.440 | 4.274 |

It can be seen in the Table 3 the best CPI rate is 0.450 and L1 miss rate is 1.698 at the size of 16384 where the mask is composed of 14-bit 1. However if the only single 14-bit filter is used at filtration, there will be fewer filtering on match candidates of text chunks. In order to increase the selectivity of filtering operation, two-stage filtering method (using $2 \times 14$-bit filters) is used therefore the number of full verification decreases. Reduced filters using in 2-stage filtering are $FilterArray_1$ and $FilterArray_2$ as shown in pseudo-code of SSEFA and both of them are composed of distinct bits from separate halves of the main 32-bit filter. $FilterArray_1$ contains filters consisted of highest 14 bits (leftmost) of 32-bit filter whereas filters of $FilterArray_2$ consist of lowest 14 bits (rightmost). Formally, if 32-bit filter is defined as $f_i = b_0^i b_1^i b_2^i ... b_{31}^i$ reduced filters are $f_{1i} = b_0^i b_1^i b_2 - ^i ... b_{13}^i$ and $f_{2i} = b_{18}^i b_{19}^i b_{20}^i ... b_{31}^i$ as represented in line 8–9 of pseudo-code of SSEFA.

In preprocessing phase, computed filter values are used as index on filter arrays while assigning the values indicating possible alignment of pattern. $FilterArray_1$ is utilized like a guard for first level filtration so $FilterArray_1[i]$ value is set 1 where filter exists otherwise set to 0. $FilterArray_2$ is used as the secondary filtering to decrease the number of verification of the all pattern and $FilterArray_2[i]$ value is set the possible beginning position of the pattern in the text where filter exists otherwise set to 0. If 2-stage filtering is passed successfully over chunk $Y^i$, a full verification is to be performed between P and $t_{32 \cdot (i-L)+j} ... t_{32 \cdot (i-L)+j+m-1}$ using j value of $FilterArray_2[f]$ where $0 \leq j < 32 \cdot L$.

### Memory Access Analysis of List and Array Structures

Filters are stored as a linked-list in SSEF algorithm [3] however accessing an element may be a little slower due to using "nodes" on linked-list. Links are allocated at random separate locations which can cause cache misses while trying to access the pointer. On the other hand, if number of the filters is fixed, the array structure can be used to hold filters which can allow fast random access. Array stores the data in contiguous memory and so improves cache spatial locality. In the following table, hardware event metric values collecting from Intel Vtune are shown while filters are stored in array and linked-list data types. As shown from tables, using array structure gives the better result than linked-list type when memory access is the major factor in processing such as accessing a value over fixed numbers of filters. Also, the linear probing method is applied on the array for collision handling of filter values.

**Table 4.** Hardware event metrics for array and linked-list type

| Structure, patlen | Array, 64 | Linked-list, 64 | Array, 512 | Linked-list, 512 |
|---|---|---|---|---|
| CPU-CLK-UNHALTED.THREAD | 598,000,897 | 612,000,918 | 592,000,909 | 606,000,909 |
| INST-RETIRED.ANY | 1,350,002,025 | 1,354,002,031 | 1,344,002,016 | 1,386,002,019 |
| MEM-LOAD-UOPS-RETIRED.L1-HIT | 992,001,488 | 996,001,500 | 996,001,488 | 996,001,494 |
| MEM-LOAD-UOPS-RETIRED.L1-MISS | 2,600,078 | 2,800,072 | 1,400,048 | 1,600,048 |
| MEM-LOAD-UOPS-RETIRED.L2-HIT | 1,800,054 | 1,600,048 | 600,018 | 800,024 |
| MEM-LOAD-UOPS-RETIRED.L2-MISS | 0 | 0 | 0 | 0 |

**Table 5.** Time and rate values for array and linked-list type

| Structure, patlen | Array, 64 | Linked-list, 64 | Array, 512 | Linked-list, 512 |
|---|---|---|---|---|
| Elapsed time | 0.205 | 0.222 | 0.191 | 0.202 |
| CPI-Rate | **0.443** | 0.455 | **0.440** | 0.453 |
| L1 miss rate | **1.925** | 2.067 | **1.041** | 1.154 |

## 4   Implementation and Experimental Results

Algorithms have been implemented in the C programming language and SMART (string matching algorithms research tool) [16] is used to compare the performances of the algorithms. GCC compiler is used with std = gnu99 mode and full optimization option is selected by -O3 flag. We used three text types: genome sequence ($|\Sigma| = 4$), protein sequence ($|\Sigma| = 20$) and natural language text (English language, $|\Sigma| = 128$) provided by the Smart research tool and dataset sizes are 200 MB. Text data is loaded to the memory in the context of 32-byte aligned by union structure using __m256i AVX2 data type. All tests run over 100 times by setting pset (size of the set of patterns) is 100. Algorithms using

**Table 6.** Test platform and data set

| CPU: | Intel Xeon E5-2680 v4 |
|---|---|
| L1d cache: | 32KB, 64B line size, 4 Latency Cycles |
| L1i cache: | 32KB, 64B line size, 4 Latency Cycles |
| L2 cache: | 256KB, 64B line size, 12 Latency Cycles |
| L3 cache: | 35MB, 64B line size, 40+ Latency Cycles |
| OS: | CentOS 7 x86-64 |
| GCC Version: 4.8.5 20150623 (UHeM System Version) | |

| | Data Set | Σ | K Value |
|---|---|---|---|
| 1 | Genome Sequence | 4 | 5 |
| 2 | Protein Sequence | 20 | 7 |
| 3 | English Language Text | 128 | 7 |

in comparison are selected by scanning all existing algorithms on SMART Tool. We only show the best result of algorithms using q-grams and these q values are reported as apices. Search times of algorithms at tables are expressed in milliseconds and best results of each pattern length have been boldfaced.

EPSMA performance is compared with the following algorithms on SMART.

- BNDM [9], BNDMq, Backward DAWG Matching algorithm [1], BSDMq [8,20];
- EBOM [21], EPSM [22], FSBNDMq [2];
- N32-freq, compares 32 characters using AVX2 where comparison order given by nondecreasing probability of pattern symbols [10];
- N32-fixed, compares 32 characters using AVX2 where comparison order is fixed [10];
- SKIPq [23], BNDMq [1]; TVSBS [14];
- UFNDMq Shift Or with q-grams [1], WFRq weak factor recognition/hashing [7];
- BOM: fast variants of backward oracle and suffix oracle matching [4];
- SSEF: Filter based fast matching by using SSE instructions [11];
- SSEFA-1: non-optimized version of SSEFA with unmasked 32-bit filter;
- SSEFA-2: reduced filter length version of SSEFA with single 28-bit filter;

**Table 7.** Times [ms] for genome sequence when pattern length $< 64$

| m | 2 | 4 | 6 | 8 | 10 | 12 | 16 | 20 | 24 | 28 | 32 | 40 | 48 | 56 | 62 |
|---|---|---|---|---|---|---|---|---|---|---|---|---|---|---|---|
| BNDMq | $194.99^{(2)}$ | $158.12^{(2)}$ | $87.28^{(4)}$ | $56.63^{(4)}$ | $49.15^{(4)}$ | $47.23^{(4)}$ | $37.81^{(4)}$ | $36.08^{(4)}$ | $32.94^{(6)}$ | $32.38^{(6)}$ | $31.40^{(6)}$ | $31.05^{(6)}$ | $30.65^{(6)}$ | $32.41^{(6)}$ | $30.54^{(6)}$ |
| BOM2 | – | – | 227.24 | 164.99 | 148.31 | 147.18 | 109.22 | 103.47 | 85.16 | 75.58 | 69.45 | 61.32 | 54.52 | 56.05 | 48.16 |
| BSDMq | $182.02^{(2)}$ | $96.07^{(3)}$ | $72.20^{(4)}$ | $49.74^{(4)}$ | $44.61^{(4)}$ | $43.72^{(4)}$ | $35.57^{(6)}$ | $33.64^{(6)}$ | $31.65^{(7)}$ | $31.45^{(6)}$ | $31.09^{(7)}$ | $30.46^{(7)}$ | $29.44^{(7)}$ | $30.94^{(7)}$ | $29.79^{(7)}$ |
| EBOM | 171.94 | 132.41 | 142.37 | 116.69 | 114.76 | 114.88 | 88.72 | 84.24 | 70.44 | 64.97 | 60.60 | 54.54 | 48.99 | 50.48 | 43.94 |
| EPSM | 31.07 | 33.29 | 43.81 | 42.81 | 44.22 | 47.26 | 33.04 | 34.03 | 31.94 | 30.91 | 29.40 | 30.00 | 29.68 | 30.65 | 29.08 |
| EPSMA | **26.86** | **28.23** | **31.25** | **29.22** | **30.94** | **31.96** | 32.86 | 31.78 | 29.88 | 28.27 | **27.84** | 28.34 | **27.31** | **27.63** | **27.49** |
| FSBNDM | – | 212.29 | 166.15 | $111.66^{(4)}$ | $94.04^{(2)}$ | $90.39^{(W2)}$ | $65.43^{(W2)}$ | $60.97^{(W2)}$ | $50.98^{(W2)}$ | $46.68^{(W2)}$ | $44.15^{(W2)}$ | $44.26^{(W2)}$ | $43.44^{(W2)}$ | $48.38^{(W2)}$ | $43.99^{(W2)}$ |
| FSBNDMq | $204.41^{(20)}$ | $106.79^{(31)}$ | $74.91^{(41)}$ | $52.38^{(41)}$ | $47.37^{(41)}$ | $46.07^{(41)}$ | $37.48^{(62)}$ | $35.27^{(62)}$ | $31.88^{(61)}$ | $31.63^{(62)}$ | $30.99^{(61)}$ | $31.00^{(61)}$ | $30.22^{(61)}$ | $32.52^{(61)}$ | $30.54^{(61)}$ |
| MEMCMP | 540.10 | 640.99 | 740.05 | 810.21 | 820.17 | 720.05 | 680.59 | 760.75 | 860.52 | 890.49 | 820.09 | 890.16 | 760.37 | 790.00 | 772.41 |
| N32-freq | $29.17^{(2)}$ | $32.10^{(5)}$ | $31.93^{(5)}$ | $30.84^{(5)}$ | $32.22^{(5)}$ | $33.02^{(5)}$ | $30.95^{(5)}$ | $32.50^{(7)}$ | $30.91^{(5)}$ | $31.72^{(5)}$ | $31.65^{(5)}$ | $31.58^{(5)}$ | $30.75^{(5)}$ | $33.01^{(5)}$ | $31.19^{(5)}$ |
| N32-fixed | $29.06^{(2)}$ | $32.05^{(5)}$ | $31.91^{(5)}$ | $30.50^{(5)}$ | $31.84^{(5)}$ | $32.65^{(5)}$ | $30.41^{(5)}$ | $32.89^{(5)}$ | $30.06^{(5)}$ | $31.24^{(5)}$ | $31.13^{(5)}$ | $31.36^{(5)}$ | $30.43^{(5)}$ | $32.65^{(5)}$ | $30.86^{(5)}$ |
| SBNDMq | $183.29^{(2)}$ | $139.13^{(2)}$ | $86.20^{(4)}$ | $56.61^{(4)}$ | $49.61^{(4)}$ | $47.53^{(4)}$ | $38.57^{(5)}$ | $37.17^{(4)}$ | $34.08^{(4)}$ | $32.84^{(6)}$ | $31.83^{(6)}$ | $31.26^{(6)}$ | $30.32^{(6)}$ | $32.53^{(6)}$ | $30.69^{(6)}$ |
| SKIPq | $173.55^{(2)}$ | $116.25^{(3)}$ | $78.29^{(4)}$ | $52.72^{(4)}$ | $46.86^{(4)}$ | $45.31^{(4)}$ | $36.81^{(6)}$ | $34.87^{(6)}$ | $31.55^{(6)}$ | $31.65^{(6)}$ | $31.60^{(6)}$ | $31.45^{(7)}$ | $29.32^{(6)}$ | $30.92^{(7)}$ | $29.30^{(7)}$ |
| SSEF | – | – | – | – | – | – | – | – | – | – | 58.74 | 49.68 | 35.92 | 37.92 | 36.40 |
| TVSBS-W8 | – | – | – | 196.23 | 175.56 | 177.76 | 131.76 | 128.31 | 99.42 | 101.02 | 96.73 | 87.72 | 84.12 | 91.63 | 80.43 |
| UFNDMq | – | – | – | $61.04^{(8)}$ | $53.96^{(8)}$ | $52.16^{(8)}$ | $40.41^{(8)}$ | $40.00^{(8)}$ | $36.21^{(8)}$ | $35.05^{(8)}$ | $35.00^{(8)}$ | $35.01^{(8)}$ | $34.06^{(8)}$ | $37.10^{(8)}$ | $34.46^{(8)}$ |
| WFRq | $213.50^{(2)}$ | $153.74^{(2)}$ | $85.73^{(3)}$ | $58.11^{(4)}$ | $51.76^{(5)}$ | $46.58^{(4)}$ | $37.42^{(5)}$ | $34.91^{(4)}$ | $33.43^{(5)}$ | $31.99^{(5)}$ | $30.97^{(5)}$ | $30.22^{(5)}$ | $29.02^{(5)}$ | $30.41^{(5)}$ | $28.97^{(5)}$ |

**Table 8.** Times [ms] for English text when pattern length $< 64$

| m | 2 | 4 | 6 | 8 | 10 | 12 | 16 | 20 | 24 | 28 | 32 | 40 | 48 | 56 | 62 |
|---|---|---|---|---|---|---|---|---|---|---|---|---|---|---|---|
| BNDMq | $129.68^{(2)}$ | $70.10^{(2)}$ | $56.46^{(2)}$ | $55.19^{(2)}$ | $47.51^{(4)}$ | $40.54^{(4)}$ | $36.30^{(4)}$ | $34.10^{(4)}$ | $32.65^{(4)}$ | $31.13^{(4)}$ | $30.34^{(4)}$ | $29.26^{(4)}$ | $29.07^{(4)}$ | $28.70^{(4)}$ | $28.58^{(4)}$ |
| BOM2 | – | 151.19 | 134.14 | 127.07 | 110.93 | 90.81 | 82.06 | 65.94 | 58.65 | 50.18 | 47.19 | 45.21 | 43.17 | 44.63 | 43.27 |
| BSDMq | $103.97^{(2)}$ | $60.44^{(2)}$ | $50.90^{(2)}$ | $46.71^{(3)}$ | $41.73^{(3)}$ | $37.74^{(4)}$ | $34.52^{(4)}$ | $32.76^{(5)}$ | $31.98^{(6)}$ | $31.80^{(6)}$ | $31.44^{(6)}$ | $30.05^{(6)}$ | $29.10^{(6)}$ | $28.58^{(6)}$ | $28.64^{(6)}$ |
| EBOM | 100.05 | 60.69 | 51.36 | 50.68 | 46.87 | 44.56 | 43.42 | 42.27 | 41.21 | 40.23 | 39.06 | 36.77 | 38.90 | 36.30 | 34.05 |
| EPSM | 31.48 | 32.54 | 36.43 | 41.52 | 38.80 | 38.13 | 32.74 | 32.67 | 31.12 | 30.56 | 28.93 | 28.01 | 27.83 | 27.07 | 26.87 |
| EPSMA | **26.94** | **27.37** | 31.81 | 31.67 | **29.73** | **29.77** | **28.70** | **28.42** | **27.03** | **26.67** | **25.80** | **25.09** | **24.71** | **24.13** | **23.26** |
| FSBNDM | 130.47 | 83.09 | 68.00 | 63.11 | $57.47^{(W4)}$ | $49.01^{(W4)}$ | $46.36^{(W4)}$ | $40.45^{(W4)}$ | $38.68^{(W4)}$ | $36.35^{(W2)}$ | $34.56^{(W4)}$ | $32.34^{(W4)}$ | $31.57^{(W4)}$ | $31.20^{(W4)}$ | $30.92^{(W4)}$ |
| FSBNDMq | $127.81^{(20)}$ | $67.39^{(20)}$ | $51.61^{(31)}$ | $47.22^{(31)}$ | $41.75^{(31)}$ | $38.96^{(31)}$ | $35.34^{(41)}$ | $33.40^{(41)}$ | $32.08^{(41)}$ | $31.43^{(41)}$ | $30.88^{(41)}$ | $29.46^{(31)}$ | $29.08^{(41)}$ | $28.75^{(41)}$ | $28.47^{(41)}$ |
| MEMCMP | 430.84 | 476.10 | 560.84 | 540.93 | 600.90 | 600.76 | 621.13 | 640.32 | 640.29 | 670.72 | 678.62 | 680.78 | 710.80 | 680.38 | 670.58 |
| N32-freq | $30.09^{(2)}$ | $29.89^{(3)}$ | $29.87^{(3)}$ | $30.73^{(3)}$ | $31.03^{(2)}$ | $30.36^{(2)}$ | $30.20^{(2)}$ | $30.07^{(2)}$ | $29.17^{(3)}$ | $29.10^{(5)}$ | $28.89^{(3)}$ | $28.48^{(2)}$ | $28.03^{(3)}$ | $28.01^{(3)}$ | $27.10^{(2)}$ |
| N32-fixed | $29.95^{(2)}$ | $29.60^{(3)}$ | $30.16^{(3)}$ | $30.78^{(3)}$ | $31.26^{(3)}$ | $30.62^{(3)}$ | $30.38^{(3)}$ | $29.45^{(3)}$ | $29.07^{(3)}$ | $29.03^{(3)}$ | $28.12^{(3)}$ | $28.13^{(3)}$ | $27.15^{(3)}$ | | |
| SBNDMq | $122.62^{(2)}$ | $67.31^{(2)}$ | $54.35^{(2)}$ | $52.68^{(2)}$ | $47.50^{(4)}$ | $44.20^{(4)}$ | $36.48^{(4)}$ | $34.39^{(4)}$ | $32.82^{(4)}$ | $31.17^{(4)}$ | $30.26^{(4)}$ | $29.83^{(4)}$ | $29.50^{(4)}$ | $29.01^{(4)}$ | $28.55^{(4)}$ |
| SKIPq | $112.14^{(2)}$ | $65.86^{(2)}$ | $53.06^{(2)}$ | $52.70^{(2)}$ | $44.60^{(4)}$ | $39.43^{(4)}$ | $35.36^{(4)}$ | $33.31^{(4)}$ | $32.98^{(4)}$ | $31.55^{(4)}$ | $31.20^{(4)}$ | $30.35^{(4)}$ | $29.44^{(4)}$ | $28.95^{(4)}$ | $28.50^{(4)}$ |
| SSEF | – | – | – | – | – | – | – | – | – | – | 58.44 | 55.68 | 40.92 | 36.92 | 35.27 |
| TVSBS-W8 | 169.07 | 98.88 | 71.21 | 64.94 | 56.84 | 48.18 | 45.17 | 39.50 | 38.21 | 36.78 | 35.68 | 35.57 | 38.41 | 37.22 | 36.80 |
| UFNDMq | $118.71^{(2)}$ | $178.53^{(2)}$ | $66.67^{(2)}$ | $68.07^{(2)}$ | $58.51^{(8)}$ | $45.96^{(2)}$ | $43.77^{(8)}$ | $38.25^{(8)}$ | $35.43^{(8)}$ | $32.34^{(8)}$ | $32.02^{(8)}$ | $31.86^{(8)}$ | $32.11^{(8)}$ | $33.15^{(8)}$ | $32.40^{(8)}$ |
| WFRq | $139.43^{(2)}$ | $77.38^{(2)}$ | $58.99^{(3)}$ | $57.83^{(2)}$ | $46.27^{(3)}$ | $39.25^{(3)}$ | $36.13^{(4)}$ | $33.58^{(4)}$ | $31.44^{(3)}$ | $31.08^{(4)}$ | $30.61^{(4)}$ | $29.20^{(4)}$ | $28.85^{(4)}$ | $28.51^{(4)}$ | $28.10^{(4)}$ |

**Table 9.** Times [ms] for protein sequence when pattern length < 64

| m | 2 | 4 | 6 | 8 | 10 | 12 | 16 | 20 | 24 | 28 | 32 | 40 | 48 | 56 | 62 |
|---|---|---|---|---|---|---|---|---|---|---|---|---|---|---|---|
| BNDMq | $121.17^{(2)}$ | $63.19^{(2)}$ | $45.54^{(2)}$ | $37.48^{(2)}$ | $37.72^{(2)}$ | $33.01^{(2)}$ | $34.75^{(2)}$ | $32.38^{(4)}$ | $31.83^{(4)}$ | $31.56^{(4)}$ | $30.15^{(4)}$ | $29.37^{(2)}$ | $29.23^{(2)}$ | $29.64^{(2)}$ | $29.12^{(2)}$ |
| BOM2 | 156.24 | 134.95 | 98.06 | 91.83 | 94.67 | 76.04 | 69.77 | 52.27 | 45.78 | 45.73 | 38.28 | 33.73 | 31.68 | 31.26 | 29.50 |
| BSDMq | $99.62^{(2)}$ | $59.44^{(2)}$ | $48.02^{(3)}$ | $38.42^{(3)}$ | $37.79^{(3)}$ | $33.21^{(3)}$ | $33.97^{(4)}$ | $32.78^{(4)}$ | $31.97^{(4)}$ | $32.20^{(4)}$ | $30.93^{(4)}$ | $29.14^{(4)}$ | $29.03^{(4)}$ | $29.12^{(4)}$ | $28.00^{(4)}$ |
| EBOM | 87.10 | 50.32 | 39.93 | 34.07 | 34.77 | 31.54 | 33.72 | 30.86 | 30.87 | 32.38 | 30.18 | 29.67 | 29.26 | 29.07 | 28.66 |
| EPSM | 31.85 | 35.47 | 33.62 | 31.07 | 33.49 | 32.36 | 34.42 | 31.90 | 31.06 | 31.66 | 30.35 | 29.57 | 29.02 | 29.38 | 28.92 |
| EPSMA | 27.73 | 28.83 | 30.62 | 27.60 | 28.29 | 28.63 | 30.34 | 27.97 | 28.12 | 29.52 | 28.33 | 27.22 | 26.18 | 26.90 | 25.45 |
| FSBNDM | 109.20 | 69.49 | 51.14 | 42.92 | 42.74 | 36.30 | 37.88 | 31.97 | 32.49 | 33.75 | $30.04^{(W4)}$ | $29.55^{(W4)}$ | $29.38^{(W4)}$ | $30.03^{(W4)}$ | $29.16^{(W4)}$ |
| FSBNDMq | $108.95^{(21)}$ | $60.35^{(20)}$ | $43.24^{(20)}$ | $36.53^{(20)}$ | $36.35^{(31)}$ | $31.78^{(31)}$ | $31.07^{(31)}$ | $30.12^{(31)}$ | $30.67^{(31)}$ | $31.42^{(31)}$ | $29.21^{(31)}$ | $28.96^{(31)}$ | $29.01^{(31)}$ | $29.09^{(31)}$ | $28.35^{(31)}$ |
| MEMCMP | 410.11 | 515.34 | 530.96 | 610.32 | 590.86 | 594.91 | 507.26 | 672.11 | 630.67 | 660.49 | 621.84 | 610.59 | 597.82 | 660.38 | 635.67 |
| N32-freq | $29.16^{(2)}$ | $30.55^{(3)}$ | $29.44^{(2)}$ | $28.05^{(3)}$ | $30.10^{(3)}$ | $28.41^{(3)}$ | $31.34^{(3)}$ | $29.05^{(3)}$ | $29.97^{(3)}$ | $31.46^{(3)}$ | $29.35^{(3)}$ | $28.62^{(3)}$ | $28.48^{(3)}$ | $29.23^{(3)}$ | $28.13^{(3)}$ |
| N32-fixed | $28.18^{(2)}$ | $30.46^{(3)}$ | $29.51^{(5)}$ | $28.26^{(3)}$ | $30.36^{(3)}$ | $28.28^{(3)}$ | $31.48^{(3)}$ | $29.55^{(3)}$ | $30.18^{(3)}$ | $31.37^{(3)}$ | $29.52^{(3)}$ | $28.88^{(3)}$ | $28.63^{(3)}$ | $29.43^{(3)}$ | $28.02^{(3)}$ |
| SBNDMq | $115.40^{(2)}$ | $60.38^{(2)}$ | $44.42^{(2)}$ | $36.60^{(2)}$ | $36.91^{(2)}$ | $32.62^{(2)}$ | $34.39^{(2)}$ | $30.25^{(2)}$ | $30.85^{(4)}$ | $31.59^{(4)}$ | $29.40^{(4)}$ | $28.48^{(2)}$ | $28.41^{(4)}$ | $29.20^{(4)}$ | $28.18^{(4)}$ |
| SKIPq | $108.73^{(2)}$ | $65.88^{(2)}$ | $53.10^{(2)}$ | $43.19^{(2)}$ | $41.55^{(4)}$ | $34.60^{(4)}$ | $34.85^{(4)}$ | $30.80^{(4)}$ | $30.89^{(4)}$ | $31.82^{(4)}$ | $29.76^{(4)}$ | $29.55^{(4)}$ | $27.52^{(4)}$ | | |
| SSEF | – | – | – | – | – | – | – | – | – | – | 58.49 | 57.52 | 35.81 | 36.60 | 35.41 |
| TVSBS-W8 | 161.27 | 98.60 | 71.25 | 54.96 | 54.79 | 45.02 | 44.48 | 35.91 | 34.51 | 35.95 | 31.28 | 29.98 | 29.73 | 29.16 | 28.09 |
| UFNDMq | $193.73^{(2)}$ | $97.48^{(2)}$ | $74.22^{(2)}$ | $59.57^{(2)}$ | $54.45^{(2)}$ | $46.19^{(2)}$ | $44.47^{(2)}$ | $35.54^{(2)}$ | $34.01^{(2)}$ | $34.10^{(2)}$ | $31.41^{(2)}$ | $30.46^{(2)}$ | $29.94^{(2)}$ | $28.73^{(2)}$ | $27.39^{(2)}$ |
| WFRq | $133.91^{(2)}$ | $75.74^{(2)}$ | $54.29^{(2)}$ | $46.53^{(2)}$ | $43.13^{(3)}$ | $34.54^{(3)}$ | $35.92^{(3)}$ | $30.43^{(4)}$ | $30.98^{(4)}$ | $32.02^{(4)}$ | $29.74^{(4)}$ | $29.02^{(5)}$ | $28.83^{(4)}$ | $28.78^{(4)}$ | $27.80^{(4)}$ |

**Table 10.** Times [ms] for genome sequence when pattern length > 64

| m | 64 | 96 | 128 | 192 | 256 | 384 | 512 | 768 | 1024 | 1280 | 1536 | 1792 | 2048 |
|---|---|---|---|---|---|---|---|---|---|---|---|---|---|
| BNDMq | $31.67^{(6)}$ | $30.46^{(6)}$ | $29.70^{(6)}$ | $29.97^{(6)}$ | $29.56^{(6)}$ | $29.80^{(6)}$ | $32.07^{(6)}$ | $29.87^{(6)}$ | $29.91^{(6)}$ | $31.06^{(6)}$ | $31.00^{(6)}$ | $31.09^{(6)}$ | $28.92^{(6)}$ |
| BOM2 | 51.89 | 39.45 | 38.04 | 35.56 | 29.67 | 29.48 | 28.10 | 24.53 | 22.82 | 22.94 | 21.83 | 21.92 | 20.77 |
| BSDMq | $30.22^{(8)}$ | $29.80^{(8)}$ | $29.82^{(8)}$ | $30.10^{(7)}$ | $27.30^{(8)}$ | $27.27^{(8)}$ | $26.84^{(7)}$ | $27.15^{(7)}$ | $27.25^{(7)}$ | $28.47^{(7)}$ | $27.61^{(7)}$ | $28.26^{(6)}$ | $27.17^{(7)}$ |
| EBOM | 47.15 | 36.86 | 35.97 | 34.79 | 31.45 | 29.13 | 28.76 | 24.14 | 22.37 | 22.63 | 21.59 | 21.55 | 20.55 |
| EPSM | 30.33 | 29.23 | 28.11 | 26.47 | 23.00 | 21.01 | 20.01 | 18.13 | 17.25 | 18.26 | 17.72 | 17.90 | 17.04 |
| FSBNDM-Wq | $48.36^{(2)}$ | $48.80^{(2)}$ | $48.49^{(2)}$ | $44.24^{(2)}$ | $43.39^{(2)}$ | $43.17^{(2)}$ | $47.80^{(2)}$ | $43.57^{(2)}$ | $43.59^{(2)}$ | $44.18^{(2)}$ | $47.60^{(2)}$ | $44.22^{(2)}$ | $42.25^{(2)}$ |
| FSBNDMq | $31.75^{(61)}$ | $30.31^{(61)}$ | $31.77^{(61)}$ | $29.86^{(61)}$ | $30.04^{(61)}$ | $29.71^{(61)}$ | $30.02^{(61)}$ | $29.84^{(61)}$ | $29.73^{(61)}$ | $30.85^{(61)}$ | $30.91^{(61)}$ | $30.88^{(61)}$ | $29.75^{(61)}$ |
| MEMCMP | 780.89 | 900.51 | 780.82 | 840.74 | 830.13 | 752.03 | 732.38 | 741.38 | 720.72 | 708.84 | 760.97 | 820.90 | 850.66 |
| N32-freq | $32.33^{(5)}$ | $31.01^{(5)}$ | $32.52^{(5)}$ | $30.44^{(5)}$ | $30.09^{(5)}$ | – | – | – | – | – | – | – | – |
| N32-fixed | $32.05^{(5)}$ | $30.70^{(5)}$ | $32.20^{(5)}$ | $30.86^{(5)}$ | $29.22^{(5)}$ | – | – | – | – | – | – | – | – |
| SBNDMq | $31.93^{(6)}$ | $30.54^{(6)}$ | $32.11^{(6)}$ | $30.10^{(6)}$ | $29.73^{(6)}$ | $28.93^{(6)}$ | $32.23^{(6)}$ | $29.97^{(6)}$ | $28.90^{(6)}$ | $31.13^{(6)}$ | $30.88^{(6)}$ | $31.03^{(6)}$ | $29.98^{(6)}$ |
| SKIPq | $30.99^{(7)}$ | $28.30^{(6)}$ | $29.50^{(6)}$ | $27.94^{(6)}$ | $26.34^{(7)}$ | $22.20^{(8)}$ | $21.73^{(8)}$ | $18.27^{(8)}$ | $17.03^{(8)}$ | $18.05^{(8)}$ | $17.58^{(8)}$ | $17.74^{(8)}$ | $16.85^{(8)}$ |
| SSEF | 33.93 | 29.89 | 29.16 | 26.78 | 24.53 | 20.08 | 18.48 | 17.66 | 16.35 | 16.23 | 16.06 | 15.81 | 15.24 |
| SSEFA | 28.26 | 27.64 | 25.52 | 23.76 | 20.66 | 17.81 | 15.66 | 14.29 | 12.97 | 13.78 | 13.62 | 12.93 | 12.78 |
| SSEFA-1 | 130.24 | 85.70 | 57.78 | 52.00 | 39.49 | 29.29 | 28.77 | 26.51 | 28.22 | 25.31 | 23.81 | 30.92 | 24.71 |
| SSEFA-2 | 70.64 | 46.37 | 39.75 | 34.28 | 30.87 | 23.53 | 21.24 | 19.72 | 23.74 | 19.28 | 19.02 | 22.53 | 19.49 |
| TVSBS-W8 | 91.12 | 77.24 | 78.45 | 75.81 | 74.20 | 75.80 | 85.59 | 76.15 | 76.94 | 78.25 | 86.23 | 79.98 | 78.61 |
| UFNDMq | $36.49^{(8)}$ | $34.38^{(8)}$ | $33.74^{(8)}$ | $33.88^{(8)}$ | $33.48^{(8)}$ | $33.81^{(8)}$ | $35.71^{(8)}$ | $33.87^{(8)}$ | $33.76^{(8)}$ | $34.86^{(8)}$ | $35.64^{(8)}$ | $34.79^{(8)}$ | $32.82^{(8)}$ |
| WFRq | $30.84^{(5)}$ | $28.75^{(5)}$ | $28.65^{(6)}$ | $27.00^{(2)}$ | $25.12^{(5)}$ | $22.12^{(6)}$ | $21.11^{(7)}$ | $18.09^{(7)}$ | $17.53^{(7)}$ | $18.33^{(4)}$ | $17.48^{(4)}$ | $17.72^{(4)}$ | $16.78^{(3)}$ |

**Table 11.** Times [ms] for English text when pattern length > 64

| m | 64 | 96 | 128 | 192 | 256 | 384 | 512 | 768 | 1024 | 1280 | 1536 | 1792 | 2048 |
|---|---|---|---|---|---|---|---|---|---|---|---|---|---|
| BNDMq | $31.76^{(2)}$ | $30.13^{(4)}$ | $31.75^{(6)}$ | $33.46^{(4)}$ | $29.21^{(4)}$ | $29.99^{(4)}$ | $31.62^{(4)}$ | $31.41^{(4)}$ | $31.77^{(4)}$ | $33.15^{(4)}$ | $32.84^{(4)}$ | $29.63^{(4)}$ | $31.38^{(4)}$ |
| BOM2 | 41.34 | 33.92 | 33.72 | 33.89 | 28.44 | 28.74 | 29.18 | 26.45 | 24.84 | 24.68 | 24.45 | 21.17 | 22.78 |
| BSDMq | $30.46^{(6)}$ | $28.44^{(6)}$ | $29.73^{(8)}$ | $31.08^{(6)}$ | $27.17^{(7)}$ | $27.37^{(6)}$ | $28.95^{(6)}$ | $28.61^{(6)}$ | $29.09^{(6)}$ | $30.06^{(6)}$ | $29.84^{(6)}$ | $26.42^{(6)}$ | $28.44^{(8)}$ |
| EBOM | 36.72 | 33.08 | 32.64 | 33.93 | 28.28 | 27.55 | 27.52 | 24.79 | 23.83 | 24.16 | 23.69 | 20.57 | 22.12 |
| EPSM | 29.72 | 29.19 | 28.85 | 26.07 | 22.02 | 19.57 | 18.70 | 18.83 | 18.76 | 18.86 | 19.68 | 17.92 | 18.77 |
| FSBNDM-Wq | $37.41^{(4)}$ | $33.69^{(4)}$ | $37.17^{(4)}$ | $38.56^{(4)}$ | $33.17^{(4)}$ | $33.92^{(4)}$ | $37.36^{(4)}$ | $35.09^{(4)}$ | $37.05^{(4)}$ | $38.24^{(4)}$ | $38.17^{(4)}$ | $33.66^{(4)}$ | $35.12^{(4)}$ |
| FSBNDMq | $31.58^{(41)}$ | $30.90^{(41)}$ | $31.41^{(41)}$ | $33.32^{(41)}$ | $29.07^{(41)}$ | $29.69^{(41)}$ | $31.60^{(41)}$ | $31.24^{(41)}$ | $31.73^{(41)}$ | $32.90^{(41)}$ | $32.69^{(41)}$ | $29.43^{(41)}$ | $31.24^{(41)}$ |
| MEMCMP | 760.81 | 711.78 | 632.58 | 600.81 | 670.06 | 633.48 | 570.78 | 580.52 | 592.52 | 612.76 | 602.17 | 610.84 | 612.23 |
| N32-freq | $30.49^{(2)}$ | $29.28^{(2)}$ | $29.56^{(2)}$ | $31.29^{(2)}$ | $27.30^{(2)}$ | – | – | – | – | – | – | – | – |
| N32-fixed | $30.89^{(3)}$ | $28.81^{(3)}$ | $30.20^{(3)}$ | $31.83^{(3)}$ | $27.88^{(3)}$ | – | – | – | – | – | – | – | – |
| SBNDMq | $31.69^{(4)}$ | $30.01^{(4)}$ | $31.51^{(4)}$ | $33.31^{(4)}$ | $29.12^{(4)}$ | $29.83^{(4)}$ | $31.51^{(4)}$ | $31.33^{(4)}$ | $31.81^{(4)}$ | $33.03^{(4)}$ | $32.99^{(4)}$ | $29.53^{(4)}$ | $31.30^{(4)}$ |
| SKIPq | $30.57^{(6)}$ | $28.91^{(4)}$ | $29.05^{(5)}$ | $30.20^{(4)}$ | $24.49^{(8)}$ | $20.88^{(8)}$ | $19.05^{(8)}$ | $17.53^{(8)}$ | $17.31^{(8)}$ | $18.36^{(8)}$ | $18.14^{(8)}$ | $15.34^{(8)}$ | $17.10^{(8)}$ |
| SSEF | 33.63 | 31.78 | 30.95 | 28.49 | 21.30 | 19.13 | 17.37 | 16.20 | 16.14 | 17.19 | 17.12 | 16.44 | 16.00 |
| SSEFA | 27.94 | 27.58 | 27.39 | 25.67 | 19.04 | 15.90 | 15.67 | 14.63 | 14.41 | 14.92 | 15.10 | 13.75 | 13.43 |
| SSEFA-1 | 78.04 | 56.75 | 54.05 | 38.50 | 33.89 | 36.32 | 26.09 | 25.40 | 24.33 | 26.42 | 25.62 | 23.81 | 22.87 |
| SSEFA-2 | 61.29 | 45.34 | 38.89 | 30.99 | 26.31 | 28.68 | 19.15 | 19.04 | 18.47 | 19.36 | 19.58 | 18.19 | 17.83 |
| TVSBS-W8 | 31.99 | 28.08 | 28.93 | 32.73 | 26.55 | 27.60 | 28.24 | 25.74 | 25.20 | 25.10 | 24.19 | 21.57 | 22.41 |
| UFNDMq | $33.96^{(2)}$ | $28.23^{(2)}$ | $30.23^{(4)}$ | $35.76^{(2)}$ | $26.43^{(2)}$ | $26.31^{(2)}$ | $27.60^{(4)}$ | $28.36^{(2)}$ | $23.23^{(2)}$ | $24.90^{(2)}$ | $24.81^{(2)}$ | $22.34^{(2)}$ | $23.43^{(2)}$ |
| WFRq | $30.23^{(4)}$ | $27.40^{(4)}$ | $28.56^{(4)}$ | $29.70^{(4)}$ | $23.59^{(4)}$ | $21.67^{(4)}$ | $20.92^{(5)}$ | $19.38^{(5)}$ | $18.94^{(3)}$ | $19.75^{(3)}$ | $19.60^{(3)}$ | $16.55^{(3)}$ | $18.16^{(3)}$ |

**Table 12.** Times [ms] for protein sequence when pattern length > 64

| m | 64 | 96 | 128 | 192 | 256 | 384 | 512 | 768 | 1024 | 1280 | 1536 | 1792 | 2048 |
|---|---|---|---|---|---|---|---|---|---|---|---|---|---|
| BNDMq | 30.10[4] | 31.16[4] | 30.21[4] | 30.32[4] | 30.33[4] | 30.34[2] | 30.25[4] | 30.25[4] | 29.27[4] | 30.69[2] | 30.36[2] | 29.19[4] | 29.31[4] |
| BOM2 | 31.48 | 31.37 | 30.45 | 30.07 | 28.01 | 25.09 | 22.57 | 21.30 | 18.97 | 19.06 | 20.21 | 19.46 | 19.89 |
| BSDMq | 29.95[4] | 30.68[4] | 29.45[4] | 29.08[4] | 29.35[4] | 28.77[4] | 29.06[4] | 28.64[4] | 27.58[4] | 29.24[4] | 28.56[4] | 27.52[4] | 27.48[4] |
| EBOM | 29.80 | 30.31 | 29.11 | 27.87 | 26.53 | 23.59 | 21.75 | 20.29 | 18.94 | 19.49 | 20.23 | 19.44 | 19.80 |
| EPSM | 29.43 | 29.86 | 29.01 | 26.02 | 23.55 | 21.03 | 18.59 | 18.77 | 17.69 | 18.12 | 18.65 | 17.71 | 17.67 |
| FSBNDM-Wq | 32.02[4] | 32.84[4] | 32.12[4] | 30.67[4] | 32.35[4] | 30.74[4] | 32.19[4] | 30.75[4] | 29.72[4] | 30.94[4] | 30.74[4] | 29.88[4] | 29.79[4] |
| FSBNDMq | 29.96[31] | 30.76[31] | 29.73[31] | 29.89[31] | 30.24[31] | 29.95[31] | 30.03[31] | 29.87[31] | 28.83[31] | 30.34[31] | 29.86[31] | 28.75[31] | 28.86[31] |
| MEMCMP | 660.50 | 590.94 | 601.14 | 596.23 | 600.87 | 587.45 | 602.25 | 607.47 | 591.54 | 613.91 | 608.38 | 620.32 | 590.18 |
| N32-freq | 30.41[3] | 31.29[3] | 30.31[3] | 30.12[3] | 30.66[3] | – | – | – | – | – | – | – | – |
| N32-fixed | 30.04[3] | 30.71[3] | 30.11[3] | 29.97[3] | 30.10[3] | – | – | – | – | – | – | – | – |
| SBNDMq | 30.38[4] | 31.08[4] | 30.22[4] | 30.24[4] | 30.40[4] | 30.22[4] | 30.31[4] | 30.28[4] | 29.17[4] | 30.42[4] | 30.26[4] | 29.08[2] | 29.19[4] |
| SKIPq | 29.79[4] | 30.05[4] | 28.28[4] | 27.33[4] | 25.86[4] | 22.08[4] | 19.78[8] | 18.41[8] | 17.11[8] | 17.48[8] | 18.00[8] | 17.04[8] | 16.97[8] |
| SSEF | 34.18 | 32.52 | 30.28 | 27.14 | 23.13 | 20.17 | 18.62 | 17.26 | 17.03 | 16.02 | 16.94 | 16.07 | 15.87 |
| SSEFA | 28.16 | 28.95 | 27.45 | 24.88 | 21.12 | 17.21 | 15.40 | 15.01 | 14.53 | 13.90 | 14.06 | 13.56 | 12.56 |
| SSEFA-1 | 88.27 | 67.20 | 48.37 | 38.91 | 34.82 | 28.84 | 26.73 | 25.28 | 24.96 | 24.50 | 23.90 | 24.69 | 23.78 |
| SSEFA-2 | 69.31 | 43.81 | 36.56 | 30.81 | 27.24 | 23.04 | 19.76 | 18.77 | 18.33 | 18.32 | 18.78 | 19.62 | 18.32 |
| TVSBS-W8 | 30.10 | 28.16 | 27.75 | 26.69 | 27.36 | 26.97 | 26.71 | 25.01 | 23.14 | 24.31 | 23.82 | 23.38 | 22.55 |
| UFNDMq | 30.03[2] | 29.76[2] | 27.79[2] | 25.89[2] | 29.28[2] | 28.41[2] | 26.45[2] | 26.44[2] | 23.42[2] | 25.50[2] | 23.59[2] | 22.38[2] | 23.86[2] |
| WFRq | 29.59[5] | 29.71[5] | 28.18[5] | 27.29[4] | 25.37[4] | 22.39[4] | 20.33[5] | 19.25[5] | 17.25[3] | 17.53[3] | 17.80[3] | 17.21[6] | 16.92[3] |

## 5 Conclusions

In this paper, we presented new state-of-the-art variations of the EPSM and SSEF algorithms by adding new techniques and instructions for the exact string matching problem. AVX2 instructions are utilized and optimizations are applied using analyzes on Intel Vtune Amplifier to improve overall performance. Besides using AVX2 instructions operated on 256-bit data for filtering algorithms; optimal bit length of the filter, 2-stage filtering technique and data structure for storing the values of filters have the significant impacts on performance. Our experiments show that new algorithms are faster than almost all previous most efficient exact string matching algorithms (more than 91.6% of all result) for various pattern lengths and alphabet sizes.

Running time difference between EPSMA and EPSM algorithms becomes more evident when pattern length is smaller than 16. Likewise, EPSMA gives better results against to the nearest competitors when pattern length is greater than 16 however the time difference between EPSMA and others is more stable in this range. In the case of longer patterns, we can also achieve fine speedups for SSEFA over old version while changing the pattern length and text type. Particularly, the time gap becomes more well-marked between SSEFA and other algorithms for very long patterns. Eventually, proposed algorithms are extremely useful for practitioners.

As future work, the new algorithms may be implemented using equivalent SIMD instructions with some modifications on other architectures like the ARM, AMD. Furthermore, the intrinsics operated on wider bit size may be used for algorithms in the near future. Nevertheless, filter length will be extremely larger again for filtering type algorithms so reduction of filter length and staggered filtering should be required in order to deal with memory access problems.

**Acknowledgements.** Computing resources used in this work were provided by the National Center for High Performance Computing of Turkey (UHeM) under grant number 4004492017.

# References

1. Durian, B., Holub, J., Peltola, H., Tarhio, J.: Tuning BNDM with q-grams. In: Proceedings of the Workshop on Algorithm Engineering and Experiments (ALENEX), pp. 29–37 (2009)
2. Peltola, H., Tarhio, J.: Variations of forward-SBNDM. In: Proceedings of the Prague Stringology Conference 2011, Prague, Czech Republic, 29–31 August 2011 (2011)
3. Durian, B., Holub, J., Peltola, H., Tarhio, J.: Improving practical exact string matching. Inf. Process. Lett. **110**(4), 148–152 (2010)
4. Allauzen, C., Crochemore, M., Raffinot, M.: Factor Oracle: a new structure for pattern matching. In: Pavelka, J., Tel, G., Bartošek, M. (eds.) SOFSEM 1999. LNCS, vol. 1725, pp. 295–310. Springer, Heidelberg (1999). https://doi.org/10.1007/3-540-47849-3_18
5. Cantone, D., Faro, S.: Searching for a substring with constant extra-space complexity. In: Ferragina, P., Grossi, R. (eds.) Proceedings of Third International Conference on Fun with Algorithms, pp. 118–131 (2004)
6. Knuth, D.E., Morris Jr., J.H., Pratt, V.R.: Fast pattern matching in strings. SIAM J. Comput. **6**(2), 323–350 (1977)
7. Cantone, D., Faro, S., Pavone, A.: Speeding up string matching by weak factor recognition. In: Stringology, pp. 42–50 (2017)
8. Faro, S.: Evaluation and improvement of fast algorithms for exact matching on genome sequences. In: Botón-Fernández, M., Martín-Vide, C., Santander-Jiménez, S., Vega-Rodríguez, M. (eds.) AlCoB 2016. LNCS. Springer, Cham (2016). https://doi.org/10.1007/978-3-319-38827-4_12
9. Navarro, G., Raffinot, M.: Fast and flexible string matching by combining bit-parallelism and suffix automata. ACM J. Exp. Algorithmics (JEA) **5**, 4 (2000)
10. Tarhio, J., Holub, J., Giaquinta, E.: Technology beats algorithms (in exact string matching). CoRR, abs/1612.01506 http://arxiv.org/abs/1612.01506 (2016)
11. Kulekci, M.O.: Filter based fast matching of long patterns by using SIMD instructions. In: Holub, J., Zdarek, J. (eds.) Proceedings of the Prague Stringology Conference 2009. Czech Technical University in Prague, Czech Republic, pp. 118–128 (2009)
12. Karp, R.M., Rabin, M.O.: Efficient randomized pattern-matching algorithms. IBM J. Res. Dev. Math. Comput. **31**(2), 249–260 (1987)
13. Boyer, R.S., Moore, J.S.: A fast string searching algorithm. Commun. ACM **20**(10), 762–772 (1977)
14. Thathoo, R., Virmani, A., Lakshmi, S.S., Balakrishnan, N., Sekar, K.: TVSBS: a fast exact pattern matching algorithm for biological sequences. Curr. Sci. **91**(1), 47–53 (2006)
15. Faro, S., Külekci, M.O.: Fast multiple string matching using streaming SIMD extensions technology. In: Calderón-Benavides, L., González-Caro, C., Chávez, E., Ziviani, N. (eds.) SPIRE 2012. LNCS, vol. 7608, pp. 217–228. Springer, Heidelberg (2012). https://doi.org/10.1007/978-3-642-34109-0_23
16. Faro, S., Lecroq, T., Borzi, S., Di Mauro, S., Maggio, A.: The string matching algorithms research tool. In: Proceedings of Stringology, pp. 99–111 (2016)

17. Faro, S.: Exact online string matching bibliography. CoRR, abs/1605.05067 http://arxiv.org/abs/1605.05067 (2016)
18. Faro, S., Lecroq T.: The exact string matching problem: a comprehensive experimental evaluation. CoRR, abs/1012.2547 http://arxiv.org/abs/1012.2547 (2010)
19. Faro, S., Lecroq, T.: The exact online string matching problem: a review of the most recent results. ACM Comput. Surv. **45**(2), 13 (2013)
20. Faro, S., Lecroq, T.: A fast suffix automata based algorithm for exact online string matching. In: Moreira, N., Reis, R. (eds.) CIAA 2012. LNCS, vol. 7381, pp. 149–158. Springer, Heidelberg (2012). https://doi.org/10.1007/978-3-642-31606-7_13
21. Faro, S., Lecroq, T.: Efficient variants of the backward-oracle-matching algorithm. In: Proceedings of the Prague Stringology Conference, pp. 146–160. Czech Technical University in Prague, Czech Republic (2008)
22. Faro, S., Külekci, M.O.: Fast packed string matching for short patterns. In: Sanders, P., Zeh N. (eds.) Proceedings of the 15th Meeting on Algorithm Engineering and Experiments, ALENEX. SIAM, New Orleans, LA, USA, pp. 113–121 (2013)
23. Faro, S.: A very fast string matching algorithm based on condensed alphabets. In: Dondi, R., Fertin, G., Mauri, G. (eds.) AAIM 2016. LNCS, vol. 9778, pp. 65–76. Springer, Cham (2016). https://doi.org/10.1007/978-3-319-41168-2_6
24. Ladra, S., Pedreira, O., Duato, J., Brisaboa, N.R.: Exploiting SIMD instructions in current processors to improve classical string algorithms. In: Morzy, T., Härder, T., Wrembel, R. (eds.) ADBIS 2012. LNCS, vol. 7503, pp. 254–267. Springer, Heidelberg (2012). https://doi.org/10.1007/978-3-642-33074-2_19
25. Chhabra, T., Faro, S., Külekci, M.O., Tarhio, J.: Engineering order-preserving pattern matching with SIMD parallelism. Softw. Pract. Exper. **47**, 731–739 (2017). https://doi.org/10.1002/spe.2433
26. https://software.intel.com/en-us/vtune-amplifier-help-intel-processor-events-reference

# A GPU-Based Metaheuristic
# for Workflow Scheduling on Clouds

Elliod Cieza[1]([☒]), Luan Teylo[1], Yuri Frota[1], Cristiana Bentes[2],
and Lúcia M. A. Drummond[1]

[1] Instituto de Computação, Universidade Federal Fluminense, Niterói, Brazil
elliodcieza@id.uff.br, {luanteylo,yuri,lucia}@ic.uff.br
[2] Eng. de Sistemas e Computação, Universidade do Estado do Rio de Janeiro,
Rio de Janeiro, Brazil
cris@eng.uerj.br

**Abstract.** Scientific workflows are being used today in a number of
areas. As they grow in complexity and importance, cloud computing emerges as an important execution environment. In this scenario,
scheduling the workflow tasks and data on the cloud ensuring proper use
of the computational resources is one of the key issues in the management of workflow execution. Although many workflow schedulers have
been proposed in the literature, few of them deal with heterogeneous
computing resources and data file assignment. The Hybrid Evolutionary Algorithm to Task Scheduling and Data File Assignment Problem
(HEA-TaSDAP) addresses these two problems simultaneously, but the
scheduling is time consuming, especially if we consider large scale workflows. In this work, we propose optimizations on HEA-TaSDAP by taking
advantage of the massive parallelism provided by GPUs, leveraging the
scheduling of larger instances in a reasonable amount of time. Our parallel solution provided about 98.83% of reductions in the scheduling time,
keeping the quality of the solutions.

## 1 Introduction

A scientific workflow is an abstraction used to model and streamline all the
steps of a computational experiment. In those systems, tasks are executed based
on their control or data dependencies and the management of the environment
is done automatically by a management system [12]. In recent years, scientific
workflows became more computationally expensive, increasing the demand for
high performance computing resources. At the same time, the adoption of cloud
computing environments to execute those kinds of applications has increased,
and the scientists start to migrate their experiments to the cloud.

Cloud computing environment has been widely employed to execute scientific workflows due to facilities in the acquisition of resources and low monetary
costs [1,4,5,11]. Unlike grid systems, cloud computing services provide a virtu-
ally unlimited amount of infrastructure on demand and a customized execution
environment, enabling scientists to execute any volume of data and tasks on

© Springer Nature Switzerland AG 2019
H. Senger et al. (Eds.): VECPAR 2018, LNCS 11333, pp. 62–76, 2019.
https://doi.org/10.1007/978-3-030-15996-2_5

the cloud. In this context, to ensure proper use of the required computational resources, a smart scheduling of those tasks and files must be performed. Among many scientific workflow schedulers, the Hybrid Evolutionary Algorithm to Task Scheduling and Data File Assignment Problem (HEA-TaSDAP), proposed in [13], is the first algorithm to directly address both the task scheduling and the data file assignment problem. HEA-TaSDAP is based on an evolutionary metaheuristic that also includes local search methods. Although HEA-TaSDAP can efficiently schedule workflows with up to 100 tasks in a relatively short period of time, workflows of this size are considered small. For example, the workflows Montage and LIGO can be modeled with 1000 tasks due to their data-intensive nature [12]. While HEA-TaSDAP can schedule instances of any size, at the current state, the scheduling of instances larger than 500 tasks can take several days to finish.

Other works in the literature, such as [9], have pointed out the importance of developing a workflow scheduler that features: (i) low scheduling overhead, (ii) is aware of heterogeneous computing resources, and (iii) directly addresses the data file assignment problem. While HEA-TaSDAP attends requirements (ii) and (iii), it falls short when it comes to the scheduling overhead.

In recent years, graphics processing units (GPUs) have become an integral part of high performance computing systems, becoming widespread in the scientific community for presenting a cost effective alternative to central processing units (CPUs) in terms of performance. In this context, the use of GPU-based parallel local searches has gained prominence in the field of optimization and metaheuristics due to its capacity to find near optimal solutions in hard problems. Coelho et al. [3] proposed four hybrid GPU/CPU neighborhoods (2-opt, swap, 2-or-opt and 1-or-opt) in a VNS heuristic for the vehicle routing problem with deliveries and selective pickups (SVRDSP). The hybrid approach achieved speedups of up to 76 times over the sequential version. This heuristic also proved to be very competitive against other SVRDSP algorithms from the literature, the algorithm improved the solution quality for 51 out of the 68 tested instances. Zhou et al. [15] developed local search metaheuristics methods (2-opt-glm, 2-opt-tex, 2-opt-tex-shm, 2-opt-shm and 2-opt-coord) for the traveling salesman problem, attaining speedups of up to 279 times over the sequential counterpart. Özçetin et al. [8] also presented parallel local search heuristics (2-opt and 3-opt) for the traveling salesman problem, analyzing the best parallelization strategies in CUDA, and obtained speedups of up to 14 times.

In this work, we aim to optimize HEA-TaSDAP execution time by taking advantage of the massive parallelism provided by GPUs, leveraging the scheduling of larger instances in a reasonable amount of time. An important factor that compels the adoption of GPUs for this problem is the availability of these resources in most diverse platforms. Cloud providers such as Amazon AWS and Google Cloud, for example, already offer virtual machines with built-in GPUs.

Thus, for this purpose, we identified the hotspots of the HEA-TaSDAP algorithm and implemented four GPU-based local search procedures. The new implementation reduced the scheduling decision time in 98.83% while keeping the same quality of the solutions.

## 2   Problem Definition

Commonly, a scientific workflow is defined as a Directed Acyclic Graph (DAG) in which vertices represent tasks, and the arcs represent the data files or dependencies between tasks. Teylo *et al.* [13], proposed a representation where data files are no longer represented as arcs, but rather as a set of vertices. According to the authors, that representation is the key for the Task Scheduling and Data Assignment Problem (TaSDAP) as it allows that the scheduling algorithm determine not only the tasks allocation but also the machines where data files generated during workflow execution are assigned.

In that problem, tasks and data files have to be allocated in a cluster of heterogeneous virtual machines (VMs) and the objective is to minimize the workflow makespan. Figure 1 shows the application and architectural models. As can be seen, the workflow is modeled as a DAG denoted by $G = (V, A, a, \omega)$, where the node set $V = N \cup D$ consists of tasks $i \in N$ and data files $d \in D$; $A$ is the set of arcs, which gives the precedence relation between tasks and data files, $a_i$ is the amount of work associated with task $i \in N$, and $\omega_{ij}$ represents the cost associated with arc $(i, j) \in A$. Note that, in the graph, a task is always preceded and succeeded by a data file as illustrated in Fig. 1(a), where $task_1$ reads data files $data_1$ and $data_2$, and writes $data_3$, which will be read later by $task_2$.

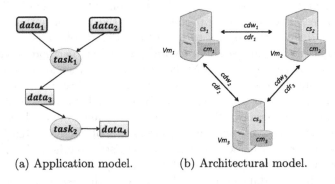

(a) Application model.              (b) Architectural model.

**Fig. 1.** Problem definition models (obtained from [13]).

The architectural model illustrated in Fig. 1(b) represents the main features of the target environment. For each VM $j \in M$, where $M$ is the set of all VMs, we consider the following characteristics: (i) the storage capacity $(cm)$; (ii) the computational slowdown index $(cs)$; (iii) the communication delay index for write operations $(cdw)$; and (iv) the communication delay index for read operations $(cdr)$. In this model the execution time of a task $i \in N$ on a VM $j \in M$ is given by $t_{ij} = a_i \cdot cs_j$ and the communication time for a task $i \in N$ executing on VM $j \in M$, to write data $d \in D$ in VM $p \in M$, where $j$ and $p$ are connected by link $l$, is given by $\overleftarrow{t}_{djp} = \omega_{id} \cdot cdw_l$ and the communication time for reading is given by $\overrightarrow{t}_{djp} = \omega_{di} \cdot cdr_l$.

# 3   The Sequential Hybrid Evolutionary Algorithm

Evolutionary Algorithms (EA) are optimization methods inspired in biology evolution mechanisms observed in nature. In an EA, each chromosome is an individual of a population which represents a possible solution to the problem. The search for the best solution is guided by a fitness function, which gives the quality of each chromosome. At each iteration of the algorithm, new individuals are generated through a crossover operation and the diversification of the population is obtained through the mutation function. In [13], a hybrid evolutionary algorithm called HEA-TaSDAP, which includes EA, local search and a path relinking method, was developed.

The representation of a chromosome in the algorithm is composed of two structures, which represent task and data assignments, and the execution order of tasks. The first structure is the *task and data assignment vector*, $AV$. In $AV$, each index $i$ represents a task or a data file, and each element $AV[i]$ contains the VM where the task or data file was assigned. The second structure is a linked list, denoted $OV$, that represents the execution order of tasks.

These two structures have a spatial complexity of $O(|V|)$ and $O(|N|)$, respectively. Therefore, local searches applied to those structures have to handle a large search space, since scientific workflows usually have hundreds of tasks and data files.

Three local search procedures were used in the sequential algorithm: (i) *swap-vm*: swap two elements in $AV$; (ii) *swap-position*: swap two elements with the same precedence order in the task order list; and (iii) *move-element*: move one task or data file to a different machine. In all the local search procedures the First-Improvement criteria was used as stop condition, i.e., the local search procedure is executed until it obtains an improvement or until all combinations have been tested.

## 3.1   Identifying Hotspots

The first step in optimizing HEA-TaSDAP execution time is to identify the hotspots. The hotspots are the functions and routines that consume the most computational time and thus are the primary targets for optimization. The identification of hotspots was accomplished using timers in the code. We divided the code into three main parts: Local Search, Crossover & Mutation and Other Functions and measured the execution time of each part. The tests were conducted using 16 well-known scientific workflows varying in size from 100 to 1000 tasks.

Table 1 presents the execution time (in seconds) of each part of the code with the percentage that this execution represents in the total execution time of HEA-TaSDAP. The results are shown for different workflows to be scheduled in a cluster with 5 VMs.

Additional tests with clusters of different sizes showed similar distributions of the execution times. So, considering that nearly 99% of the scheduling time is concentrated on the local search functions, paralellizing this part is expected to give the best results.

**Table 1.** Distribution of execution time for the sequential version using 5 VMs.

| Workflow (# of tasks) | Local search | Crossover & Mutation | Other functions |
|---|---|---|---|
| Montage (100) | 929 s (97.58%) | 10 s (1.05%) | 13 s (1.37%) |
| Montage (200) | 7680 s (98.12%) | 15 s (0.19%) | 132 s (1.69%) |
| Montage (300) | 15054 s (96.85%) | 16 s (0.1%) | 473 s (3.04%) |
| Montage (400) | 16980 s (98.02%) | 11 s (0.06%) | 332 s (1.92%) |
| Montage (500) | 40180 s (97.38%) | 17 s (0.04%) | 1062 s (2.57%) |
| Cybershake (100) | 247 s (97.24%) | 3 s (1.18%) | 4 s (1.57%) |
| Cybershake (200) | 986 s (98.21%) | 4 s (0.4%) | 14 s (1.39%) |
| Cybershake (300) | 4252 s (98.75%) | 5 s (0.12%) | 49 s (1.14%) |
| Cybershake (400) | 10627 s (99.74%) | 7 s (0.07%) | 21 s (0.2%) |
| Cybershake (500) | 124013 s (99.68%) | 10 s (0.04%) | 68 s (0.28%) |
| Sipht (100) | 1802 s (98.52%) | 3 s (1.91%) | 23 s (1.26%) |
| Sipht (300) | 13491 s (98.86%) | 10 s (1.09%) | 133 s (0.97%) |
| Sipht (400) | 60537 s (98.41%) | 12 s (0.58%) | 947 s (1.54%) |
| Sipht (500) | 43491 s (97.26%) | 15 s (0.63%) | 1188 s (2.66%) |
| Epigemonics (100) | 650 s (92.46%) | 1 s (5.88%) | 42 s (5.97%) |

## 4  Proposed GPU-Based Local Searches

GPUs are increasingly popular these days due to their higher performance and lower energy consumption compared to traditional multicore CPUs. GPUs support a massive amount of parallelism at relatively low cost. In the case of NVIDIA GPUs and the CUDA programming model, *kernels* are offloaded to the GPU. The kernel code is executed by multiple parallel threads running on different GPU cores.

As discussed previously, the current local search procedures produce a significant scheduling overhead, making HEA-TaSDAP very inefficient when scheduling workflows with more than 100 tasks. In order to increase the metaheuristic efficiency, allowing the scheduler to deal with larger instances, we propose the algorithm Parallel HEA-TaSDAP (PHEA-TaSDAP). The main idea of our algorithm is to implement the local search on the GPU. In PHEA-TaSDAP, we propose different local search procedures to take better advantage of the fine-grain massive parallelism of the GPU.

PHEA-TaSDAP implements on the GPU the local searches *move-element* and *swap-vm*, and also includes 2-opt *move-element* and 4-opt *move-element*.

The GPU-accelerated neighborhoods were implemented with two kernels. The first kernel is responsible for evaluating all the possible move operations in $AV$. The second kernel performs a reduction in the shared memory to find best improving move. Once all of the neighborhoods are finished executing, the best moves of each neighborhood are combined in a single solution, following the

Partial-GPU-CPU Multi Improvement [10] strategy, in which the combination is performed by the CPU.

## 4.1 Move-Element

In this local search, a new chromosome is generated by altering one position in $AV$, moving one task or data file to a different virtual machine. In the evaluation kernel, one thread is assigned to each position of $AV$ and is responsible for evaluating the best VM allocation for its position. For a workflow of $n$ tasks and a set of $|M|$ VMs, the first kernel performs a total of $|M| \cdot n$ evaluations, where $n$ evaluations are performed in parallel.

Figure 2(a) shows an example of the *move-element* neighborhood with a workflow of 7 tasks and 3 VMs. In this case, 7 threads will compute in parallel the cost of moving one element of $AV$ to another VM.

## 4.2 2-opt *move-element*

Similar to the *move-element* neighborhood, in 2-opt *move-element*, a new chromosome is obtained by moving two tasks or data files to different virtual machines in $AV$, as shown in Fig. 2(b), that illustrates only 3 out of 21 possible movements.

Since there are $C_{n,2} = \frac{n!}{2!(n-2)!} = \frac{n \cdot (n-1)}{2}$ possible combinations of pairs of different tasks in a workflow of $n$ tasks, the first kernel is launched with this number of threads. Thus, each pair ($x$ and $y$) of distinct positions in $AV$ is assigned to a thread that performs $|M|^2$ evaluations. To guarantee that a unique pair of indexes is mapped to a different GPU thread, an efficient mapping

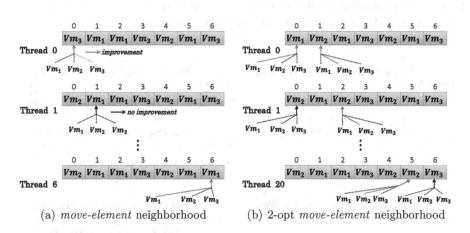

(a) *move-element* neighborhood    (b) 2-opt *move-element* neighborhood

**Fig. 2.** Example of the *move-element* and 2-opt *move-element* neighborhoods for a workflow of 7 tasks scheduled into a cluster with 3 virtual machines.

function, described in [7], is used, where each thread $i$ computes the pair of indexes $x$ and $y$ as follows:

$$x = n - 2 - \left\lfloor \frac{\left( \sqrt{8 \cdot \left( \frac{n \cdot (n-1)}{2} \right) - 8 \cdot i - 7} - 1 \right)}{2} \right\rfloor \text{ and } , y = 1 + i - x \cdot (n-1) + \frac{x \cdot (x+1)}{2}$$

### 4.3   Swap-Vm

The *swap-vm* local search swaps two elements in $AV$, Fig. 3(a) illustrates an example of 3 possible movements. Analogous to the 2-opt move-element neighborhood, the are $C_{n,2}$ possible swaps of pairs in $AV$ where each thread of the evaluation kernel evaluates if its correspondent swapped pair of elements resulted in an improvement or not. However, swapping a pair of elements in $AV$ requires a single operation regardless of the amount of virtual machines, hence the number of evaluations executed per thread is 1.

### 4.4   4-opt *move-element*

The 4-opt *move-element* moves four tasks or data files to different virtual machines in $AV$, as shown in Fig. 3(b), that illustrates a small subset of 3 movements. In this neighborhood, the number of combinations of 4 tasks out of $n$ tasks is enormous. So, we created a matrix structure with an arbitrary number of combinations. The indexes of these combinations are generated and sorted in lexicographical order in the CPU, that guarantees indexes without repetition. The matrix with the indexes is copied to the GPU that executes the evaluation and the reduction kernels.

In the evaluation kernel, each thread responsible for a combination of four tasks, tests all possible combinations of virtual machines for the given 4 tasks in $AV$. Note that the number of evaluations each thread performs is $|M|^4$.

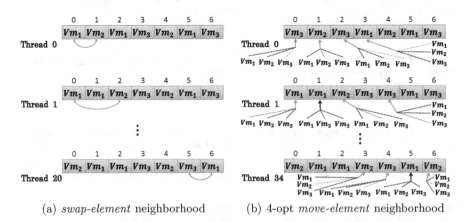

(a) *swap-element* neighborhood          (b) 4-opt *move-element* neighborhood

**Fig. 3.** Example of the *swap-element* and 4-opt *move-element* neighborhoods for a workflow of 7 tasks scheduled into a cluster with 3 virtual machines.

# 5    Experimental Results

In this section, we evaluate the solutions produced by PHEA-TaSDAP concerning scheduling time and quality of the solution. We compare PHEA-TaSDAP against the sequential version proposed in [13] and also compared against a scheduling heuristic used by the Pegasus system [6] called Heterogeneous Earliest Finish Time (HEFT) [14].

HEFT is one of the four site selection (scheduling) algorithms supported by the Pegasus Site Selector module. The other three algorithms(*Random, Group* and *RoundRobin*) were not included in our experiments because they did not improve the solution quality as much as HEFT.

The experiment test bed comprises a heterogeneous set of synthetic virtual machines based on Amazon EC2 detailed in Tables 2 and 3, and a synthetic workflow generator proposed in [2] to generate instances with 100 to 1000 tasks.

**Table 2.** Virtual machine specification.

| VM type | Slowdown | Storage | Bandwidth |
|---------|----------|---------|-----------|
| m3.medium | 1.53 | 8 GB | 4 Mbps |
| m3.large | 0.77 | 32 GB | 9 Mbps |
| m3.xlarge | 0.38 | 80 GB | 10 Mbps |
| m3.2xlarge | 0.19 | 160 GB | 10 Mbps |

For the benchmark instances, we selected four scientific workflow applications: Montage, an astronomy application used to generate custom mosaics of the sky; Cybershake, an application used to characterize earthquake hazards; Epigemonics, a biology application designed to execute genome sequencing operations; SIPHT, a biotechnology application created to search for untranslated small RNAs. Montage, Cybershake and Epigemonics are data intensive workflows and SIPHT is a compute intensive workflow [2].

The parallel version of the algorithm was implemented in C++ and CUDA version 9.1.85. All experiments (parallel and sequential) were executed in a computer with AMD Ryzen R7 1800X processor at 3.9 GHz, with 32 GB of memory and NVIDIA GeForce RTX 2080 Ti (Pascal architecture) GPU running Ubuntu 18.04.

We first analyze the quality of the scheduling in terms of the makespan of the solution. Figure 4 shows the makespan results in minutes for small instances executing on up to 20 VMs. We can observe in the graphs of this figure, that for Montage and SIPHT, both the sequential HEA-TaSDAP (CPU) and the parallel PHEA-TaSDAP (GPU) generated better makespan results than HEFT. For Cybershake and Epigemonics, the CPU and GPU implementations also outperfomed HEFT solutions, but with a smaller gap. Comparing the makespan solutions generated by the CPU and GPU versions, we can observe that they are similar, except for the cases when a small number of VMs is used.

**Table 3.** Virtual machine allocation for each cluster.

| # of VMs | Virtual machine distribution |
|---|---|
| 2 | 2 × m3.2xlarge |
| 3 | 3 × m3.2xlarge |
| 4 | 3 × m3.2xlarge, 1 × m3.xlarge |
| 5 | 3 × m3.2xlarge, 2 × m3.xlarge |
| 6 | 3 × m3.2xlarge, 3 × m3.xlarge |
| 7 | 3 × m3.2xlarge, 3 × m3.xlarge, 1 × m3.large |
| 8 | 3 × m3.2xlarge, 3 × m3.xlarge, 2 × m3.large |
| 9 | 3 × m3.2xlarge, 3 × m3.xlarge, 2 × m3.large, 1 × m3.medium |
| 10 | 3 × m3.2xlarge, 3 × m3.xlarge, 2 × m3.large, 2 × m3.medium |
| 11 | 3 × m3.2xlarge, 3 × m3.xlarge, 3 × m3.large, 2 × m3.medium |
| 12 | 3 × m3.2xlarge, 3 × m3.xlarge, 3 × m3.large, 3 × m3.medium |
| 13 | 4 × m3.2xlarge, 3 × m3.xlarge, 3 × m3.large, 3 × m3.medium |
| 14 | 4 × m3.2xlarge, 4 × m3.xlarge, 3 × m3.large, 3 × m3.medium |
| 15 | 4 × m3.2xlarge, 4 × m3.xlarge, 4 × m3.large, 3 × m3.medium |
| 16 | 4 × m3.2xlarge, 4 × m3.xlarge, 4 × m3.large, 4 × m3.medium |
| 17 | 5 × m3.2xlarge, 4 × m3.xlarge, 4 × m3.large, 4 × m3.medium |
| 18 | 5 × m3.2xlarge, 5 × m3.xlarge, 4 × m3.large, 4 × m3.medium |
| 19 | 5 × m3.2xlarge, 5 × m3.xlarge, 5 × m3.large, 4 × m3.medium |
| 20 | 5 × m3.2xlarge, 5 × m3.xlarge, 5 × m3.large, 5 × m3.medium |

We also analyzed the quality of the makespan for larger workflows. Four sets of large instances that vary the number of tasks from 200 to 500 were analyzed. Due to space limitations, we present only the results for the Montage workflow, notwithstanding the other workflows presented analogous results. Figure 5 presents the makespan results in minutes for large instances of Montage executing on up to 20 VMs. We can observe in the graphs that the CPU and GPU versions consistently generated better makespan results than HEFT. Comparing the results of the CPU and GPU versions, we observe similar makespan results for more than 4 VMs.

Next, we present an analysis of the time required to compute the scheduling solution and the speedup obtained by the parallel implementation. We did not include HEFT in this analysis because it provided poorer makespan results. When the problem becomes harder to solve for large instances, HEA-TaSDAP and PHEA-TaSDAP make a more intelligent search in the solution space.

Figure 6 shows the scheduling time in seconds for the CPU and GPU versions for small instances executing on up to 20 VMs. The graphs show that the GPU scheduling time increases proportionally to the number of VMs, while the CPU scheduling time presents an irregular behaviour. In Epigemonics, for example, the CPU scheduling times are surprisingly low with 9 VMs, outperforming

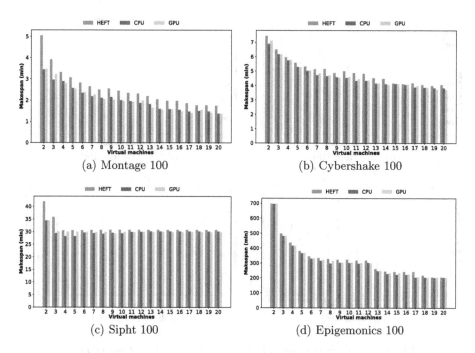

**Fig. 4.** Comparison of the solution quality for Montage, Cybershake, Epigemonics and Sipht workflows.

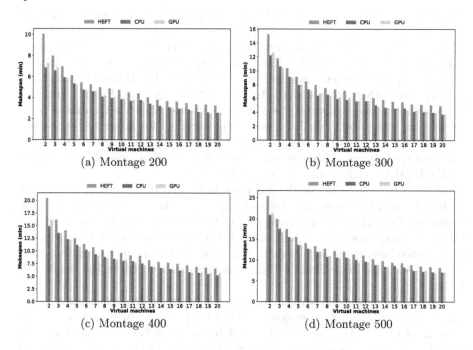

**Fig. 5.** Comparison of the solution quality for Montage instances.

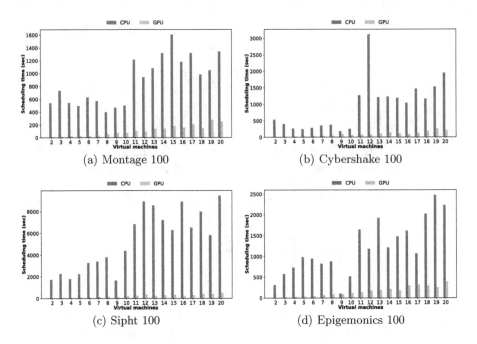

**Fig. 6.** Comparison of the scheduling time for different workflows.

the GPU. It occurs because all GPU-based local search procedures use the best improvement strategy, generating all possible combinations of neighborhoods, while the CPU local search uses the first improvement one. Thus, in CPU procedures the local search execution times may vary a lot. However, except for this particular case of Epigemonics, we can observe that the GPU scheduling time is quite small when compared to the CPU scheduling time. Figure 7 presents the scheduling time results for the Montage instance when the number of tasks varies from 200 to 500. Similar results were obtained for larger instances, but the difference between the CPU and the GPU time is significantly higher. For the Montage instance with 500 tasks, the difference is so large that is hard to see the GPU scheduling time in the graph.

In order to better disclose the difference in the scheduling computation time of the CPU and GPU versions, Tables 4 and 5 show the execution times and the speedups of the GPU version compared to the CPU version for the small and large instances, respectively. Table 4 shows that clusters with more VMs achieved smaller speedups. It happens because the 4-opt *move-element* was implemented only in GPU, and its execution time is strongly influenced by the number of VMs.

Table 4 shows that the performance gains of Montage depend on the instance size, we observe an average speedup of 227.2 for Montage 1000, and an average speedup of 14.9 for Montage 100. This difference occurs because small instances cannot take full advantage of the GPU capabilities. Since the CPU version could

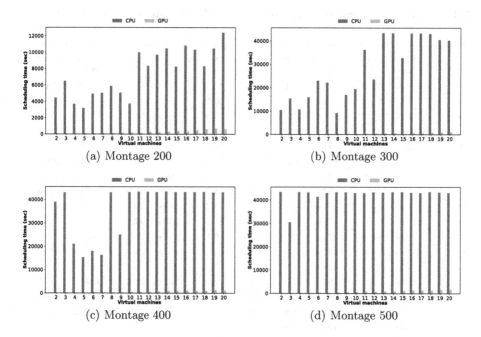

(a) Montage 200

(b) Montage 300

(c) Montage 400

(d) Montage 500

**Fig. 7.** Comparison of the scheduling time for Montage instances.

**Table 4.** GPU scheduling times (in seconds) and the speedups for small instances.

| # of VMs | Montage 100 | | Cybershake 100 | | Epigemonics 100 | | Sipht 100 | |
|---|---|---|---|---|---|---|---|---|
| | Sched time | Speedup | Sched time | Speedup | Sched time | Speedup | Sched time | Speedup |
| 2 | 10 s | 52.2 | 14 s | 39.1 | 7 s | 43.3 | 19 s | 89.8 |
| 3 | 14 s | 52.2 | 12 s | 33.5 | 16 s | 36.0 | 51 s | 44.6 |
| 4 | 25 s | 21.4 | 19 s | 14.1 | 29 s | 24.9 | 64 s | 28.0 |
| 5 | 28 s | 17.9 | 20 s | 12.3 | 36 s | 27.3 | 96 s | 23.4 |
| 6 | 25 s | 24.8 | 31 s | 9.2 | 49 s | 19.5 | 87 s | 37.8 |
| 7 | 34 s | 17.0 | 40 s | 8.9 | 68 s | 12.1 | 128 s | 26.7 |
| 8 | 51 s | 7.9 | 46 s | 8.2 | 84 s | 10.4 | 166 s | 22.9 |
| 9 | 72 s | 6.5 | 92 s | 2.0 | 90 s | 1.2 | 139 s | 11.9 |
| 10 | 74 s | 6.7 | 62 s | 4.1 | 116 s | 4.4 | 213 s | 20.6 |
| 11 | 105 s | 11.6 | 76 s | 16.7 | 138 s | 11.9 | 250 s | 27.3 |
| 12 | 93 s | 10.1 | 73 s | 42.7 | 179 s | 6.6 | 351 s | 25.4 |
| 13 | 139 s | 7.8 | 106 s | 11.5 | 15292 s | 10.0 | 251 s | 34.1 |
| 14 | 141 s | 9.4 | 138 s | 8.9 | 218 s | 5.6 | 281 s | 25.7 |
| 15 | 181 s | 8.9 | 107 s | 11.1 | 186 s | 8.0 | 332 s | 18.9 |
| 16 | 157 s | 7.5 | 92 s | 11.3 | 297 s | 5.4 | 248 s | 35.8 |
| 17 | 209 s | 6.3 | 124 s | 11.8 | 318 s | 3.4 | 314 s | 20.7 |
| 18 | 150 s | 6.5 | 198 s | 5.9 | 297 s | 6.8 | 431 s | 18.5 |
| 19 | 280 s | 3.7 | 261 s | 5.9 | 253 s | 9.8 | 417 s | 13.9 |
| 20 | 253 s | 5.3 | 221 s | 8.8 | 388 s | 5.8 | 514 s | 18.4 |

**Table 5.** GPU scheduling times (in seconds) and the speedups for Montage instances.

| # of VMs | Montage 200 | | Montage 300 | | Montage 400 | | Montage 500 | | Montage 1000 | |
|---|---|---|---|---|---|---|---|---|---|---|
| | Sched time | Speedup | Sched time | Speedup | Sched time | Speedup | Sched time | Speedup | Sched time | Speedup |
| 2 | 10 s | 52.2 | 14 s | 39.1 | 7 s | 43.3 | 19 s | 89.8 | 47 s | 1074.8 |
| 3 | 14 s | 52.2 | 12 s | 33.5 | 16 s | 36.0 | 51 s | 44.6 | 77 s | 396.2 |
| 4 | 25 s | 21.4 | 19 s | 14.1 | 29 s | 24.9 | 64 s | 28.0 | 122 s | 759.5 |
| 5 | 28 s | 17.9 | 20 s | 12.3 | 36 s | 27.3 | 96 s | 23.4 | 179 s | 465.1 |
| 6 | 25 s | 24.8 | 31 s | 9.2 | 49 s | 19.5 | 87 s | 37.8 | 119 s | 347.9 |
| 7 | 34 s | 17.0 | 40 s | 8.9 | 68 s | 12.1 | 128 s | 26.7 | 184 s | 269.6 |
| 8 | 51 s | 7.9 | 46 s | 8.2 | 84 s | 10.4 | 166 s | 22.9 | 340 s | 345.1 |
| 9 | 72 s | 6.5 | 92 s | 2.0 | 90 s | 1.2 | 139 s | 11.9 | 469 s | 127.8 |
| 10 | 74 s | 6.7 | 62 s | 4.1 | 116 s | 4.4 | 213 s | 20.6 | 357 s | 120.4 |
| 11 | 105 s | 11.6 | 76 s | 16.7 | 138 s | 11.9 | 250 s | 27.3 | 530 s | 85.7 |
| 12 | 93 s | 10.1 | 73 s | 42.7 | 179 s | 6.6 | 351 s | 25.4 | 625 s | 71.3 |
| 13 | 139 s | 7.8 | 106 s | 11.5 | 192 s | 10.0 | 251 s | 34.1 | 1216 s | 35.6 |
| 14 | 141 s | 9.4 | 138 s | 8.9 | 218 s | 5.6 | 281 s | 25.7 | 809 s | 56.7 |
| 15 | 181 s | 8.9 | 107 s | 11.1 | 186 s | 8.0 | 332 s | 18.9 | 1267 s | 35.7 |
| 16 | 157 s | 7.5 | 92 s | 11.3 | 297 s | 5.4 | 248 s | 35.8 | 1255 s | 34.5 |
| 17 | 209 s | 6.3 | 124 s | 11.8 | 318 s | 3.4 | 314 s | 20.7 | 2172 s | 20.8 |
| 18 | 150 s | 6.5 | 198 s | 5.9 | 297 s | 6.8 | 431 s | 18.5 | 1868 s | 24.0 |
| 19 | 280 s | 3.7 | 261 s | 5.9 | 253 s | 9.8 | 417 s | 13.9 | 1941 s | 22.7 |
| 20 | 253 s | 5.3 | 221 s | 8.8 | 388 s | 5.8 | 514 s | 18.4 | 1818 s | 24.3 |

take days, or even weeks to finish processing the workflows presented in Table 5, we limited the CPU scheduling time to 12 h. The speedups of the GPU execution in Table 5 considered a 12-h CPU execution time.

Considering that most real life workflows present thousands of tasks, we evaluated PHEA-TaSDAP with a 1000 task instance (Montage 1000). The makespan and scheduling results are shown in Fig. 8. In comparison to the CPU results, the GPU version presented smaller makespans in all cases.

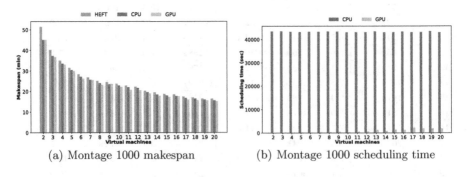

(a) Montage 1000 makespan          (b) Montage 1000 scheduling time

**Fig. 8.** Comparison of the makespan and scheduling time for Montage 1000.

## 6 Conclusion Remarks

In this paper we proposed a parallel implementation for the HEA-TaSDAP, called PHEA-TaSDAP, to improve the scheduling decision time. The computational results demonstrated that the GPU implementation yielded satisfactory results, reducing computational times by two orders of magnitude while preserving the solution quality. With the new implementation, it is now possible to schedule larger workflows that would have taken days with the CPU implementation.

Future research should investigate parallel metaheuristics that might be best suited for this problem, such as particle swarm, and implement it whilst maintaining all of HEA-TaSDAP constraints.

## References

1. Abrishami, S., Naghibzadeh, M., Epema, D.H.: Deadline-constrained workflow scheduling algorithms for infrastructure as a service clouds. Future Gener. Comput. Syst. **29**(1), 158–169 (2013)
2. Bharathi, S., Chervenak, A., Deelman, E., Mehta, G., Su, M.H., Vahi, K.: Characterization of scientific workflows. In: 2008 Third Workshop on Workflows in Support of Large-Scale Science, WORKS 2008, pp. 1–10, November 2008
3. Coelho, I., Munhoz, P., Ochi, L., Souza, M., Bentes, C., Farias, R.: An integrated CPU-GPU heuristic inspired on variable neighbourhood search for the single vehicle routing problem with deliveries and selective pickups. Int. J. Prod. Res. **54**(4), 945–962 (2016)
4. de Oliveira, D., Baião, F.A., Mattoso, M.: Towards a taxonomy for cloud computing from an e-science perspective. In: Antonopoulos, N., Gillam, L. (eds.) Cloud Computing. CCN, pp. 47–62. Springer, London (2010). https://doi.org/10.1007/978-1-84996-241-4_3
5. De Oliveira, D., Ocaña, K.A., Ogasawara, E., Dias, J., GonçAlves, J., Baião, F., Mattoso, M.: Performance evaluation of parallel strategies in public clouds: a study with phylogenomic workflows. Future Gener. Comput. Syst. **29**(7), 1816–1825 (2013)
6. Deelman, E., et al.: Pegasus: mapping scientific workflows onto the grid. In: Dikaiakos, M.D. (ed.) AxGrids 2004. LNCS, vol. 3165, pp. 11–20. Springer, Heidelberg (2004). https://doi.org/10.1007/978-3-540-28642-4_2
7. Luong, T.V., Melab, N., Talbi, E.G.: Neighborhood structures for GPU-based local search algorithms. Parallel Process. Lett. **20**(04), 307–324 (2010)
8. Özçetin, E., Öztürk, G.: A hybrid genetic algorithm for the quadratic assignment problem on graphics processing units. Anadolu Univ. J. Sci. Technol.-A Appl. Sci. Eng. **17**(1), 167–180 (2016)
9. Pandey, S., Wu, L., Guru, S.M., Buyya, R.: A particle swarm optimization-based heuristic for scheduling workflow applications in cloud computing environments. In: 24th International Conference on Advanced Information Networking and Applications (AINA), pp. 400–407. IEEE (2010)
10. Rios, E., Coelho, I.M., Ochi, L.S., Boeres, C., Farias, R.: A benchmark on multi improvement neighborhood search strategies in CPU/GPU systems. In: 2016 International Symposium on Computer Architecture and High Performance Computing Workshops (SBAC-PADW), pp. 49–54. IEEE (2016)

11. Szabo, C., Sheng, Q.Z., Kroeger, T., Zhang, Y., Yu, J.: Science in the cloud: allocation and execution of data-intensive scientific workflows. J. Grid Comput. **12**(2), 245–264 (2013)
12. Taylor, I.J., Deelman, E., Gannon, D.B., Shields, M.: Workflows for e-Science: Scientific Workflows for Grids. Springer, New York (2006). https://doi.org/10.1007/978-1-84628-757-2
13. Teylo, L., de Paula, U., Frota, Y., de Oliveira, D., Drummond, L.M.: A hybrid evolutionary algorithm for task scheduling and data assignment of data-intensive scientific workflows on clouds. Future Gener. Comput. Syst. **76**, 1–17 (2017)
14. Topcuouglu, H., Hariri, S., Wu, M.: Performance-effective and low-complexity task scheduling for heterogeneous computing. IEEE Trans. Parallel Distrib. Syst. **13**(3), 260–274 (2002)
15. Zhou, Y., He, F., Qiu, Y.: Optimization of parallel iterated local search algorithms on graphics processing unit. J. Supercomput. **72**(6), 2394–2416 (2016)

# A Systematic Mapping on High-Performance Computing for Protein Structure Prediction

Gesiel Rios Lopes[✉], Paulo Sergio Lopes de Souza[✉],
and Alexandre C. B. Delbem[✉]

Institute of Mathematical and Computer Sciences (ICMC),
University of São Paulo (USP), São Carlos, SP, Brazil
gesielrios@usp.br, pssouza@icmc.usp.br, acbd@icmc.usp.br

**Abstract.** The problem of Protein Structure Prediction (PSP) is one of the major challenges in computational biology, which has attracted the interest of many researchers in several areas. However, determining the three dimensional structure is an expensive and a time-consuming taks, even considering the current advances made in High-Performance Computing (HPC) systems. This paper presents a systematic mapping on HPC for PSP problems, aiming to determine: protein energy models applied to solve PSP problems with HPC, parallel programming models considered in such HPC solutions, and the heuristics and metaheuristics implemented with HPC for PSP. We considered 5732 papers published until January 2018 and, from this set, a total of 72 studies were selected for this paper. Our results show an increasing interest to apply HPC for this hard computing problem, using MPI as programming model and clusters as infrastructure to solve PSP problems. Some hybrid programming models with OpenMP and CUDA can also be found. There is a recurrent use of genetic algorithms to optimize PSP problems and the full atom model was the widest energy representation applied.

**Keywords:** Protein structure prediction · Parallel computing ·
High-performance computing · Systematic mapping

## 1 Introduction

Proteins are biological macromolecules, consisting of one or more long chains of a linear chain of amino acid residues, called a polypeptide, which performs essential functions for the creation and maintenance of life [7]. Proteins perform a vast array of functions, such as enzymatic actions, catalyzing metabolic reactions, DNA replication, responding to stimuli, and transporting molecules from one location to another. Many proteins are extracellular signals such as insulin, transmitting signals to distant tissues, or are binding proteins, which

H. Senger et al. (Eds.): VECPAR 2018, LNCS 11333, pp. 77–91, 2019.
https://doi.org/10.1007/978-3-030-15996-2_6

carry biomolecules to different places in the body, performing vital organic functions. The execution of all these activities depends exclusively on the protein having an active biological function, which in turn depends on its native state, which is closely associated with its three-dimensional structure [1,6].

The Protein Structure Prediction (PSP) has been a tool for development in aid of research in areas that require the determination of structures of new proteins by computational simulation. The PSP problem consists of determining the tertiary structure from a sequence of amino acids (primary sequence) of a given protein. The tertiary structure that the protein takes depends on the interactions between their atoms and those with the atoms of the environment (solvent) [6]. Finding the tertiary structure of a protein means knowing the relative position of atoms in three-dimensional space. Therefore, this problem has been considered one of the main challenges of Cellular Molecular Biology [19,24].

Most of the protein structures already determined were obtained using experimental methods such as X-ray Crystallography (CRX) and Nuclear Magnetic Resonance (NMR). Such methods, in general, require relatively significant financial resources and development time. Furthermore, it is not always possible to determine the structure by these methods. Therefore, it is indispensable to develop computational methods to predict 3D protein structures from protein sequences, in a faster, reliable and inexpensive way, since the number of these sequences increases each day [13].

Over last years several computational methods have been proposed as a solution to the PSP problem. However, despite advances made in recent years, the development of methodologies capable of achieving a high degree of predictability and accuracy remains an important challenge. PSP problem is classified in computational complexity theory as NP-complete problems [17]. Therefore, due to the complexity presented by the PSP problem and the inefficiency of the use of exact methods to solve NP-Complete problems, the use of approximate strategies, such as the metaheuristics[1], allied with the application of high-performance computing techniques (HPC) has been a compelling alternative to obtain acceptable solutions to the PSP problem [10].

Therefore, the choice of the prediction models and their associated algorithms should take in the context of the computer hardware environment in which they will run because algorithms designed to take advantage of the maximum performance in a particular hardware architecture may become less effective on different hardware. This concern becomes more evident nowadays since we are witnessing the consolidation of heterogeneous systems (i.e, systems that use more than one kind of processors), motivated mainly by the exacerbated power consumption in the current high-performance architectures.

In this sense, despite advances made in recent years, the development of methodologies and use of appropriate techniques capable of achieving a high

---

[1] Metaheuristic it is a general rule architecture that, formed from a common theme, can serve as a basis for solving generically optimization problems (usually from the area of combinatorial optimization) [15].

degree of predictability and accuracy remains a major challenge. For that reason to solve the PSP problem, if imperative to investigate the application of parallel processing in the energy potentials used to differentiate structures potentially near or far from the native state or in the optimization process used to find the native state, considering the use of more robust and comprehensive programming models, mainly those considering the use of heterogeneous processing, with CPUs and processing accelerators such as Graphics Processing Units (GPU), and Xeon Phi.

This paper shows a Systematic Mapping Study (SMS) to provide an overview of the state of the art of high-performance computing techniques that are currently used to solve the PSP problem. We focus on the techniques that have been applied to coarse-grain protein models and also the underlying hardware and programming models that have been used to execute those algorithms.

The remaining of this paper is organized as follows. Section 2 presents a brief overview of the aspects related to the PSP problem; Sect. 3 discusses the research method used to perform the mapping study. Results are presented in Sect. 4. Section 5 discusses the results and their implications. Finally, the conclusions are summarized in Sect. 6.

## 2   Protein Structure Prediction Problem

Proteins are basic structures of all living beings made up from 20 L-$\alpha$-amino acids which fold into a particular 3D structure that is unique to each protein. The folding of proteins has a compact form in relation to polypeptides, also generating the structural diversity necessary for proteins to perform and acquire a specific set of biological functions. It is known that better understanding the protein folding process results in medical advancements and development of new drugs [3]. Each amino acid contains N, C, O, $C_\alpha$ and H atoms and a specific side chain. Amino acids are joined through a peptide bond, formed between CO-NH groups [8]. A polypeptide is a continuous structure of many amino acid sequences which are bonded with a peptide bond. An amino acid unit in the polypeptide chain is called residue.

The 3D structure is responsible for the biology function of the protein. There are four levels of protein structure, like 'primary', 'secondary', 'tertiary' and 'quaternary'. The primary structure of the protein is also the amino acid sequence itself that differentiates one protein from another, this level of molecular organization is the simplest and most important because it originates the spatial arrangement of the molecule. The conformation that the protein will assume depends primarily on that amino acid sequence. The secondary structure refers to segments of the primary structure that form isolated folds. There are three main types of secondary structures: $\alpha$-helix, $\beta$-sheet and the loops (also called coils). The combination of all secondary structures of a protein forms a tertiary structure, which corresponds to the final form that a protein will assume. Several tertiary structures bind to other tertiary structures to form a more complex structure, known as quaternary structures [8].

The PSP problem refers to the determination of the 3D configuration of given protein from its amino acid sequence. This problem is not trivial [5]. The three-dimensional structure that the protein assumes depends on the interactions between its atoms and these with the atoms of the medium (solvent) [6]. Therefore, finding the tertiary structure of the protein means knowing the relative position of atoms in three-dimensional space, a task that requires a high computational effort. Despite the significant advances in scientific computing in recent years, mainly regarding the enlargement of the processing capacity of parallel computers at relatively low costs, the development of methodologies capable of achieving a high degree of predictability and accuracy in PSP remains one of the main challenges of Molecular and Cellular Biology [19,24].

The first methods developed for the PSP problem were organized according to three main groups: Comparative Modeling, Fold Recognition (or Threading) and first principle (or *ab initio*). These methods differ in the use of information available in the databases of experimentally resolved three-dimensional structures of proteins. Comparative modeling is the methodology most dependent on this information, with *ab initio* being totally independent (see Fig. 1) [25].

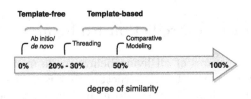

**Fig. 1.** Relation between methods of protein structure prediction and the use of experimentally resolved structures. Adapted from [25].

With recent advances in the area of PSP, it can be noted that the separation among these three methods is increasingly tenuous. Besides, a quick found to the latest CASP[2] shows that many of the methods can be included in more than one category. For example, the separation between the prediction of protein folding and comparative modeling is increasingly difficult, and the use of some structural/experimental information is widely observed even in so-called first principles. Therefore, the classification below is currently used when evaluating and comparing methods objectively [25]:

1. **Template-free:** uses only information from an amino acid sequence of a protein and a force field that models the interactions among atoms, in order to restrict the dihedral angles for values that correspond to feasible folds [2];

---

[2] Critical Assessment of Protein Structure Prediction - CASP is a world-wide biannual meeting that aims at establishing the current state of the art in protein structure prediction of the different methodologies developed, identifying what progress has been made, and highlighting where future effort may be most productively focused [20].

2. **Template-based:** prioritize structures (conformations) for a protein by considering its similarity to protein sequences obtained by other methods such as for example, CRX, and NMR [14].

In this classification, methods called of *de novo* are those that use some structural information, such as protein fragments, secondary structure prediction and statistical potentials, derived from proteins. In this way, what will indicate the choice of the method to be applied is the presence or not of structures solved experimentally, and deposited in banks of structures such as the Protein Data Bank (PDB), that can be used as a template for the modeling of the target sequence. The choice of a method is intrinsically related to the obtained from the alignment among the target sequence and possible template candidates.

The conformations associated with the global minimum of an energy function are considered the probable native conformations that the protein adopts under physiological conditions. Thus, methods of protein structure prediction must have, in their methodologies, the following common characteristics [25]:

 (i) One representation of the protein structure and a set of degrees of freedom that define the search space of conformations;
 (ii) Energy functions compatible with the representation of protein structure;
(iii) Search algorithms to efficiently select an energetically favorable conformation.

In the literature, one can also find several others classifications of the methods used to solve the PSP problem, as described in Floudas [11] and Dorn [10], for example. This others classifications, will not be addressed in this work, due to limited space.

## 3   Research Method

The research method for the mapping study presented in this paper is based on the guidelines given by Kitchenham and Charters [18] that consists of a method capable of identifying, interpret and evaluate scientific studies on a specific topic or research question. Its method involves three main phases: **(i) Planning** - refers to the pre-review activities, and aims at establishing a review protocol defining the research questions, inclusion and exclusion criteria, sources of studies, search string, and mapping procedures; **(ii) Conducting** - searches and selects the studies, in order to extract and synthesize data from them; **(iii) Reporting** - final phase that aims at writing up the results and circulating them to potentially interested parties. The motivation for this method is to provide a possible synthesis of existing evidence, regarding treatment or technology, identify topics for future researchers and/or for development of theoretical background related to new areas of research [21].

## 3.1  Research Questions

The main goal of the study provides an updated overview of high-performance computing techniques, currently used to solve the PSP problem. Therefore, the following research questions (RQ) have been addressed:

$RQ_1$: What protein energy model representation is used to solve the PSP problem through the proposed high-performance computing solutions?

$RQ_2$: What heuristics, metaheuristics or other methods are applied to solve the PSP problem through the proposed high-performance computing solutions?

$RQ_3$: What parallel programming models are used to solve the PSP problem through the proposed high-performance computing solutions?

## 3.2  Study Selection

For retrieving the studies, we performed a selection process in which, among others, the following aspects were addressed: (i) terms and search string definition; (ii) source selection for searching; (iii) inclusion and exclusion criteria definition; and (iv) how to store data.

## 3.3  Search String

The search string considers two areas - Protein Structure Prediction and High-Performance Computing - and it was applied in three meta-data fields: title, abstract and keywords. The search string went through syntactic adaptations according to particularities of each source and was elaborated and refined according to an initial set of key papers selected and based on the opinion of experts in that area. During the string validation, these papers must always be retrieved from electronic databases. Although subjective, this control enabled the string calibration and identification of possibly relevant studies.

We defined the search string considering the following keywords: prediction, protein structure, PSP, tertiary structure, computing method, computational model, optimization, optimizing, high-performance, HPC, parallelization, parallel, concurrent, graphics processing unit, GPU, graphics accelerator, FPGA, field programmable gate array and Boolean operations. Figure 2 shows the search string elaborated.

```
(( "prediction" ) AND ( "protein structure" OR "psp" OR "tertiary structure" OR "ab initio" OR "template
free" ) AND ( "computing method" OR "computational model" OR "optimizing" OR "optimization" OR
    "high performance" OR "hpc" OR "parallelization" OR "parallel" OR "concurrent" OR "graphics
processing unit" OR "gpu" OR "graphic accelerator" OR "field programmable gate array" OR "fpga" ))
```

**Fig. 2.** Search string.

## 3.4    Sources

To select the adequate databases for our search, we considered the criteria discussed by Dieste and Padua [9] and were selected the following databases, namely: ACM Digital Library, EI Compendex, IEEE Xplore, Science Direct, Scopus and Web of Science.

## 3.5    Inclusion and Exclusion Criteria

The selection criteria are organized in one inclusion criterion (IC) and seven exclusion criteria (EC). The inclusion criterion is: (**IC-1:**) Techniques or approaches of high-performance computing that are used for the prediction of protein tertiary. The exclusion criteria are: (**EC-1:**) The study is not written in English; (**EC-2:**) In the case of duplicated studies, the most complete one is considered; (**EC-3:**) The study does not relate techniques or approaches of high-performance computing to solve PSP problems; (**EC-4:**) The study does not relate prediction of protein tertiary; (**EC-5:**) The study does not relate details about implementation used; (**EC-6:**) The primary study is a table of contents, short course description, tutorial, keynotes, copyright form or summary of an event (e.g., a conference or a workshop); **EC-7:** The study is published in the grey literature[3].

## 3.6    Data Extraction and Synthesis

In the search process, we have used a data extraction form to answer the review questions, presented in Table 1. The search was performed between November 2017 and January 2018. The outcoming data was published and is freely available[4].

**Table 1.** Contents of data extraction form

|  | Attributes |
|---|---|
| *Metada* | ID and date |
| *Content* | Title, author, year, keywords, abstract, doi, document type (i.e. conference or journal), source, affiliation, country/territory and search database |
| *Data Extracted* | (1) Computational methods; (2) Energy model representation; (3) Programming model; (4) Metaheuristic |

In this phase, the primary studies were identified from databases and analyzed. Web of Science returned a larger set of studies (2603). ACM Digital Libary,

---

[3] Grey literature uses materials/research made available by organizations not belonging to the academic or traditional commercial publishing.

[4] http://bit.ly/sm-psp-hpc.

EI Compendex, IEEE Xplore, Science Direct and Scopus returned 150, 2086, 78, 438 and 2352, respectively (Fig. 3). The duplicated studies (1975 papers) were identified and removed. A set of 738 papers were selected according to the inclusion and exclusion criteria, in the selection phase, based on the partial reading (titles and abstracts). After a full reading, only 72 papers were selected, as shown in Fig. 3. We aimed to be as conservative as possible and, therefore, the search string has become generic to retrieve many studies from electronic databases, even if it would require a larger effort in the selection process. Many papers were introduced as primary studies, but only a few of them had more contributions and/or more significant impacts.

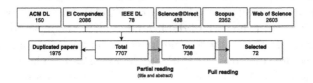

**Fig. 3.** Distribution of papers (conduction phase).

### 3.7 Classification Scheme

A systematic mapping requires a classification scheme [21]. We considered different facets, one for each research question. We only looked at the main findings found as benefits and problems related to the implementation of high-performance computing solutions used to solve the PSP problem reported by the selected studies. The categories comprising other facets were defined following two approaches: (i) based on categories already considered in the literature; and (ii) taking the selected studies into account. Following, The categories of these facets are presented in Sect. 4.

## 4   Results

This section discusses an overview of on selected primary studies in this study. The Fig. 4(a) presents the disposal of the primary studies selected from each database. It is possible to verify that were selected in our study only primary studies from Scopus with 34 papers (47.2%), IE Compendex with 26 papers (36.1%), Web of Science with 11 papers (15.3%) and Science Direct with one paper (1.4%).

Figure 4(b) displays the disposition of the primary studies selected from the publishing vehicle, conference or journal. It is possible to observe that the papers from conferences correspond to 51.4% of the papers selected and the other 48.6% of the papers selected were papers published in journals.

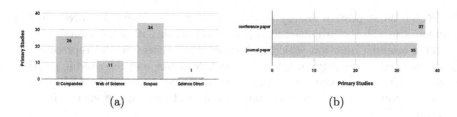

**Fig. 4.** (a) Distribution of primary studies per source database. (b) Quantity of primary studies selected from conferences and journals.

Figure 5(a) shows the distribution of primary studies selected per year. Although the automatic search in search engines have not been limited to a specific period, the last decade concentrates most of the papers. This points out that research aiming to make possible the resolution of the PSP problem through high-performance computing techniques has increased in the last years.

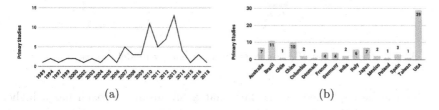

**Fig. 5.** (a) Distribution of primary studies selected over the years. (b) Quantity of primary studies selected per countries.

Our study counted 191 authors in the 72 primary studies. Researchers are located in 16 different countries, as shows Fig. 5(b). The sum of publications in each country exceeds the number of studies selected because some studies were developed in cooperation with different researchers and countries. The USA is the most prolific country with studies in the area (29 articles), followed by Brazil (11 articles) and China (10 articles), which shows a great interest of these countries in researchers in this area.

## 5   Discussion

In this Section, we present the discussion the main idea of the selected primary studies considering each research questions proposed in Sect. 3.1. We performed the mapping study according to the steps described in Sect. 3 and we used a form (see Table 1) with all papers selected, its bibliographic reference, and including the facets of the classification schema aforementioned. This form was used to extract the answers to each research question. Thus, each research question was answered considering the 72 papers selected by our mapping study.

$RQ_1$: What protein energy model representation is used to solve the PSP problem through the proposed high-performance computing solutions?

This research question seeks to discover what energy model representation has been used to simplify both the polypeptide chains and the residue positions of an atomic model since one of the major obstacles to solve the PSP problem is to determine energy functions that can accurately measure energy free of a conformation [5].

Figure 6 shows the disposal of the primary studies selected from protein energy model representation that is used to solve the PSP problem through the proposed high-performance computing solutions. We can observe that the full atom approach is the most adopted energy model representation for the use of high-performance computing techniques for solving the PSP problem, with 37 papers (47.4%).

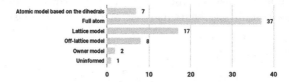

**Fig. 6.** Distribution of primary studies per energy model representation.

This can be explained by the fact that a full atom approach has a higher representation of the interactions among the atoms of the protein, this is due to the fact that in a full atom representation each residue that constitutes the protein is represented by its dihedral angles ($\phi$ and $\psi$) and by its side chain angles ($\chi$). We also have that a full atom approach is computationally challenging because it presents computational complexity of the order $O(g^{2r})$, where $g$ is the number of degrees of freedom of the dihedral angles, and $r$ is the number of residues of the primary structure, providing an environment of new opportunities for the application of high-performance computing [3,4].

It is also possible to observe in Fig. 6 that the second most used energy model representation was the lattice model with 17 papers (23.6%), which indicates that although the model is the most used one, as indicated by [23], the parallelism of the lattice model is little explored. Off Lattice model and the Atomic model based on the dihedrals angle base between the C-alpha also has been found, with eight papers (11.1%) and seven papers (9.7%), respectively. Finally, Fig. 6 also shows that in two papers were found an energy model defined by the authors as an own model and in another paper, the authors did not mention which model was used.

$RQ_2$: What heuristics, metaheuristics or other methods are applied to solve the PSP problem through the proposed high-performance computing solutions?

This question aims to identify what heuristics, metaheuristics or other methods are used to support the resolution of the PSP problem with the support of high-performance computing techniques since for complicated problems, heuristics/metaheuristics are often able to offer a better trade-off between solution quality and computation time [16].

Figure 7 shows the results for this question founded in the primary studies. We can observe that the Genetic Algorithm is the most used metaheuristics to explore the search space of candidate solutions with 17 papers. This is most likely due to the Genetic Algorithms perform search procedures in the space of feasible solutions, using probabilistic rules to combine solutions to obtain quality improvements [15]. Unfortunately in 12 primary studies, corresponding to 16.7% of then, it was not possible to identify the details of the methods used.

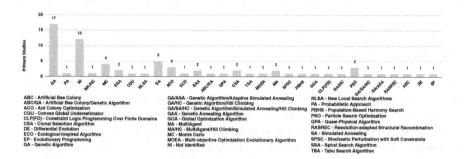

**Fig. 7.** Distribution of primary studies per heuristics, metaheuristics or other methods.

$RQ_3$: What parallel programming models are used to solve the PSP problem through the proposed high-performance computing solutions?

Our interest in this question is to find out which programming models are used to decrease the complexity of the algorithms used to solve the PSP problem. Programming models describe a parallel computing system in terms of the semantics of the programming language or programming environment, and this view is influenced by the architectural design and the language, compiler, or the runtime libraries [22]. It should be noted that the goal of a programming model is to provide a mechanism that the programmer can specify parallel programs.

Figure 8 presents the distribution of the programming models used in the solutions to the PSP problem. Most of the adopted solutions found in the selected primary studies use Message Passing as programming model through MPI (37.5%). A possible reason to use MPI is that several computers have a larger computational capacity than a single one and the problem presents a low computation/communication rate.

It is also possible to observe in Fig. 8 the use of hybrid approaches with MPI/Pthreads (7.0%) and MPI/OpenMP (4.2%). Shared Memory as the programming model is represented by Multithread C (5.5%), Multithread Java (8.3%) and OpenMP (8.3%). We also identify the use of the many-core architectures through GPU, using CUDA (8.3%) and OpenCL (1.4%). Our mapping also identified the use of Field Programmable Gate Array (FPGA) with six papers (8.3%). Other mapped programming models were JavaSpace and NetSolve with

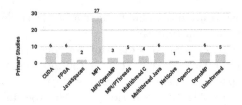

**Fig. 8.** Distribution of primary studies per programming models.

2.8% and 1.4% respectively, and in six papers the authors did not mention which models were used.

### 5.1 Future Research Directions

A computational approach to PSP problem requires a model that represents it abstractly, in a given level of atomic interactions. Based on well-established thermodynamic laws, PSP is generally modeled as an optimization problem where the corresponding free energy value is minimized, in relation to the possible conformations that a protein can reach. However, a successful PSP computational approach requires two essential parts: (1) to define the simplified mathematical model corresponding to the protein energy function of the protein, and (2) to develop an efficient optimization method to find the global minimum of the potential energy function.

In general, the potential energy function of a protein is defined with the positions of its atoms and calculated using force field models, as observed in our research question $RQ_1$. However, this approach has a very high computational cost [3], so the use of parallel processing is essential to allow us to obtain good quality results in reasonable computing time.

Another aspect observed in the selected primary studies is the lack of approaches and methodologies that can give a degree of predictability for the performance of the calculation of energy potentials. This type of approach could identify and mitigate key programming issues, such as load balancing, data sharing, and finalization detection.

Efficient solutions for the PSP problem require to overcome challenges, mainly related to the development of algorithms capable of identifying good regions in the universe of viable solutions and making more efficient searches for restricted areas in the solution search space. Population-based metaheuristic techniques are the most common, as observed in our research $RQ_2$. In such techniques, a collection of agents "collaborate" to find an optimal (or at least a satisfactory) solution. Due to the parallel nature of such techniques, the parallel, distributed and GPU architectures can be seen as appropriate to solve many of the challenges. However, it is still imperative to investigate new models to optimize local and temporal localities, in order to take advantage of the potential offered by parallel computing in this context.

Finally, in a general sense, the Protein Structure Prediction is a relevant problem, and its solution is not an easy task, which requires more research to be done in an efficient way. The development of new strategies, the adaptation, and investigation of new methods and the combination of existing computational methods and techniques for the 3-D PSP problem is clearly needed.

# 6  Conclusion

This paper has addressed a systematic mapping study to find evidences about the application of solutions based on the high-performance computing techniques that are currently used to solve the protein structure prediction problem. In order to provide a mapping of research topics, a set of 5,732 primary studies was analyzed, of which 72 were selected for discussion.

We have defined three research questions that reflect the scope of the study to map the contributions and challenges. Based on our results, it is possible to identify a trend in the use of distributed memory with MPI as the programming model to solve PSP problems. However, this may indicate underutilization of the available resources of the architecture used and makes the solutions non-scalable. This situation leads to the development of hybrid programming model, as proposed by [12]. Another point observed in our mapping study was the recurrent use of genetic algorithms as an alternative to optimize the PSP problem. Nevertheless, one of the disadvantages of the genetic algorithm in optimization problems is the slower convergence in problems as PSP. They can suffer from excessively slow convergence rate due to the high number of needed calculations. In order to avoid such problem, a possible alternative would be the development of solutions merging evolutionary algorithms and other metaheuristics or machine learning techniques.

The full atom model was the widest energy model representation used in the primary studies selected. Although the full atom model has shown impressive results. So, many other models need to be proposed, which consider other interactions levels. It is worth mentioning that solving the problem of the prediction of protein structure, it is not an easy task, and the use of high-performance computing techniques will be a decisive resource to solve this mission-critical science problem.

This general discussion of parallel hardware/software possibilities emphasizes the need for collaborative research when addressing the design and implementation of solutions through high-performance computing techniques to PSP problem.

**Acknowledgements.** The authors thank CAPES (PROEX), CNPQ and FAPESP (under the process 2013/07375-0) for the financial support. We also thank ICMC-USP and LaSDPC for offering the necessary infrastructure for this study.

# References

1. Anfinsen, C.B.: Principles that govern the folding of protein chains. Science **181**(4096), 223–230 (1973)
2. Berg, J., Tymoczko, J., Stryer, L.: Biochemistry, pp. 988–990. W. H. Freeman, New York (2002)
3. Bonetti, D.R.F.: Algoritmos de estimação de distribuição para predição ab initio de estruturas de proteínas. Ph.D. thesis, ICMC - USP (2012)
4. Brasil, C.R.S.: Algoritmo evolutivo de muitos objetivos para predição ab initio de estrutura de proteínas. Ph.D. thesis, ICMC - USP (2012)
5. Brasil, C.R.S., Delbem, A.C.B., da Silva, F.L.B.: Multiobjective evolutionary algorithm with many tables for purely ab initio protein structure prediction. J. Comput. Chem. **34**(20), 1719–1734 (2013)
6. Bujnicki, J.M.: Prediction of Protein Structures, Functions, and Interactions. Wiley, Hoboken (2008)
7. Carter, C.W., Wolfenden, R.: tRNA acceptor stem and anticodon bases form independent codes related to protein folding. Proc. Natl. Acad. Sci. **112**(24), 7489–7494 (2015)
8. Creighton, T.E.: Proteins: Structures and Molecular Properties. Macmillan, New York (1993)
9. Dieste, O., Padua, A.G.: Developing search strategies for detecting relevant experiments for systematic reviews. In: First International Symposium on Empirical Software Engineering and Measurement (ESEM 2007), pp. 215–224 (2007)
10. Dorn, M., e Silva, M.B., Buriol, L.S., Lamb, L.C.: Three-dimensional protein structure prediction: methods and computational strategies. Comput. Biol. Chem. **53**, 251–276 (2014)
11. Floudas, C.A.: Computational methods in protein structure prediction. Biotechnol. Bioeng. **97**(2), 207–213 (2007)
12. Gang, W., Xiaoguang, L., Jing, L.: Parallel algorithm for protein folds prediction. In: 2006 International Conference on Computational Intelligence and Security, vol. 1, pp. 470–473 (2006)
13. Gibas, C., Jambeck, P.: Developing Bioinformatics Computer Skills. O'Reilly Media, Inc., Sebastopol (2001)
14. Ginalski, K.: Comparative modeling for protein structure prediction. Curr. Opin. Struct. Biol. **16**(2), 172–177 (2006)
15. Goldbarg, M.C., Goldbarg, E.G., Luna, H.P.L.: Otimização Combinatória e Metaheurísticas: algoritmos e aplicações, vol. 1. Elsevier, Amsterdam (2016)
16. Jana, N.D., Das, S., Sil, J.: Backgrounds on protein structure prediction and metaheuristics. In: Jana, N.D., Das, S., Sil, J. (eds.) A Metaheuristic Approach to Protein Structure Prediction. ECC, vol. 31, pp. 1–28. Springer, Cham (2018). https://doi.org/10.1007/978-3-319-74775-0_1
17. Kenneth Jr., M., LeGrand, S.M., et al.: The Protein Folding Problem and Tertiary Structure Prediction. Springer, Heidelberg (2012)
18. Kitchenham, B., Charters, S.: Guidelines for performing systematic literature reviews in software engineering (2007)
19. Koehl, P.: Protein Structure Prediction, pp. 1–34. Humana Press, Totowa (2010)
20. Moult, J., Fidelis, K., Kryshtafovych, A., Schwede, T., Tramontano, A.: Critical assessment of methods of protein structure prediction (CASP)—Round XII. Proteins Struct. Funct. Bioinf. **86**, 7–15 (2018)

21. Petersen, K., Vakkalanka, S., Kuzniarz, L.: Guidelines for conducting systematic mapping studies in software engineering: an update. Inf. Softw. Technol. **64**, 1–18 (2015)

22. Rauber, T., Rünger, G.: Parallel Programming: For Multicore and Cluster Systems. Springer, Heidelberg (2013). https://doi.org/10.1007/978-3-642-37801-0

23. Sar, E., Acharyya, S.: Genetic algorithm variants in predicting protein structure. In: 2014 International Conference on Communication and Signal Processing, pp. 321–325 (2014)

24. Setubal, J.C., Meidanis, J.: Introduction to Computational Molecular Biology. PWS Pub., Boston (1997)

25. Verli, H.: Bioinformática: da biologia à flexibilidade molecular, 1ª edn. Sociedade Brasileira de Bioquímica e Biologia Molecular, São Paulo (2014). ISBN 978-85-69288-00-8

# Performance Evaluation of Deep Learning Frameworks over Different Architectures

Rafael Gauna Trindade[1]([⊠])(iD), João Vicente Ferreira Lima[2](iD),
and Andrea Schwerner Charão[2]

[1] Computer Science Graduate Program (PPGCC),
Universidade Federal de Santa Maria, Santa Maria, Brazil
[2] Department of Languages and Computer Systems,
Universidade Federal de Santa Maria, Santa Maria, Brazil
`jvlima@inf.ufsm.br`

**Abstract.** We evaluate the performance of two well-known Deep Learning frameworks – Caffe and TensorFlow – on two different types of computing devices – GPU and NUMA CPU architecture – using two popular network models as benchmark – AlexNet and GoogLeNet. We variate batch sizes between trainings and estimate the average training time per iteration and per image on each configuration. Both frameworks presented similar times for the AlexNet model, and TensorFlow outperforms Caffe by presenting times up to 2 times lower than Caffe for the GoogLeNet Model. The work also presents the impact of lack of support by the frameworks for NUMA Architectures, and relates a problem stated on loss computation by the Caffe Framework.

**Keywords:** Deep Learning · Caffe · TensorFlow · NUMA · GPU

## 1 Introduction

The popularity of Deep Learning (DL) methods to solve machine learning problems, like object's detection and classification on images, has presented a crescent rate in the last years. From 2006 to 2016, the number of DL papers published by year growth approximately 238% [16], while the number of searches for term 'deep learning' on Google raised about 3300% from 2004 to 2017, with a visible growth starting from 2012 [5] – same year when AlexNet model won the ILSVRC[1].

To create an application from scratch that can be able to train a DL neural network is not a trivial task. Several DL frameworks were released in order to simplify this task. Among them, two framework are highlighted by their popularities: Caffe[2] and TensorFlow[3]. Both of them help reducing the implementation

---

[1] http://www.image-net.org/challenges/LSVRC/.
[2] http://caffe.berkeleyvision.org.
[3] https://www.tensorflow.org.

© Springer Nature Switzerland AG 2019
H. Senger et al. (Eds.): VECPAR 2018, LNCS 11333, pp. 92–104, 2019.
https://doi.org/10.1007/978-3-030-15996-2_7

time for DL models, in distinct ways. Beside that, both frameworks also have support for different CPU architectures and accelerators like GPUs.

Given this compatibility with different kinds of systems, it is important to measure the performance of these frameworks on such systems. This work proposes to evaluate the performance of Caffe and TensorFlow on different types of heterogeneous computer architectures, and investigate why the performance can be different on some cases.

The remainder of the paper is organized as follows. Section 2 presents the related work about performance evaluations of DL frameworks. Section 3 gives a brief description of evaluated frameworks, and Sect. 4 describes the methodology applied on this work. Our experimental results are presented in Sect. 5. Finally, Sect. 6 presents the discussion and concludes the paper.

## 2 Related Work

Some papers related to DL frameworks performance evaluation can be found in the literature.

Shams et al. [13] evaluate the performance of Caffe, Apache SINGA and TensorFlow on different HPC architectures, with TensorFlow being evaluated with an older version (0.12 version). The authors restrict the evaluation to measure time spent with training, varying metrics as batch size. The frameworks were compiled and evaluated in environments with multiple GPUs - interconnected by PCIe3 and NVLink technologies - and environments with one or more computational nodes, in order to evaluate the scalability of frameworks. Among the hardware used by the work are the NVIDIA Tesla P100 GPU and the Intel Xeon Phi Knights Landing (KNL) CPU, the latter using the Omni-Path feature for multi-node communication. Five different types of network models were evaluated, with more emphasis on the AlexNet, GoogLeNet and VGG-19 models. Shams et al. [13] show that the Caffe framework had expressively smaller training times in almost all the metrics used, but indicates that for large networks such as VGG-19, the TensorFlow framework can achieve similar time to Caffe. All frameworks showed good scalability results, although TensorFlow does not perform well when using the KNL CPU in conjunction with Omni-Path. As for the GPU results, the use of NVLink technology showed better results than PCIe3.

Bahrampour et al. [3] present a comparative study of five deep learning frameworks, namely Caffe, Neon, TensorFlow, Theano, and Torch, on three aspects: extensibility, hardware utilization, and speed. The evaluation was conducted on a single machine with a Intel Xeon E5-1650 CPU and a NVIDIA GeForce GTX Titan X, using two different kinds of CNNs (LeNet and AlexNet), stack autoencoders and Long Short-Term Memory network (LSTM). At the time, Theano and Torch presented better results than Caffe and TensorFlow, using a pip[4] installation of the latter of an old version (0.6.0 version), without compiling Eigen to

---

[4] https://pypi.org/project/pip/.

enable support for vectorized instructions of the Intel CPU utilized and using an older CUDA and cuDNN version than other frameworks being compared.

Shi and Chu [14] also evaluate performance of DL frameworks in different execution environments, with one or four GPUs and four computational nodes. The frameworks evaluated were the following: Caffe-MPI (extension for distributed execution), CNTK, MXNet and TensorFlow (1.2.1 version). Three network models were used in the evaluation: AlexNet, GoogLeNet and ResNet-50, with fixed lot sizes for each. The authors identified different overheads and bottlenecks that may be the targets of optimizations. The work also provides descriptions of the different gradient optimization algorithms used, as well as an analysis of the parallelism used by the libraries to read the input files, as well as the storage format that each library uses. As a result of training times, Caffe-MPI again presents smaller times in all environments for almost all the networks used, besides presenting better scalability values both in the use of multiple GPUs and in the use of multiple nodes.

Following a different course from the other authors, Pena et al. [11] evaluate the combination of performance combined with energy consumption on the use of DL frameworks for CNN training in embedded architectures. The evaluated frameworks were Caffe and TensorFlow (1.0.1 version) for the AlexNet, GoogLeNet, NiN, VGG_F, and Cifar-10 CNN models. The tests were conducted on three different types of embedded systems: USB Neural Compute Stick NCS), Intel Joule 570X and Raspberry Pi 3 Model B. The lot size employed was 1, a relatively small number and generally not advised for actual training due to large variance of loss through training. As a result, the Caffe library has lower energy consumption rates than TensorFlow – up to 2.8 times on Raspberry Pi – albeit in conjunction with longer inference times - up to 4.7 times on Intel Joule.

## 3    Deep Learning Frameworks

We selected two frameworks for evaluation: Caffe and TensorFlow, as shown in Table 1, and a comparative overview can be seen on Table 2. The frameworks were selected on a combination of popularity and compatibility with different CPU architectures. To ensure a fair comparison between frameworks over different architectures, only the original implementations of frameworks were used – and not architecture-specific ports like Intel Caffe[5].

**Table 1.** Deep learning frameworks for evaluation.

| Framework | Version | CPU BLAS library | GPU BLAS library |
|-----------|---------|------------------|------------------|
| Caffe | 1.0 | OpenBLAS 0.2.19 | cuBLAS 8.0 |
| TensorFlow | 1.9 | Eigen 3.3.4 | cuBLAS 8.0 |

---

[5] https://github.com/intel/caffe.

**Table 2.** Frameworks comparative overview.

| Property | Caffe | TensorFlow |
|---|---|---|
| Development team | BVLC | Google |
| Implementation language | C++ | C++ |
| Supported languages | C++, Python, Matlab | C++, Python |
| Programming paradigm | Declarative and Imperative | Imperative |
| CPU support | Yes | Yes |
| BLAS on CPU | OpenBLAS, Atlas, Intel MKL | Eigen, Intel MKL |
| Multiple nodes | No | Yes |
| GPU support | Yes | Yes |
| BLAS on GPU | cuBLAS, OpenCL | cuBLAS |
| Multiple GPUs | Yes | Yes |
| Supported ANN models[a] | CNN, RNN, DBN, LNN | CNN, RNN, DBN, LNN, LSTM |
| Synchronization model | Synchron | Synchron and Asynchron |
| Communication model | No | Parameter server |
| Fault tolerance mechanism | Checkpoint-and-resume | Checkpoint-and-recovery |

[a]This information may be incomplete.

Caffe offers at compile time the possibility to choose the BLAS library to be used by the framework on CPU. Currently, three library are supported: OpenBLAS[6], Atlas[7] and Intel MKL[8]. For this work, we choose OpenBLAS due to its simplicity and compatibility with several different types of CPU architectures.

## 3.1 Caffe

Caffe is a well-known Deep Learning framework, developed and maintained by Berkeley Vision and Learning Center (BVLC), and written in C++ in a clean way, making it a simple but powerful and highly extensible tool. The BVLC provides also a collection of reference models, allowing newcomers to evaluate the framework with pre-existents models like AlexNet [8]. The two Caffe-related network models used in this work derive from this collection.

The framework has a large number of built-in layer types, like convolutional and pooling layers, and allows the network designer to prototype an entire network by only using the Google Protocol Buffer language – a relatively simple way to describe structured data in a serialized form. Moreover, Caffe also provides bindings to another languages than C++ like Python and MATLAB, allowing the developer to write new layers that the framework doesn't have.

The Caffe implementation delegates to linear algebra subroutine (BLAS) libraries the responsability to provide lower training/inference times on multi-core and manycore processor architectures like CPU and GPU. The framework

---

[6] https://www.openblas.net.
[7] http://math-atlas.sourceforge.net.
[8] https://software.intel.com/en-us/mkl.

itself does not provide any way to use model or data parallelism, neither has a distributed implementation, evaluating the provided network in a serialized way, independently of the network structure.

### 3.2   TensorFlow

TensorFlow is presented as an open source software library for high performance numerical computation [1]. Developed and maintained by Google, TensorFlow has an active development cycle, with new releases in short periods of time. Its flexible architecture allows deployment of computation across a variety of processing units (CPUs, GPUs, TPUs), and different architectures, like x86 or ARM.

Computational works are commonly described on TensorFlow through a directed acyclic graph (DAG) of computations [1], and Deep Learning networks are not different. Such graph is used to distribute workloads to different *TensorFlow workers*, allowing model parallelism. The network designer can also attribute a part of the network to a specific target device, like GPU, allowing asynchronous computations with different kinds of devices [1]. Both the network definition and training routines must be hard-coded in a programming language (C++ or Python), making it a more complex tool when compared to Caffe. In exchange, the nature of the framework does not restrict its use to Deep Learning, allowing it to be used in a wider range of scientific problems.

TensorFlow comes with an API, TF-Slim, that provides several pre-coded commmonly used deep learning layers, simplifying a bit the work for the network designer. This API is used to model the networks that this work uses for performance evaluation of TensorFlow.

## 4   Methodology

In order to analyse the performance of Caffe and TensorFlow frameworks, we chose four parameters: The batch size, number of epochs, network model, and target architecture.

Batch size is an DL hyperparameter that can change between trains. It corresponds to number of images trained in the same batch, and its size is proportional to the memory usage of frameworks, since it determinates the size of intermediate data between layers (*blobs* on Caffe and *tensors* on TensorFlow). We experiment varying batch size from 16 to 512, in powers of 2. Larger sizes like 1024 does not fit into memory of the GPU used by this work, and its efficiency on real world DL training makes it generally a bad option [9]. Smaller sizes than 32 are generally bad for training routines since it introduces much noise to loss computation (few images, more variance), but the inclusion of size 16 is interesting for measure how the frameworks scale.

An epoch is the amount of iterations required for each signal (images in our case) from input dataset to pass one time through the network. We set a small number of trainings epochs – 4 epochs per setting – since we are only interested on training time and not in training efficiency. Considering this, the dataset also is small: a subset of ImageNet with 1024 images of just one category. This configuration will make any setting result in overfitting, making this kind of result an expected behavior.

Two well known network models were used to evaluate the frameworks: **AlexNet** [10] (Fig. 1a) and **GoogLeNet** [15] (Fig. 1b). Both winners of ILSVRC on different years (2012 and 2014), they are convolutional neural networks (CNN) with relevant differences with each other. Although deep, AlexNet is shallowest than GoogLeNet, which is also wider than AlexNet, with some groups of layers that can be computed in parallel (if the framework supports model parallelism). Such model results in a high number of layers, and consequently a higher need for memory availability to store its intermediate data and a higher computational time to make the inference and back propagation processes.

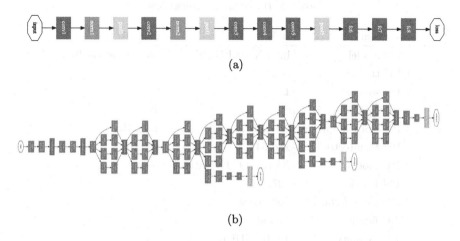

(a)

(b)

**Fig. 1.** AlexNet (a) and GoogLeNet (b) network models. Blue nodes (`conv`) on graphs refer to convolutional layers – the layer type that demands most computational power on a CNN. (Color figure online)

The models were implemented for each framework, using the Protocol Buffer language for Caffe and the Slim API for TensorFlow.

The trainings in each framework were done in NUMA or GPU, if available on physical machine. With TensorFlow it is possible to perform a training using both CPU and GPU at same time, but there is no dynamic scheduler on framework to distribute the computation between devices – a manual and static scheduling must be done per layer (vertex) on network (computational graph) –, so we do not cover this feature. A specification overview of the hardware present in these environments is shown in Table 3.

**GPU.** Both Caffe and TensorFlow have support for CPU and NVIDIA GPUs on x86 systems. The main computing device can also be switched at any point between layers computation with the two frameworks. All the data transfers needed are done implicitly by the frameworks. This work evaluates the frameworks on an environment with a NVIDIA Titan X GPU (lsc5). The GPU has around 12 GB of dedicated memory, managing to train batches of up to 512 images for the network models used in this work.

**NUMA Architecture.** The non-uniform memory accesses are an important point on training CNNs on NUMA architectures. Despite the large memory capacity – which allows it to easily store the stipulated maximum batch sizes by the work –, reference times to read/write data can have different values depending on where the data is located and which CPU the data request come from. This work evaluates the performance of frameworks on a NUMA machine with 8 NUMA nodes and 48 CPU cores/threads (blade01).

**Table 3.** Hardware specifications.

| Specification | lsc5 | blade01 |
|---|---|---|
| CPU model | Intel Xeon E5620 | Intel Xeon E5-4617 |
| CPU threads | 8 | 6 |
| CPU sockets | 1 | 8 |
| CPU total threads | 8 | 48 |
| CPU clock frequency | 2.4 GHz | 2.9 GHz |
| CPU architecture | x86_64 | x86_64 |
| GPU model | NVIDIA GTX Titan X | - |
| GPU threads | 3072 | - |
| GPU clock frequency | 1000 MHz | - |
| GPU family | Pascal | - |
| GPU memory | 12 GB GDDR5 | - |
| Memory (RAM) | 11 GB | 488 GB |
| RAM technology | DDR3 1066 MHz | DDR3 1600 MHz |
| NUMA nodes | 1 | 8 |
| Swap memory | 14 GB | 7.4 GB |
| Operating system | Debian buster | Debian stretch |

## 5  Experimental Results

### 5.1  Average Iteration Time by Batch Size

One of the first charts to be analyzed is the average training iteration time for all settings, by varying the input batch size (Fig. 2). The Caffe framework has a smaller average time in most cases on both environments for the AlexNet model, but in many of them its standard deviation meets the standard deviation of the TensorFlow times, making this advantage entirely questionable.

Through these charts it is also possible to see that the GPU (lsc5) training for the GoogLeNet network found a limit that did not reach the batch size of 512 for both frameworks. However, it is possible to see that TensorFlow has made better use of the dedicated memory available, being able to train lots of size 256, while Caffe could not exceed 128.

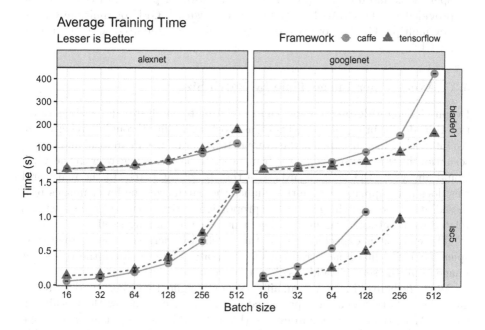

**Fig. 2.** Average iteration time for all evaluated settings.

On the other hand, the TensorFlow framework achieves times up to approximately 2 times smaller in comparison to Caffe for the GoogLeNet network in both environments. There are two reasons that contribute to this scenario:

1. Model Parallelism: TensorFlow benefits from the use by default of model parallelism in multicore environments by dividing the network model computational graph between multiple jobs scattered through CPU or GPU cores [6] – wider networks like GoogLeNet can improve performance in its training time due to the existence of layers that can be computed in parallel – besides relying on the parallelism provided by the cuBLAS and Eigen linear algebra subroutines libraries.

2. Use of batched GEMMs (General Matrix-Matrix Multiplication): The TensorFlow implementation for GPU makes use of a relatively recent feature of the cuBLAS 8.0 library [4] that consists of running multiple matrix multiplications in parallel – and that can outperform classical GEMM approaches [2]. Such feature can provide greater performance since in most cases the matrix multiplications performed by the convolution layers are not large enough to

require the full potential of processing power that a GPU like Titan X can deliver. Such GEMM operation recently was also released for Intel Xeon Phi KNL manycore processors [7], although not have full support on these frameworks. In contrast, although compiled with the same version of the cuBLAS and cuDNN libraries, the Caffe framework only makes use of simple GEMM operations and does not provide any other form of parallelism than the one provided by the BLAS library for systems with a GPU or multiple CPUs. For multiple GPUs, however, data parallelism is supported with the use of NCCL[9].

## 5.2    Average per Image Time by Batch Size

Despite having widespread usage, charts relating to batch size and average iteration time do not bring all the sights on network scalability through batch growth. An interesting measure then is the average time per image: In an ideal and unreal scenario, the time consumed by the framework to pass an image over the network would always be the same regardless of the size of the batch. In the real world this does not happen, because the smaller the batch size, the fewer images processed at a time, and the greater the proportion of time spent with instructions related to in-network training management, not the training itself.

Therefore, it is expected that as the batch size increases, the average time spent for individual image training will decrease. Figure 3 shows the times per image of all the settings addressed by this work.

With the help of Fig. 3, we can affirm some thoughts that Figs. 2 and 4 already gave clues - both frameworks presented a performance far below the possible in the NUMA architecture environment (blade01). The average time per image varies by the sizes of batches in both networks. In addition, training times in this environment have been too high, and the framework itself is to blame: both do not have decent support for machines with NUMA architecture. Due to non-uniformity in memory access time, a lot of time is spent with I/O because the intermediate data of the networks are not designed to be allocated efficiently through the NUMA nodes. Fortunately, some recent efforts can be found in the literature in order to take advantage of this type of architecture [12].

In the GPU environment (lsc5), we can observe that TensorFlow – in addition to present times averagely smallers than the competitor – presents a gradual reduction in the average time per image, showing signs of GPU scalability. Caffe also features gradual reduction of time, but on a smaller scale.

All timings gathered on this evaluation were extracted from iteration/step times reported by the frameworks. It is important to note that the initial iteration for the mean calculations is 32, due to the fact that in most settings, the TensorFlow framework presented peaks of time variance prior to this iteration followed by a stability, as shown in Fig. 4. It presents peaks at isolated iterations in which the time is up to 5 times greater than the time of the other iterations.

---

[9] https://developer.nvidia.com/nccl.

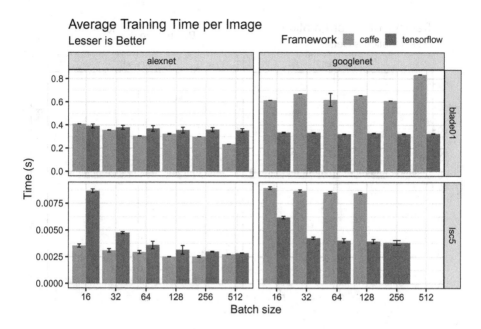

**Fig. 3.** Average training times per image, by varying batch size.

The AlexNet-`blade01` (NUMA) setting presents instability in the times through-out the training, however there is no variation greater than 7% in relation to the mean. This variation is the reason for relatively large standard deviation values, as shown below in this section.

One of the reasons for this variation may be the allocation of memory on demand (lazily), as done by Caffe [8], but only in the first iteration of trainings.

### 5.3 Caffe Loss Calculation Problem

Aside from performance evaluation, we also detected a problem during training in Caffe. The framework presented an unexpected behavior with some training settings: the reported loss reached a negative value, as shown in Fig. 5. In DL, loss can be categorized as a quantitative of how much the network predictions differ from the expected result, i.e. it is theoretically impossible to the loss value be negative. Loss is inversely proportional to the correctness of the model, that is, the greater the loss, the less accurate the model. It is common (and desired) that loss values reduce in a continuous way and that reduction is not so abrupt, which could lead the network to an overfitting.

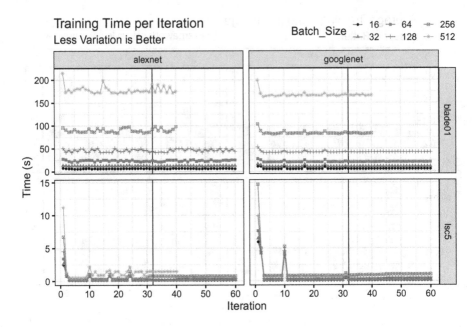

**Fig. 4.** Training times per iteration for TensorFlow framework. The vertical line on charts delimits the 32th iteration, from where the timing variation softens in mostly of our cases.

The actual value presented by Caffe is not the loss obtained in the current iteration: it is a moving average of a ring buffer with the last `average_loss` iterations (present in the `caffe::Solver<DType>::UpdateSmoothedLoss`[10] method). After the buffer is initially filled in, for each new value to be inserted into the buffer, the difference between the new value and the value to be replaced is divided by the buffer size and added to the current average. Thus, if the new value is less than the value to be replaced, the average is reduced because a negative value is added. However, it is impossible for the moving average to reach a negative value without negative values being added to the ring buffer itself, that is, negative loss values are actually returned from the inference/forward step of the network, stating an anomalous behavior. In previous experiments such behavior can be seen in both implementations (CPU and GPU) and in this work such characteristic was presented in the configuration with GoogLeNet, GPU, batch size of 32 and 64, and GoogLeNet, NUMA, batch size of 256. Such a problem may never have been detected by previous work because common evaluated training datasets generally generate good results in the evolution of loss during trainings. We believe that exposing this flaw of the tool also counts as a form of secondary contribution of the work.

---

[10] https://github.com/BVLC/caffe/blob/master/src/caffe/solver.cpp.

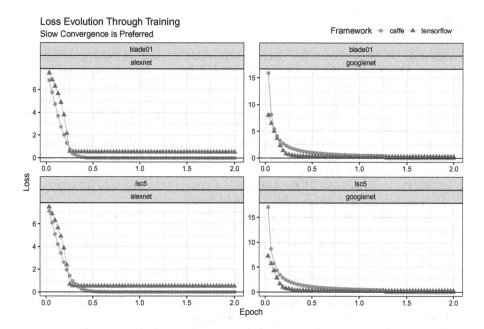

**Fig. 5.** Loss evolution through the initial training epochs for the dataset used with batch size of 32. The loss rate reaches negative values for Caffe in the combination `lsc5` (GPU) and GoogLeNet, while reaching very small positive values in the other configurations, but still valid

# 6 Conclusion

This work presented a performance evaluation of Caffe and TensorFlow frameworks on a NUMA machine and a cutting-edge GPU device. The frameworks presented similar times for the AlexNet model on both environments, but also presented a considerable difference on GoogLeNet model. In its 1.9 version, TensorFlow offers higher performances than before, whereas Caffe presented better training times [11,13,14]. The use of model parallelism and modern linear algebra subroutines like batched GEMM allows to TensorFlow lower training times.

However, the lack of specific support for NUMA architectures is notorious. Previous experiments on a single old Intel Core 2-Quad CPU achieved lower training times than the NUMA architecture for both frameworks. The NUMA architecture has enough potential to achieve good results in tasks such as machine learning, however this lack of support leads to training times up to 100 times greater than GPU training.

**Acknowledgments.** We thank CNPq for supporting the development of this work, and NVIDIA support with the donation of the NVIDIA GTX Titan X GPU used for our experiments.

# References

1. AAbadi, M., et al.: Tensorflow: large-scalemachine learning on heterogeneous distributed systems (2016). CoRR abs/1603.04467. http://arxiv.org/abs/1603.04467
2. Abdelfattah, A., Haidar, A., Tomov, S., Dongarra, J.: Performance, design, and autotuning of batched GEMM for GPUs. In: Kunkel, J.M., Balaji, P., Dongarra, J. (eds.) ISC High Performance 2016. LNCS, vol. 9697, pp. 21–38. Springer, Cham (2016). https://doi.org/10.1007/978-3-319-41321-1_2
3. Bahrampour, S., Ramakrishnan, N., Schott, L., Shah, M.: Comparative study of caffe, neon, theano, and torch for deep learning (2015). CoRR abs/1511.06435. http://arxiv.org/abs/1511.06435
4. Cecka, C.: Pro Tip: cuBLAS Strided Batched Matrix Multiply, July 2018. https://devblogs.nvidia.com/cublas-strided-batched-matrix-multiply/
5. Google: Deep Learning - Google Trends, May 2018. https://trends.google.com.br/trends/explore?date=all&q=%2Fm%2F0h1fn8h
6. Google Inc.: TensorFlow Architecture, July 2018. https://www.tensorflow.org/extend/architecture
7. Intel Corporation: Introducing Batch GEMM Operations, July 2018. https://software.intel.com/en-us/articles/introducing-batch-gemm-operations
8. Jia, Y., et al.: Caffe: convolutional architecture for fast feature embedding (2014). CoRR abs/1408.5093. http://arxiv.org/abs/1408.5093
9. Keskar, N.S., Mudigere, D., Nocedal, J., Smelyanskiy, M., Tang, P.T.P.: On large-batch training for deep learning: generalization gap and sharp minima (2016). CoRR abs/1609.04836. http://arxiv.org/abs/1609.04836
10. Krizhevsky, A., Sutskever, I., Hinton, G.E.: ImageNet classification with deep convolutional neural networks. In: Pereira, F., Burges, C.J.C., Bottou, L., Weinberger, K.Q. (eds.) Advances in Neural Information Processing Systems, vol. 25, pp. 1097–1105. Curran Associates, Inc. (2012). http://papers.nips.cc/paper/4824-imagenet-classification-with-deep-convolutional-neural-networks.pdf
11. Pena, D., Forembski, A., Xu, X., Moloney, D.: Benchmarking of CNNs for low-cost, low-power robotics applications. In: Robotics: Science and Systems (RSS 2017) Workshop - New Frontier for Deep Learning in Robotics, July 2017
12. Roy, P., Song, S.L., Krishnamoorthy, S., Vishnu, A., Sengupta, D., Liu, X.: NUMA-Caffe: NUMA-aware deep learning neural networks. ACM Trans. Archit. Code Optim. 15(2), 24:1–24:26 (2018). https://doi.org/10.1145/3199605
13. Shams, S., Platania, R., Lee, K., Park, S.J.: Evaluation of deep learning frameworks over different HPC architectures. In: 2017 IEEE 37th International Conference on Distributed Computing Systems (ICDCS), pp. 1389–1396, June 2017. https://doi.org/10.1109/ICDCS.2017.259
14. Shi, S., Chu, X.: Performance modeling and evaluation of distributed deep learning frameworks on GPUs (2017). CoRR abs/1711.05979. http://arxiv.org/abs/1711.05979
15. Szegedy, C., et al.: Going deeper with convolutions. In: 2015 IEEE Conference on Computer Vision and Pattern Recognition (CVPR), pp. 1–9, June 2015. https://doi.org/10.1109/CVPR.2015.7298594
16. Vargas, R., Mosavi, A., Ruiz, L.: Deep learning: a review. In: Advances in Intelligent Systems and Computing (2017). https://www.researchgate.net/publication/318447392_DEEP_LEARNING_A_REVIEW

# Non-uniform Domain Decomposition for Heterogeneous Accelerated Processing Units

Gabriel Freytag[1]([✉]), Philippe Olivier Alexandre Navaux[1],
João Vicente Ferreira Lima[2], Lucas Mello Schnorr[1], and Paolo Rech[1]

[1] Universidade Federal do Rio Grande do Sul, Porto Alegre, RS 9500, Brazil
{gfreytag,navaux,schnorr,prech}@inf.ufrgs.br
[2] Universidade Federal de Santa Maria, Santa Maria, RS 1000, Brazil
jvlima@inf.ufsm.br

**Abstract.** The use of heterogeneous architectures has become indispensable in optimizing application performance. Nowadays, one of the most popular heterogeneous architectures is discrete CPU+GPU. Despite the high computational power present in such architectures, in many cases, memory data transfers between CPU and GPU are significant performance bottlenecks. As an attempt to mitigate performance costs involved in data transfers, chipmakers started to integrate CPU and GPU cores in the same fabric sharing the same main memory but with different memory address spaces in architectures denominated APUs (Accelerated Processing Unit). To efficiently exploit heterogeneous CPU+GPU architectures it is needed to split the data so that both processing units (PUs) can perform the computations in parallel. Although this approach results in significant performance improvements, some applications can also be functionality split, as is the case of the Lattice-Boltzmann Method (LBM). In this work, we evaluate the performance of each kernel resulting from the functional decomposition of an OpenCL Lattice-Boltzmann method implementation using non-uniform domain decomposition between CPU and GPU on an APU to better understand the performance impact of different non-uniform domain decompositions between CPU and GPU on each kernel. The experimental results performed on an AMD APU A10-7870K show that uniform domain decompositions between each kernel on the same PU but non-uniform domain decompositions between CPU and GPU affect each kernel differently. These results suggest that non-uniform domain decompositions between each kernel on the same PU and not only between the different PUs can improve even more the performance of the application.

**Keywords:** Lattice-Boltzmann Method · LBM ·
Heterogeneous architectures · APU · OpenCL

© Springer Nature Switzerland AG 2019
H. Senger et al. (Eds.): VECPAR 2018, LNCS 11333, pp. 105–118, 2019.
https://doi.org/10.1007/978-3-030-15996-2_8

# 1   Introduction

Graphics Processing Units (GPUs) are currently crucial components to accelerate large-scale applications from science to industry in different areas. Such applications usually require large computational power to be performed in a computationally acceptable time, and the use of GPUs to accelerate large-scale applications partially fulfills this need. As the computations performed by this kind of applications are usually highly parallel and applied to a wide range of data, they can take full advantage of the computational power present in GPUs.

However, not all stages of large-scale applications are suitable to be performed by GPUs. In some stages of the applications there may be data dependencies or even weak parallelism preventing the full exploitation of processing capabilities exposed by GPUs. Although these stages do not benefit from the high parallelism of GPUs, they usually can be efficiently processed by CPUs which are often only used to orchestrate the GPUs, remaining idle during most of the application execution time in common CPU+GPU heterogeneous computing platforms.

While on the one hand the concurrent use of CPUs and GPUs makes it possible to achieve significantly performance improvements in large-scale applications compared to the use of GPUs only, the biggest performance bottleneck in these systems are the memory transfers between CPU and GPU. As GPUs are normally connected to the CPU through PCIe connections, the transfer of data to and from GPUs are highly costly and impact significantly the performance of applications. To try to mitigate this overhead, chip makers began to incorporate CPU and GPU Processing Units (PUs) in the same chip so that both could share the same memory space in the system and, therefore, no longer need copies of data between CPU and GPU. These heterogeneous computing platforms composed of CPU cores and GPU cores integrated in the same chip are called Accelerated Processing Units (APUs).

One of the keynote steps in the parallelization of applications to make it possible to take full advantage of the parallelism present in most CPU+GPU heterogeneous computing platforms are the domain and functional decomposition steps. While the domain decomposition step consists in the partitioning of the data manipulated by the application in smaller pieces called subdomains, functional decomposition step consists in the partitioning of the computations performed by the application in smaller pieces. Both decomposition techniques are widely used, however, domain decomposition is the most commonly used strategy to parallelize applications.

Lattice-Boltzmann Method (LBM) is a numerical method for fluid flow simulations and fluid physics modeling. It is frequently adopted as an alternative technique for computational simulations of fluid dynamics instead of using discrete Navier-Stokes equations solvers or other conventional numerical schemes. As there are some well defined computations that are performed over a large amount of data, both functional and domain decompositions can be used to parallelize the method. However, as the different stages of the computations have different complexities the performance of each stage resulting from the functional decomposition can achieve different performances on each PU. Therefore, an uniform domain decomposition may not exploit to the maximum the performance of each stage in the respective PU in which it has the best performance.

Therefore, the objectives of this paper are to evaluate the performance of each stage resulting from the functional decomposition in combination with different non-uniform domain decompositions of the LBM in an APU. Moreover, we also intend to evaluate the performance of the method using functional decomposition combined with domain decomposition and allocating the data used by the method in two different ways: on the host-visible memory space; and in device's memory space.

## 2   Related Work

Performance improvements of Lattice Boltzmann method parallelization in a wide range of architectures are constantly being studied due to its intrinsic high parallelism [1,6,7,12,14]. Most parallel implementations in CPU+GPU heterogeneous computing platforms decompose the LBM domain in uniform subdomains that are then computed by either the CPU or the GPU. [4] present a multiphase flow implementation of the LBM where the mass transport phase is performed in the CPU and the momentum transport phase is performed in the GPU. In this work the domain is decomposed in uniform subdomains that are processed by the CPU and the GPU. The results of the experiments show that the heterogeneous CPU-GPU approach outperforms the GPU-only approach approximately 1.8 times and 3 times the multicore CPU-only approach. [3] present a LBM implementation for heterogeneous CPU-GPU clusters in which the domain is decomposed in uniform subdomains that are distributed between the CPUs and GPUs of a cluster. The results of the experiments show that the implementation has a significant performance efficiency in weak scaling, but in strong scaling using multiple GPUs it is significantly less efficient than running CPU-only implementation. Already [13] present a heterogeneous CPU-GPU LBM implementation with mesh refinement and using two different meshes: multi-domain and irregular. In multi-domain mesh the CPU and GPU process concurrently two independent tasks in each step and in irregular mesh the CPU processes a smaller subdomain while the GPU processes a greater subdomain. The results show that the performance of the irregular implementation outperforms the multi-domain implementation, especially in problems with large refined regions, about 4.5 times faster.

However, some studies achieved significant performance improvements with balanced data distributions between the CPU and the GPU using uniform or even non-uniform subdomains. [15] implemented an entropic LBM for heterogeneous CPU-GPU systems using uniform domain decomposition. They use a load balancing model to estimate the optimal data distribution between CPU and GPU to minimize the execution time. Performing experiments they conclude that the overall computing time improvements with the optimal load balancing model range from 16.2% to 82.4% compared to the CPU-only and GPU-only configurations. Already [8] present a scalable LBM implementation for heterogeneous CPU-GPU clusters. They also decompose the domain in uniform subdomains and implement a load balancing strategy by means of which it is possible to specify the ratio of the subdomain that is processed by the CPU and the GPU. With this strategy the data of a subdomain is divided based on the Y dimension, increasing or decreasing the amount to be performed by each device. The results of the experiments show that the performance improvement in comparison to a GPU-only version is up to 16.22% on a cluster with a domain size $512 \times 512 \times 128$ and a data distribution ratio equal to 20%/80% (CPU/GPU).

The use of APUs, on the other hand, turns it possible to share the same data space between the CPU and the GPU cores and, therefore, reduce the high overhead introduced by data transfers between both computing units in discrete heterogeneous computing platforms where GPUs are usually connected with the CPU through PCIe connections. [16] accelerated an image convolution filtering algorithm on an APU partitioning the image in two pieces, one piece for the CPU and another for the GPU, relatively to the performance of each processing unit. They achieved performance improvements of 2.5 to 4.8 times compared to single-GPU executions. [9] evaluated the performance and efficiency of a 3D acoustic reverse time migration application in a CPU, GPU, and an APU. They used a domain decomposition where each OpenCL work-item applied its computations over uniform slices of data along the z-axis. In the APU they also compare the performance using two different data placement strategies: one on which copies of data between CPU and GPU are made explicitly; and one on which both computing units access the same data through a virtual memory space. They show that the APU reduces or suppresses the CPU-GPU data transfer overhead which could become a stronger performance bottleneck on clusters with more than 16 nodes.

## 3    Lattice-Boltzmann Method

Lattice-Boltzmann Method (LBM) is a numerical method for fluid flow simulations and fluid physics modeling. The Method originated from Lattice Gas (LG) automata, a discrete particle kinetics utilizing a discrete lattice and discrete time [2]. It is frequently adopted as an alternative technique for computational simulations of Fluid Dynamics instead of using discrete Navier-Stokes equations solvers [11] or other conventional numerical schemes based on discretizations of macroscopic continuum equations [2].

The Lattice Gas Automaton (LGA) is constructed as a simplified, fictitious molecular dynamic in which space, time, and particle velocities are all discrete [2]. Thus, in the LBM the space, time and velocity of the particles are also all discrete. A lattice is formed by discrete points, each one with a fixed number of discrete displacement directions and at each iteration, particles realize a space displacement among the lattice points, enabling simulations of physical properties of fluid flows in a simple way [11].

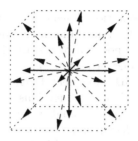

**Fig. 1.** D3Q19 lattice geometry

The LBM is an evolution of the LGA model and replaces the boolean site populations by real numbers between 0 and 1 in LGA, representing the average value and their time evolution controlled by a Boltzmann Equation (BE), derived from the LG model [5]. The fundamental idea of the LBM is to construct simplified kinetic models that incorporate the essential physics of microscopic or mesoscopic processes so that the macroscopic averaged properties obey the desired macroscopic equations [2].

In this paper we consider only a three-dimensional lattice structure with 18 propagation directions, as shown in Fig. 1. As the propagation can be null, one more propagation direction is added to the eighteen directions, resulting in a D3Q19 structure.

The possible directions of the D3Q19 model are defined by [11]:

- A static point at coordinate $(0,0,0)$, where the particle has zero velocity. The value of $\omega_i$ in this case is $1/3$.
- Six nearest directions $(-1,0,0)$, $(+1,0,0)$, $(0,-1,0)$, $(0,+1,0)$, $(0,0,-1)$ and $(0,0,+1)$, with unity velocity and $\omega_i = 1/18$.
- Twelve diagonal line neighbors $(1,1,0)$, $(-1,1,0)$, $(1,-1,0)$, $(-1,-1,0)$, $(1,0,1)$, $(-1,0,1)$, $(1,0,-1)$, $(-1,0,-1)$, $(0,1,1)$, $(0,-1,1)$, $(0,1,-1)$ and $(0,-1,-1)$, with velocity $\sqrt{2}$ and $\omega_i = 1/36$.

To deal with the collisions against the boundaries, a mechanism called Bounce-back is used [11]. It consists in the inversion of the speed vectors directions each time that a collision occur against static points in the boundary. This method prevents the forces leaving, returning them to the fluid.

## 4  The LBM OpenCL Implementation

The OpenCL implementation of the three-dimensional (3D) Lattice-Boltzmann method presented in our work is based on the implementation for distributed memory architectures presented by [10]. In this study the authors presented a two-dimensional (2D) and a 3D implementation of the LBM where the whole LBM computation was decomposed in smaller phases that were executed sequentially over the same data, each of it depending on the computation performed by the previous stage of computation. Each of these phases is performed in parallel by all remote nodes on different uniform subdomains (all having the same size) resulting from the decomposition of the LBM domain in $n$ subdomains, where $n$ is equal to the number of remote hosts used for the computation of the method. In both 2D and 3D implementations presented by the authors the domain was decomposed in each of its dimensions and in different uniform sizes, whose performance was subsequently analyzed to find out the most efficient domain decomposition for each implementation.

In our work, the decomposition of the LBM computations in smaller phases was kept, but the domain decomposition was modified. We modified the domain decomposition so that the domain is decomposed in two subdomains, one for each device when both are used for the computations of the LBM, and that the proportion of data assigned to each device may be non-uniform, that is so that they can have different sizes. In this way, it is possible to assign a smaller, equal or greater proportion of the domain to be processed by the CPU and the counterpart by the GPU, and vice versa. The domain proportion assignment to the devices is performed in relation to the Z dimension of the domain and, therefore, the subdomains have the same size in X and Y dimension (the same as the original domain) but have different sizes in Z dimension, according to the domain proportion chosen. For example, a domain proportion of 25% of a domain of size $128 \times 128 \times 128$ for the CPU and the remaining 75% of this domain for the GPU corresponds to a subdomain of size $128 \times 128 \times 32$ being processed by the CPU and a subdomain of size $128 \times 128 \times 96$ being processed by the GPU.

Figure 2 shows the main steps of the LBM OpenCL implementation algorithm. Initially, to be able to execute something in the devices of the OpenCL platform, it is needed to create an OpenCL context using the IDs of the desired OpenCL devices. As in our case, the CPU and GPU devices will be used to perform computations concurrently and need to share some resources, a single OpenCL context is created using both devices IDs. After the creation of the context, for each device, it is needed to create a command queue where all computations to be performed by the device will be enqueued.

To be able to compute the phases resulting from the LBM functional decomposition in the devices, first, it is needed to create a program object with the source code of the phases implementation and then build (compile and link) the program. With the program created and built, for each of the phases it is needed to create an OpenCL kernel object, which are functions declared in the program. This kernels are created once and enqueued countless times.

Before starting the computation of the method, it is needed to assign the attributes of each kernel. The kernels, besides other attributes, need the address in memory where the LBM data structures are allocated. This data structures need to be allocated in the previously created OpenCL context so that the data structures can be shared by both devices.

In Fig. 2 we present the 5 kernels that compose the computations done by the LBM as well as the loop that iterates over the maximum time steps ($t\_max$)

1: Get IDs of desired OpenCL devices
2: Creates OpenCL context with devices' IDs
3: Creates devices' command queues
4: Creates and builds program object
5: Creates the kernels
6: Creates memory objects for LBM data structures
7: Sets devices' kernels arguments
8: Enqueues INITIALIZE kernel
9: **for** Each time step **do**
10:    Enqueues REDISTRIBUTE kernel
11:    Enqueues PROPAGATE kernel
12:    Enqueues BOUNCEBACK kernel
13:    Enqueues RELAXATION kernel
14: **end for**
15: Wait for all kernels to finish
16: Sums devices' kernels execution times
17: Releases allocated memory objects

**Fig. 2.** Main steps of the LBM OpenCL implementation.

of the simulation. The *initialize* kernel is the first to be executed by a device over its corresponding subdomain and is responsible for assign the initial density values for each particle of the fluid in the subdomain. Unlike *initialize* kernel, the four remaining kernels are executed *t_max* times by a device over the subdomain. The *redistribute* kernel is responsible for calculating the macroscopic density and speed of the particles and the *propagate* kernel is responsible for propagating de forces of the particles in the fluid to the neighbor points. Already the *bounceback* kernel is responsible to compute the collisions of the particles against obstacles present in the flow and against the borders of the pipe, inverting the speed directions when collisions occur against static points. The *relaxation* kernel, in turn, emulates the shock among the particles.

As each kernel must be executed in the same order that they are enqueued in the same device's queue, for each kernel are associated events relative to the previous kernel enqueued in the respective queue so that the execution of a kernel only begins after completion of the execution of the previous kernel on which it depends. Therefore, kernels enqueued in the same queue need to be executed sequentially, while kernels enqueued in different queues can be executed in parallel and asynchronously by the respectively associated devices, with the exception of the propagate kernel that must be executed synchronously in different queues due to neighboring dependencies.

The events used to ensure the correct order of execution of the kernels in a queue, at the end of the execution of the application are used to obtain the execution time of each kernel in each device. These events store, among other information, the moment when the execution of the kernel started as well as when it finished. Thus, to obtain the total execution time of a kernel, the execution times of each enqueuing of the kernel in a queue are summed from the information stored in the respective events.

In addition, two modes of memory allocation: *device*, in which memory is allocated in the device-visible memory space; and *host*, in which memory is allocated in the host-visible memory space. In the *device* memory allocation mode, the allocation is performed in the device memory by means of the *clCreateBuffer()* method using only the *CL_MEM_READ_WRITE* flag and passing a null pointer. Already in the *host* memory allocation mode the allocation is performed in the host pinned memory through the *clCreateBuffer()* method in which, in addition to the *CL_MEM_READ_WRITE* flag, the *CL_MEM_ALLOC_HOST_PTR* flag and a null pointer are still used. The latter allows the use of the same pointer to access the data stored in memory on both the host and the devices, requiring only a mapping of the pointer to a temporary pointer to access the memory directly on the host without the need to perform memory copies.

## 5     Experimental Results

In this section, we present the results of experiments performed on an APU using different non-uniform domain decomposition sizes in executions only in the CPU, only in the GPU and collaboratively in the CPU and in the GPU.

### 5.1     Platform and Environment

The experiments were performed on a platform composed of an AMD A10-7870K APU that has 4 CPU cores and 8 GPU cores integrated in the same chip, 6 GB of RAM memory and Ubuntu 14.04 (trusty) operating system with 3.13.0-149-kernel-generic. The OpenCL Software Development Kit (SDK) used was AMDAPPSDK-3.0, the compiler was Clang 7.0, and the compilation flags -*O3 -march=native -mavx*.

Experiments with domain sizes of 32, 64, 96 and 128 were executed. For each domain size and mode of memory allocation (device and host), experiments were performed only on the CPU, only on the GPU and experiments in which the CPU and the GPU worked collaboratively. The maximum number of time steps (*t_max*) was 200 and each experiment was repeated 20 times.

Each of the domain sizes experimented had an obstacle at its center in order to hinder the flow of the fluid and increase the complexity of computing. In Fig. 3 is presented a representation of a domain of size 128 and the respective obstacle present in its center.

### 5.2     Performance Evaluation

Figures 4 and 5 present the execution times of each kernel using only the CPU device, only the GPU device and using both CPU and GPU devices with a domain of size $128 \times 128 \times 128$ and using device-visible memory space and host-visible memory space, respectively. Comparing the execution times of each kernel only in the CPU device using the *device* and *host* memory allocations modes it is possible to observe that there is a minimum variation in the execution times

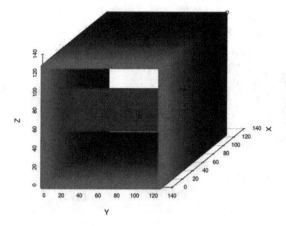

**Fig. 3.** The representation of a domain and the obstacle located at the center.

but does not affect the performance of the application. However, comparing the execution times of the kernels only in the GPU device it is possible to observe that with the *host* memory allocation mode the execution time of each kernel practically tripled in propagate, bounceback and relaxation kernels, while in initialize and redistribute kernels the execution time is approximately six times greater. As for the GPU to access the memory in host-visible memory space, the OpenCL runtime needs to translate the address used by the GPU device to the address used by the CPU device to handle the data, this translation harms significantly the performance in the GPU.

Comparing the execution times of each kernel using both CPU and GPU devices and a uniform domain decomposition with a proportion of 50% for each device this also happens. However, in this case, while the execution times of the initialize, redistribute and propagate are reduced by half compared with using only the GPU, the execution times of the bounceback and relaxation kernels are even greater than with using only the GPU device.

By analyzing the execution times of each kernel only in the CPU device, only in the GPU device and in a collaborative way using both CPU and GPU devices presented in Fig. 4, it is possible to observe that both GPU-only and CPU+GPU outperform the performance of the CPU-only. Despite the execution time of propagate, bounceback, and relaxation kernels decreasing in the GPU compared to their CPU execution times, there was an increase in initialize and redistribute kernels.

Now, comparing the execution times of the kernels in the GPU with the times using both CPU and GPU devices it is possible to notice that, with the exception of the relaxation and bounceback kernels, there was a decrease in the execution time of the other kernels. Although the relaxation kernel execution time has increased considerably, what stands out is the significant increase in bounceback kernel execution time. Since this kernel has similar performance on

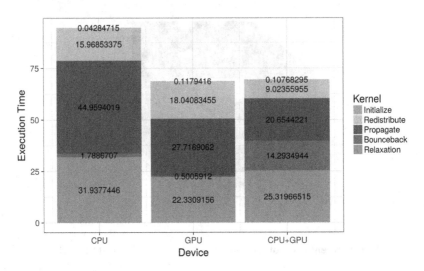

**Fig. 4.** CPU-only, GPU-only and CPU+GPU execution times of each kernel in device memory allocation mode.

both the CPU- and GPU-only, collaborative processing of the kernel should not increase its execution time, at least not so abruptly.

Analyzing the execution times of each kernel only in the CPU device, only in the GPU device and in both CPU and GPU devices with a uniform domain decomposition with a proportion of 50% for each device and using the *host* memory allocation mode presented in Fig. 5 it is possible to observe that the CPU-only outperforms both GPU-only and CPU+GPU. Although the execution times of practically all kernels are significantly smaller in the CPU-only experiments, with the exception of the bounceback kernel which has a slightly greater execution time compared to in GPU-only. Moreover, what is even more evident is the dissonance between bounceback kernel execution time in CPU+GPU compared to the CPU-only and GPU-only execution times.

Figure 6 shows the execution times of each kernel by varying the proportion of the domain assigned to each device, from execution only on the CPU ($128 \times 0$), the decrease of the relative proportion to CPU and the consecutive increase of the ratio relative to GPU up to execution only on the GPU ($0 \times 128$), in *device* memory allocation mode. As can be seen, as the CPU proportion decreases and the GPU proportion increases, the execution time of each kernel (with the exception of the bounceback kernel) decreases up to the $80 \times 48$ proportion. With this domain decomposition the shortest execution times were obtained for the total execution and also for the propagate and relaxation kernels.

The variability in the execution times of the kernels shown with the use of non-uniform domain decomposition indicates that traditional uniform domain decomposition approaches may not efficiently exploit the computational power of underlying architectures. In addition, uniform domain decomposition does not consider the possibility of applications not executing efficiently in an architecture

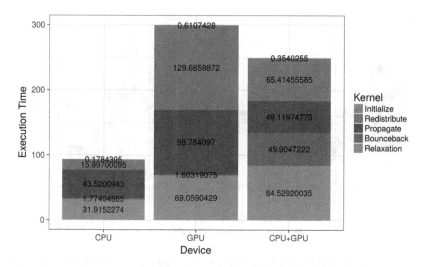

**Fig. 5.** CPU-only, GPU-only and CPU+GPU execution times of each kernel in host memory allocation mode.

and, thus, undermining the performance of the application as a whole, as can be seen in Fig. 6 where the uniform proportion at $64 \times 64$ does not efficiently explore devices capabilities such as the non uniform $80 \times 48$ proportion does.

In addition, by looking more closely at the bounceback kernel in all non-uniform domain decomposition proportions, it is possible to observe that as the GPU proportion increases and the CPU proportion decreases, the kernel execution time increases considerably, and when executed only on the GPU with no CPU proportion, the best execution time is obtained. As no different operations are performed when the domain is decomposed but rather divided between the devices, one hypothesis is that exists some problem with the domain, more specifically with the obstacle into the domain.

Moreover, using a non-uniform domain decomposition where each device has a different domain proportion for each of its kernels can further optimize application performance. An example of this can be seen in Fig. 6, where the best execution times for the propagate and relaxation kernels are obtained with an $80 \times 48$ proportion, while in initialize and redistribute kernels it is obtained with a $96 \times 32$ proportion and in the bounceback kernel with a $0 \times 128$ proportion. Combining this different non-uniform domain decomposition that provides the best performance for the respective kernels the performance of the application can possibly be further improved.

Finally, Fig. 7 shows the execution times of each kernel by varying the proportion of the domain assigned to each device, from execution only in the CPU ($128 \times 0$), the decrease of the relative proportion of CPU and the consecutive increase of the proportion relative to the GPU up to execution only in the GPU ($0 \times 128$) in *host* memory allocation mode. In this case, however, the proportion of the domain performed by the devices that provided better performance

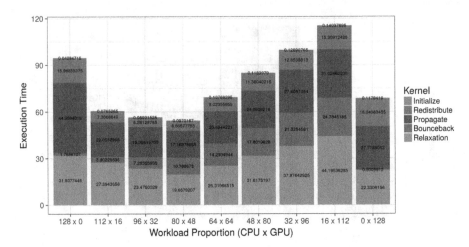

**Fig. 6.** Execution times of each kernel for different non-uniform subdomains using only CPU device, only GPU device and both CPU and GPU devices and using a *device* memory allocation mode.

improvements was the $112 \times 16$ proportion. Since the GPU doesn't have a good performance in this memory allocation mode, this is the only proportion it is possible to outperform the CPU-only execution. In this proportion, all kernels (with exception of the bounceback kernel) achieve the shortest execution times. The bounceback kernel, in turn, achieves the shortest execution time with a $0 \times 128$ proportion and, as well as in the *device* memory allocation mode, the

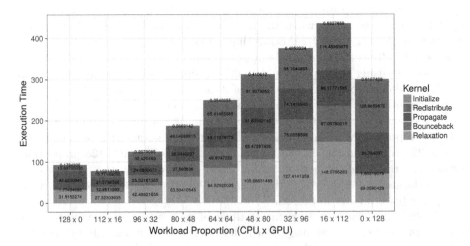

**Fig. 7.** Execution times of each kernel for different non-uniform subdomains using only CPU device, only GPU device and both CPU and GPU devices and using a *host* memory allocation mode.

execution time of this kernel increases significantly as the proportion of the domain assigned to the GPU also increases.

# 6  Conclusion

In this work, we implemented an OpenCL Lattice-Boltzmann Method based on a 3D model in which it is possible to decompose the domain in non-uniform subdomains that are then assigned to each of the devices available in an APU architecture. The LBM is also functionally decomposed so that the computations of the method over the subdomains are performed in phases, that in our work were transformed in OpenCL kernels. In addition, two different memory allocation modes were also implemented.

The results show that non-uniform domain decomposition can improve the performance by efficiently exploiting the devices parallelism. When analyzing the execution times of each kernel when both CPU and GPU devices are used for the computations it is possible to observe that each kernel benefits from different non-uniform domain decompositions in each device. This indicates that using different non-uniform domain decomposition for each kernel on the same device can improve the performance of the application by efficiently exploiting the parallelism accordingly to the complexity of each kernel.

Therefore, as future works, we suggest the implementation of mixed non-uniform domain decompositions on the same device where each kernel performs its computations over different proportions of the domain. Moreover, we also suggest the exploitation of the HSA shared memory features present in the APU used in our experiments to analyze if it is possible to minimize the memory access overheads and also analyze the behavior of the kernels with different non-uniform domain decomposition proportions for each device.

# References

1. Calore, E., Gabbana, A., Kraus, J., Pellegrini, E., Schifano, S.F., Tripiccione, R.: Massively parallel lattice-Boltzmann codes on large GPU clusters. Parallel Comput. **58**, 1–24 (2016). https://doi.org/10.1016/j.parco.2016.08.005
2. Chen, S., Doolen, G.D.: Lattice Boltzmann method for fluid flows. Ann. Rev. Fluid Mech. **30**(1), 329–364 (1998). https://doi.org/10.1146/annurev.fluid.30.1.329
3. Feichtinger, C., Habich, J., Köstler, H., Hager, G., Rüde, U., Wellein, G.: A flexible patch-based lattice Boltzmann parallelization approach for heterogeneous GPU-CPU clusters. Parallel Comput. **37**(9), 536–549 (2011). https://doi.org/10.1016/j.parco.2011.03.005
4. McClure, J.E., Prins, J.F., Miller, C.T.: A novel heterogeneous algorithm to simulate multiphase flow in porous media on multicore CPU-GPU systems. Comput. Phys. Commun. **185**(7), 1865–1874 (2014). https://doi.org/10.1016/j.cpc.2014.03.012
5. McNamara, G.R., Zanetti, G.: Use of the Boltzmann equation to simulate lattice-gas automata. Phys. Rev. Lett. **61**(20), 2332–2335 (1988). https://doi.org/10.1103/PhysRevLett.61.2332

6. Meadows, L., Ishikawa, K.: OpenMP tasking and MPI in a lattice QCD benchmark. In: de Supinski, B.R., Olivier, S.L., Terboven, C., Chapman, B.M., Müller, M.S. (eds.) IWOMP 2017. LNCS, vol. 10468, pp. 77–91. Springer, Cham (2017). https://doi.org/10.1007/978-3-319-65578-9_6

7. Nagar, P., Song, F., Zhu, L., Lin, L.: LBM-IB: a parallel library to solve 3D fluid-structure interaction problems on manycore systems. In: Proceedings of the International Conference on Parallel Processing, December 2015, pp. 51–60 (2015). https://doi.org/10.1109/ICPP.2015.14

8. Riesinger, C., Bakhtiari, A., Schreiber, M., Neumann, P., Bungartz, H.J.: A holistic scalable implementation approach of the lattice Boltzmann method for CPU/GPU heterogeneous clusters. Computation 5(4), 48 (2017). https://doi.org/10.3390/computation5040048. http://www.mdpi.com/2079-3197/5/4/48

9. Said, I., Fortin, P., Lamotte, J., Calandra, H.: Leveraging the accelerated processing units for seismic imaging: a performance and power efficiency comparison against CPUs and GPUs. Int. J. High Perform. Comput. Appl. (2017). https://doi.org/10.1177/1094342017696562

10. Schepke, C., Diverio, T.A.: Distribuição de Dados para Implementações Paralelas do Método de Lattice Boltzmann. Ph.D. thesis, Universidade Federal do Rio Grande do Sul (2007)

11. Schepke, C., Maillard, N., Navaux, P.O.A.: Parallel lattice Boltzmann method with blocked partitioning. Int. J. Parallel Program. 37(6), 593–611 (2009). https://doi.org/10.1007/s10766-009-0113-x

12. Tang, P., Song, A., Liu, Z., Zhang, W.: An implementation and optimization of lattice Boltzmann method based on the multi-node CPU+MIC heterogeneous architecture. In: 2016 International Conference on Cyber-Enabled Distributed Computing and Knowledge Discovery (CyberC), no. 1, pp. 315–320 (2016). https://doi.org/10.1109/CyberC.2016.67, http://ieeexplore.ieee.org/document/7864252/

13. Valero-Lara, P., Jansson, J.: Heterogeneous CPU+GPU approaches for mesh refinement over lattice-Boltzmann simulations. Concurr. Comput. 29, 1–20 (2017). https://doi.org/10.1002/cpe.3919

14. Xian, W., Takayuki, A.: Multi-GPU performance of incompressible flow computation by lattice Boltzmann method on GPU cluster. Parallel Comput. 37(9), 521–535 (2011). https://doi.org/10.1016/j.parco.2011.02.007

15. Ye, Y., Li, K., Wang, Y., Deng, T.: Parallel computation of entropic lattice Boltzmann method on hybrid CPU-GPU accelerated system. Comput. Fluids 110, 114–121 (2015). https://doi.org/10.1016/j.compfluid.2014.06.002

16. Zhou, Y., He, F., Qiu, Y.: Accelerating image convolution filtering algorithms on integrated CPU-GPU architectures. J. Electron. Imaging 27(3) (2018). https://doi.org/10.1117/1.JEI.27.3.033002

# Performance Evaluation of Two Load Balancing Algorithms for Hybrid Clusters

Tiago Marques do Nascimento[✉], Rodrigo Weber dos Santos,
and Marcelo Lobosco

Graduate Program on Computational Modeling, UFJF,
Campus Universitário, Juiz de Fora, MG 36036-900, Brazil
tiago.nascimento@uab.ufjf.br, {rodrigo.weber,marcelo.lobosco}@ufjf.edu.br
http://www.ufjf.br/pgmc

**Abstract.** The use of hybrid environments, composed by CPUs and accelerators, imposes new challenges to the programmer that wants to use all the processing power available on the hardware. Although standards such as OpenCL and OpenACC can help in the task of writing parallel code for hybrid platforms, some issues remain open. In particular, multiprocessors and accelerators are different architectures and for this reason present distinct performances. As a result, data parallel applications have to find a data division that distributes the same amount of work to all devices, i.e, they have to finish their work in approximately the same time. This work uses a simulator of the Human Immune System (HIS) to evaluate two load balancing algorithms, a static and a dynamic ones, that can be used for this purpose. The results have shown that the dynamic load balancing algorithm outperforms the static one by a factor of up to 1.07.

**Keywords:** Load balancing · Hybrid cluster · GPUs · Multiprocessors

## 1 Introduction

Six out of the ten fastest supercomputers in the world are hybrid architectures [20], merging multicore CPUs and accelerators, such as GPUs, in a single computational platform. In order to use all resources available in hybrid distributed memory systems, programmers can mix traditional parallel programming tools and libraries used to develop application for those environments, such as MPI, with new ones, such as OpenCL(Open Computing Language) [12]. OpenCL is a parallel programming framework that allows programmers to write parallel code that can be compiled and executed for a large number of target platforms, including CPUs, APUs and distinct accelerators. With OpenCL, all devices available in a single machine can be simultaneously used in parallel computations, which

M. Lobosco—The authors would like to thank UFJF and the Brazilian agencies FAPEMIG, CAPES, and CNPq.

ⓒ Springer Nature Switzerland AG 2019
H. Senger et al. (Eds.): VECPAR 2018, LNCS 11333, pp. 119–131, 2019.
https://doi.org/10.1007/978-3-030-15996-2_9

can be specially useful for data parallel programs. However, programmers that want to explore data parallelism in all devices of a hybrid platform must take performance differences into account, since they can impact the way the code is written and executed. A load balancing (LB) algorithm can help in this task. In this work we use the term LB in the sense of the data division that makes all devices in a hybrid cluster composed by CPUs and GPUs finish their computing in approximately the same time.

An automatic LB scheme based on the master-worker parallel pattern [10,12] can be implemented in OpenCL through the use of command-queues, specially those that implements the out-of-order execution. Command-queues are used to allow the interaction between the host, which is responsible for interacting with the user program, and the devices, such as CPU cores and GPUs. Commands are sent to the command-queue and wait there until they are executed on a device. There are three types of commands that can be issued: kernel execution, memory and synchronization commands. The commands within a single queue can execute in the same order they appear in the command-queue (in-order execution), or out-of-order. The programmer can enforce an order constraint using explicit synchronization mechanisms.

The automatic LB scheme based on the master-worker parallel pattern is particularly suited for problems based on task parallelism [10], not for an in-order execution for problems based on data parallelism. In previous work we proposed two distinct algorithms to implement an automatic data partition for data parallel programs running on APUs, which is an hybrid shared memory architecture: a static [14] and a dynamic version [15], which were them evaluated [16]. Both LB algorithms measures, during the execution of the application, the amount of data each device will receive to compute. The difference is that the static version keeps the division until the end of the computation, while the dynamic one may change it along the execution. Finally, the dynamic LB algorithm was implemented in a hybrid distributed shared memory environment [17].

When implemented in a hybrid distributed shared memory environment, the dynamic LB algorithm may have a disadvantage: the communication costs to rebalancing data across distinct machines. Some questions arose from our previous work: in which cases this cost would compensate, i.e., in which cases the gain from rebalancing would be greater than the costs to rebalancing? Would the static version, if implemented in the same environment, perform better, since it removes the communication costs resulting from load rebalancing? In this work, we try to answer these questions. The main contributions of this work are the following: (a) the introduction of a static LB algorithm, implemented and evaluated in a previous work [16], to the hybrid distributed shared memory environment composed of CPUs and GPUs that the dynamic LB algorithm was evaluated [17]; (b) the evaluation of both algorithms using a regular, data-parallel application (HIS, Human Immune System Simulator); and (c) the identification of an initial and unexpected irregular phase in this regular application due to the initial amount of zeros that must be computed by each device, that affects the performance of the static LB algorithm.

The remaining of this work is organized as follows. Section 2 presents the related work. Section 3 briefly explains the implementation of the application used to evaluate the LB algorithms. Section 4 presents the implementation details of both LB algorithms and Sect. 5 presents the results obtained using the HIS simulator as a benchmark. Finally, the last Section presents the conclusions and plans for future works.

## 2   Related Work

A significant amount of research has been done on hybrid computing techniques [11]. Harmony [2] is a runtime supported programming and execution model that uses a data dependency graph to schedule and run independent kernels in parallel hybrid architectures. This approach is distinct from ours because we focus on data parallelism, while Harmony focus on task parallelism. Merge [8] is a library system that deals with map-reduce applications on hybrid system. Qilin [9] is an API that automatically partitions threads to one CPU and one GPU. SKMD [6] is a framework that transparently distributes the work of a single parallel kernel across CPUs and GPUs. SOCL [4] is an OpenCL implementation that allows users to dynamically dispatch kernels over devices. StarPU [1] is a task programming library for hybrid architectures that provides support for hybrid scheduling. Our approach is distinct because we are not proposing a new library, API, framework or OpenCL implementation, nor we limit the number of CPUs or GPUs that can be used as Qilin does. Also, StarPU does not perform inter-node load-balancing as our approach does. Since the proposed LB algorithms are implemented in the application code, we do not have to pay the overheads imposed by the frameworks, runtime systems or APIs.

## 3   The HIS Simulator

A three dimensional simulator of the HIS [18,19] was used to evaluate the performance of the two LB algorithms. The simulator implements the model using a set of eight Partial Differential Equations (PDEs) to describe how some cells and molecules involved in the innate immune response, such as neutrophils, macrophages, protein granules, pro and anti-inflammatory cytokines, react to an antigen, which is represented by lipopolysaccharides. The diffusion of some cells and molecules are described by the mathematical model, as well as the process of chemotaxis. Chemotaxis is the movement of immune cells in response to chemical stimuli by pro-inflammatory cytokine. Neutrophils and macrophages move towards the gradient of pro-inflammatory cytokine concentration. A detailed discussion about the model can be found in [18,19] and a simplified model of the HIS is presented in Fig. 1.

The discretized points of the region of infected tissue are represented computationally by a tridimensional mesh of floating point values. The numerical method used in the computational implementation of the mathematical model

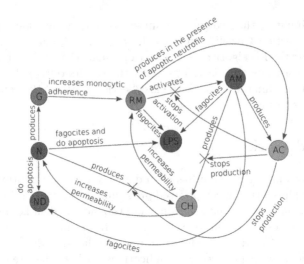

**Fig. 1.** Relations among the components of the model.

was the Finite Difference Method [7], a method commonly used in the discretization of PDEs. The computation of the convective term (the chemotaxis term) is a complex part in the resolution of the PDEs. Our implementation is based on the finite difference method for the spatial discretization and the explicit Euler method for the time evolution. First-Order Upwind scheme [3] is used in the discretization of the chemotaxis term. More details about the numerical implementation, specially how the Laplace operator, that simulates the diffusion phenomenon, is implemented in 3D, can be found in a previous work [19]. This previous work used C and CUDA in the implementation, using only GPUs in the computation, while this work uses C and OpenCL, using simultaneously all resources (CPUs and GPUs) available in the cluster.

There are two ways to divide the data mesh that represent the discretized points: division by planes and division by individual elements. The division by individual elements allows the algorithm to use of a fine-grain data partition in the LB. In a previous work [16], we have found that the division by individual elements performs better and, for this reason, this division will be used in this work for both LB algorithms.

## 4   Static LB Algorithm

Hybrid computers represent a big challenge to the development of data parallel applications due to the distinct hardware characteristics. Some architectures, such as CUDA [5], have fixed the roles for each device: GPUs have been used to handle data parallel work while CPUs handle all the rest. The use of this fixed role may impact performance, since CPUs are idle while GPUs are handling the data parallel work. Actually, multicore CPUs could handle part of the work submitted to the GPU.

OpenCL [12] is an interesting alternative to this model, since it is easy to program parallel codes that use simultaneously all devices available to operate in data items. The point is that the programmer is responsible for the data division between CPUs and GPUs. A good data division would give each device a distinct amount of data proportional to its relative performance. For example, if device $A$ is 1.5 times faster than device $B$, it should receive 1.5 times more data to compute than device $B$.

In previous works we have presented two distinct LB algorithms [13,15] to be used with data parallel OpenCL codes running on an APU. The key idea behind the two algorithms is similar: data is split into two parts, one of which will be computed by the CPU, while the other one will be computed by the GPU. The amount of data that will be assigned to the CPU and GPU depends on their relative computing capabilities, which is measured in both LB algorithms during the execution of the application. Later, the dynamic algorithms was implemented in a different hardware platform: a hybrid cluster [17].

This work presents the implementation of the static LB algorithm in a hybrid cluster. Since an APU merges GPUs and CPUs cores on a single silicon chip, some modifications have to be done in the algorithm to deal with multiple GPUs and CPUs available in distinct nodes of a cluster, as we did in the dynamic implementation [17]. Also, the algorithm does not assume that all machines in a cluster have the same configuration, i.e., the same number and types of CPUs and GPUs.

Both LB algorithms can be used in a wide variety of data parallel applications. Usually these applications have at least two aligned loops, in which the inner loop performs the same operations on distinct data items. Each step of the inner loop (or a collection of loops, if a multidimensional data structure is used) could be executed in any order, since no data dependency occurs between two distinct loop iterations. The number of steps the outer loop iterates is determined by the nature of the problem, but usually a dependency exists between two consecutive steps: a new step cannot proceed without the result of a previous one, since their results will be used during the computation of the new step. In many applications the outer loop is related to the progress of a simulation over time, and for this reason will be referred in this work as time-steps. The LB algorithms will decide the amount of data each device will receive to compute in the inner loop. During the computation of each data item, some applications may also require access to its neighbor's data, located at distinct memory spaces due to data splitting between CPUs and GPUs. These data, called boundaries, must be updated after each iteration of the outer loop. This update requires the introduction of synchronization operations and the explicit copy of data. In the case of a hybrid cluster, this copy may occur inside a machine (e.g., copying data between two distinct GPUs or between the memory space of a CPU and a GPU, and vice-versa) or between machines, which imposes the use of remote communication primitives. Both data copy and synchronization operations are expensive, deteriorating performance, and for this reason should be avoided.

The static LB algorithm is presented in Algorithm 23 and works as follows. To determine the amount of data each device will receive to compute, two probing phases are used. In the first one (first for loop), that lasts a single time-step, all GPUs and CPUs receive an equal amount of data to compute (data size divided by the total number of devices) and the time required to compute them is recorded using the OpenCL routine *clGetEventProfilingInfo()*. This information is then used in the second probing phase (second for loop), that uses a larger number of steps to determine the relative computing power of each device. Finally, the data division computed in the second probing phase are kept until the end of the simulation (last for loop). The amount of data each device will receive in the second probing phase and in the remaining computing steps are computed using Eq. 1.

```
 1: initialize MPI and OpenCL;
 2: allocate memory in each device's memory space;
 3: divide data equally among all devices;
 4: start clock;
 5: for a single time-step do
 6:     call cpus/gpus to compute their data;
 7:     synchronize;
 8: end for
 9: finish clock;
10: compute Pᵢ⁽ᵗ⁾ and transfer data accordingly;
11: start clock;
12: for a configurable number of time-steps do
13:     call cpus/gpus to compute their data;
14:     synchronize;
15: end for
16: finish clock;
17: compute Pᵢ⁽ᵗ⁾ and transfer data accordingly;
18: for all remaining time-steps do
19:     call cpus/gpus to compute border points;
20:     synchronize;
21:     call cpus/gpus to compute interior points and transfer border points in parallel;
22:     synchronize;
23: end for
```

**Algorithm 1.** The static LB algorithm

$$P_i^{(t)} = \frac{P_i^{(t-1)}}{T_i^{(t-1)} \times \sum_{k=1}^{N} \frac{P_k^{(t-1)}}{T_k^{(t-1)}}}, \tag{1}$$

where $P_i^{(t)}$ is the percentage of data the device $i$ will receive to compute in the next time-step $t$, $P_i^{(t-1)}$ is the percentage of data the device $i$ received in the previous time-step, $T_i^{(t-1)}$ is the time in which device $i$ executed the previous time-step and $N$ is the total number of devices available in the hybrid cluster.

In the first time-step ($t = 0$), the percentage of data each device will receive to compute is divided equally among all devices.

In the APU version of the static LB algorithm, a single probing phase was used to determine the data division that would be used for the entire computation, the initial division used in this probe phase was determined by the user, and the data division was computed once. In this paper, two probing phases are used, each device will receive the same amount of data to compute in the first probing phase, and the data division is computed twice: the first one to be used in the second probing phase, and the last one to be used during all remaining computing steps. The change was motivated by the observation that performance was hurt if the user guesses a bad data division to be used during the probing phase. The proposed solution uses a single time-step to guess a good data division to be used during the second probing phase.

A final optimization is done in order to reduce the communication costs. Each device divides its data into two subsets: borders and interior points. The border points are composed by the points that must be exchanged with the neighbors, whereas the interior points are not exchanged. The device compute first the border points. While computing the interior points, the device exchange borders with its neighbors, so computation and communication overlap.

## 5 Performance Evaluation

This section evaluates the performance of both LB algorithms, static and dynamic, using for this purpose a simulator of the HIS [18,19]. This simulator was chosen because it is a representative of data parallel algorithm: the same set of operations must be executed on a large amount of data.

All tests were executed on a small cluster composed by 6 nodes. The node has a two AMD 6272 processors CPU, each one with 16 computing cores, (totalling 32 computing cores), 32 GB of main memory, two Tesla M2075 GPUs, each one with 448 CUDA cores, and 6 GB of global memory. Linux 3.10.0, OpenMPI version 3.2 and gcc version 4.8.5 were used to run and compile all codes. The machines are connected by a Gigabit Ethernet network. Although the AMD CPUs totals $32 \times 6 = 192$ cores, one Float-Point Unit (FPU) is shared by two cores, as a result, only 96 FPUs are available in the cluster.

A mesh of size $50 \times 50 \times 3200$ was used in the experiments. The values used to set the initial conditions and parameters of HIS are the same used in our previous work [16], and are detailed in [21]. A total of 100,000 time-steps were executed. For the dynamic version of the algorithm, the LB interval is equal to 1% of the time-steps, and the LB threshold is equal to 200 elements. The dynamic LB algorithm executes from time to time, defined by the LB interval, to adjust the amount of data each device will receive till the end of the computation. If the difference between $P_i^{(t)}$ and $P_i^{(t-1)}$ in Eq. 1 is lower than the LB threshold, the devices remain with their previous loads until another load balancing step is reached [16].

Four versions of the HIS were executed: a sequential one, a version that used the static LB algorithm, a version that used the dynamic LB algorithm and one that did not use LB. In the version that did not use the LB, the mesh size was divided equally among all devices that were used to execute the code. Each HIS version was executed at least 3 times, and all standard deviations of the execution time were below 2%. The cluster uses a queue system that guarantees that each user access a set of machines in a exclusive way.

## 5.1 Results

Table 1 presents the results. Due to the large execution time for the sequential code, its total execution time was estimated using $10,000$ time-steps. A typical simulation of $1,000,000$ time-steps would require more than 46 days of computation. The parallel version of the simulator that does not use the LB algorithm executes up to 202 times faster. But the use of the LB algorithms improved the performance even more: using the same configuration, the application executed up to 730 times faster than the sequential one and up to 5.8 times faster than the version that does not use the LB algorithms. When both algorithms are compared, it can be observed that the dynamic version always outperforms the static one: their gains range from 1.02 to 1.08.

**Table 1.** Experimental results for the parallel version of the code in a small cluster. Average execution time(s), standard deviation and gains of the best LB algorithm (the dynamic one). The last gain presented relates to the dynamic LB executed with all devices compared to the sequential one. SLB is a short for Static LB, and DLB for Dynamic LB. CCs is a short for computing cores

| Platform | w/o LB | SLB | DLB | Gain |
|---|---|---|---|---|
| 32 CPU CCs/896 GPU CCs | $7,586.1 \pm 0.2\%$ | $2,352.1 \pm 0.5\%$ | $2,282.4 \pm 0.0\%$ | 3.3 |
| 64 CPU CCs/1792 GPU CCs | $4,493.3 \pm 0.8\%$ | $1,317.6 \pm 0.8\%$ | $1,290.6 \pm 0.3\%$ | 3.5 |
| 96 CPU CCs/2688 GPU CCs | $3,035.9 \pm 0.8\%$ | $929.9 \pm 0.5\%$ | $899.0 \pm 0.4\%$ | 3.4 |
| 128 CPU CCs/3584 GPU CCs | $4,211.4 \pm 0.4\%$ | $783.2 \pm 0.1\%$ | $727.7 \pm 0.7\%$ | 5.8 |
| 160 CPU CCs/4480 GPU CCs | $2,003.4 \pm 0.5\%$ | $626.1 \pm 1.4\%$ | $606.4 \pm 1.0\%$ | 3.3 |
| 192 CPU CCs/5376 GPU CCs | $2,800.6 \pm 0.2\%$ | $565.7 \pm 2.0\%$ | $554.4 \pm 0.5\%$ | 5.1 |
| Sequential | $404,919.0 \pm 1.0\%$ | | | 730.4 |

Although the dynamic algorithm outperforms the static one in the hybrid shared memory environment, we did not expect that this behavior would be

**Table 2.** Execution time breakdown for the dynamic LB algorithm. Times in seconds.

|  | Computation of internal points and border swap | Computation of borders | Load balancing |
|---|---|---|---|
| 1 node | 2, 204.5 | 76.7 | 0.1 |
| 2 nodes | 1, 275.5 | 78.9 | 0.4 |
| 3 nodes | 886.7 | 81.1 | 0.5 |
| 4 nodes | 694.3 | 96.3 | 0.7 |
| 5 nodes | 655.9 | 90.1 | 0.9 |
| 6 nodes | 603.5 | 96.9 | 1.4 |

also observed in the hybrid distributed shared memory environment because we believed that the communication costs involved in the LB operations would be prohibitive. To investigate this hypothesis, an execution time breakdown of the dynamic LB algorithm was done. Their results are presented in Table 2. The dynamic LB algorithm performed a total of 100 data rebalancings along 100, 000 time-steps, and their costs, as Table 2 shows, are negligible.

To better understand why the dynamic LB algorithm outperformed the static one, a second instrumentation of the code was done. We measure, for each algorithm, both the execution time in each device as well as the amount of data they received to compute. Table 3 presents the execution time, for each device and configuration. In this table, we consider that each machine is composed by three devices: two GPUs and one multicore CPU. In other words, parallel execution time of all CPU cores are presented as a single device. Figure 2 shows the amount of data each device received to compute. In this figure, the amount of data for the dynamic LB algorithm is the one received in the last rebalancing.

As one can observe, Table 3 shows that the static LB algorithm suffers from an unbalancing in the execution time. For example, using four machines to execute the code, the performance difference between the fastest device and slowest one is about 1.3 times. For the dynamic LB algorithm, the biggest difference among devices is 2.8%. The reason for this unbalancing is due to the slightly higher load percentage the CPUs received when compared to the dynamic LB algorithm, as Fig. 2 shows. Why the static LB algorithm decided to give more data to CPUs compute than the dynamic algorithm did?

## 5.2  How the Dataset and the CPU Optimizations Impact Performance

The answer to the previous question is related to the dataset used: this effect occurs due to an imbalance in the execution time in the initial and final time-steps of the application. The cause of the imbalance is an optimization done by the compiler: in the beginning of the execution, due to the values used as initial conditions, there are a lot of float-point multiplications by zero, which

**Table 3.** Computing time in each device for the static (first figures) and dynamic LB algorithms. Times in seconds. Highlighted values indicate inbalances caused by the static LB.

| | 1 Node | 2 Nodes | 3 Nodes | 4 Nodes | 5 Nodes | 6 Nodes |
|---|---|---|---|---|---|---|
| GPU#1 | 2,097.1/2,113.4 | 1,070.3/1,074.0 | 721.7/725.2 | 546.0/550.2 | 440.8/445.0 | 372.9/375.5 |
| GPU#2 | 2,105.2/2,113.6 | 1,066.0/1,074.1 | 722.5/725.4 | 543.3/550.3 | 441.2/445.1 | 372.0/375.6 |
| CPU#1 | **2,242.0**/2,117.2 | **1,095.0**/1,075.8 | **751.5**/726.9 | **592.4**/552.7 | **505.8**/447.7 | **429.0**/378.6 |
| GPU#3 | | 1,073.2/1,074.1 | 725.5/725.3 | 549.4/550.2 | 436.8/445.0 | 371.2/375.5 |
| GPU#4 | | 1,066.7/1,074.2 | 723.5/725.3 | 546.7/550.4 | 439.6/445.1 | 374.9/375.6 |
| CPU#2 | | **1,147.8**/1,077.1 | **768.4**/727.2 | 549.6/552.8 | **512.6**/447.2 | **417.7**/377.7 |
| GPU#5 | | | 726.1/725.3 | 543.5/550.2 | 439.0/445.0 | 374.2/375.5 |
| GPU#6 | | | 720.0/725.4 | 543.7/550.3 | 439.5/445.1 | 373.7/375.6 |
| CPU#3 | | | **819.4**/728.4 | **703.4**/565.8 | 470.4/446.7 | **415.5**/377.4 |
| GPU#7 | | | | 538.8/550.2 | 441.2/445.0 | 371.5/375.5 |
| GPU#8 | | | | 542.0/550.3 | 443.5/445.1 | 374.8/375.5 |
| CPU#4 | | | | **610.7**/555.1 | **488.6**/447.3 | **437.7**/377.3 |
| GPU#9 | | | | | 473.6/446.6 | **394.4**/377.5 |
| GPU#10 | | | | | 458.5/445.3 | 376.1/375.6 |
| CPU#5 | | | | | 435.3/445.1 | 366.4/375.8 |
| GPU#11 | | | | | | **422.5**/379.1 |
| GPU#12 | | | | | | 380.3/375.6 |
| CPU#6 | | | | | | 377.5/375.7 |

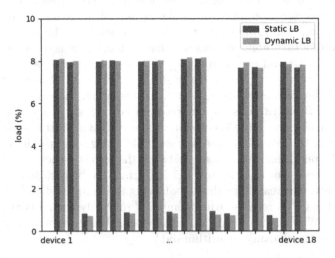

**Fig. 2.** Amount of data assigned to each device when running in 6 nodes.

are detected and results in an early exit since the execution of the entire multiplication pipelining is not required to obtain the final result. However, for the non-zero values, the multiplication demands the execution of the entire processing pipelining, which takes dozens of clock cycles. So, some devices can be idle while others are very busy. If a slice of the mesh, composed by zero values, is allocated in the CPU, for example, its computing time will be recorded with a lower value, and the CPU will receive more data than it can in fact handle. As the non-zero values propagate through the mesh, this optimization isn't performed and the computation time becomes regular, but just the dynamic LB algorithm can adjust to this new information. At the end of the computation, the number of zero values increases again, and both algorithms suffer its effects. We collected the number of non-zero positions in the mesh, as time goes by, using $1,000,000$ of time-steps. The results were collected at each $10,000$ simulation steps. Figure 3 presents the results.

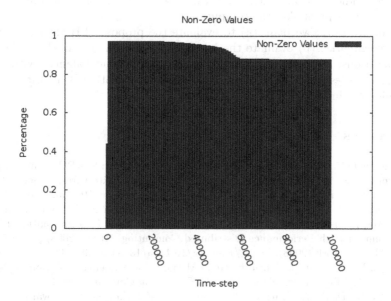

**Fig. 3.** Percentage of non-zero values in a mesh. The results were collected at each $10,000$ time-steps.

## 6   Conclusion and Future Work

This paper presented the performance evaluation of two LB algorithms in a hybrid cluster environment, composed by GPUs and multicore CPUs. Their key idea is to split data items of an application that explore data parallelism into multiple parts that will be computed simultaneously by CPUs and GPUs. The amount of data that will be assigned to CPUs and GPUs depends on their relative computing capabilities, which is measured during the execution of the application. In the static algorithm, after a data division is established, it is kept until the end of the computation. The dynamic LB algorithm measures the execution time and updates the amount of data each device computes during all the execution of the application. The Human Immune System simulator was used to evaluate both algorithms.

The results have shown that the algorithms were very effective in their purposes, resulting in gains up to 1,482-fold in execution time compared to the sequential one. Compared to the version that did not use the LB, the gains in performance were up to 5.8 times. We have also shown that the dynamic LB algorithm outperformed the static one. The reason is that the dynamic LB algorithm adapts to changes in the initial phase of the application, in which a large amount of zeros are used in the computation. CPUs skip multiplication operations by zero, finishing to compute faster than if they had to compute the result. This optimization makes the LB algorithms to allocate more data to CPUs than they can handle, specially because, as time goes by, the amount of zeros reduce, and the CPUs cannot skip the computation.

As future work, we plan: (a) to evaluate the proposed LB algorithm using other benchmarks; (b) evaluate the impacts of the algorithm in the scalability of applications; (c) compare the performance of our load balancer with other existing libraries; and (d) Analyse the efficiency of both LB algorithms and determine the impact of communication on it.

# References

1. Augonnet, C., Thibault, S., Namyst, R., Wacrenier, P.A.: StarPU: a unified platform for task scheduling on heterogeneous multicore architectures. Concurr. Comput. : Pract. Exper. **23**(2), 187–198 (2011). https://doi.org/10.1002/cpe.1631
2. Diamos, G.F., Yalamanchili, S.: Harmony: an execution model and runtime for heterogeneous many core systems. In: Proceedings of the 17th International Symposium on High Performance Distributed Computing, HPDC 2008, pp. 197–200. ACM, New York (2008). https://doi.org/10.1145/1383422.1383447
3. Hafez, M.M., Chattot, J.J.: Innovative Methods for Numerical Solution of Partial Differential Equations. World Scientific Publishing Company (2002)
4. Henry, S., Denis, A., Barthou, D., Counilh, M.-C., Namyst, R.: Toward OpenCL automatic multi-device support. In: Silva, F., Dutra, I., Santos Costa, V. (eds.) Euro-Par 2014. LNCS, vol. 8632, pp. 776–787. Springer, Cham (2014). https://doi.org/10.1007/978-3-319-09873-9_65
5. Kirk, D.B., Hwu, W.M.: Programming Massively Parallel Processors: A Hands-on Approach, 2nd edn. Morgan Kaufmann Publishers Inc., San Francisco (2013)
6. Lee, J., Samadi, M., Park, Y., Mahlke, S.: Transparent CPU-GPU collaboration for data-parallel kernels on heterogeneous systems. In: Proceedings of the 22nd International Conference on Parallel Architectures and Compilation Techniques, PACT 2013, pp. 245–256. IEEE Press, Piscataway (2013). http://dl.acm.org/citation.cfm?id=2523721.2523756
7. LeVeque, R.: Finite Difference Methods for Ordinary and Partial Differential Equations: Steady-State and Time-Dependent Problems (Classics in Applied Mathematics Classics in Applied Mathemat). Society for Industrial and Applied Mathematics, Philadelphia (2007)
8. Linderman, M.D., Collins, J.D., Wang, H., Meng, T.H.: Merge: a programming model for heterogeneous multi-core systems. In: Proceedings of the 13th International Conference on Architectural Support for Programming Languages and Operating Systems, ASPLOS XIII, pp. 287–296. ACM, New York (2008). https://doi.org/10.1145/1346281.1346318

9. Luk, C.K., Hong, S., Kim, H.: Qilin: exploiting parallelism on heterogeneous multi-processors with adaptive mapping. In: Proceedings of the 42nd Annual IEEE/ACM International Symposium on Microarchitecture, MICRO 42, pp. 45–55. ACM, New York (2009). https://doi.org/10.1145/1669112.1669121

10. Mattson, T., Sanders, B., Massingill, B.: Patterns for Parallel Programming, 1st edn. Addison-Wesley Professional, Boston (2004)

11. Mittal, S., Vetter, J.S.: A survey of CPU-GPU heterogeneous computing techniques. ACM Comput. Surv. **47**(4), 1–35 (2015)

12. Munshi, A., Gaster, B., Mattson, T.G., Fung, J., Ginsburg, D.: OpenCL Programming Guide, 1st edn. Addison-Wesley Professional, Boston (2011)

13. do Nascimento, T.M., de Oliveira, J.M., Xavier, M.P., Pigozzo, A.B., dos Santos, R.W., Lobosco, M.: On the use of multiple heterogeneous devices to speedup the execution of a computational model of the human immune system. Appl. Math. Comput. **267**, 304–313 (2015)

14. do Nascimento, T.M., dos Santos, R.W., Lobosco, M.: Use of multiple GPUs to speedup the execution of a three-dimensional computational model of the innate immune system. J. Phys. **490**, 012075 (2014). https://doi.org/10.1088/1742-6596/490/1/012075

15. do Nascimento, T.M., dos Santos, R.W., Lobosco, M.: On a dynamic scheduling approach to execute OpenCL jobs on APUs. In: Osthoff, C., Navaux, P.O.A., Barrios Hernandez, C.J., Silva Dias, P.L. (eds.) CARLA 2015. CCIS, vol. 565, pp. 118–128. Springer, Cham (2015). https://doi.org/10.1007/978-3-319-26928-3_9

16. do Nascimento, T.M., dos Santos, R.W., Lobosco, M.: Performance evaluation of two load balancing algorithms on a hybrid parallel architecture. In: Malyshkin, V. (ed.) PaCT 2017. LNCS, vol. 10421, pp. 58–69. Springer, Cham (2017). https://doi.org/10.1007/978-3-319-62932-2_5

17. do Nascimento, T.M., dos Santos, R.W., Lobosco, M.: Dynamic load balancing algorithm for heterogeneous clusters. In: Wyrzykowski, R., Dongarra, J., Deelman, E., Karczewski, K. (eds.) PPAM 2017. LNCS, vol. 10778, pp. 166–175. Springer, Cham (2018). https://doi.org/10.1007/978-3-319-78054-2_16

18. Pigozzo, A.B., Macedo, G.C., Santos, R.W., Lobosco, M.: On the computational modeling of the innate immune system. BMC Bioinform. **14**(Suppl. 6), S7 (2013)

19. Rocha, P.A.F., et al.: A three-dimensional computational model of the innate immune system. In: Murgante, B., et al. (eds.) ICCSA 2012. LNCS, vol. 7333, pp. 691–706. Springer, Heidelberg (2012). https://doi.org/10.1007/978-3-642-31125-3_52

20. Strohmaier, E., Dongarra, J., Simon, H., Meuer, M.: Top500 supercomputer sites (2018). http://top500.org

21. Xavier, M.P., Santos, R.W., Lobosco, M.: Implementação paralela de um ambiente de múltiplas GPUs de um modelo 3D do sistema imune inato (2013)

# An Improved OpenMP Implementation of the TVD–Hopmoc Method Based on a Cluster of Points

Frederico Cabral[1], Carla Osthoff[1], Roberto Pinto Souto[1], Gabriel P. Costa[1],
Sanderson L. Gonzaga de Oliveira[2], Diego N. Brandão[3(✉)],
and Mauricio Kischinhevsky[4]

[1] LNCC, Petrópolis, RJ, Brazil
{fcabral,osthoff,rpsouto,gcosta}@lncc.br
[2] Universidade Federal de Lavras, Lavras, MG, Brazil
sanderson@dcc.ufla.br
[3] CEFET/RJ, Rio de Janeiro, RJ, Brazil
diego.brandao@eic.cefet-rj.br
[4] Universidade Federal Fluminense, Niterói, RJ, Brazil
kisch@ic.uff.br

**Abstract.** This paper concentrates on an OpenMP implementation of
the TVD–Hopmoc method with executions performed on Intel® Many
Integrated Core and Xeon® Scalable Processor architectures. Specifically, this paper evaluates an improved OpenMP implementation of
the TVD–Hopmoc method based on a cluster of points when applied
to the convection–diffusion equation in 1–D. Aiming at avoiding fine-
grained parallelism employed in a basic OpenMP implementation of the
TVD–Hopmoc method, this approach groups variables (located at stencil points) to be calculated simultaneously in parallel instead of calculating them individually. Numerical experiments performed on Intel®
Many Integrated Core and Scalable Processor architectures show that the
improved OpenMP implementation of the TVD–Hopmoc method based
on a cluster of points provides further worthwhile gains when compared
both with our previous implementation based only on parallel chunk
loops and a basic OpenMP implementation of this method.

**Keywords:** High perfomance computing · Parallel processing ·
Convection–diffusion equation

## 1 Introduction

The Hopmoc method was designed to solve parabolic convective–dominated
problems in parallel architectures (see [2] and references therein). It devises a
spatial partition of stencil points that allows how to minimize communication
among threads. The Hopmoc method subdivides the set of unknowns into two
subsets. Thus, the Hopmoc method divides each time step into two time semi-
steps. The unknowns containing in these subsets are calculated alternately by

© Springer Nature Switzerland AG 2019
H. Senger et al. (Eds.): VECPAR 2018, LNCS 11333, pp. 132–145, 2019.
https://doi.org/10.1007/978-3-030-15996-2_10

explicit and implicit approaches during the first and second time semi–steps, respectively. The Hopmoc method evaluates time semi–steps along characteristic lines using a Semi-Lagrangian approach taking into account concepts of the Modified Method of Characteristics [11].

Discretization of the convective term in transport equations is frequently afflicted with severe complications. To avoid spurious numerical oscillations, Harten [3] introduced the concepts of Total Variation Diminishing (TVD) techniques and flux–limiter formulations, which are stable higher–order accurate solutions of convection–diffusion equations. The TVD–Hopmoc [4] uses a flux-limiter formulation to calculate the value at the foot of the characteristic line based on the Lax–Wendroff scheme and increase the accuracy of the original Hopmoc method [4,8].

We evaluated a simple (or naive) OpenMP-based TVD–Hopmoc method. This implementation was analyzed using the Intel® Parallel Studio XE software development product so that we followed its recommendations and proposed our previous OpenMP-based TVD–Hopmoc method [8]. A further analysis using this software led us to improve our earlier implementation. This paper presents this enhanced OpenMP implementation and compares its results both with the naive and our initial version of the TVD–Hopmoc method [8]. We investigate here an approach that groups variables (located at stencil points) to be calculated concomitantly in parallel instead of calculating them separately.

Various publications have been proposing to improve performance on Intel Xeon Phi accelerators. These problem-solving techniques have been trying to handle the challenge presented in this architecture to achieve linear speedups, principally in OpenMP implementations. For example, Ma et al. [5] proposed strategies to optimize the OpenMP implicit barrier constructs. These authors revealed how to remove the OpenMP inherent barrier constructs when there is no data dependence. Their second strategy uses a busy-waiting synchronization. Their optimized OpenMP implementation obtained better results than the basic OpenMP strategies. Caballero et al. [6] introduced a tree-based barrier that uses cache locality along with SIMD instructions. Their approach achieved a speedup of up to 2.84x over the basic OpenMP barrier in the EPCC barrier micro-benchmark. Cabral et al. [7] evaluated the original Hopmoc method in different parallel programming paradigms. The authors, however, did not perform the implementations on Intel® Xeon® Phi accelerators. A previous publication [8] showed that a simple OpenMP implementation of the TVD-Hopmoc method suffers from high load imbalance caused by the fine-grained parallelism used inherently by the OpenMP standard. This implementation employed a parallel chunk loop strategy to avoid the fine-grained parallelism, which improved its performance in approximately 50%.

The remainder of this paper is structured as follows. Section 2 presents the TVD–Hopmoc method in details. Section 3 explains a simple OpenMP implementation of the TVD–Hopmoc method. Section 4 describes an improved OpenMP-based TVD–Hopmoc method. Finally, Sect. 6 addresses the conclusion and discusses future directions in this work.

## 2   The TVD–Hopmoc Method

We describe below the Hopmoc method in details (see [2] and references therein). Consider the one–dimensional convection–diffusion equation in the form

$$u_t + v u_x = d u_{xx}, \tag{1}$$

with adequate initial and boundary conditions, where $v$ represents a constant positive velocity, $d$ is a positive constant of diffusivity, and $0 \le x \le 1$. In Eq. (1), $u_t$ refers to the time derivative and not $u$ evaluated at the discrete time step $t$. Nevertheless, we abuse the notation and now use $t$ to denote a discrete time step so that $0 \le t \le T$, for $T$ time steps.

Consider also a conventional finite–difference discretization for this equation, with $\Delta t = u^{t+1} - u^t$, and $\delta t = \frac{\Delta t}{2} = u^{t+\frac{1}{2}} - u^t$ represents a time semi–step of the method. A characteristic line permits to obtain $\overline{u}\left(\overline{x}_i^{t+\frac{1}{2}}\right)$ and $\overline{\overline{u}}\left(\overline{\overline{x}}_i^t\right)$ in the previous two time semi–steps, for $\overline{x}_i^{t+\frac{1}{2}} = x_i - v \cdot \delta t$ and $\overline{\overline{x}}_i^t = x_i - 2v \cdot \delta t$, respectively, and the variable values $\overline{\overline{u}}\left(\overline{\overline{x}}_i^t\right)$ are obtained using an interpolation technique [2], as described below. For clarity, a variable in a previous time semi–step and in a previous time step are written as $\overline{u}_i^{t+\frac{1}{2}} = u\left(\overline{x}_i^{t+\frac{1}{2}}\right)$ and $\overline{\overline{u}}_i^t = u\left(\overline{\overline{x}}_i^t\right)$, respectively. Additionally, $\overline{u}_i^{t+\frac{1}{2}}$ is the variable in the previous time semi–step at the foot of the characteristic line originated at $x_i^{t+1}$. Moreover, we use a uniform spatial discretization so that $\Delta x = x_{i+1} - x_i$ [2].

We use a three–point finite–difference scheme in the discretization of diffusive terms and $\overline{\overline{u}}_i^{t+1}$ is a numerical approximation of $u$ in $(x_i, u^{t+1})$ when $t$ is even. Using the finite-difference operator $L_h\left(u_i^t\right) = d\frac{u_{i-1}^t - 2u_i^t + u_{i+1}^t}{\Delta x^2}$, the consecutive time semi–steps of the Hopmoc method can be written as $\overline{u}_i^{t+\frac{1}{2}} = \overline{\overline{u}}_i^t + \delta t\left(\theta_i^t L_h\overline{\overline{u}}_i^t + \theta_i^{t+1} L_h\overline{u}_i^{t+\frac{1}{2}}\right)$ or $u_i^{t+1} = \overline{u}_i^{t+\frac{1}{2}} + \delta t\left(\theta_i^t L_h\overline{u}_i^{t+\frac{1}{2}} + \theta_i^{t+1} L_h u_i^{t+1}\right)$, for $\theta_i^t = 1 \, (= 0)$ if $t + i$ is even (odd).

The discretization of the convective term demands to calculate the values of the concentration at midpoints of the sides of each grid interval. The method obtains these values using a TVD scheme [4,8].

Our numerical simulations were performed for a Gaussian pulse with amplitude 1.0, whose initial center location is 0.2, with velocity $v = 1$ and diffusion coefficient $d = \frac{2}{Re} = 10^{-3}$ (where $Re$ stands for Reynolds number), $\Delta t = 10^{-7}$, $\Delta x$ is set as $10^{-5}$, $10^{-6}$, and $10^{-7}$ (i.e., $10^5$, $10^6$, and $10^7$ stencil points, respectively), and $T$ is established as $10^4$, $10^5$, and $10^6$.

## 3   A Basic OpenMP Implementation of the TVD–Hopmoc Method

This section outlines a simple (or naive) OpenMP-based TVD–Hopmoc method. We implemented the algorithms using the C++ programming language. Specifically, we used the icpc (Intel C++ compiler) version 2018, with the optimization flags -xHost and -O3. Additionally, in Xeon Scalable Processors, the -qopt-zmm-usage=high flag was used.

In short, this basic OpenMP implementation (i.e., using the OpenMP *parallel for* directive) consists of the "main" time loop that performs two steps. Firstly, the method computes the MMOC step, where the TVD Van Leer flux–limiter scheme is implemented. Secondly, it executes the first and second (explicit and implicit) semi–steps.

The simplistic approach to parallelize the TVD–Hopmoc method in executions on Intel® Many Integrated Core Architecture is to insert OpenMP directives in specific loops of the code, for example, in loops that solve the explicit and implicit operators. Algorithm 1 shows a fragment of pseudo-code that delineates how this naive implementation performs a time step of the Hopmoc method. This fragment of pseudo-code shows four for loops that calculate the two time semi–steps of the algorithm using alternately explicit and implicit approaches. The first and second (third and fourth) for loops calculate unknowns $\bar{u}_i^{t+\frac{1}{2}}$ $\left(u_i^{t+1}\right)$ using explicit and implicit approaches in the first (second) time semi–step. In this naive implementation, we observed no improvement when using other forms of OpenMP thread schedulings, such as OpenMP dynamic and guided schedulings. The ANNOTATE_ITERATION_TASK macro instructs the Intel® Advisor shared memory threading assistance tool that these loops must be analyzed to generate the performance estimates.

Algorithm 2 shows a fragment of a pseudo-code that is used to obtain the suitability analysis carried out by the Intel® Advisor shared memory threading assistance tool. This fragment of pseudo-code shows an OpenMP parallel region composed of a loop that iterates the time steps of the TVD–Hopmoc method. Thus, this while loop is identified as a parallel region to be analyzed by the Intel® Advisor shared memory threading assistance tool.

We executed experiments with this simple OpenMP-based TVD–Hopmoc method performed on a machine containing an Intel® Xeon™ CPU E5-2698 v3 @ 2.30 GHz composed of 32 physical cores. To evaluate our source code, we analyzed it using the Intel® Advisor shared memory threading assistance tool. This analysis revealed that even with most of the implementation vectorized, the gains using the OpenMP standard is limited. The reason for this is because the calculations in the method are implemented using an approach with very fine granularity to take full advantage of parallelism and HPC capabilities.

Figure 1 exhibits the results of an experiment performed with the support of the Intel® VTune™ Amplifier performance profiler. This figure shows that this simple OpenMP implementation obtains an inefficient performance in a multicore environment in a simulation with $T = 10^6$ and $\Delta x = 10^{-5}$, i.e., in a mesh composed of $10^5$ stencil points. Specifically, Fig. 1 reveals that the execution of this implementation obtained high spin (imbalance or serial spinning) time caused by the use of the implicit OpenMP strategies. Additionally, Fig. 1 exhibits a high clock ticks per Instructions Retired (CPI) rate (1.301) achieved by the basic OpenMP-based TVD–Hopmoc method.

**Algorithm 1.** A time step composed of four for loops that iterate the first and second time semi–steps of a naive OpenMP-based TVD–Hopmoc method.

1: #pragma omp for
{First time semi–step of the Hopmoc method, where $\alpha = d * \frac{\delta t}{(\delta x)^2}$}
2: **for** $i \leftarrow head + 1; i \leq n - 2; i \leftarrow i + 2$ **do**
3:    ANNOTATE_ITERATION_TASK (loop_HOP_EXP_1);
   $\overline{u}_i^{t+\frac{1}{2}} \leftarrow \alpha \cdot \left( \overline{\overline{u}}_{i-1}^{t} + \overline{\overline{u}}_{i+1}^{t} \right) + (1 - 2\alpha)\overline{\overline{u}}_i^{t};$
4: **end for**
{First time semi–step of the Hopmoc method using an implicit approach}
5: #pragma omp single
6: $head \leftarrow (head + 1)\%2;$
7: #pragma omp for
8: **for** $i \leftarrow head + 1; i \leq n - 2; i \leftarrow i + 2$ **do**
9:    ANNOTATE_ITERATION_TASK (loop_HOP_IMP_1);
   $\overline{u}_i^{t+\frac{1}{2}} \leftarrow \dfrac{\overline{\overline{u}}_i^{t} + \alpha \cdot \left( \overline{u}_{i-1}^{t+\frac{1}{2}} + \overline{u}_{i+1}^{t+\frac{1}{2}} \right)}{1+2\alpha};$
10: **end for**
{Second time semi–step of the Hopmoc method using an explicit approach}
11: #pragma omp single
12: $head \leftarrow (head + 1)\%2;$
13: #pragma omp for
14: **for** $i \leftarrow head + 1; i \leq n - 2; i \leftarrow i + 2$ **do**
15:    ANNOTATE_ITERATION_TASK (loop_HOP_EXP_2);
   $u_i^{t+1} \leftarrow \alpha \cdot \left( \overline{u}_{i-1}^{t+\frac{1}{2}} + \overline{u}_{i+1}^{t+\frac{1}{2}} \right) + (1 - 2\alpha) \cdot \overline{u}_i^{t+\frac{1}{2}};$
16: **end for**
{Second time semi–step of the Hopmoc method using an implicit approach}
17: #pragma omp single
18: $head \leftarrow (head + 1)\%2;$
19: #pragma omp for
20: **for** $i \leftarrow head + 1; i \leq n - 2; i \leftarrow i + 2$ **do**
21:    ANNOTATE_ITERATION_TASK (loop_HOP_IMP_2);
   $u_i^{t+1} \leftarrow \dfrac{\overline{u}_i^{t+\frac{1}{2}} + \alpha \cdot \left( u_{i-1}^{t+1} + u_{i+1}^{t+1} \right)}{1+2\alpha};$
22: **end for**

Figure 2 displays a CPU usage histogram extracted from Advanced Hotspots Analysis performed by the Intel® VTune™ Amplifier performance profiler. This figure shows that the basic OpenMP-based TVD–Hopmoc method uses a small number of cores concurrently. In particular, this implementation used on average 19 cores at the same time (in a machine composed of 32 cores).

Figure 3a shows a screen captured from the suitability report performed by the Intel® Advisor shared memory threading assistance tool. This figure shows that the naive OpenMP-based TVD–Hopmoc method suffers from high load imbalance and reaches 100% of runtime overhead. To provide specific detail, a suitability analysis performed by the Intel® Advisor shared memory threading assistance tool indicated that the simple OpenMP-based TVD–Hopmoc method

**Algorithm 2.** Pseudo-code outlining how to obtain the suitability analysis performed by the Intel® Advisor shared memory threading assistance tool.

```
1: t_beg ← omp_get_wtime();
2: #pragma omp parallel
3: {
4: ANNOTATE_SITE_BEGIN(time_loop);
5: while (t < T) do
6:     [...]
7: end while
8: ANNOTATE_SITE_END();
9: }
10: t_end ← omp_get_wtime();
```

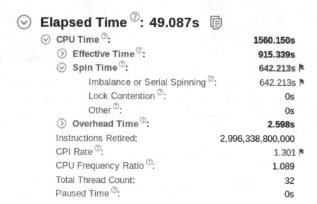

**Fig. 1.** Execution time obtained by a basic OpenMP-based TVD–Hopmoc method when analyzed with the support of the Intel® VTune™ Amplifier performance profiler.

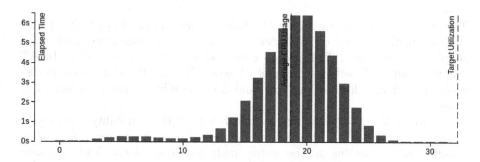

**Fig. 2.** CPU usage histogram produced with the results of an execution of the basic OpenMP-based TVD–Hopmoc method. This histogram was taken from Advanced Hotspots Analysis performed by the Intel® VTune™ Amplifier performance profiler. It displays a percentage of the wall time.

presents 75% of load imbalance and high runtime overhead, including high thread scheduling time, due to fine-grained parallelism employed in this implementation. Additionally, there is no scalability gain when executing this implementation. Intel® Advisor shared memory threading assistance tool advises that this implementation is too fine-grain, and it is not adequate for multi-threading. This software suggested to increase task granularity, reduce task overhead, or consider vectorization in this implementation.

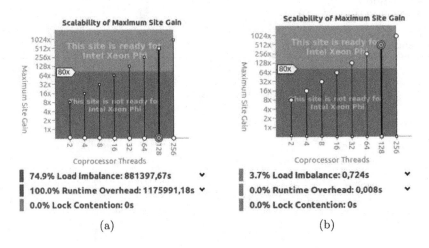

**Fig. 3.** Intel Advisor's predictions.

## 4    An Improved OpenMP Implementation of the TVD–Hopmoc Method Based on a Cluster of Points

This section presents an improved OpenMP implementation of the TVD–Hopmoc method based on a cluster of points. As mentioned, we analyzed a simple OpenMP-based TVD–Hopmoc method with the support of the Intel® Parallel Studio XE software for Intel's Haswell/Broadwell architectures to discover the vulnerabilities of our code and consequently to propose solutions to them.

Figure 3b shows another screen captured from the suitability report performed by the Intel® Advisor shared memory threading assistance tool when enabling task chunking in the naive implementation of the TVD–Hopmoc method (reported in Sect. 3). According to the Intel® Advisor shared memory threading assistance tool, using this technique would reduce load imbalance to 4% with no runtime overhead. Figure 3b also shows that the expected scalability would be high if this approach were employed. Chunking is a strategy that merges several tasks into a single one, i.e., they are executed together as a chunk, with little or no overhead between them. In the case of using parallel chunk loops in the source code, the programmer merges loops inside the analyzed site into a single one. An implementation based on parallel chunk loops groups some of them to consequently obtain a smaller number of parallel loops. Therefore, the code employs a coarse–grained approach. However, data dependency limits the use of this approach. In the case of the TVD–Hopmoc method, unknowns that are approximated using an implicit approach depend on unknowns that are solved using an explicit approach. Thus, it was not possible to integrally follow this recommendation because of limitations in data dependency to calculate variable values in the TVD–Hopmoc method. Therefore, we adopted an intermediate solution. We referred to it as an implementation based on parallel chunk loops in an earlier version [8].

We conducted then a further data dependency analysis with the objective of building an implementation that groups stencil points to calculate them in parallel. This analysis led us to implement an improved OpenMP-based TVD–Hopmoc method that merges all operators in the Hopmoc method into two loops, instead of using four loops as the original Hopmoc method performs (see Algorithm 1). To provide further details, we analyzed data dependency to guarantee that the loops are suitable for parallelism, i.e., to assure that tasks inside loops are computed concurrently. Each of these two loops executes over a cluster of four grid points. The first cluster of points, called I-cluster, is composed of the two unknowns $\overline{u}_{i-1}^{t+1}$ and $\overline{u}_{i+1}^{t+1}$, which are solved using an implicit approach, and the unknown $\overline{u}_i^{t+1}$, which is solved using an explicit approach during the second time semi–step of the TVD–Hopmoc method (see Fig. 4a). Additionally, the unknown $u_i^{t+\frac{1}{2}}$ belongs to this cluster of points. It is solved using an implicit approach in the first time semi–step of the TVD–Hopmoc method.

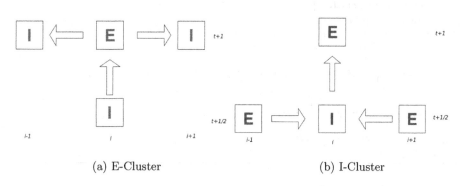

(a) E-Cluster                    (b) I-Cluster

**Fig. 4.** Two strategies for clustering points.

Figure 4b shows the second cluster of points employed in this scheme, called E-cluster. This cluster of points is also composed of four unknowns. The E-cluster is composed of an unknown $\overline{u}_i^{t+1}$ that is solved using an explicit approach during the second time semi–step and three unknowns that are solved during the first time semi–step of the TVD–Hopmoc method: $u_i^{t+\frac{1}{2}}$, $u_{i-1}^{t+\frac{1}{2}}$, and $u_{i+1}^{t+\frac{1}{2}}$.

The finite-difference mesh can be composed of these two types of a cluster of points [8]. In particular, this scheme allows that balancing load to be evaluated during runtime so that adjacent clusters of points in a level $l$ can be grouped again to form a larger cluster of points in a level $l + 1$.

Algorithm 3 shows a fragment of pseudo-code that illustrates the first and second time semi–steps of the Hopmoc method. Specifically, Algorithm 3 displays that the four parallel for loops outlined in Algorithm 1 (from a naive OpenMP implementation) are substituted by two parallel for loops that calculate all E-clusters and I-clusters. Using this scheme to cluster points, our OpenMP-based TVD–Hopmoc method avoids data dependency and increases parallelism.

---

**Algorithm 3.** Pseudo-code depicting the first and second time semi–steps of the improved OpenMP-based TVD–Hopmoc method.

---

1: [...]
   {Compute all E-clusters}
2: #pragma omp for
3: **for** $i \leftarrow 2;\ i \leq n - 3;\ i \leftarrow i + 4$ **do**
4: $\quad \bar{u}_{i-1}^{t+\frac{1}{2}} \leftarrow \alpha \cdot \left( \bar{\bar{u}}_{i-2}^{t} + \bar{\bar{u}}_{i}^{t} \right) + (1 - 2\alpha) \cdot \bar{\bar{u}}_{i-1}^{t};$
5: $\quad \bar{u}_{i+1}^{t+\frac{1}{2}} \leftarrow \alpha \cdot \left( \bar{\bar{u}}_{i+2}^{t} + \bar{\bar{u}}_{i}^{t} \right) + (1 - 2\alpha) \cdot \bar{\bar{u}}_{i+1}^{t};$
6: $\quad \bar{u}_{i}^{t+\frac{1}{2}} \leftarrow \frac{\bar{\bar{u}}_{i}^{t} + \alpha \cdot \bar{u}_{i-1}^{t+\frac{1}{2}} + \alpha \cdot \bar{u}_{i+1}^{t+\frac{1}{2}}}{1 + 2\alpha};$
7: $\quad u_{i}^{t+1} \leftarrow \alpha \cdot \left( \bar{u}_{i-1}^{t+\frac{1}{2}} + \bar{u}_{i+1}^{t+\frac{1}{2}} \right) + (1 - 2\alpha) \cdot \bar{u}_{i}^{t+\frac{1}{2}};$
8: **end for**
   {Compute all I-clusters}
9: #pragma omp for
10: **for** $i \leftarrow 2;\ i \leq n - 5;\ i \leftarrow i + 4$ **do**
11: $\quad \bar{u}_{i}^{t+\frac{1}{2}} \leftarrow \frac{\bar{u}_{i}^{t} + \alpha u_{i-1}^{t+1}}{1 + 2\alpha};$
12: $\quad u_{i}^{t+1} \leftarrow \alpha \cdot \left( \bar{u}_{i-1}^{t+\frac{1}{2}} + \bar{u}_{i+1}^{t+\frac{1}{2}} \right) + (1 - 2\alpha) \cdot \bar{u}_{i}^{t+\frac{1}{2}};$
13: $\quad u_{i-1}^{t+1} \leftarrow \frac{\bar{u}_{i-1}^{t+\frac{1}{2}} + \alpha \cdot \left( u_{i}^{t+1} + u_{i-2}^{t+1} \right)}{1 + 2\alpha};$
14: $\quad u_{i+1}^{t+1} \leftarrow \frac{\bar{u}_{i+1}^{t+\frac{1}{2}} + \alpha \cdot \left( u_{i}^{t+1} + u_{i+2}^{t+1} \right)}{1 + 2 \cdot \alpha};$
15: **end for**

---

Figure 5a exhibits the results of an experiment performed with our previous implementation [8] and the support of the Intel® VTune™ Amplifier performance profiler. In an experiment with $T = 10^6$ and $\Delta x = 10^{-5}$, i.e., in a mesh composed of $10^5$ stencil points, this figure displays that our previous OpenMP-based TVD–Hopmoc method [8] obtained lower execution time (1159 s) than the basic OpenMP implementation of this method (1560 s; see Fig. 1). Furthermore, Fig. 5a exhibits that our previous OpenMP-based TVD–Hopmoc method [8] obtained lower wall time (36 s) than the basic OpenMP implementation of this method (49 s). On the other hand, Fig. 5a shows a high Clockticks per Instructions Retired (CPI) rate (1.418) yielded by our previous OpenMP implementation of the TVD–Hopmoc method based uniquely on parallel chunk loops [8].

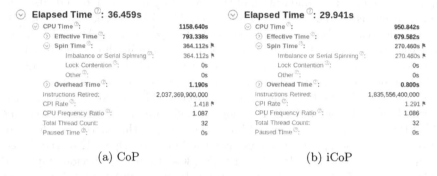

|  | (a) CoP | (b) iCoP |

Fig. 5. Execution time obtained by the simple and the improved cluster of points implementations of the TVD–Hopmoc method when analyzed with the support of the Intel® VTune™ Amplifier performance profiler.

Figure 6a displays a CPU usage histogram taken from Advanced Hotspots Analysis performed by the Intel® VTune™ Amplifier performance profiler. This figure displays that our previous method [8] used on average 22 cores concurrently when performed on the machine aforementioned.

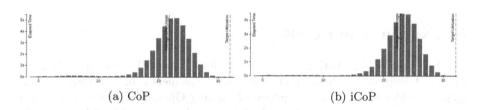

|  | (a) CoP | (b) iCoP |

Fig. 6. CPU usage histogram produced in an execution of simple and the improved OpenMP implementation of the TVD–Hopmoc method based on a cluster of points. This histogram was captured from Advanced Hotspots Analysis produced by the Intel® VTune™ Amplifier performance profiler.

Also with the objective of avoiding fine-grained parallelism, we improved our previous OpenMP-based implementation of the TVD–Hopmoc method [8] by combining two time steps in the same while loop. With this improvement, data are updated straightforwardly to the next iteration instead of performing this explicitly as our previous implementation carried out [8]. Then, to distinguish this implementation from the earlier algorithm [8], we will refer the new version as improved OpenMP implementation of the TVD–Hopmoc based on a cluster of points (iCoP for short). Both codes are thread-safe codes.

According to the Intel® Advisor shared memory threading assistance tool, both implementations present 71% of vectorization efficiency. Our OpenMP-based TVD–Hopmoc method is 50% faster than the naive implementation.

Experiments with the use of our previous implementation [8] and the improved OpenMP implementation of the TVD–Hopmoc method were also performed on a machine containing an Intel® Xeon™ CPU E5–2698 $v3$ @ 2.30 GHz with 32 physical cores. Again, we established $T = 10^6$ and $\Delta x = 10^{-5}$, i.e., the mesh was composed of $10^5$ stencil points. Figure 5b shows the results of an experiment performed with the improved OpenMP implementation of the TVD–Hopmoc method based on a cluster of points and the support of the Intel® VTune™ Amplifier performance profiler. This figure shows that the improved OpenMP-based TVD–Hopmoc method obtained lower execution time (951 s) than our previous OpenMP implementation of this method (1159 s; see Fig. 5a). Furthermore, Fig. 5b shows that the improved OpenMP-based TVD–Hopmoc method obtained lower wall time (30 s) than our previous OpenMP implementation [8] of this method (36 s). Furthermore, this figure displays that the improved OpenMP implementation of the TVD–Hopmoc method based on cluster of points reaches a lower Clockticks per Instructions Retired (CPI) rate (1.291) than both the simple OpenMP implementation (1.301) and our previous OpenMP implementation of the TVD–Hopmoc method based exclusively on parallel chunk loops (1.418).

Figure 6b shows a CPU usage histogram generated from the use of the Intel® VTune™ Amplifier performance profiler. This figure shows that the improved OpenMP implementation of the TVD–Hopmoc method [8] used on average 23 cores simultaneously when performed on the machine aforementioned.

## 5    Experimental Results

The first part of this section shows the results of OpenMP implementations of the TVD–Hopmoc method. Intel's OpenMP implementation specifies environment variables that define the policy of binding OpenMP threads to physical processing units (i.e., cores). Thread affinity can have a considerable impact on the computing time of the application. Although this also depends on the system (machine) topology and operating system, we evaluated our OpenMP implementation of the TVD–Hopmoc method based on a cluster of points along with three thread binding policies, namely balanced, compact, and scatter policies.

Figure 7 shows speedups obtained by those three OpenMP implementations of the TVD–Hopmoc method when applied to the same meshes described earlier in executions performed on a machine containing an Intel® Xeon Phi™ Knights-Corner (KNC) accelerator 5110P, 8 GB DDR5, 1.053 GHz, 60 cores, 4 threads per core. The highest speedup reached by the improved implementation based on cluster of points, implementation based only on parallel chunk loops [8], and simple implementation were 56x, 49x, and 28x (106x, 105x, and 95x) [80x, 72x, and 58x], respectively, when applied to a mesh comprised of $10^5$ $\left(10^6\right)$ $\left[10^7\right]$

stencil points and $T$ set as $10^6$ $(10^5)$ $[10^4]$. The results of our OpenMP-based TVD–Hopmoc presented in Fig. 7 employed the scatter policy. This binding policy yielded the same maximum speedup as the two other policies evaluated when applied to this machine.

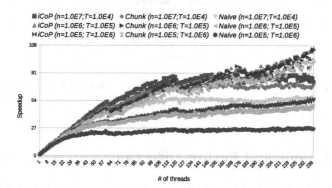

**Fig. 7.** Speedups obtained by three OpenMP implementations of the TVD–Hopmoc method (iCoP, *chunk* loops [8], and naive implementation) applied to meshes composed of $10^5$, $10^6$ and $10^7$ stencil points and $T$ specified as $10^6$, $10^5$, and $10^4$, respectively, in executions performed on an Intel® Xeon Phi™ KNC accelerator.

Figure 8 shows the results of two OpenMP implementations in runs performed on a machine containing an Intel® Xeon® Platinum 8160 CPU @ 2.10 GHz, with two nodes with 24 cores, 2 threads per core. This figure reveals that our iCoP approach of the TVD–Hopmoc method alongside the balanced binding policy obtained a speedup of approximately 17x (using 95 threads) in this experiment, against a speedup of 11x reached by our previous implementation of the TVD–Hopmoc method [8].

The balanced binding policy distributes threads among physical cores before assigning them to logical cores. Keeping in mind that the system contains two sockets, where each of them holds 24 cores with two threads per core, the balanced (compact) policy assigns threads to both sockets when using more than 24 (48) threads, and consequently, a higher inter-socket communication arises when the system uses this number of threads. Then, when using from 25 to 80 (from 48 to 96) threads, the speedups obtained by the iCoP approach along with the balanced (compact) binding policy significantly vary (see Fig. 8). The same characteristic occurs when employing the CoP approach [8].

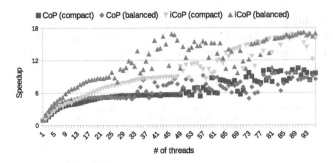

**Fig. 8.** Speedups of two OpenMP implementations of the 1-D TVD–Hopmoc method applied to meshes composed of $10^6$ stencil points and $T$ established as $10^5$, in runs performed on an Intel® Xeon® Scalable Processor architecture.

## 6  Conclusions and Future Directions

This work used Intel® Parallel Studio XE tools to analyze a simple OpenMP-based TVD–Hopmoc method in simulations performed on a machine containing an Intel® Xeon™ CPU E5-2698 v3 @ 2.30 GHz composed of 32 physical cores. As a result, this paper proposed an improved OpenMP implementation of this method based on a cluster of points that obtained a speedup up to 106x (against a speedup of 95x of a naive OpenMP implementation) when applied to a mesh composed of $10^6$ stencil points in runs carried out on an Intel® Xeon Phi™ KNC accelerator. Our improved OpenMP implementation of the method achieved a speedup up to 17x (against a speedup of 11x obtained by our previous OpenMP implementation) when applied to a mesh composed of $10^6$ stencil points in runs performed on an Intel® Xeon® Scalable Processor. In particular, this work shows how to improve a parallel algorithm based on parallel loops that present high load imbalance by employing a strategy based on parallel chunk loops when analyzing data dependence.

The speedup obtained by our improved method based on a cluster of points was smaller when setting a small number of time steps $T$ than establishing a large number of iterations $T$ (see Fig. 7). In future studies, we intend to investigate the reasons for high cache miss rates and consequently lower speedups in simulations establishing a small number of time steps. Moreover, new studies will be carried out to obtain an implementation that boosts data locality and, hence, generates high cache hit rates. Additionally, we also plan to investigate a coarse–grained implementation that employs an explicit synchronization mechanism capable of providing high speedups in an OpenMP-based TVD–Hopmoc method, even in simulations with a small number of time steps.

**Acknowledgement.** The Conselho Nacional de Desenvolvimento Científico e Tecnológico (CNPq), Coordenação de Aperfeiçoamento de Pessoal de Nível Superior (CAPES), and Fundação de Amparo à Pesquisa do Estado do Rio de Janeiro (FAPERJ) supported this work. We would like to thank the Núcleo de Computação Científica at Universidade Estadual Paulista (NCC/UNESP) for letting us execute our simulations on its heterogeneous multi-core cluster. These resources were partially funded by Intel® through the projects entitled Intel Parallel Computing Center, Modern Code Partner, and Intel/Unesp Center of Excellence in Machine Learning.

# References

1. Holstad, A.: The Koren upwind scheme for variable gridsize. Appl. Num. Math. **37**, 459–487 (2001)
2. Oliveira, S.R.F., de Oliveira, S.L.G., Kischinhevsky, M.: Convergence analysis of the Hopmoc method. Int. J. Comput. Math. **86**, 1375–1393 (2009)
3. Harten, A.: High resolution schemes for hyperbolic conservation laws. J. Comput. Phys. **49**, 357–393 (1983)
4. Brandão, D.N., Gonzaga de Oliveira, S.L., Kischinhevsky, M., Osthoff, C., Cabral, F.: A total variation diminishing hopmoc scheme for numerical time integration of evolutionary differential equations. In: Gervasi, O., et al. (eds.) ICCSA 2018. LNCS, vol. 10960, pp. 53–66. Springer, Cham (2018). https://doi.org/10.1007/978-3-319-95162-1_4
5. Ma, H., Zhao, R., Gao, X., Zhang, Y.: Barrier optimization for OpenMP program. In: Proceedings of 10th ACIS International Conference on Software Engineering, Artificial Intelligences, Networking, Parallel and Distributed Computing, pp. 495–500 (2009)
6. Caballero, D., Duran, A., Martorell, X.: An OpenMP* barrier using SIMD Instructions for Intel® Xeon Phi™ coprocessor. In: Rendell, A.P., Chapman, B.M., Müller, M.S. (eds.) IWOMP 2013. LNCS, vol. 8122, pp. 99–113. Springer, Heidelberg (2013). https://doi.org/10.1007/978-3-642-40698-0_8
7. Cabral, F.L., Osthoff, C., Kischinhevsky, M., Brandão, D.: Hybrid MPI/OpenMP/OpenACC implementations for the solution of convection diffusion equations with HOPMOC Method. In: Proceedings of 14th International Conference on Computational Science and Its Applications (ICCSA), pp. 196–199 (2014)
8. Cabral, F.L., Osthoff, C., Costa, G.P., Brandão, D., de Oliveira, S.L.G.: Tuning up TVD HOPMOC method on Intel MIC Xeon Phi architectures with Intel Parallel Studio Tools. In: Proceedings of the International Symposium on Computer Architecture and High Performance Computing Workshops (SBAC-PADW), pp. 19–23 (2017)
9. Gourlay, A.R., McKee, S.: The construction of Hopscotch methods for parabolic and elliptic equations in two space dimensions with mixed derivative. J. Comput. Appl. Math. **3**, 201–206 (1977)
10. van Leer, B.: Towards the ultimate conservative difference schemes. J. Comput. Phys. 361–370 (1974)
11. Douglas Jr., J., Russel, T.F.: Numerical methods for convection-dominated diffusion problems based on combining the method of characteristics with finite element or finite difference procedures. SIAM J. Num. Anal. **19**, 871–885 (1982)

# A Scheduling Theory Framework for GPU Tasks Efficient Execution

Antonio-Jose Lázaro-Muñoz⬤, Bernabé López-Albelda⬤,
Jose María González-Linares⁽✉⁾⬤, and Nicolás Guil⬤

Department of Computer Architecture, University of Málaga, Málaga, Spain
{alazaro,blopeza,jgl,nguil}@uma.es

**Abstract.** Concurrent execution of tasks in GPUs can reduce the computation time of a workload by overlapping data transfer and execution commands. However it is difficult to implement an efficient runtime scheduler that minimizes the workload makespan as many execution orderings should be evaluated. In this paper, we employ scheduling theory to build a model that takes into account the device capabilities, workload characteristics, constraints and objective functions. In our model, GPU tasks scheduling is reformulated as a flow shop scheduling problem, which allow us to apply and compare well known methods already developed in the operations research field. In addition we develop a new heuristic, specifically focused on executing GPU commands, that achieves better scheduling results than previous techniques. Finally, a comprehensive evaluation, showing the suitability and robustness of this new approach, is conducted in three different NVIDIA architectures (Kepler, Maxwell and Pascal).

**Keywords:** Makespan reduction on GPUs · Scheduling theory · Flow shop

## 1 Introduction

In a typical application executed in current heterogeneous parallel architectures, some parts are executed in the CPU or host, while others parts are delegated (offloaded) to the GPU. Besides, GPUs are broadly used in multitask environments, e.g. data centers, where applications running on CPUs offload specific functions to GPUs in order to take advantage of the device performance. This way, it is probable to have several independent tasks ready to run concurrently in a GPU. In this context, several works have been published that try to improve the way tasks are scheduled on GPUs [2,9]. The most recent ones propose hardware [15,20,21] or software [3,22,23] solutions that support preemption and offer responsiveness, fairness or quality of service capabilities. The proposed solutions are focused on kernel execution and they do not take into account the transfer

---

This work has been supported by the Ministry of Education of Spain (TIN2016-80920-R) and the Junta de Andalucía of Spain (TIC-1692).

H. Senger et al. (Eds.): VECPAR 2018, LNCS 11333, pp. 146–159, 2019.
https://doi.org/10.1007/978-3-030-15996-2_11

of data required to compute those kernels. In many cases, the time taken by these transfers is not negligible and can affect the performance of the applied scheduling policy. In addition, software approaches typically require to modify the original kernels.

The impact of transfers on the total execution time is given by the fact that the computation on the device must wait for the transfer of input data from CPU memory to GPU memory to be finished. This delay entails an overhead that can be alleviated by overlapping data transfers with computation. Some Application Programming Interfaces (API) such as CUDA [12] and OpenCL [7] provide features that allow to overlap communication and computation, e.g., CUDA streams or OpenCL commands queues. These features rely on the use of asynchronous communications and hardware managed command queues, and a large performance gain can be obtained when properly configured.

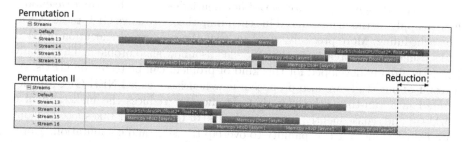

**Fig. 1.** Profile views of 4 independent tasks launched on a Nvidia K20c card. Matrix Multiplication, Black Scholes, Matrix Transposition and Vector Addition are launched by streams 13, 14, 15, and 16 respectively. Top view corresponds to the ordering selected by an scheduling heuristic, while bottom view shows the ordering selected by another heuristic. The makespan reduction is solely due to the launching tasks different orderings.

The importance of properly configuring the concurrent execution of several tasks can be seen in the next example, where one single host process launches tasks onto an Nvidia K20c GPU. Figure 1 shows two time-lines corresponding to the execution of four independent tasks in a different order. The tasks have been selected from CUDA SDK [13] and they are scheduled employing a different stream per task. More precisely, the tasks are Matrix Multiplication (Stream 13), Black Scholes (Stream 14), Matrix Transposition (Stream 15) and Vector Addition (Stream 16). Time-lines include the time spent in data transfer commands from host to device (HtD) and from device to host (DtH), and the kernel computation commands in the GPU (Kernel) for every stream. As it can be seen from Fig. 1, there is no overlapping between kernels execution from different tasks as these tasks are able to exhaust at least one of the available GPU resources (registers, shared memory, etc.). Nevertheless, the total execution time for the bottom execution order is shortened by around 10% thanks to a higher overlap between the transfer times of some tasks and the kernel execution times of other tasks. The current Nvidia hardware scheduler solely utilizes the kernel resource requirements to select the order that kernels blocks are launched in the GPU, thus either of these orderings is possible. These results show the importance of choosing the best execution order for a set of GPU tasks so that overlapping between data transfers and kernel computation is optimized.

On the other hand, scheduling theory is a field of applied mathematics that deals with the problem of optimal ordering of a set of jobs. It is used in many areas like management, production, transportation or computer systems. In scheduling theory, a flow shop is an ordered set of processors $P = < P_1, P_2, \ldots, P_m >$ such that the first operation of each job is performed on processor $P_1$, the second on processor $P_2$, and so on, until the job completes execution on $P_m$ [5]. Many works have been published on the problem of scheduling a collection of jobs on a flow shop, to optimize measures like the maximum finishing time or the utilization of the machines [17].

Previous works that have studied tasks scheduling on GPUs either ignore transfers overlapping [3] or propose ad-hoc heuristics [8]. In this paper we expose how to apply methods introduced in scheduling theory to solve GPU tasks execution scheduling. More precisely, we show that the concurrent execution of GPU tasks using CUDA streams can be modelled as a flow shop problem. Thus, many heuristic already developed for this kind of problem can be tested on GPUs. As a result of our study we also propose a new heuristic, called NEH-GPU, implemented in a run-time scheduler that significantly reduces the makespan of a workload and, consequently, increases the use of the GPU. It takes into account data transfers and GPU capability to overlap transfers and computation. Moreover, in contrast with other software scheduling approaches, original kernels of the tasks do not need to be modified.

The rest of the paper is organized as follows. First, scheduling theory is reviewed in Sect. 2, with a focus on GPU tasks scheduling using the flow shop problem. Next, in Sect. 3, several heuristics obtained from the operations research field are discussed, and a new algorithm that merges the previous theory with a GPU tasks execution model is presented. Then, several experiments that show the suitability and robustness of this new approach are conducted in Sect. 4. Finally, conclusions are drawn.

## 2   Scheduling Theory Applied to GPU Tasks Execution

The problem of launching N tasks in a GPU can be studied using scheduling theory. Scheduling is a decision-making process where $n$ jobs are allocated to $m$ machines. Following the notation introduced by Graham et al. [6], the problem can be identified by three fields, $\alpha$ (that describes the machine environment), $\beta$ (the processing characteristics and constraints), and $\gamma$ (the objective function). Each of these fields can accept one or more values and, below, the most relevant ones in a GPU tasks launching context are explained.

Launching a task (job in scheduling terminology) in a NVIDIA GPU typically involves executing in order three types of commands: Host to Device transfer (HtD), kernel command (K), and Device to Host transfer (DtH). There can

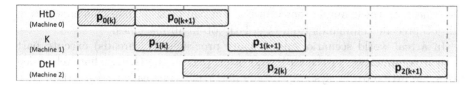

**Fig. 2.** GPU tasks launching as a 3-machine flow shop problem. HtD commands are executed by machine 0, K commands by machine 1 and DtH commands by machine 2. Commands from $k$th job precede commands from $(k + 1)$th job in all machines (permutation flow shop). $p_{i(j)}$ corresponds to the processing time of job $j$ in machine $i$.

be zero, one or more of each of these commands; in this case we consider them as a single command that encompasses all of them. Transfer commands are executed in DMA engines and kernel commands in the GPU itself (through the Grid Management Unit). Although current NVIDIA architectures allow Concurrent Kernel Execution if kernels do not exhaust any of the hardware resources (memory, registers, etc), most kernels in real applications are designed to fully utilize these resources, thus we restrict our analysis to kernels that do not execute concurrently. On the other side, modern GPUs have two DMA engines that allow simultaneous transfer commands in opposite directions, thus we can consider 3 machines in our environment (two DMA engines plus the GPU). This corresponds to a flow shop problem, that is, a problem where each job must be processed on each machine following a given order. Then, field $\alpha$ is represented by $F3$ to describe a 3-machine flow shop problem. Figure 2 shows an example with two jobs in a 3-machine flow shop problem.

A generalization of this problem is the flexible flow shop (also known as hybrid flow shop), where instead of $m$ machines in series there are $c$ stages in series. Each stage includes a number of identical machines in parallel and can be used to describe a cluster of GPUs. Thus, there would be 3 stages (one stage for each command type), with as many machines as GPUs in the cluster, and the problem would be represented as $FF3$.

Regarding the processing characteristics and constraints, several values can be taken into account. For example, a common type of flow shop problems considers that every machine operates under the assumption of First Come First Served policy. This policy does not hold under devices with HyperQ[1] unless events are used to enforce an ordering. On the other hand, it is known that for $F3$ systems there always exist optimal schedules that do not require sequence changes between machines [16] and, in that case, some simplifications can be made that make easier to find an optimal schedule. Thus, in this work events are used to enforce the same ordering in all the machines. This type of flow shop problem is called permutation flow shop and it is noted using the word *prmu* in

---

[1] HyperQ is a feature of modern GPUs since Kepler architecture, where several hardware managed queues can schedule different kernel commands, but can also change the execution order of these commands.

the $\beta$ field. In the example shown in Fig. 2 it can be seen than commands from $k$th job precede commands from $(k + 1)$th job in all machines.

In a real world scenario, one or more processes (or threads) execute part of their computation in the CPU and other part in the GPU. Thus, scheduled tasks can arrive to the system at some particular time called release date $(r_j)$. These tasks cannot be launched before its release date and this can be noted adding this value, $r_j$, to the $\beta$ field. Moreover, each process could execute many different tasks in the GPU, with some precedence constraints among them to ensure correct execution. This constraints are typically encoded using a directed acyclic graph and can be expressed using the word *prec* in the $\beta$ field. Finally, tasks could belong to different users thus they must be launched in different GPU contexts. In scheduling theory this is equivalent to job families, that is, jobs in the same family can be processed one after another without any delay, but switching from one family to another requires a setup time, $s$, before jobs are launched. This setup time is the time that takes to create a GPU context, and in the scheduling theory notation is expressed adding the word *fmls* to the $\beta$ field.

It is also possible to include information about the job characteristics in this $\beta$ field, like its processing time or its priority. For example, we will refer to $p_{ij}$ as the processing time of job $j$ in machine $i$ (as in Fig. 2, where $p_{0(k)}$ is the processing time of $k$th job in machine 0 and so on). Although it is possible to obtain an estimation of the processing time of each command in advance, the real transfer times depend on whether there is another transfer in the opposite direction or not [8]. Therefore, these sources of uncertainties may lead to sub-optimal schedules when solving the objective function. A priority factor can also be assigned to each job using a weight value, $w_j$, that can be taken into account in the objective function. Furthermore, due dates $d_j$ that reflect the completion date of job $j$ can be also included in the $\beta$ field.

Finally, the objective function that defines the optimal schedule must be considered. The completion time of job $j$ can be denoted by $C_j$. The most common function in flow shop problems is to minimize the makespan $C_{max}$, defined as $\max(C_1, ..., C_n)$, and it is equivalent to minimize the completion time of the last job to leave the system. In this type of problems it is almost equivalent to maximize the usage of the machines that is our main objective. Another useful objective function is the total weighted completion time ($\sum w_j C_j$), also referred as the weighted flow time, that takes into account the priority factors given by the weight values.

Table 1 resumes these values with their meaning and a short description. All or some of these parameters can be combined to express different real world situations and to select an appropriate solution from the existing literature [1,4]. The only requisite is to obtain the right notation that captures the problem. For example, a simple scenario with a single GPU and several independent tasks, ready to be executed using the same context, can be modelled as a $F3|prmu|Cmax$ problem. On the other side, a more complex scenario like a multi-GPU system where several users launch independent tasks at different

**Table 1.** Scheduling theory notation summary

| Field | Value | Meaning | Description |
|---|---|---|---|
| $\alpha$ | $Fm$ | Flow shop with $m$ machines | Each job is processed following a given order |
| | $FFc$ | Flexible flow shop with $c$ stages | As $Fm$ but using c stages of identical machines |
| $\beta$ | $prmu$ | Permutation | Machines operate under FIFO policy |
| | $r_j$ | Release dates | Tasks arrive at some particular release dates |
| | $w_j$ | Priority factors | Tasks are assigned a weight factor |
| | $d_j$ | Due dates | Tasks are assigned due dates |
| | $prec$ | Precedence constraints | Tasks must follow a directed acyclic graph |
| | $fmls$ | Job families | Tasks belong to different users |
| $\gamma$ | $C_{max}$ | Makespan | Minimize completion time of last task |
| | $\sum w_j C_j$ | Total weighted completion time | Priority factors are included |

release dates can be studied as a $FF3|r_j, fmls|Cmax$. As a practical example, in next section we will study the $F3|prmu|Cmax$ problem that arises when several threads launch independent kernels that can be computed using the same GPU context.

## 3 Flow Shop Scheduling

The problem presented in this section is typical in many situations where one or more threads launch several tasks that can be computed using the same GPU context. For example, in a video surveillance application, there could be several threads analyzing different video streams and part of the computation could be offloaded to a GPU to accelerate the whole process. In a similar way to CUDA MultiProcess-Service (MPS, [11]), a proxy thread could be used to collect all tasks, and launch them using the same GPU context to improve concurrency among tasks.

Each task consists of several commands (i.e., HtD, K and DtH commands) that are executed by the DMA engines and the GPU. The total execution time (the makespan $C_{max}$) can be reduced by selecting the right schedule. Thus, this problem can be modelled as a $F3|prmu|Cmax$, where these commands (*jobs*) are scheduled in the three *machines* to minimize the makespan.

It can be proved that $F3||Cmax$ is strongly NP-hard. In fact, for a $N$ tasks flow shop problem, there are $N!$ different permutations, thus many heuristics have been presented to solve efficiently this problem [17]. These heuristics can be classified as *constructive* or *improvement* depending on if they compute the schedule from scratch or by improving a previous solution. In this paper we are interested on real time scheduling, thus we will consider only lightweight algorithms. In next subsections, we present four heuristics that can be used in our run-time scheduler. For comparison purposes, the two first heuristics are classical ones as they do no model the data transfer overlapping. The last two heuristics employ an execution model that takes into account this overlapping.

## 3.1  Slope Index

Some heuristics that take into account an arbitrary number of machines, like for example the Slope heuristic [14], have been proposed in the literature to find quasi-optimal schedules for the flow shop problem. This heuristic gives priority to the tasks having the strongest tendency to progress from short times to long times in the sequence of processes. In our GPU problem this means that tasks with short HtD times and long DtH times are prioritized over tasks with long HtD times and short DtH times. This priority is established by computing a slope index $A_j$ for job $j$ as $A_j = -\sum_{i=1}^{m}(m - (2i - 1))p_{ij}$, where $m$ is the number of machines (3 in our GPU problem), and the jobs are sequenced in decreasing order of the slope index. We will refer to this heuristic as SI (Slope Index).

## 3.2  NEH Heuristic

Nawaz, Enscore and Ham developed in [10] an algorithm for solving the flow shop problem that is regarded as one of the best scheduling heuristics. This algorithm is typically noted as NEH and it is a constructive heuristic that iterates to compute a solution:

1. For each task compute its total processing time and sort them in non-increasing order.
2. Pick the first two tasks and find the best sequence by computing the makespan for the two possible sequences.
3. For each of the following tasks, $i = 3, \ldots, n$, find the best schedule by placing it in all the possible $i$ positions in the sequence of tasks that are already scheduled and computing the makespan.

Most heuristics try to schedule first the *best*, i.e. shortest, tasks, but this heuristic starts probing the *worst* (longest) tasks and accommodates the remaining tasks to minimize the makespan. The only drawback is the makespan must be computed $[n(n + 1)/2] - 1$ times, of which $n$ are complete sequences and the rest are partial schedules, but it can consistently obtain better results than other heuristics [18].

## 3.3  Single Queue

Previous approach assume all processing times are fixed but in fact they depend on the commands that are currently being processed. More precisely, if both a HtD and a DtH command are executing at the same time, their processing times will change [8]. This is due to the fact that, although the PCIe bus is bidirectional and modern GPUs have two DMA engines, the memory system is shared between both copy operations and the bandwidth of the HtD and DtH commands is reduced. A transfer model that do not consider overlapping can incur in errors above 10%. Therefore, these previous heuristics will likely fail to obtain an optimum schedule.

In [8], a GPU tasks execution model and a heuristic based on an overlapping transfers model were presented. That model uses an estimation of the HtD, K and DtH commands of each task to simulate the execution of a permutation of the tasks. HtD and DtH times are updated online to reflect the effect of overlapping transfers, achieving an average simulation error below 1.5%. Nevertheless, to obtain a correct estimation, Hyper-Q must be restrained. Any change in the original order performed by Hyper-Q could introduce a significant error in the simulation, thus Hyper-Q is disabled by forcing a single hardware managed queue.

The heuristic presented in that work uses the execution model to perform an online simulation of the execution to choose the tasks that better overlap in each instant. The reasoning behind the heuristic implemented on that work is similar to the Slope Index, but using the tasks execution model to select, in an iterative manner, the task that better adapt to the current tasks commands. Tasks with short HtD commands are selected first, while next tasks are chosen looking for the best fit between the remaining K commands of the previous selected tasks and the HtD command of the new task, and between the remaining DtH commands of the previously selected tasks and the K command of the new task. We will refer to this heuristic as SQ (Single Queue).

### 3.4   NEH Heuristic with a GPU Tasks Execution Model

In the original NEH heuristic, the makespan is computed using a fixed duration for each command, but in a GPU the length of two overlapping transfer commands can vary more than 10%. Therefore, the predicted makespan can have a large error that may lead to an erroneous order selection. In this work we propose to combine the NEH method with a GPU tasks execution model that can predict more accurately the makespan. We will refer to this heuristic as NEH-GPU (NEH heuristic with GPU tasks execution model).

To illustrate the advantages of using the execution model, we discuss again Fig. 1 (in Introduction section). This picture compares the results obtained by the original NEH (Permutation I) with NEH-GPU (Permutation II) when scheduling four independent tasks: matrix multiplication (MM), Black-Scholes (BS), matrix transposition (TM) and vector adition (VA). For each task it is given, in the left side of Table 2, the duration of its HtD, K and DtH commands, and its total makespan if it is launched alone. Also, in the right side of the same table, the partial makespans computed by each heuristic are shown. The two longest taks, 3 and 0, are tried in the first iteration. Each algorithm computes the makespan using the data on the left and, although they predict a different makespan for permutation 3–0, they select the same permutation, 0–3, as the one with the best partial makespan. In the second iteration they try all possible permutations inserting task 2 in ordering 0–3 and predict different makespans that lead them to select different permutations, 0–3–2 for NEH and 2–0–3 for NEH-GPU. Finally, in the last iteration, each heuristic inserts the remaining task obtaining different schedules. The NEH heuristic predicts a makespan of 27.32 when scheduling 0–3–2–1, but the real execution using this permutation takes 29.79. On the other side, NEH-GPU predicts a makespan of 26.58 when scheduling 1-0-3-2 and the real execution takes 26.97. That is, the GPU model predicts very accurately the real execution time, which leads to a better schedule decision.

**Table 2.** Computation of 4 independent tasks optimal ordering using NEH and NEH-GPU. Left table show the HtD, K and DtH commands duration of 4 tasks, and right table the tested orderings and predicted makespans using each method.

| | | | | | | | NEH | | NEH-GPU | |
|---|---|---|---|---|---|---|---|---|---|---|
| | | | | | | | Ordering | Makespan | Ordering | Makespan |
| | | | | | | 1st | 3-0 | 24.43 | 3-0 | 25.32 |
| | | | | | | | 0-3 | **19.37** | 0-3 | **19.37** |
| | Task | HtD | K | DtH | Total | 2nd | 2-0-3 | 24.40 | 2-0-3 | **25.57** |
| 0 | MM | 2.52 | 10.61 | 1.26 | 14.39 | | 0-2-3 | 24.35 | 0-2-3 | 26.26 |
| 1 | BS | 0.73 | 8.50 | 0.49 | 9.72 | | 0-3-2 | 24.35 | 0-3-2 | 26.26 |
| 2 | TM | 5.03 | 0.31 | 4.98 | 10.32 | 3rd | 1-0-3-2 | 31.06 | 1-2-0-3 | **26.58** |
| 3 | VA | 10.04 | 0.37 | 4.98 | 15.39 | | 0-1-3-2 | 32.08 | 2-1-0-3 | 31.28 |
| | | | | | | | 0-3-1-2 | 27.47 | 2-0-1-3 | 33.04 |
| | | | | | | | 0-3-2-1 | **27.32** | 2-0-3-1 | 29.30 |

## 4    Experiments

All the experiments in this work have been conducted using a set of real kernels obtained from the CUDA and Rodinia SDK like in [8]. Tasks with different transfer and kernel processing times have been selected (see Table 3). There are tasks with a short HtD command and a long K command, tasks with long HtD and DtH commands and short K commands, and so forth. Although some of these tasks have several commands of the same type (for example, matrix multiplication must transfer two matrices from host to device, or pathfinder launches several kernel commands in order), the scheduler considers there is a single command that encompasses all the commands of the same type.

In order to represent a more varying computational load, different input parameters have been selected to increase the number of tasks to 21. Moreover, to extend the applicability of the results, three GPU architectures, a K20c (Kepler), a GTX980 (Maxwell) and a Titan X (Pascal), have been considered. Finally, to avoid the effect of outliers, every experiment is executed fifteen times to record a mean makespan.

### 4.1    Statistical Analysis

First, we will analyze statistically our concurrent tasks execution model to assess the validity of the new heuristic and compare it with the previous heuristics. With this aim, we have obtained every possible combination of 4 tasks, with repetition, from the set of 21 tasks. This represents a total of $\left(\binom{21}{4}\right) = 10626$ benchmarks of four tasks each one. For each benchmark there are $4! = 24$ different schedules, thus there are 255024 different experiments that have been executed 15 times to record a mean makespan for each one. We have selected the

**Table 3.** Tasks used in the experiments. They are classified as Dominant Kernel (DK) or Dominant Transfer (DT) depending on the duration of the HtD, K and DtH commands. *CONV* task can be DK (CONV1) or DT (CONV2) depending on the input parameters.

| Kernel | Source | Description | Dominance |
|--------|--------|-------------|-----------|
| MM | CUDA SDK | Matrix Multiplication | DK |
| BS | CUDA SDK | Black Scholes | DK |
| PF | Rodinia | Path Finder | DK |
| PAF | Rodinia | Particle Filter | DK |
| CONV | CUDA SDK | Separable Convolution | DK/DT |
| VA | CUDA SDK | Vector Addition | DT |
| TM | CUDA SDK | Matrix Transposition | DT |
| FWT | CUDA SDK | Fast Walsh Transform | DT |

median and minimum makespan for each benchmark as well as the makespan obtained by each heuristic. Finally, we have computed the speed-up of each heuristic with respect to the median per benchmark, and for comparison purposes the speed-up of the minimum with respect to the median (best speed-up). These values are represented in Fig. 3a using box plots to visualize their statistical properties [19]. On each box, the central mark corresponds to the median, the edges of the box are the 25th and 75th percentiles, the whiskers are drawn with dashed lines and extend to the most extreme datapoints not considered to be outliers (about $\pm 2.7\sigma$ and 99.3% coverage), the outliers are plotted individually with '+' signs, and there are notches at the median marks for comparison intervals. Two medians are significantly different at the 5% significance level if their intervals do not overlap.

The leftmost box of Fig. 3a corresponds to the Slope Index heuristic. This heuristic is very simple but the results are poor. Thus, its median value is very close to 1 (that is, almost no speed-up is obtained) and in many samples the speed-up is below 1. Next box shows the results of the NEH algorithm. Results are much better, with a median speed-up close to 1.05, and most speed-up values are above 1 although the lower whisker extends below 0.9. The box at the center corresponds to the Single Queue heuristic. Results are better than SI but not as good as NEH. Most speed-up values are above 1 and the lower whisker extends below 0.9 as in the NEH algorithm. Finally, the two last boxes correspond to the new algorithm presented in this work, NEH-GPU, and the best attainable speed-up. NEH-GPU obtains results very close to the best, with a slightly lower median and the lower whisker extended above 0.9. Compared with the other heuristics, its median speed-up value is higher and it has no outliers below the lower whisker. Notches in all boxes are very narrow but none of them overlap, thus every heuristic is significantly different at the 5% significance level.

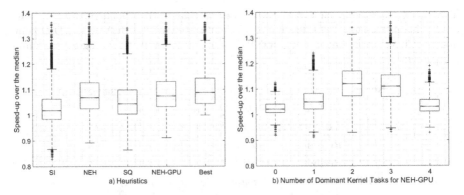

**Fig. 3.** Box plots of speed-up over mean makespan values of 10626 benchmarks of 4 tasks in K20c, GTX980 and TitanX devices. Central marks correspond to median values, boxes encompass the second and third quartiles, whiskers extend to cover 99.3% of the values, outliers are plotted individually with '+' signs, and notches at the median marks can be used for comparison intervals. Leftmost figure (a) shows results for each heuristic (SI, NEH, SQ and NEH-GPU) and for the best makespan (Best). Rightmost figure (b) shows results for the NEH-GPU heuristic and different combinations of DK and DT tasks (left box considers only benchmarks with 4 DT tasks, in next column benchmarks with 1 DK task and 3 DT tasks, and so on).

Both NEH-GPU and Best results show there are many experiments where speed-ups up to 1.40 can be obtained, and it would be interesting to ascertain what type of experiments can obtain more benefits from a good schedule selection. A sensible approach could be to study the overlapping opportunities among several tasks; for example, tasks with long K commands can be easily overlapped with tasks with long HtD commands. Therefore, we have classified the tasks as dominant transfer (DT) or dominant kernel (DK) depending on whether the transfer time dominates over the kernel time, or the other way round, and we have analyzed the results obtained by different combinations of DT and DK tasks. Figure 3b shows the box plots of the speed-up values obtained by the NEH-GPU algorithm separating the results by the number of DK tasks. Leftmost box corresponds to experiments where there are no DK tasks (the four tasks are DT), next box takes into account experiments with only one DK task and three DT tasks, and so on. It can be seen that experiments where all the tasks are of the same type get little benefit from a good schedule, but experiments with a fair mix of DK and DT tasks have more opportunities to overlap and speed-up values can be much higher.

## 4.2   Applicability and Scalability

In this section the four heuristics will be evaluated in a demanding multithreaded scenario (e.g. heterogeneous computing server) where several threads running applications (workers) offload tasks onto a device. All workers send task information regarding CUDA API calls to a buffer that is constantly polled by a host proxy thread. This thread is in charge of reordering the set of tasks found in the buffer using one of the four heuristics, and submitting the corresponding commands to the device.

The scalability of each heuristic is tested by increasing the number of tasks from 4 to 8 and 16. This number of tasks represents a very large number of different benchmarks, $\left(\binom{21}{8}\right) \approx 310^6$ for 8 tasks and $\left(\binom{21}{16}\right) \approx 10^9$ for 16 tasks. Besides, there are $8! = 40320$ possible schedules with 8 tasks, and $16! \approx 10^{13}$ with 16 tasks. Therefore, a random subset of different benchmarks have been selected for each combination of number of tasks (4, 8 and 16) and GPU architectures (K20c, GTX 980 and Titan X), and only the results obtained by each heuristic have been computed. For comparison purposes, the best makespan $(BM)$ obtained for each benchmark in each architecture has been recorded to establish a minimum reference value. Then, for every experiment, the makespan obtained by each heuristic $(HM)$ is compared with this reference value to assess the proximity value. This proximity is computed by dividing both values $(BM/HM \cdot 100)$ to obtain a percentage with maximum value of 100% (the higher the better). Results include the overhead of schedule computation incurred by each heuristic. This overhead ranges from $1\,\mu s$ for SI to less than $1\,ms$ for the rest of heuristics when 16 tasks are scheduled. Thus, taking into account the makespan duration, scheduling overhead is negligible.

Figure 4 shows the average of the results obtained with this experiment per each heuristic. In order to extract conclusions they are grouped attending to the number of tasks, the proportion of dominant kernel tasks, and the different GPU architectures, respectively. A proximity value closer to 100% means that heuristic obtains the best makespan, or a value very close to it, most of the times. It can be seen that the new NEH-GPU heuristic consistently obtains better proximity values than the other heuristics in all the situations and GPU architectures.

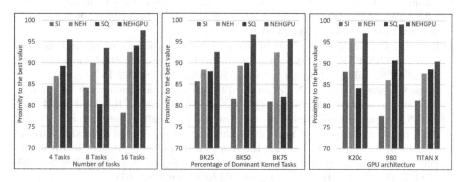

**Fig. 4.** Proximity to the best values with different number of tasks (left plot), different proportion of dominant kernel tasks (center plot), and different GPU architectures (right plot)

## 5    Conclusions

There have been several previous works studying tasks scheduling policies on GPUs. As far as we know, this is the first paper that discusses how to apply scheduling theory concepts to the problem of task scheduling on GPUs. It has been shown that the concurrent execution of GPU tasks using CUDA streams can be modelled as a flow shop problem. The most important advantage of this approach is that an objective function can be defined and an appropriate solution from the existing literature can be selected. As a practical example, it has been studied the $F3|prmu|Cmax$ problem that arises when several threads launch independent kernels that can be computed using the same GPU context. Several solutions found in both the scheduling and the GPU literature have been presented. Besides, a new heuristic called NEH-GPU, that combines an existing heuristic with a GPU tasks execution model, has been developed. This heuristic can also be included as runtime support because it does not modify the original kernels and it has a low overhead.

Several experiments have been conducted to show the suitability and robustness of this new approach. Three different GPU architectures, Kepler, Maxwell and Pascal, have been evaluated using several real kernels from the CUDA and Rodinia SDK. A statistical analysis has been conducted to assess the significance of the NEH-GPU heuristic and to show its advantage over other heuristics. Furthermore, the number of tasks has been varied to assess the scalability of the heuristics. In all of them NEH-GPU has obtained the closest results to the best makespan obtained by any heuristic.

## References

1. Allahverdi, A., Ng, C., Cheng, T., Kovalyov, M.Y.: A survey of scheduling problems with setup times or costs. Eur. J. Oper. Res. **187**(3), 985–1032 (2008). https://doi.org/10.1016/j.ejor.2006.06.060
2. Basaran, C., Kang, K.D.: Supporting preemptive task executions and memory copies in GPGPUs. In: 2012 24th Euromicro Conference on Real-Time Systems, pp. 287–296, July 2012. https://doi.org/10.1109/ECRTS.2012.15
3. Chen, G., Zhao, Y., Shen, X., Zhou, H.: EffiSha: a software framework for enabling effficient preemptive scheduling of GPU. In: Proceedings of the 22nd ACM SIGPLAN Symposium on Principles and Practice of Parallel Programming. PPoPP 2017, pp. 3–16. ACM, New York (2017). https://doi.org/10.1145/3018743.3018748
4. Framinan, J., Gupta, J., Leisten, R.: A review and classification of heuristics for permutation flow-shop scheduling with makespan objective. J. Oper. Res. Soc. **55**, 1243–1255 (2004). https://doi.org/10.1057/palgrave.jors.2601784
5. Garey, M.R., Johnson, D.S., Sethi, R.: The complexity of flowshop and jobshop scheduling. Math. Oper. Res. **1**(2), 117–129 (1976)
6. Graham, R., Lawler, E., Lenstra, J., Kan, A.: Optimization and approximation in deterministic sequencing and scheduling: a survey. Ann. Discrete Math. **5**(C), 287–326 (1979). https://doi.org/10.1016/S0167-5060(08)70356-X
7. Khronos Group: OpenCL 2.0 API Specification, October 2014. https://www.khronos.org/registry/cl/specs/opencl-2.0.pdf

8. Lázaro-Muñoz, A.J., González-Linares, J., Gómez-Luna, J., Guil, N.: A tasks reordering model to reduce transfers overhead on GPUs. J. Parallel Distrib. Comput. **109**, 258–271 (2017). https://doi.org/10.1016/j.jpdc.2017.06.015
9. Lee, H., Al Faruque, M.A.: GPU-EvR: run-time event based real-time scheduling framework on GPGPU platform. In: Proceedings of the Conference on Design, Automation and Test in Europe. DATE 2014, pp. 220:1–220:6. European Design and Automation Association, Leuven (2014)
10. Nawaz, M., Enscore, E.E., Ham, I.: A heuristic algorithm for the m-machine, n-job flow-shop sequencing problem. Omega **11**(1), 91–95 (1983). https://doi.org/10.1016/0305-0483(83)90088-9
11. NVIDIA: CUDA Multi-process Service, March 2015. https://docs.nvidia.com/deploy/pdf/CUDAMultiProcessServiceOverview.pdf
12. NVIDIA: CUDA Programming Guide, September 2015. http://docs.nvidia.com/cuda/cuda-c-programming-guide/index.html
13. NVIDIA: CUDA Samples, September 2015. http://docs.nvidia.com/cuda/cuda-samples/index.html
14. Palmer, D.S.: Sequencing jobs through a multi-stage process in the minimum total time–a quick method of obtaining a near optimum. J. Oper. Res. Soc. **16**(1), 101–107 (1965). https://doi.org/10.1057/jors.1965.8
15. Park, J.J.K., Park, Y., Mahlke, S.: Chimera: collaborative preemption for multi-tasking on a shared GPU. In: Proceedings of the Twentieth International Conference on Architectural Support for Programming Languages and Operating Systems. ASPLOS 2015, pp. 593–606. ACM, New York (2015). https://doi.org/10.1145/2694344.2694346
16. Pinedo, M.: Scheduling: Theory, Algorithms, and Systems. With CD-ROM, 3rd edn. Springer, New York (2008)
17. Ruiz, R., Maroto, C.: A comprehensive review and evaluation of permutation flow-shop heuristics. Eur. J. Oper. Res. **165**(2), 479–494 (2005). https://doi.org/10.1016/j.ejor.2004.04.017
18. Taillard, E.: Some efficient heuristic methods for the flow shop sequencing problem. Eur. J. Oper. Res. **47**, 65–74 (1990)
19. Tukey, J.W.: Exploratory Data Analysis. Addison-Wesley Publishing Company, Boston (1977)
20. Wang, Z., Yang, J., Melhem, R., Childers, B., Zhang, Y., Guo, M.: Simultaneous multikernel GPU: multi-tasking throughput processors via fine-grained sharing. In: 2016 IEEE International Symposium on High Performance Computer Architecture (HPCA), pp. 358–369, March 2016. https://doi.org/10.1109/HPCA.2016.7446078
21. Xu, Q., Jeon, H., Kim, K., Ro, W.W., Annavaram, M.: Warped-Slicer: efficient intra-SM slicing through dynamic resource partitioning for GPU multiprogramming. In: Proceedings of the 43rd International Symposium on Computer Architecture. ISCA 2016, pp. 230–242. IEEE Press, Piscataway (2016). https://doi.org/10.1109/ISCA.2016.29
22. Zhong, J., He, B.: Kernelet: high-throughput GPU kernel executions with dynamic slicing and scheduling. IEEE Trans. Parallel Distrib. Syst. **25**(6), 1522–1532 (2014). https://doi.org/10.1109/TPDS.2013.257
23. Zhou, H., Tong, G., Liu, C.: GPES: a preemptive execution system for GPGPU computing. In: 21st IEEE Real-Time and Embedded Technology and Applications Symposium, pp. 87–97, April 2015. https://doi.org/10.1109/RTAS.2015.7108420

# A Timer-Augmented Cost Function
# for Load Balanced DSMC

William McDoniel$^{(\boxtimes)}$ (iD) and Paolo Bientinesi

RWTH Aachen University, 52062 Aachen, Germany
`mcdoniel@aices.rwth-aachen.de`

**Abstract.** Due to a hard dependency between time steps, large-scale simulations of gas using the Direct Simulation Monte Carlo (DSMC) method proceed at the pace of the slowest processor. Scalability is therefore achievable only by ensuring that the work done each time step is as evenly apportioned among the processors as possible. Furthermore, as the simulated system evolves, the load shifts, and thus this load-balancing typically needs to be performed multiple times over the course of a simulation. Common methods generally use either crude performance models or processor-level timers. We combine both to create a timer-augmented cost function which both converges quickly and yields well-balanced processor decompositions. When compared to a particle-based performance model alone, our method achieves 2× speedup at steady-state on up to 1024 processors for a test case consisting of a Mach 9 argon jet impacting a solid wall.

**Keywords:** DSMC · Load balancing

## 1 Introduction

For the simulation of rarefied gas flows, where collisions between molecules are both important and sufficiently rare that the gas cannot be treated as a continuum, the approach of choice is Direct Simulation Monte Carlo (DSMC) [2]. DSMC finds applications across many fields, spanning a huge range of time and length scales, and treating a wide variety of physics, from flow in and around microelectromechanical systems (MEMS) [7], to the highly reactive flows around a spacecraft during atmospheric re-entry [10], to entire planetary atmospheres [9], and even extending to the evolution of solar systems and galaxies [14]. DSMC is a particle-based method where the interactions among individual computational molecules are simulated over time. A major challenge in running 3D, time-varying DSMC simulations on supercomputers is load balancing, which is not a simple matter of assigning or scheduling independent tasks until all are finished. In this paper, we propose and test a new method for estimating the computational load in regions of an ongoing DSMC simulation, which is used to divide the physical domain among processors such that each has to do a roughly equal amount of computation.

© Springer Nature Switzerland AG 2019
H. Senger et al. (Eds.): VECPAR 2018, LNCS 11333, pp. 160–173, 2019.
https://doi.org/10.1007/978-3-030-15996-2_12

When run on many cores, each process in a DSMC simulation owns a region of space and all of the particles in it. The simulation proceeds in time steps, repeatedly executing three actions. First, all particles move a distance proportional to their velocities. Second, particles which have moved to regions owned by different processors are communicated. Third, pairs of nearby particles are tested for collisions and may (depending on random number draws) collide. In order to determine the effect of collisions on the gas, processors must know about all of the local particles. Effectively, this introduces a dependency between the movement of particles on all processors and the collisions on a single processor. All of the processors must proceed through the simulation synchronously, and so performance degrades if one processor is doing more computation per time step than others, since all of the others will be forced to wait for it each time step. A single processor that takes twice as long as the others to simulate a time step will cause the whole simulation to proceed half as quickly as it otherwise might.

The load balancing of a simulation in which processes own regions of space in a larger domain boils down to the determination of where processor boundaries should be drawn, with the goal of dividing the domain into regions that require roughly equal amounts of computation each time step. Almost all methods for load balancing physics simulations rely on a "cost function", which may be implicit in a more complex balancing scheme, or explicitly computed and used as the basis for decomposing the domain. A cost function maps points in space to estimated computational load; a simulation is load-balanced if the integral of the (accurate) cost function over a processor's subdomain is the same for all processors. Cost functions can be produced from performance models, by analyzing the method. Sometimes this is straightforward. For example, many finite difference or finite element solvers predictably do work proportional to the number of elements or grid points; consequently, such simulations can be load balanced by evenly apportioning elements to processors. By contrast, the computational cost of DSMC is hard to model. Because of this, load balancers tend to either use approximate models (which have errors and so lead to imbalance) or ignore the details of the method entirely and look only at actual time spent by different processors (thus producing a coarse cost function). We propose to combine both sorts of estimates to achieve better balance than either can by itself.

## 2   DSMC

DSMC is a stochastic, particle-based method which has been in use for decades [3]. The main idea is to use a relatively small number of computational particles (millions to billions) to represent the very large number of real particles in a macroscopic system, where real particle densities can easily be $10^{20}$ particles per cubic meter or larger, and the system could be an entire planet's atmosphere or more. "Particles" are generally molecules (as with the test case in this paper) but may be dust grains, ions, or even electrons. In DSMC, each computational particle behaves much like a real particle most of the time, e.g., moving in response to external forces. Collisions between computational particles have a random element. Random number draws determine post-collision velocities and energies, whether or not chemical reactions occur when particles collide, and even whether or not a collision between two particles occurs at all. Because each computational particle's properties change over time in the way that a random real particle's might, a relatively tiny number of computational particles can capture the statistical properties of the real flow.

DSMC produces approximate solutions to the Boltzmann equation. Unlike the dense (often liquid) flows for which molecular dynamics is suited, in a rarefied gas molecules are almost always so far from their nearest neighbors that intermolecular forces are essentially nonexistent. Molecules interact with other molecules for relatively short amounts of time in between long periods of ballistic motion. Using the dilute gas approximation, DSMC treats these interactions as instantaneous pair-wise collisions which can be de-coupled from molecular motion within a time step. As a particle-based method, rather than a differential equation solver, DSMC is also highly extensible, and modular physics packages can be quickly implemented, making it easy to use for many different kinds of problems. DSMC is expensive relative to traditional partial differential equation solvers for fluid flow, and becomes more so as flow densities increase. Still, the method is used because it is much more accurate than traditional solvers at low densities (more precisely, it is more accurate when the mean free path between collisions is not small relative to other length scales in the problem).

A major challenge to load balancing in DSMC is that, unlike with many continuum finite element methods, it is difficult to model its cost (the difficulty of load-balancing DSMC is also discussed in [5]). The amount of computation performed scales roughly linearly with the number of particles, but this is not an exact relation. Most particles need to be moved once per time step, and this is often simple. Most particles are moved by multiplying their velocities by the time step size and adding the result to their positions. But particles which are near a surface or domain boundary may impact it and bounce off, in which case the code must find when and where they intersected the surface and then compute a new move from that point with the remaining time.

Not only are some particles easier to move than others, the number of collisions that a processor needs to compute depends on many factors. DSMC domains are typically divided into a grid, and the grid cells are used to locate neighbors which are potential collision partners. The number of collisions to perform in a cell is (on average) proportional to the square of the number of particles in the cell and to the time step size. When collisions are a significant factor in a simulation's cost, high-density regions are often more expensive than low-density regions, even when both have the same total number of particles. The number and type of collisions actually performed depends further on local temperature, on the species present, on which chemical reactions are being considered, etc.

Furthermore, particle creation (for inflow at a boundary, for example) might also be a significant cost. Created particles need to be assigned some initial properties, like velocity, which are typically sampled from probability distributions.

The computational cost of each of these major functions of a DSMC code is difficult to model by itself, and the relative importance of each depends on specific features of the problem being simulated. In general, it is not feasible to develop a "one size fits all model" that predicts computational cost from the state of a simulation.

# 3   Load Balancing

We conceive of load balancing as a two step process. The first step is to find a way to predict whether a proposed domain decomposition will prove to be well-balanced, or at least better balanced than the current decomposition (for dynamic balancing). This is the purpose of a cost function, which can be applied to the space owned by a processor to obtain an estimate of the computational load associated with that space; a simulation is well-balanced if all processors are performing roughly equal amounts of work. The focus of this paper is on this first step: We want to provide a better estimate of the simulation's true cost function. The second step is to actually assign parts of the simulation domain to each processor such that the new decomposition is predicted to be balanced by this cost function. For this step, there exist many techniques for splitting up a domain which are suitable for DSMC. This is a space partitioning problem, and we stress that the two steps are in general separable. Many different kinds of cost function can be used as input for a given decomposition algorithm (as in this paper), and a given type of cost function can be used with many different decomposition algorithms. For this work, we implemented a recursive coordinate bisection (RCB) algorithm [1] to test various cost functions: Given a map of computational load in a 3D domain, we cut in the longest dimension so that half of the work is in each new subdomain; this is applied recursively until one subdomain can be assigned to each processor.

While we will not discuss the partitioning problem in detail, it is important to recognize that it can be expensive. This is unimportant for a static problem, since the balancing must only be performed once, but time-varying simulations will need to be periodically re-balanced. Many methods of re-partitioning a domain will often produce a new processor map that has little overlap with the old one. That is, after a repartitioning many processors will own entirely different regions of space. When this happens, there is a large amount of communication as many (and often most) of the particles in the domain will need to be sent to new processors, and computation must wait until a processor is given the particles contained within the region of space it now owns. Therefore it is undesirable to load balance too frequently, and it is important to have an accurate cost function which does not require multiple balance iterations to obtain a good result.

## 3.1  State of the Art

We now briefly discuss the four methods[1] in common use for load balancing parallel DSMC simulations, highlighting the advantages and disadvantages of each.

1. Random scattering (e.g., [5]): Since DSMC performance is hard to model and load-balancing itself can be costly, this method seeks to quickly and cheaply balance a simulation by dividing the domain up into many small elements and then simply randomly assigning elements to processors, ignoring topology, adjacency, etc. Each processor will own a large number of often non-contiguous elements. If the elements are small relative to length scales in the problem, it is likely that each processor is doing a roughly equal amount of work. This method might not even require re-balancing for dynamic problems, though re-balancing can be necessary if the collision grid changes. However, these benefits come with a significant drawback. By assigning small, non-contiguous chunks of space to each processor, random scattering drastically increases the number of particles that move between processors each time step. Each processor also neighbors a very large number of other processors (likely neighboring almost *every* other processor), and it is difficult to determine which processor owns a particular point in space.

2. Cell Timers (e.g., [11]): One solution to the problem of not knowing where the load is just to measure it. By inserting timers into a code at the cell level, one obtains a resolved map of load in the simulation. However, this is difficult to do because many computationally expensive parts of a DSMC simulation are not naturally performed with an awareness of the grid structure. The grid is irrelevant to moving particles around, for example, and typically only matters for finding collision partners. Additional indexing to keep track of which cells particles are in may be required, with a very large number of cell-level timers turning on and off many times each time step.

3. Processor Timers: A popular class of load-balancer abstracts away almost all of the details of the method and just looks to see which processors are taking longer than others. Some distribution of the load inside each processor is assumed (typically uniform) and boundaries are periodically redrawn to attempt to achieve a balanced simulation. Because the map of load as a function of space is very coarse, this method might require multiple iterations to achieve balance, even given a static simulation. It can also become unstable, and so is typically integrated into a partitioning scheme which will move small amounts of space between processors very frequently (as in [5,12], or [13]).

4. Particle Balancing (perhaps first applied to DSMC in [11] and used in codes like UT's PLANET [8] or Sandia's SPARTA [http://sparta.sandia.gov]): Another popular balancing method uses particle count as a proxy for load. Processor boundaries are drawn such that each processor owns space containing roughly equal numbers of particles. This is essentially just a crude

---

[1] The names of the methods are our own labels for them.

performance model, and it often works well for small numbers of processors. Particle count is also an excellent proxy for memory requirements, and so this method naturally helps ensure that memory use is balanced as well. However, because this method only approximates the true load, error can yield significant imbalance, especially for simulations using many processors.

The last three of these methods all implicitly or explicitly depend on a cost function. They intend to balance the simulation by assigning space to processors such that the integral of the cost function is the same over each processor's subdomain. Two try to measure this cost function, finely or coarsely, and one estimates it with a performance model.

The processor timer and particle balancing methods are convenient and easy to implement, but error in their estimated cost functions can be a significant problem when using a large number of processors. This is easily seen with the particle balancing method. Suppose that there is a small region of the domain where the load is twice as large as would be expected from the number of particles present in it. Perhaps there is a lot of particle creation occurring here, or there is some complex geometry in the flow and moving the particles takes longer here as they interact with the object, or this is a very hot region and expensive chemical reactions are more likely to occur. With a small number of processors, particle balancing will still yield a satisfactory result. The load-intense region is small, and so the extra work done by the processor which owns it will be negligible compared to the work it does in surrounding regions where the estimated cost function works well. The ratio of the work this processor does to the work some other processor does will still be near unity. However, as the number of processors increases, eventually there will be a processor which *only* owns part of this load-intense region. This processor is assigned twice as much work per time step as the typical processor, and the simulation will proceed at roughly 50% efficiency.

Meanwhile, the processor timer method is blind to the distribution of load within each processor – it assumes a uniform cost function inside each processor's subdomain. This causes problems at high processor counts because it will often have to perform multiple balancing passes to achieve a good result. It is even possible for it to produce a less-balanced partitioning than the one it started from. This is an overshooting problem, and can be addressed with damping terms or other schemes for shifting processor boundaries slowly over multiple passes, but these worsen its performance in the typical case and lead to the method requiring multiple iterations to balance even a flow with very little spatial variation.

We propose to combine the best features of these two methods to produce a hybrid timer-augmented cost function, mitigating the individual drawbacks of the particle balancing and processor timer methods while still being cheap to compute and simple to implement. We will demonstrate a clear improvement over particle balancing at steady state and show that the hybrid method outperforms a simple implementation of the timer-based method for our test case.

# 4    Timer-Augmented Cost Function

The chief advantage of particle balancing is its quick convergence to a good-enough solution, while a processor timer method may require more iterations but is expected to eventually converge on a more balanced set of processor boundaries. Although on the surface the two appear to be radically different approaches, they can be combined in such a way as to obtain both the quick convergence of particle balancing and the superior converged solution of processor timing. We call this hybrid method a timer-augmented cost function (TACF).

To show how this can be done, we first sketch the process of building a cost map (Fig. 1) for a particle balancer. A cost map is just the discretized cost function. We take a grid spanning the entire simulation domain, where each cell has only a single variable: number of particles. Each processor will go over all of its particles, determine in which grid cell each belongs, and increment that cell's counter. In the end we have a high-resolution map of particles for the whole domain, which will be given to the partitioner.

However, there is no reason that every particle should contribute the same weight (i.e., same estimated computational load) to the map. If performing a multi-species simulation, where one class of particle is significantly more expensive to move or collide than another, a user or developer might choose for these particles to have a disproportionate effect on the cost map – perhaps each cell's counter is incremented by 2 instead of 1 for these expensive particles. Then when the partitioner operates on the cost map, it will give fewer total particles to processors which end up with more of the expensive particles.

Our insight is that we can instead (or in addition) weight particles' contributions to the cost map by processor-level timer results. If a processor containing $N$ particles took $T$ seconds to compute the previous time step, then when it contributes to the cost map it will not add 1 to each cell per particle, but instead $T/N$. In total, it will contribute $T$ to the cost map, distributed across the cells that overlap its subdomain in proportion to where its particles are located. When every processor does this, each with its own values of $T$ and $N$, the sum across all cells in the resulting map is just the total time taken by all processors for the previous time step. The amount of this quantity in a region of space is an estimate of the time required to compute a time step for that region. When the partitioner evenly apportions this quantity, each processor will end up with an amount of "time" which is closer to the average. We are essentially taking a reasonably good performance model that nevertheless has some systematic error and augmenting it with processor-level timers to drive its converged error to zero. Where particle balancing converges on an even distribution of particles (and therefore an almost-even distribution of computational load), this timer-augmented method just converges on an even distribution of computational load.

This augmented cost model can also be conceived of starting from the timers. If all we have are processor-level timers, then we must guess at a distribution of the load within each processor. We may assume that it is uniform for lack of better options. Instead, we can suppose that the load is distributed in the same way as the particles, and this will work fairly well because particle count

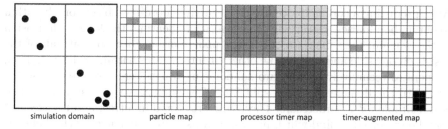

**Fig. 1.** Schematic of various methods for generating a cost map. The simulation domain is shown on the left, with particles in black and processor boundaries in red. The other figures are cost maps, with darker shades indicating higher estimated cost (scale differs between maps). Particle balancing produces a map which is proportional to particle density. Processor timers best reflect the true cost of the computation, but are blind to the distribution of load within each processor. The timer-augmented map resolves the spatial distribution of particles while also reflecting the extra cost associated with, e.g., particularly dense gas.

is a reasonably good proxy for load. This does not change the converged result, since eventually all processors should be taking equal amounts of time either way. What we gain is faster convergence. Imagine a processor which takes twice as long as the average processor, and which contains a highly non-uniform particle distribution. All of the particles are in just one half of its volume. If our partitioner is blind to the distribution of the load inside each processor, it might re-draw boundaries in useless or counter-productive ways. It might donate the empty half of the over-worked processor's volume to other processors, achieving nothing. It might donate the half containing all of the particles, leaving the original processor with nothing to do and over-working another processor. Such a system can be made to eventually converge, but it will require multiple iterations. And we stress that these iterations are expensive. Not only does a balancing pass itself require a great deal of communication, but the simulation cannot simply repeatedly build cost maps and partition processors, since the system needs timer data for the new processor distribution to perform a new balancing pass.

## 5   Method

We implemented a load balancer with the ability to produce a cost map using particle balancing, processor timers, and with our TACF in a simple 3D DSMC code. The base code essentially follows along with the treatment in [4]. It is parallelized with MPI.

To determine processor boundaries, we use a cost map consisting of a uniform grid with 1000 cells per processor, with the cells distributed so as to keep the map's resolution similar in all three dimensions. At initialization we set the cost map to a constant value everywhere, and then we periodically produce new cost maps from the particles and/or timer results of the ongoing simulation.

After producing a cost map, we use the recursive coordinate bisection algorithm to obtain boundaries. Essentially, this algorithm identifies the longest dimension in the domain, then makes a cut in the plane normal to it so that half of the cost is on one side and half on the other (it interpolates within grid cells). Then it operates recursively on the two subdomains which were just created by the cut, until the domain has been split into $2^n$ subdomains with estimated equal cost, suitable for $2^n$ processors. These cuts are stored in a tree, and the tree can then be traversed to find which processor owns a given particle by checking the particle's position against the cut position at each of $n$ levels. This is a simple technique that only works for processor counts which are powers of two, but we believe our results would also apply to other partitioning methods.

Simulations were run on Intel Xeon E5-2680 v3 Haswell CPUs, with two CPUs (16 cores total) and 128 GiB of memory per node. The authors gratefully acknowledge the computing time granted through JARA-HPC on the supercomputer JURECA at Forschungszentrum Jülich [6].

## 5.1  Test Case

Our test case is an argon jet shooting upwards into a vacuum towards a solid wall, shown in Fig. 2. The domain is a cube with side length 80 cm. Each time step, argon flowing upwards at 2900 m/s (Mach 9) is created in a cylinder on the bottom boundary at 0.01 kg/m$^3$ and 300 K.

The resulting argon jet starts at the bottom of the domain and expands upwards, becoming faster, colder, and less dense. A strong shock forms just off of the solid boundary at the top of the domain, which specularly reflects incoming molecules. The gas behind this shock is much denser and hotter, and is now subsonic. It then accelerates towards the vacuum boundaries on the sides of the domain.

This case features typical spatial non-uniformity. Density varies by many orders of magnitude, temperatures range from nearly 0 to more than 5000 K, and there is both supersonic and subsonic flow. Molecules are created each time step in a small region of the domain, and there are both vacuum and solid boundaries. Further, only the boundary conditions and creation mechanism are known a priori. The flow-field in Fig. 2 is the eventual steady state of a time-varying 3D DSMC simulation. In short, it would be very hard to specify an appropriate domain decomposition in advance, and the optimal decomposition will change as the flow develops from an initially-empty domain.

Figure 2 also shows an example of how the problem is partitioned. Large processor subdomains are placed over the nearly empty bottom corners of the domain while many small processors are clustered over the domain's centerline, where most of the molecules are.

To make our findings reproducible, we now detail the various parameters we chose for our simulations. We use a time step of $1.427 \times 10^{-7}$ s. The ratio of real molecules to simulated molecules is $2.4 \times 10^{12}$ per processor, and each processor has roughly 100,000 cells, distributed in as close to a regular, uniform grid as possible within its subdomain. That is, as the number of processors increases, the physical flow being simulated is unchanged, but we use more computational molecules and more cells – this is very close to weak scaling. Processor boundaries are initialized to be uniform, and for the first 50 time steps argon is created at 1% of its nominal density (so as not to run out of memory on the small number of processors which own the creation region before any load-balancing occurs). We load balance every 25 time steps for the first 100 time steps, then every 50 time steps thereafter, or when any processor owns more than 4 million molecules (again to avoid running out of memory). The simulation reaches steady state around the 600th or 700th time step. After the 900th time step, we stop load balancing and run for 100 more time steps. The frequency of load-balancing is not optimized here, and optimizing this is itself a difficult problem, which is why we mainly focus on the balance at steady state.

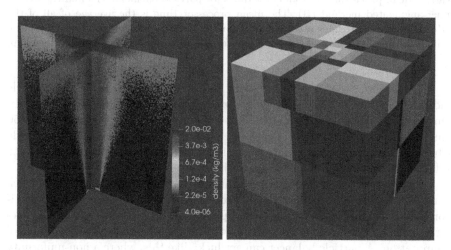

**Fig. 2.** (left) Contours of density along two planes which cut through the center of the domain. (right) A sample processor decomposition for our test case at steady state, using particle balancing with 64 processors.

# 6  Results

We can directly compare particle balancing to TACF by looking at the quality of the decomposition each produces. We obtain the wall clock time for a time step by starting a timer just after molecules are communicated (after they move and potentially arrive in other processors' subdomains) and stopping it at the same point in the next time step. We obtain a "processor time" for a single processor (that is, a core) for a time step by starting a timer just after molecules are communicated and stopping it just before they are communicated in the next time step. This measure is capturing nearly all of the computation that a processor is doing while excluding time that it spends waiting for other processors. This is the quantity that each processor contributes to the cost map and is what we attempt to balance with the aim of minimizing the wall clock time.

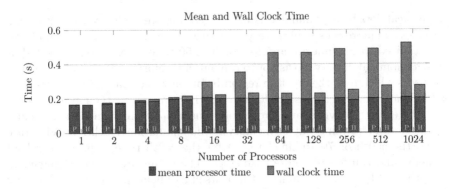

**Fig. 3.** Mean processor and wall clock times for particle balancing (P) and the hybrid timer-augmented method (H). The mean processor time is the average of all of the individual processor times used as inputs for the timer-augmented load balancer. The wall clock time is the actual time required for the simulation to complete a time step.

Figure 3 shows the mean processor times and wall clock times for particle and timer-augmented balancing for a range of processor counts, with the problem scaled to match per Sect. 5.1. Measurements were taken over the final 50 time steps of the simulation. The mean processor times are shown to provide a baseline. Wall clock times in excess of the mean processor times are due to either imbalance or communication overhead.

Up to 8 cores, both methods perform well – there is little excess wall clock time. The test case is symmetric on two of the coordinate axes, and the partitioner makes its first cuts parallel to the planes in Fig. 2, so even particle balancing produces four mirrored subdomains which all do basically equal amounts of computation. A particle balancer can get lucky like this, where a non-uniformity in one processor is balanced by a similar non-uniformity in another. This can even happen without symmetry. Especially when processor counts are small, it is likely that subdomains are large enough to contain a variety of flow regimes such that expensive regions and cheap regions average out.

However, the particle balancer falls behind the timer-augmented balancer starting at 16 cores. By 64 cores, the particle balancer is producing a decomposition where processors are on average spending more time waiting for other processors than on computation. The inefficiency due to imbalance does not grow without bound, though. After quickly growing between 16 and 64 cores, it grows only very slowly up to 1024 (and this growth may be largely due to communication costs). This is predicted by our theoretical discussion of the advantages and disadvantages of different load balancers in Sect. 3.1. There is a limit to how imbalanced a particle balancer can get, which is determined by how expensive the most expensive particles in the simulation are and how cheap the cheapest particles in the simulation are.

Meanwhile, the TACF balancer performs much better for large processor counts. It sees only slow growth in wall clock time as processor count increases, as might be expected of a weak scaling plot. The practical benefits are clearly significant – the simulation using the TACF balancer is able to perform time steps about twice as quickly on many cores.

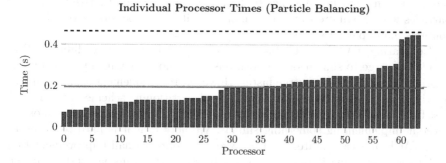

**Fig. 4.** Processor times for the particle balancing method. The red line shows the mean processor time and the dashed line shows the wall clock time. Deviations from the mean indicate imbalance. (Color figure online)

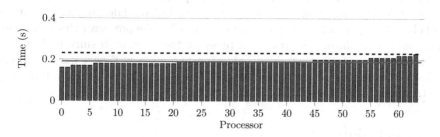

**Fig. 5.** Processor times for the timer-augmented balancing method. The red line shows the mean processor time and the dashed line shows the wall clock time. Deviations from the mean indicate imbalance. (Color figure online)

We now look more closely at the efficacy of each load balancer by examining distributions of processor times. Figure 4 shows the (sorted) processor times for the 64-core particle-balanced simulation. Most processors are more than 20% off of the mean time. The high wall clock time seen earlier is driven by four particularly slow processors which cover the most expensive parts of the flow. By contrast, the distribution of times for the TACF balancer (Fig. 5) are much more even, with almost all processors within 10% of the mean time and no significant outliers.

The TACF method achieves this improved load balance by recognizing that not all particles are equally costly, so it requires more memory. In all of the particle balancing simulations, there were approximately 650,000 molecules in each processor's subdomain. While this is true of the average processor with TACF, there is significant particle imbalance starting at 16 processors. With 16, one processor has 1 million molecules. On 64, one has 1.44 million. On 1024, one has 1.8 million. If memory use is a constraint, TACF could be modified to cap the maximum particle imbalance by finding a minimum alternative weight that particles will contribute to the cost map even if their processor is very fast and contains many particles.

Comparing TACF to the processor timer method is more difficult. Both should converge to similar decompositions after enough balance passes, but the hybrid method should converge faster. However, real implementations of processor timer methods make use of sophisticated partitioning schemes with implicit cost functions to try to address this issue, and so a fair comparison is impossible without implementing something similar. We note that it is hard to do better than TACF at steady state, per Figs. 3 and 5 – only a small improvement from better load-balancing is possible. To try to study the transient performance of each, we can run our test case with processor timer balancing by using a damping factor, such that processors contribute a weighted average of their individual processor times and the mean processor time to the cost map. When we do this (including tuning the damping factor), the simulation takes significantly longer (at least $2\times$ longer when using more than 16 processors) to complete than with particle balancing or TACF. Further, we must perform an ten extra load balance passes at steady state to obtain a reasonably well-balanced decomposition with a wall clock time per time step comparable to TACF. The processor timer method performs poorly during the transient phase of the simulation since it does not make sense to perform many load balancing passes every time a new partition is desired, whereas particle balancing and TACF perform about as well during the transient phase as at steady state.

## 7 Conclusion

Large-scale DSMC simulations require load balancing in order to be feasible. As part of this, many methods use a model of the load as a function of space to guide the decomposition of the domain into processors' subdomains. We discussed several models, and proposed a timer-augmented cost function which combines the quick convergence of a particle balancer and the low error of processor timers.

Not only does a timer-augmented cost function yield a significantly more balanced domain decomposition than the one achieved by partitioning on the basis of particles alone, it is also an easy improvement to make in code. In the case of our code, the only difference between a particle balancer and the TACF balancer is that, with TACF, each processor contributes a different constant value to the cost map instead of the same constant value. All other aspects of the load balancer and partitioner can remain the same, which makes it easy to realize significant performance gains ($\sim2\times$ at steady state for our test case). In fact, a timer-augmented balancing method was recently adopted by the developers of SPARTA, and is now an option for users of this open-source code.

# References

1. Berger, M.J., Bokhari, S.H.: A partitioning strategy for nonuniform problems on multiprocessors. IEEE Trans. Comput. **5**, 570–580 (1987)
2. Bird, G.A.: The DSMC Method. CreateSpace Independent Publishing Platform, Scotts Valley (2013)
3. Bird, G.A.: Molecular Gas Dynamics. NASA STI/Recon Technical Report A **76** (1976)
4. Boyd, I.D., Schwartzentruber, T.E.: Nonequilibrium Gas Dynamics and Molecular Simulation. Cambridge University Press, Cambridge (2017)
5. Ivanov, M., Markelov, G., Taylor, S., Watts, J.: Parallel DSMC strategies for 3D computations. North-Holland, Amsterdam (1997). https://doi.org/10.1016/B978-044482327-4/50128-5, http://www.sciencedirect.com/science/article/pii/B9780444823274501285
6. Jülich Supercomputing Centre: JURECA: general-purpose supercomputer at Jülich supercomputing centre. J. Large-Scale Res. Facil. **2**(A62) (2016). https://doi.org/10.17815/jlsrf-2-121, http://dx.doi.org/10.17815/jlsrf-2-121
7. Karniadakis, G.E., Beskok, A., Aluru, N.: Microflows and Nanoflows: Fundamentals and Simulation, vol. 29. Springer, New York (2006). https://doi.org/10.1007/0-387-28676-4
8. McDoniel, W.J., Goldstein, D.B., Varghese, P.L., Trafton, L.M.: Three-dimensional simulation of gas and dust in Io's Pele plume. Icarus **257**, 251–274 (2015). https://doi.org/10.1016/j.icarus.2015.03.019. http://www.sciencedirect.com/science/article/pii/S0019103515001190
9. McDoniel, W.J., Goldstein, D.B., Varghese, P.L., Trafton, L.M.: The interaction of Io's plumes and sublimation atmosphere. Icarus **294**, 81–97 (2017). https://doi.org/10.1016/j.icarus.2017.04.021. http://www.sciencedirect.com/science/article/pii/S0019103517303068
10. Moss, J.N., Bird, G.A.: Direct simulation of transitional flow for hypersonic re-entry conditions. Therm. Desi. Aeroassisted Orbital Transf. Veh. **96**, 338–360 (1985)
11. Nance, R.P., Wilmoth, R.G., Moon, B., Hassan, H., Saltz, J.: Parallel DSMC solution of three-dimensional flow over a finite flat plate. NASA Technical report (1994)
12. Olson, S.E., Christlieb, A.J., Fatemi, F.K.: PID feedback for load-balanced parallel gridless DSMC. Comput. Phys. Commun. **181**(12), 2063–2071 (2010). https://doi.org/10.1016/j.cpc.2010.06.045. http://www.sciencedirect.com/science/article/pii/S0010465510002985
13. Taylor, S., Watts, J.R., Rieffel, M.A., Palmer, M.E.: The concurrent graph: basic technology for irregular problems. IEEE Parallel Distrib. Technol.: Syst. Appl. **4**(2), 15–25 (1996)
14. Weinberg, M.D.: Direct simulation monte carlo for astrophysical flows-II. Ram-pressure dynamics. Mon. Not. R. Astron. Soc. **438**(4), 3007–3023 (2014)

# Accelerating Scientific Applications on Heterogeneous Systems with HybridOMP

Matthias Diener$^{(\boxtimes)}$, Daniel J. Bodony, and Laxmikant Kale

University of Illinois at Urbana-Champaign, Urbana, USA
{mdiener,bodony,kale}@illinois.edu

**Abstract.** High Performance Computing relies on accelerators (such as GPGPUs) to achieve fast execution of scientific applications. Traditionally these accelerators have been programmed with specialized languages, such as CUDA or OpenCL. In recent years, OpenMP emerged as a promising alternative for supporting accelerators, providing advantages such as maintaining a single code base for the host and different accelerator types and providing a simple way to extend support for accelerators to existing code. Efficiently using this support requires solving several challenges, related to performance, work partitioning, and concurrent execution on multiple device types. In this paper, we discuss these challenges and introduce a library, HybridOMP, that addresses several of them, thus enabling the effective use of OpenMP for accelerators. We apply HybridOMP to a scientific application, PlasCom2, that has not previously been able to use accelerators. Experiments on three architectures show that HybridOMP results in performance gains of up to 10x compared to CPU-only execution. Concurrent execution on the host and GPU resulted in additional gains of up to 10% compared to running on the GPU only.

**Keywords:** GPGPU · Heterogeneous computing · OpenMP · Accelerators

## 1 Introduction

The HPC community has recently seen a large increase in demand for processing power, especially for use by large scientific applications. As a response to this demand, many modern cluster systems consist of heterogeneous nodes that contain accelerators, such as a GPGPUs, in addition to the CPUs. Programming such a heterogeneous system is challenging, as few programming models support executing code on accelerators, leading to the use of specialized solutions such as CUDA [11] or OpenCL [9]. Newer proposals in this area are Kokkos [4], Legion [2], C++AMP [7], XKAAPI [6], OmpSs [14], and StarPU [1], among several others.

© Springer Nature Switzerland AG 2019
H. Senger et al. (Eds.): VECPAR 2018, LNCS 11333, pp. 174–187, 2019.
https://doi.org/10.1007/978-3-030-15996-2_13

Such specialized languages have the advantage of being able to result in the best performance in many cases, as they can often provide support for special device features and offer good code generation for specific device types. However, this performance comes at a cost. Existing application code can often not be reused and must be rewritten in a new language. Also, code is often not portable between different device types (for example, between CPU and GPU, or between GPUs of different vendors), such that various devices may require different implementations, compilers, and runtime libraries, leading to duplicated code and an increased difficulty of code maintenance and verification, increasing the burden for developers and users.

For many scientific applications, adding support for using heterogeneous systems is easier when existing code (often written in C/C++/Fortran) can be reused on several types of accelerators without having to duplicate the code. Furthermore, applications should be able to support different hardware and software environments with this approach. Supporting *concurrent* execution on the host and offloading devices to use all available computing resources efficiently should also be a goal.

In this context, an interesting alternative to support accelerator devices are recent versions of the OpenMP standard [13]. Since version 4.0, the standard supports accelerators through *offloading*, which allows the compilation and execution of largely unmodified code on such devices, provided that the compiler and runtime contain support for the device. Using OpenMP provides advantages compared to prior solutions, by removing the need to duplicate code, and allowing the use of existing code, programming languages, and runtimes with only minimal changes. Furthermore, OpenMP can target different types of devices, and support is not limited to specific compilers or hardware architectures. Many of these properties are shared with OpenACC [12], but OpenMP has a higher developer familiarity and a bigger existing code base.

Figure 1 contains a simplified example of a floating-point ZAXPY code, which calculates the equation $Z = aX + Y$, for the vectors $Z$, $X$, and $Y$, and a scalar $a$. ZAXPY is similar to a standard DAXPY operation, but stores its result in a separate vector instead of updating an input vector. In the code example, the omp target pragma in line 3 indicates to the compiler that the following section of code should be compiled for the host system and the accelerator, and indicates to the OpenMP runtime library to transfer data structures used in the section to the device, execute the *offloaded* code, and transfer back the results. This closely matches the traditional usage of accelerators with libraries such as CUDA. However, if no device is available at runtime, the OpenMP code is executed on the host's CPUs. In this way, code can execute on various types of devices or even the host, while having only a single version of the application code.

To support concurrent execution, an approach that can be taken is to create multiple OpenMP threads, of which only some are offloaded. This is illustrated in Fig. 2. In this example, one thread (thread 0) is offloaded, while the other thread (thread 1) executes on the host. Work is partitioned between these threads depending on a parameter, $M$, that determines which part of the problem is

```
1   double x[N], y[N], z[N], a;
2
3   #pragma omp target
4   {
5     for(int i=0; i<N; i++)
6       z[i] = a * x[i] + y[i];
7   }
```

**Fig. 1.** Example of OpenMP offloading code for the ZAXPY operation $(Z = aX + Y)$.

```
1   double x[N], y[N], z[N], a;
2
3   #pragma omp parallel num_threads(2)
4   {
5           if (omp_get_thread_num()==0) {
6   #pragma omp target
7   {
8           for (int i=0; i<M; i++)
9                   z[i] = a*x[i] + y[i];
10  }
11          } else {
12          for (int i=M; i<N; i++)
13                  z[i] = a*x[i] + y[i];
14          }
15  }
```

**Fig. 2.** Example of concurrent execution of OpenMP on host and device for the ZAXPY operation.

executed on the CPU and on the offloading device. This pattern can be used to implement concurrent execution.

In this paper, we introduce a library, *HybridOMP*, that implements this pattern and allows scientific applications to leverage heterogeneous architectures with few changes. HybridOMP handles data partitioning between the host and accelerators based on a performance estimate. We apply HybridOMP to a scientific application, *PlasCom2*, and perform experiments on three heterogeneous systems. Performance results show significant improvements (up to 10×) from offloading itself, while concurrent execution on CPU+GPU provided additional gains of up to 10%.

The remainder of this paper is organized as follows. The next section analyzes the performance of OpenMP offloading compared to CUDA. Section 3 provides a brief overview of our application, *PlasCom2*, and discusses the choice of using OpenMP for heterogeneous execution. Our HybridOMP library is presented in Sect. 4. Section 5 describes our experimental methodology, while performance results are analyzed in Sect. 6. Related work is presented in Sect. 7. Finally, Sect. 8 discusses our conclusions and ideas for future work.

## 2    OpenMP Offloading Performance

An important aspect of using OpenMP for accelerators is the performance of the offloaded code compared to other solutions. Several prior studies [3,8] evaluated certain performance aspects of OpenMP offloading. In this section, we show how OpenMP offloading performance compares to CUDA, as well as running OpenMP on the host. For the experiments in this section, we run three versions of a ZAXPY code similar to the one shown in Fig. 1 on two different hardware platforms with Nvidia GPUs (x86+K20X and Power9+V100, respectively). These platforms and their software environments will be described in more detail in Sect. 5. We measure the execution time for the actual ZAXPY operation, while varying the number of (double) vector elements used in the calculation, up to the memory limitations of each device. As OpenMP uses `cudaMemcpy` for data movement, we only measure the performance of the calculation, without data movements.

Results for the two hardware platforms are shown in Figs. 3 and 4. On both platforms, running on the CPU is faster than on the GPU for small input sizes, due to kernel startup overheads, as expected. Compared to CUDA, OpenMP offloading has a significantly higher startup overhead. However, for larger input sizes, starting at approximately $2^{25}$ vector elements for ZAXPY, performance between the offloaded OpenMP code and CUDA becomes comparable, with less than 10% difference between them on the Power9 system.

The point at which it becomes profitable to offload therefore depends highly on the input size and hardware/software characteristics, and indicates a need for a careful profile to determine what operations to offload. Furthermore, these results show that even for larger input sizes, running on the CPU concurrently with the GPU could provide performance gains for the overall execution.

## 3    PlasCom2

PlasCom2 is a next-generation multiphysics simulation application [5]. It is built up from modular, reusable components designed to be adapted to modern, heterogeneous architectures. PlasCom2 supports uncertainty quantification, optimization and control, and repeatability through provenance. The parallelization model of PlasCom2 uses domain decomposition with hybrid MPI+X, with X currently as OpenMP. PlasCom2's frontend code is written mostly in C++. Its computational kernels are written in Fortran 90 for performance reasons.

PlasCom2 follows a development model in which the code base only consists of easy-to-maintain code, written in standard languages, without hand optimizations or hardware-dependent code. Automatic code transformation tools and runtime systems are then used to optimize execution for each target architecture PlasCom2 is running on.

In such a development model, there are several advantages of using OpenMP to execute PlasCom2 on GPUs compared to other solutions. First, PlasCom2's development model is supported directly, and changes have to be made only to

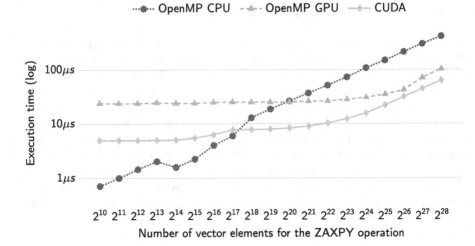

**Fig. 3.** Performance results for the ZAXPY code on the x86 system.

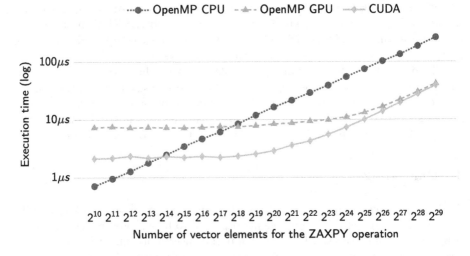

**Fig. 4.** Performance results for the ZAXPY code on the Power9 system.

the frontend code that manages the parallel execution, while the kernels can be left mostly untouched. Second, PlasCom2 already uses OpenMP for parallelization within each cluster node, and developers are familiar with its development model. Finally, OpenMP offloading already provides ways to transfer data between CPU and GPU, either implicitly (all data is transferred) or explicitly (the application specifies which data needs to be transferred). This solution also has disadvantages compared to others. Most importantly, offloading support in

OpenMP requires very recent compiler and runtime versions. Furthermore, as the previous section has shown, performance is not always the same as more traditional solutions such as CUDA, especially for smaller input sizes.

# 4 The HybridOMP Library

We propose *HybridOMP*, an OpenMP library that supports applications with offloading execution to devices. The library builds on top of OpenMP 4.5. It consists of 3 main parts, which are handled automatically during execution:

1. Work partitioning.
2. Data movement.
3. Code execution.

## 4.1 Work Partitioning

To perform work partitioning between host and devices, HybridOMP executes one PlasCom2 kernel on the host and device and measures its execution time. The resulting performance ratio is used to calculate the work partitioning between host and devices. As an illustrative example, Fig. 5 shows a comparison of homogeneous partitioning on CPU-only and heterogeneous partitioning with HybridOMP, considering a four-core system with two GPGPUs.

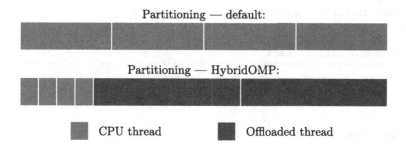

**Fig. 5.** Overview of work partitioning with HybridOMP.

## 4.2 Data Movement

Data movement in HybridOMP is handled locally inside each kernel. The reason for this is that we want to be independent of which kernels are actually called at runtime, and in which order they are called. Nevertheless, data is not copied between host and device for each kernel execution, but data is maintained on each device as long as possible and copied only when necessary. Figure 6 shows an overview of the data movement. At the beginning of each kernel, input parameters are transferred to the device if the thread executing the kernel is a thread that should be offloaded. This is done with the target enter data statement which only transfers data if it is not already located on the device. At the end of execution, changed output data is transferred back to the host and the other devices.

```
1  SUBROUTINE applyoperator(...)
2  mydev = hyb_tid_to_device(tid) ! HybridOMP - offload this thread?
3  !$omp target enter data(...) device (mydev) if (mydev>=0)
4  [...]
5  ! for host and all other devices:
6  !$omp target update(output data)
```

**Fig. 6.** Data movement with HybridOMP.

### 4.3 Code Execution

Code execution is handled similarly as data movement, with each kernel handling its own execution, for the same reasons as before. Figure 7 shows an example of the execution. The `target teams` directive starts the offloaded code section. For the outermost loops, the `distribute parallel do` directive distributes loop iterations among the hardware threads on the device.

```
1  SUBROUTINE applyoperator(...)
2  mydev = hyb_tid_to_device(tid) ! HybridOMP - offload this thread?
3  !$omp target teams device(mydev) if (mydev>=0)
4  [...]
5  !$omp distribute parallel do
6  DO K = opInterval(5), opInterval(6) ! outermost loop
7  [...]
8  !$omp end target teams
```

**Fig. 7.** Code execution with HybridOMP.

### 4.4 Implementation

HybridOMP is implemented as a set of library functions written in C. HybridOMP does not rely on external libraries and only requires a working OpenMP version 4.5 compiler and runtime. When integrating HybridOMP into PlasCom2, we use a stencil kernel to measure relative performance for the work partitioning for all kernels. In a future version, we intend to evaluate different partitions for different kernels.

## 5 Experimental Methodology

We performed multiple experiments to evaluate the performance of OpenMP offloading with HybridOMP in PlasCom2. This section discusses the methodology of our experiments.

## 5.1    Hardware Environment

We run experiments on the following hardware platforms.

- **Power9:** An IBM Power9 system with two CPUs, and four NVIDIA Volta V100 GPUs. The P9 system represents a newer type of machine with unified memory between host and accelerator.
- **Power8 (Ray):** An IBM Power8 system with two CPUs, and four NVIDIA Pascal P100 GPUs.
- **Blue Waters (XK7 nodes):** An AMD x86 system with AMD Interlagos CPUs, and an NVIDIA Kepler K20X GPU. The x86 system represents an older type of machine with non-unified memory between host and accelerator.

Our main results are shown for a single node, but we also run a strong scaling experiment on the Power8 and Blue Waters machines.

## 5.2    Software Environment

On the x86 system, all software was compiled with gcc version 7.2.0, while we used the IBM XL compiler version 13.1.7 (beta2) on the Power9 and Power8 machines. The CUDA version on both Power systems is 9.1, while we use CUDA 7.5 on Blue Waters.

## 5.3    PlasCom2 Configuration

We run a scalability test case of PlasCom2 with 200,000 points and 10 time steps. Overall memory consumption of this test case is approximately 1 GByte. For the strong scaling experiments, we run with 4× of the number of points.

**Table 1.** Overall execution time results (in seconds) on the Power9 system.

|                         | Host  | 1 GPU | 4 GPU | HybridOMP |
|-------------------------|-------|-------|-------|-----------|
| Right Hand Side (RHS)   | 21.12 | 7.28  | 4.12  | 3.96      |
| Total execution time    | 23.65 | 9.81  | 6.39  | 6.21      |

## 5.4    Execution

For the experiments, we create a single OpenMP thread per GPU for offloading. Each thread then creates multiple teams per thread for executing the code on the device. For all experiments, we run with 20 CPU threads per node on the Power systems and 8 CPU threads on Blue Waters, which resulted in the highest performance on each system. We show average values of three executions.

## 6  Results

### 6.1  Single-Node Experiments

Figures 8, 9 and 10 show the performance results of PlasCom2, broken down by
kernel. On the Power9 machine, the highest performance gains were achieved
for the stencil operators, ApplyOperator and ApplyDissOperator, achieving a
speedup of 10× over using the host only. Most other operators have lower
improvements of 2×–5×. By using HybridOMP, performance was only improved
by 0%–5% over using only GPUs. The reason for this is that the GPUs on this
system are very fast and the IBM XL compiler is producing efficient code for
the GPU. Overall, total application performance was improved by up to 5×
with offloading, as shown in Table 1, in which the Right Hand Side (RHS) row
refers to the time the application spends for calculation, without communication
or I/O.

For the Power8 system, performance results are very similar to Power9. Overall performance is a bit lower, as expected. Total application performance was
improved by 4× (Table 2).

On the Blue Waters system, performance improvements from offloading are
lower than on the Power systems. The reason is that the GPU is much older, as
well as the fact that GCC is not producing as efficient code as IBM XL. Due to

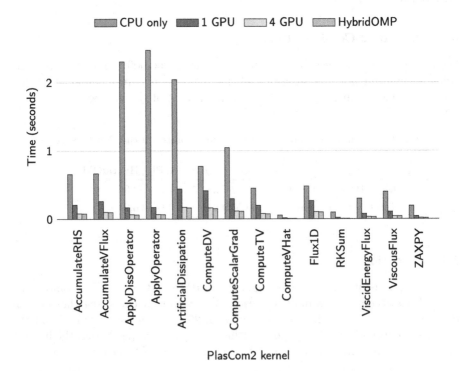

**Fig. 8.** PlasCom2 kernel results on the Power9 system.

**Table 2.** Overall execution time results (in seconds) on the Power8 system.

|  | Host | 1 GPU | 4 GPU | HybridOMP |
|---|---|---|---|---|
| Right Hand Side (RHS) | 27.58 | 10.25 | 6.98 | 6.61 |
| Total execution time | 29.73 | 11.31 | 8.15 | 7.95 |

**Table 3.** Overall execution time results (in seconds) on the Blue Waters system.

|  | Host | 1 GPU | HybridOMP |
|---|---|---|---|
| Right Hand Side (RHS) | 63.43 | 30.91 | 27.11 |
| Total execution time | 67.55 | 34.55 | 30.93 |

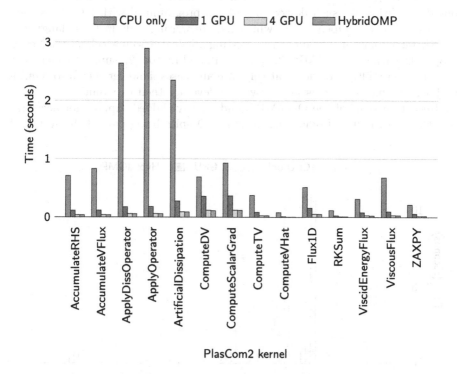

**Fig. 9.** PlasCom2 kernel results on the Power8 system.

the same reason, HybridOMP can benefit from concurrent execution on the host and devices, improving performance by up to 10%. For the stencil operators, performance is improved approximately by 5× compared to the host. For the other kernels, gains are between 1.5× and 5×. Overall, performance on Blue Waters is improved by 2.2× with HybridOMP (Table 3).

## 6.2   Multi-node Experiments

Performance results of the strong scaling experiments for 1–8 nodes on Ray and Blue Waters are shown in Figs. 11 and 12. The input size is 4 times higher than for the single-node experiments. For both systems, we can see that HybridOMP continues to be faster than using only the host even when using multiple nodes. As performance gains for smaller inputs tend to be smaller for GPU offloading, the performance difference decreases for higher node numbers.

## 7   Related Work

Many solutions to program accelerator devices such as GPGPUs have been proposed. Traditionally, such devices have been programmed with languages such as CUDA [11] and OpenCL [9], which require writing code in those languages and therefore make it difficult to run existing applications on accelerators. Newer proposals, such as C++AMP [7], Kokkos [4], and Legion [2], support concurrent execution on multiple devices natively in many cases, however they also require major code changes to existing software to leverage their capabilities.

Recent versions of the OpenMP standard have added support for accelerators through the use of offloading pragmas. Despite being part of the standard

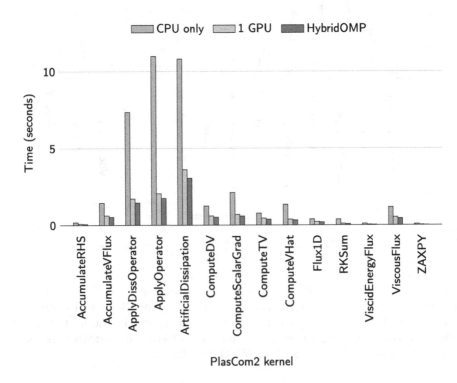

**Fig. 10.** PlasCom2 kernel results on the Blue Waters XK7 system.

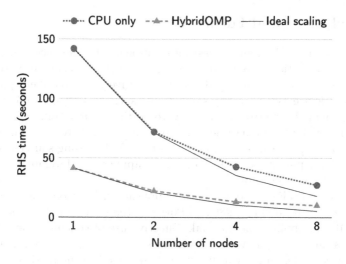

**Fig. 11.** Scaling results on the Ray (Power8+Nvidia P100) system.

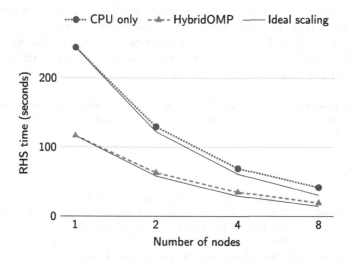

**Fig. 12.** Scaling results on the Blue Waters (x86+Nvidia K20X) system.

for some time now, actual compiler support for OpenMP offloading in released versions is relatively recent. Several recent papers discuss some aspects of the performance of OpenMP offloading [3,8]. In this paper, we add to these evaluations by measuring the impact of the input size on OpenMP performance comparisons.

Multiple benchmarks suites for evaluating heterogeneous architectures and concurrent execution on them have been proposed [10,15]. Most of these are implemented in one of the languages mentioned above. In this paper, we use a full scientific application to evaluate the benefits of heterogeneous computing.

# 8   Conclusions and Future Work

OpenMP has emerged as an interesting solution for heterogeneous computing, with a device-agnostic, annotation-based way to enable code and data offloading to accelerator devices, such as GPUs. To effectively run parallel applications on different device types at the same time (such as CPU+GPU), we introduced HybridOMP in this paper, which extends the OpenMP offloading support. HybridOMP enables running scientific applications on heterogeneous systems, while maintaining the simple philosophy of OpenMP of using source-code annotations, without putting a major burden on application developers. It can be added easily to existing code.

We added HybridOMP to a scientific application, PlasCom2, and performed experiments on three different x86 and Power systems. Results show that through HybridOMP, an application can make effective use of concurrent execution on accelerators and the host, with performance gains of up to 10x on some kernels compared to host-only execution, and up to 10% compared to GPU-only execution.

For the future, we intend to make the work scheduling to multiple devices dynamic, such that different device types and uneven work difficulty can be handled better. We will also address concurrent execution on the host and on offloaded devices, by executing part of the work on the CPUs, in order to improve utilization of the whole system.

**Acknowledgments.** This material is based in part upon work supported by the Department of Energy, National Nuclear Security Administration, under Award Number DE-NA0002374.

# References

1. Augonnet, C., Thibault, S., Namyst, R., Wacrenier, P.A.: StarPU: a unified platform for task scheduling on heterogeneous multicore architectures. Concurr. Comput.: Pract. Exp. **23**(2), 187–198 (2011). https://doi.org/10.1002/cpe.1631
2. Bauer, M., Treichler, S., Slaughter, E., Aiken, A.: Legion: expressing locality and independence with logical regions. In: International Conference for High Performance Computing, Networking, Storage and Analysis (SC) (2012). https://doi.org/10.1109/SC.2012.71
3. Bercea, G.T., et al.: Performance analysis of OpenMP on a GPU using a CORAL proxy application. In: International Workshop on Performance Modeling, Benchmarking, and Simulation of High Performance Computing Systems (PBMS), pp. 1–11 (2015). https://doi.org/10.1145/2832087.2832089
4. Carter Edwards, H., Trott, C.R., Sunderland, D.: Kokkos: enabling manycore performance portability through polymorphic memory access patterns. J. Parallel Distrib. Comput. **74**(12), 3202–3216 (2014). https://doi.org/10.1016/j.jpdc.2014.07.003
5. Diener, M., White, S., Kale, L.V., Campbell, M., Bodony, D.J., Freund, J.B.: Improving the memory access locality of hybrid MPI applications. In: European MPI Users' Group Meeting (EuroMPI), pp. 1–10. ACM Press, New York (2017). https://doi.org/10.1145/3127024.3127038

6. Gautier, T., Lima, J.V.F., Maillard, N., Raffin, B.: XKaapi: a runtime system for data-flow task programming on heterogeneous architectures. In: International Parallel and Distributed Processing Symposium (IPDPS), pp. 1299–1308 (2013). https://doi.org/10.1109/IPDPS.2013.66
7. Gregory, K., Miller, A.: C++ AMP: Accelerated Massive Parallelism with Microsoft Visual C++. Microsoft Press (2012)
8. Jacob, A.C., et al.: Efficient fork-join on GPUs through warp specialization. In: 2017 IEEE 24th International Conference on High Performance Computing (HiPC), pp. 358–367. IEEE, December 2017. https://doi.org/10.1109/HiPC.2017.00048
9. Khronos Group: OpenCL 2.2 Reference Guide. Technical report (2017)
10. Gomez Luna, J., et al.: Collaborative heterogeneous applications for integrated-architectures. In: ISPASS 2017 - IEEE International Symposium on Performance Analysis of Systems and Software, pp. 43–54 (2017). https://doi.org/10.1109/ISPASS.2017.7975269
11. Nvidia: CUDA C programming guide, version 9.1. Technical report (2018)
12. OpenACC-Standard.org: OpenACC Programming and Best Practices Guide. Technical report, June 2015
13. OpenMP Architecture Review Board: OpenMP Application Program Interface, Version 4.0 (2013)
14. Planas, J., Badia, R.M., Ayguadé, E., Labarta, J.: Self-adaptive OmpSs tasks in heterogeneous environments. In: PAR International. pp. 138–149 (2013). https://doi.org/10.1109/IPDPS.2013.53
15. Sun, Y.G., et al.: Hetero-mark, a benchmark suite for CPU-GPU collaborative computing. In: Proceedings of the 2016 IEEE International Symposium on Workload Characterization, IISWC 2016, pp. 13–22 (2016). https://doi.org/10.1109/IISWC.2016.7581262

# A New Parallel Benchmark for Performance Evaluation and Energy Consumption

Adriano Marques Garcia$^{(\boxtimes)}$ ⓘ, Claudio Schepke ⓘ,
Alessandro Gonçalves Girardi ⓘ, and Sherlon Almeida da Silva ⓘ

Laboratório de Estudos Avançados em Computação (LEA),
Universidade Federal do Pampa (UNIPAMPA), Alegrete, Brazil
adriano1mg@gmail.com,
{claudio.schepke,alessandro.girardi}@unipampa.edu.br,
sherlonalmeidadasilva@gmail.com

**Abstract.** This paper presents a new benchmark to evaluate performance and energy consumption of different Parallel Programming Interfaces (PPIs). The benchmark is composed of 11 algorithms implemented in PThreads, OpenMP, MPI-1 and MPI-2 (spawn) PPIs. Previous studies have used some of these applications to perform this type of evaluation in different architectures, since there is no benchmark that offers this variety of PPIs and communication models. In this work we measure the energy and performance of each application in a single architecture, varying the number of threads/processes. The goal is to show that this set of applications has enough features to form a parallel benchmark. The results show that there is no single best case that provides both better performance and low energy consumption in the presented scenarios. However, PThreads and OpenMP achieve the best trade-offs between performance and energy in most cases.

**Keywords:** Benchmark · Performance · Energy consumption

## 1 Introduction

In recent years, the increase in the complexity of applications and data size has demanded a great search for computational and energetic efficiency. Moreover, many countries are limiting the use of existing supercomputers because of their high energy consumption [1]. This shows that energy consumption is currently a concern in many different computer systems. The popularization of Green500, which lists computers from the TOP500 list of supercomputers in terms of energy efficiency, shows that reducing energy consumption is one of the directions of high-performance computing [1]. So the challenge should not only be to increase performance, but also to consume less energy.

Supported by CAPES.

H. Senger et al. (Eds.): VECPAR 2018, LNCS 11333, pp. 188–201, 2019.
https://doi.org/10.1007/978-3-030-15996-2_14

The performance increase is reached with even faster multiple parallel processors. Parallel computing aims to use multiple processors to execute different parts of the same program simultaneously [14]. However, processors should be able to exchange information at a certain point in execution time. While tasks parallelism makes it possible to increase the performance, the use of more processors and the need for communication among them can lead to an increase in energy consumption.

The parallelism can be explored with different Parallel Programming Interfaces (PPIs), each one having specific peculiarities in terms of synchronization and communication. In addition, the performance gain may vary according to processor architecture and hierarchical memory organization, communication model of each PPI, and also with the complexity and other characteristics of the application.

The scenario here presented shows that, although parallelism allows performance gains, this can lead to higher energy consumption. This energy consumption grows mainly according to the amount of processors that are used in parallel and the volume of communication by them. On the other hand, the reduction in execution time allowed by the parallelization causes the decrease in the total energy consumption in some cases. It is fundamental to use adequate benchmarks to define which parallelization strategy compensates for the increase in energy consumption in a particular architecture. However, there is not a benchmark that offers a good set of applications, fully parallelized, using multiple PPIs and different models of communication among tasks. The most commonly used parallel benchmarks have only partial parallel sets using more than one PPI.

To fill this gap, this work proposes a set of 11 applications developed with the purpose of evaluating the performance and energy consumption in multi-core architectures. These applications were developed and classified according to different criteria in previous studies [4,8–10].

These studies have shown that these applications have characteristics that are distinct enough to represent different scenarios. The objective of this work is to show the impact of these distinct characteristics on the performance and energy consumption of different applications and also the impact of the implementations using different PPIs.

To achieve this goal, applications were run on a multi-core machine. For each application, the execution time and the total power consumption of the processor were measured. Different numbers of threads/processes were used for the parallelization. The data were analyzed side by side with the result obtained by the sequential version of each application.

The remainder of this work is organized as follows. In the Sect. 2 we present the PPIs in which the applications are implemented. The related works are discussed in Sect. 3, where we compare our work with similar benchmarks. The Sect. 4 presents the set of applications and the techniques used to parallelize them, bringing more details about the historic of classifications. The Sect. 5 discusses the results and, finally, Sect. 6 draws the final considerations and future works.

## 2    Parallel Programming Interfaces

There are several computational models used in parallel computing, such as: data parallelism, shared memory, exchange of messages, and operations in remote memory. These models differ in several aspects, such as whether the available memory is locally shared or geographically distributed, and volume of communication [6]. In this work, the set of applications were implemented using two communication models with the four PPIs: PThreads, OpenMP, MPI-1 and MPI-2.

The OpenMP pattern consists of a series of compiler directives, function libraries, and a set of environment variables that influence the execution of parallel programs [14]. These directives are inserted into the sequential code and the parallel code is generated by the compiler from them. This interface operates on the basis of the thread fork-join execution model.

Different from OpenMP, in POSIX Threads (PThreads) the parallelism is explicit through library functions. That is, the programmer is responsible for managing *threads*, workload distribution, and execution control [2]. PThreads comprises some subroutines that can be classified into four main groups: thread management, mutexes, condition and synchronization variables.

MPI-1 standard API specifies point-to-point and collective communications operations, among other characteristics. In a program developed using MPI-1 all processes are statically created at the start of the execution So, the number of processes remains unchanged during program execution. At the start of the program, an initialization function of the execution environment MPI is executed by each process. This function is `MPI_Init()`. A process MPI is terminated by calling the function `MPI_Finalize()`.

Traditionally, applications deployed with MPI-2 begin the execution with a single process. The primitive `MPI_Comm_spawn()` is used for the creation of processes dynamically. A process of an MPI application, which will be called by the parent, invokes this primitive. This invocation causes a new process, called child, to be created, which not need to be identical to the parent. After creating a child process, it will belong to an intra-communicator and the communication between parent and child will occur through this communicator. In the child process, the execution of the function `MPI_Comm_get_parent()` is responsible for returning the intercom that links it to the parent. In the parent process, the intercom that binds the child is returned in the execution of the function `MPI_Comm_spawn()`.

## 3    Related Work

There are several benchmarks developed to serve different purposes. Through a bibliographic study, we searched for benchmarks that have similar purposes and the same target architectures of the benchmark proposed in this work. Therefore, we have considered benchmarks that provide a set of parallel applications for embedded or general-purpose multi-core architectures. In this way, we identify the following benchmarks: ALPBench, PARSEC, ParMiBench, SPEC, Linpack, NAS and Adept Project.

## 3.1   Similar Benchmarks

ALPBench consists of a set of parallelized complex media applications gathered from various sources, and modified to expose thread-level and data-level parallelism. It consists of 5 applications parallelized with PThreads. This benchmark is focused on general-purpose processors and has open source license.

PARSEC (Princeton Application Repository for Shared-Memory Computers) is an open source benchmark suite composed of multi-threaded programs. It consists of 11 applications, some parallelized using OpenMP, or PThreads or Intel TBB. The suite focuses on emerging workloads and was designed to contain a diverse selection of applications that is representative of next-generation shared-memory programs for chip-multiprocessors.

ParMiBench is an open source benchmark that specifically serves to measure performance on embedded systems that have more than one processor. This benchmark organize its applications into four categories and domains: industrial control and automotive systems, networks, office devices and security. Its set consists of 7 parallel applications implemented using PThreads.

SPEC is a closed source benchmark, but offers academic licenses. This benchmark is intended for general purpose architectures, but is subdivided into several groups with specific target architectures, and can be used for several purposes, such as: Java servers, file systems, high performance systems, CPU tests, among others. We consider the following groups of SPEC: SPEC MPI2007, SPEC OMP2012 and SPEC Power. SPEC MPI2007 is a set of 18 applications deployed in MPI focused on testing high performance computers. SPEC OMP2012 uses 14 scientific applications implemented in OpenMP, offering optional power consumption metrics based on SPEC Power. Finally, SPEC Power tests the power consumption and performance of servers using CPU/Memory-Bound applications implemented in C and Fortran.

HPL consists of a software package that solves arithmetic dual floating-point precision random linear systems in high performance architectures. It runs a testing and timing program to quantify the accuracy of the solution obtained, as well as the time it took to compute. HPL code is open and consist of 7 applications form a collection of subroutines in Fortran, mostly CPU-Bound. Parallel implementations use MPI. HPL is the benchmark that makes up the so-called *High-Performance Computing Benchmark Challenge*, which is a list of the 500 fastest high performance computers in the world.

The NAS Parallel Benchmarks (NPB) is a set of open source programs generally used to evaluate the performance of parallel supercomputers. The benchmark is derived from physical applications of fluid dynamics and consists of four cores and three pseudo-applications in the original "pencil-and-paper" specification (NPB 1). It is an open source benchmark and the main set of applications is implemented with MPI and OpenMP.

**Table 1.** Comparison of our benchmark with the similar ones

| Rating criteria | ALPBench | PARSEC | ParMiBench | SPEC | HPL | NPB | Adept | Our benchmark |
|---|---|---|---|---|---|---|---|---|
| Number of applications | 5 | 11 | 7 | 14-18 | 7 | 12 | 10-12 | 11 |
| Number of PPIs | 1 | 3 | 1 | 2 | 1 | 2 | 3 | 4 |
| Number of communication models | 1 | 1 | 2 | 1 | 1 | 2 | 2 | 2 |
| Set of applications implemented in multiple PPIs | | | | | | | X | X |
| Open source | X | X | X | | X | X | X | X |

The Adept Benchmark is used to measure the performance and energy consumption of parallel architectures. Its code is open and is divided into 4 sets: Nano, Micro, Kernel and Application. The Micro suite, for example, consists of 12 sequential and parallel applications with OpenMP, focusing on specific aspects of the system, such as process management, caching, among others. On the other hand, the Kernel set has 10 applications implemented sequentially and parallel with OpenMP, MPI and one of them in UPC (Unified Parallel C).

## 3.2    Comparison Among the Benchmarks

The benchmark addressed in this work consist of 11 applications implemented in C and their complexities range from $O(n)$ to $O(n^3)$. All applications are parallelized in 4 PPIs: PThreads, OpenMP, MPI-1 and MPI-2. These PPIs are the target of this work because they are the most widespread in the academic field and also because they are supported by most multi-core architectures, both embedded and general purpose. Therefore, the purpose of this benchmark is to provide the user a tool to evaluate the performance and power consumption of different PPIs in embedded and general purpose multi-core architectures.

We analyze the main characteristics of the related parallel benchmarks and compare to the benchmark we propose in this work in Table 1. In relation to the benchmarks, some use only one PPI while others use more than one. However, some of those who use more than one PPI do not have the whole set of applications paralleled by all PPIs. They implement parts of the set with one PPI and other parts with another PPI. Three of these benchmarks use PThreads, five of them use OpenMP, and four use MPI. ALPBench also uses Intel TBB and Adept uses UPC.

Thus, even if some of these benchmarks implement three different PPIs, none of them allow an efficient comparison among these PPIs and communication models. Also, they do not exploit the parallelism with dynamic process creation that MPI-2 offers. In this way, we do not find any other benchmark that use different PPIs, different communication models and a completely parallelized set of applications. The exception is the NPB, but it only offers two PPIs. Therefore, none of them meets the objective of comparing parallel programming interfaces, which is the main objective of the benchmark we are proposing in this work.

# 4    Benchmark Applications

This section presents the 11 applications of the benchmark.

They were developed with the purpose of establishing a relation between performance and energy consumption in embedded systems and general purpose architectures [11]. Below are listed the applications detailing briefly each.

- **Gram-Schmidt**- The Gram-Schmidt process is a method for orthonormalising a set of vectors in an inner product space.
- **Matrix Multiplication** - This algorithm multiplies the lines of a matrix $A$ by the columns of a matrix $B$.
- **Dot Product** - The dot product is an algebraic operation that multiplies two equal-length sequences of numbers.
- **Odd-Even Sort** - It is a comparison sort algorithm related to bubble sort.
- **Dijkstra** - It finds a minimal cost path between nodes in a graph with non-negative edges.
- **Discrete Fourier Transform** - The discrete Fourier transform (DFT) converts a finite sequence of equally-spaced samples of a function into an equivalent-length sequence of equally-spaced samples of the discrete-time Fourier transform (DTFT), which is a complex-valued function of frequency.
- **Jacobi Method** - The Jacobi method is an algorithm for determining the solutions of a diagonally dominant system of linear equations.
- **Harmonic Sums** - The Harmonic Sums or Harmonic Series is a finite series that calculates the sum of arbitrary precision after the decimal point.
- **PI Calculation** - It applies the Gregory-Leibniz formula to find $\pi$.
- **Numerical Integration** - This algorithm integrates an $f(x)$ function in a given interval, using approximation techniques to define an area.
- **Turing ring** - It is a space system in which predators and prey interact in the same place. The system simulates the iteration and evolution of preys and predators through the use of differential equations.

These algorithms are used in the most diverse computing areas. Four of them are directly related to linear algebra. However, some other areas are also represented, some of them are: molecular dynamics, electromagnetism, digital signal processing, image processing, mathematical optimization, among others.

## 4.1    Parallelizing the Applications

Parallelize a sequential program can be done in several ways. However, inappropriate techniques can negatively impact the performance of an application. To minimize this problem, all parallel implementations in this work were based on statements from [2,3,6,14]. [14] propose that the parallelization be done in a systematic way, according to them, there are three fundamental steps for the parallelization of a sequential application, which are: computation decomposition; assigning tasks to processes/threads; mapping processes/threads into physical processing units.

The decomposition of the computation and assignment of tasks to processes/threads occurred explicitly in the parallelization with PThreads and MPI 1 and 2, in order to obtain the best workload balancing. Also were included message exchange functions among processes, as well as the dynamic creation of processes in MPI-2. For Parallelization with OpenMP, parallel loops with thin and coarse granularity were used. According to [3,14], this technique is most appropriate for parallelizing applications that perform iterative calculations and traverse contiguous data structures (eg matrix, vector, etc.). For each data structure a specific parallelization model was adopted.

### 4.2    Applications History

The set of applications that compose the benchmark have already been investigated in previous works. The applications were used in these works to analyze performance and energy consumption on embedded systems and general purpose processors. In [8,9,11] the authors classified the applications in CPU-Bound, Weakly Memory-Bound and Memory-Bound, according to the following criteria:

1. **Reads/writes to memory** - represents the number of accesses to the shared and private memory addresses of the processor, considering read and write operations for each application;
2. **Data dependence** - means that at least one thread/process can only start its execution when the computation result of one or more threads/processes is over. This shows the existence of communication among threads/processes;
3. **Synchronization points** - determine that at certain times during the execution of an application, all threads/processes will need to be synchronized before a new task starts.
4. **Thread-Level Parallelism** - shows how busy the processor is during application execution;
5. **Communication rate** - represents the volume of communication required by threads/processes during application execution.

In [10], the authors used the number of data exchange operations as criteria for classification. In the PPI target, these operations represents barriers, locks/unlocks and threads/processes creation or termination. Using this criteria, the applications were divided in High and Low Communication. The main problem with both classifications is that they were not done uniformly with all applications. The first classification used some applications with a specific interface, while another configuration was used to do a second classification. Hence, the four PPIs were never evaluated together. TLP, for example, was collected only for 9 applications and using only PThreads.

Already using the first criterion (access read/write to shared memory), the applications were classified in CPU-Bound and Memory-Bound. However, this type of data does not indicate how much CPU was actually used by a particular application. An application that performs many accesses to shared memory could also have a high CPU usage. In the opposite case, an application with few accesses to memory and previously classified as CPU-Bound, could also make less use of CPU in relation to the other application classified as Memory-Bound.

After that, in [4,5] the authors investigated the impact of each PPI in the use of CPU and memory. In these studies the authors classified the applications in such a way that all scenarios analyzed contained at least one application with: high CPU usage and high memory usage; high CPU usage and low memory usage; low CPU usage and high memory usage; or low CPU and memory usage. Finally, [12] used some of these applications to verify the best performance and energy consumption in different multi-core architectures.

Thus, gathering all these previous studies, it was concluded that this set contained applications diverse enough to characterize a benchmark. After all, they were already being used as a benchmark, but an effort was needed to unify them, to analyze the whole set together and prepare them for use by others. This is one of the main objectives of this work

## 5  Results

This section presents the methodology for evaluate the applications, presenting its complexity and the result for energy consumption and performance.

### 5.1  Methodology

The results presented in this section are the average of 30 executions disregarding the extreme values. This number of executions was established as indicated in [7]. In this study the authors perform experiments that show that the minimum number of executions is MPI in order to obtain statistically acceptable results. Following the indications of this study, the results in MPI-1 and MPI-2 showed a standard deviation below 0.5 in the worst cases. OpenMP and PThreads showed a standard deviation below 0.1 in all cases. During the experiments the computer remained locked to ensure that other applications did not interfere actively with the results.

The toolkit Intel® Performance Counter Monitor (PCM) 2.0 was used to measure energy consumption. It has a tool to monitor the power states of the processor and DRAM memory. For the runtime, the time at the beginning and at the end of the main function of each application was measured and the difference of these values was used.

One thing that is not simple to do when comparing different parallel applications is to set a workload that is equivalent to all of them. That way, we tested applications with small, medium, and large inputs. However, we choose to present in this work only the data referring to the medium sized inputs, since they allowed a better visualization of the results for most cases and are the same ones used in the previous works.

The Table 2 shows the size of the inputs used for each application, as well as the acronym used to identify each application in the following sections.

**Table 2.** Details about the applications

| Data structures | Problem size | Acronym | Application | Complexity |
|---|---|---|---|---|
| Unstructured data | 1 billion | NI | Numerical Integration | $O(n)$ |
| | 4 billion | PI | PI Calculation | |
| | 15 billion | DP | Dot Product | |
| Vector | 100000 | HA | Harmonic Sums | $O(n*d)$ |
| | 150000 | OE | Odd-Even Sort | $O(n^2)$ |
| | 32768 | DFT | Discrete Fourier Transf. | |
| Matrix | $2048 \times 2048$ | TR | Turing Ring | $O(m*n)$ |
| | | DJ | Dijkstra | $O(n^3)$ |
| | | JA | Jacobi Method | |
| | | MM | Matrix Multiplication | |
| | | GS | Gram-Schmidt | |

## 5.2 Complexity

The last column of the Table 2 presents the algorithmic complexity by application. Only the serial applications were used for this complexity analysis, which is based on the arithmetic operations of the algorithm. The complexity analysis for parallel applications is mainly based on execution time. However, several factors influence the complexity of parallel applications, such as load balancing and parallelization model, as [13] explain in their works.

The analysis of sequential complexities showed that the set of applications range from $O(n)$ to $O(n^3)$, with several other intermediate complexities. In this way, it is possible to conclude that the benchmark has enough diversity in this aspect to evaluate performance in different architectures.

## 5.3 Performance and Energy Consumption

The next experiments were carried out on a computer equipped with 2 Intel® Xeon® E5-2650 v3 processor. Each processor has 10 physical cores and 10 virtual cores operating at the standard 2.3 GHz frequency and turbo frequency of 3 GHz. Its memory system consists of three levels of cache: a 32 KB cache L1 and a 256 KB cache L2 for each core. Level L3 has a 25 MB cache for each processor using Smart Cache technology. The main memory (RAM) is 126 GB in size and DDR3 technology. The operating system is Linux version 4.4.0-128 using Intel® ICC 18.0.1 compiler with optimization flags.

The results of energy consumption and performance are arranged in the same graphs. Bars show the energy consumption in joules and correspond to the y-axis values on the left. The time in seconds is represented by the marker X and is aligned to the y-axis on the right. Each chart displays the results of each application individually. These results refer to running using 2, 4, 8, and 16 parallel threads/processes for each PPI. In addition, the first result of each graph represents the sequential execution of the respective application. The other sets refer to each of the PPIs, nominated at the top of each graph.

In all the graphs in Fig. 1, the scales of the two y-axes were adjusted so that both energy consumption and performance values for the sequential application were aligned at the same point. This allows an easier visualization of the impact of variation on the number of threads/processes.

Our initial hypothesis was that a higher use of the processor and memory system should cause an increase in energy consumption in proportion to the number of parallel threads/processes. But in addition, reducing the execution time of each application should reduce its consumption in proportion to the performance achieved over the sequential application. However if the sequential results were proportionally aligned in a graph, we should note that this proportion does not appear in the parallel versions. This is because there are other factors that impact on energy consumption, such as the need for communication among tasks and increasing the complexity of the control structures that the operating system has to deal with.

In Fig. 1, the applications between (a) and (i) in general show a result as expected in our initial hypothesis. However, the results show that the energy consumption of MPI-1 and MPI-2 is slightly higher in most cases. In addition, in applications that do more communication among tasks, such as GS and JA, energy consumption and runtime were about ten times higher for both MPI PPIs than the others. Following, the TR (Fig. 1d) application showed a different behavior when using PThreads. Except when using 16 threads, in the other cases this PPI had an increase in execution time in relation to the others. However, the energy consumption did not increase in a proportional way to the time, remaining close to the result of the other PPIs. A similar behavior, but with a worse scalability with PThreads, can be seen in OE.

OpenMP showed that its best trade-off between performance and energy consumption occurs using 8 threads. Observing the results of NI, TR, DP and OE, we can see that although there is a slight reduction in execution time with 16 threads, the energy consumption does not follow this reduction and it is the same seen with 8 threads. If we compare the three applications that only do iterative computation (DP, PI and NI), it can be seen that the execution time of DP and NI is smaller than PI (which still scaling with 16 threads). Therefore, the loss of scalability in the other two applications is certainly related to the size of the problem that was not adequate. In addition, all OpenMP results with 8 threads were smaller than the others in almost all cases. The easy structuring of parallelism with OpenMP ends up playing a fundamental role in these results when compared to manual parallelism using PThreads.

Regarding Odd-Even Sort (Fig. 1h), the results show that we obtained performance gains in all cases with both MPI-1 and MPI-2. However, with 16 OpenMP threads there was no performance gain or PThreads with 16 and 8 threads. What we have concluded, is that the average workload initially set, is not large enough for all cases. OE is a memory-bound application, so the overhead of communication/synchronization among threads begins to impact negatively earlier in

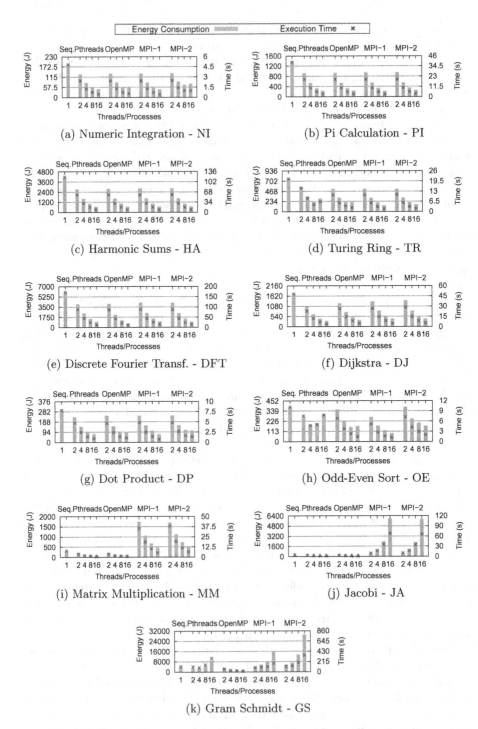

**Fig. 1.** Energy consumption and performance graphs for each application.

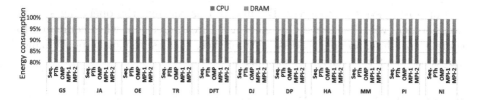

**Fig. 2.** Percentage of energy consumed by DRAM memory in relation to consumption by the CPU using 8 threads/processes.

these cases. With MPI, performance only begins to converge after 32 processes for this workload, but this result is not included in this work, because we are still implementing efficient workload distribution for many tasks in some applications.

It is expected that the more robust the architecture, the better the MPI results can be. In this way it was possible to observe a good scalability of MPI in the first cases. However, considering the last 3 cases, we can conclude that MPI is the worst case overall. In these three cases MPI did not have a good scalability and presented worse results than the sequential version. Considering only MPI-1 and MPI-2, the second one was the one with the worst results. A similar behavior was observed by the authors in [12]. Additionally, the applications that presented the worst results for MPI are the only ones in [4] and [5] that showed a higher memory usage than CPU usage during execution. In this way we can conclude that a high memory use has a strong negative impact on energy consumption.

The worst results among all the applications were obtained with GS. Not considering OpenMP, the other PPIs did not present a superior scalability in relation to the sequential version. It was also the application that obtained the highest energy consumption among all, with a peak of about 30.000 joules with 16 processes in MPI-2, but with a much shorter execution time. One of the reasons that MPI uses more energy than OpenMP accessing memory for the GS case is not that MPI is just inherently less efficient at accessing memory, but that using distributed memory requires redundant memory accesses. This way, more memory accesses are made.

Finally, we present in Fig. 2 the energy consumption results divided by CPU consumption and memory consumption. For all amounts of threads/processes the results did not vary much, therefore we only present the graph for 8 threads/processes. In this graph we can see that DRAM energy consumption is stable among PPIs in some cases, representing on average 10% of total consumption. In other cases, MPI-1 and MPI-2 always have a larger portion of energy destined for memory. In addition, the highest memory energy consumption occurs with MPI in GS. We will have to carry out another study to analyze the relation of this with the results obtained in Fig. 1.

The difference in these PPIs can be explained in the context of threads and processes. Threads are often referred as a lighter type of process for the system, while processes are heavier. Thread shares with other threads its code area, data, and operating system resources. Because of this sharing, the operating system needs to deal with less scheduling costs and thread creation, when compared to context switching among processes. All of these factors impact on performance and consequently on energy consumption.

# 6    Conclusions and Future Work

In this paper we present a set of applications that can be used as a benchmark. The main purpose of this benchmark is to analyze energy consumption and performance of PPIs in multi-core architectures. We first compared our proposed benchmark with the main parallel benchmarks that are currently used for the same purpose. This comparison showed that there is no benchmark that meets the proposed goal: to offer a simpler way to compare PPIs. In addition we did a study of the history of the applications, where we showed that there were already authors using them for the same purpose. This fact meant that there was no other benchmark that would efficiently meet this demand, so it was necessary to create one from scratch.

Our experimental results showed that the applications generally have a good performance gain. In addition, the overhead caused by the energy consumption showed a behavior proportional to the number of threads/processes used in parallel. The exceptions are two applications (JA and GS) that demonstrated an unexpected behavior, but equal with MPI-1 and MPI-2. Both should be further investigated in the course of our study to verify the relationship of these results to the fact that they have been classified as highly memory-bound applications in previous studies.

Some applications in our benchmark still require a few more adjustments, as you could see in the results. However most applications showed a pattern in relation to gain performance. In many cases we have achieved near optimal performance, reducing runtime twice with 2 threads, 4 times with 4 threads, and so on. In addition, energy consumption has also been reduced in the same proportion for this majority of cases. We conclude that after these adjustments, the applications will already be ready to be made available to the community for use in other studies.

As future works, we intend to verify how the distribution of threads/processes among different cores and processors affects our experiments. We should also repeat the experiments using another compiler, such as gcc without optimization flags. The next step is to check the scalability of our applications, so we will increase the number of threads/processes by varying the size of the workload (some preliminary tests have shown that MPI gets better trade-offs in these cases). Finally, we also consider including more PPIs such as Intel TBB, Cilk or UPC.

# References

1. Bourzac, K.: Supercomputing poised for a massive speed boost. Springer Nat. Int. J. Sci. (2017)
2. Butenhof, D.R.: Programming with POSIX Threads. Addison-Wesley Professional, Boston (1997)
3. Foster, I.: Designing and Building Parallel Programs. Addison Wesley Publishing Company, Boston (1995)
4. Garcia, A.M.: Classificação de um benchmark paralelo para arquiteturas multinúcleo (2016)
5. Garcia, A.M., Schepke, C.: Uma proposta de benchmark paralelo para arquiteturas multicore. XVIII Escola Regional de Alto Desempenho, pp. 285–289 (2018)
6. Gropp, W., Lusk, E., Thakur, R.: Using MPI-2: Advanced Features of the Message-Passing Interface. MIT press, Cambridge (1999)
7. Hunold, S., Carpen-Amarie, A.: Reproducible MPI benchmarking is still not as easy as you think. IEEE Trans. Parallel Distrib. Syst. **27**(12), 3617–3630 (2016)
8. Lorenzon, A.F., Cera, M.C., Beck, A.C.S.: Optimized use of parallel programming interfaces in multithreaded embedded architectures. In: VLSI (ISVLSI), Computer Society Annual Symposium on 2015 IEEE, pp. 410–415. IEEE (2015)
9. Lorenzon, A.F.: Avaliação do desempenho e consumo energético de diferentes interfaces de programação paralela em sistemas embarcados e de propósito geral. Master's thesis, Universidade Federal do Rio Grande do Sul (2014)
10. Lorenzon, A.F., Sartor, A.L., Cera, M.C., Beck, A.C.S.: The influence of parallel programming interfaces on multicore embedded systems. In: 2015 IEEE 39th Annual Computer Software and Applications Conference (COMPSAC), vol. 2, pp. 617–625. IEEE (2015)
11. Lorenzon, A.F., Cera, M.C., Beck, A.C.S.: Performance and energy evaluation of different multi-threading interfaces in embedded and general purpose systems. J. Sig. Process. Syst. **80**(3), 295–307 (2014)
12. Lorenzon, A.F., Cera, M.C., Beck, A.C.S.: Investigating different general-purpose and embedded multicores to achieve optimal trade-offs between performance and energy. J. Parallel Distrib. Comput. **95**, 107–123 (2016)
13. Mikloško, J., Kotov, V.E.: Complexity of parallel algorithms. In: Mikloško, J., Kotov, V.E. (eds.) Algorithms, Software and Hardware of Parallel Computers, pp. 45–63. Springer, Heidelberg (1984). https://doi.org/10.1007/978-3-662-11106-2_2
14. Rauber, T., Rünger, G.: Parallel Programming: For Multicore and Cluster Systems. Springer, Heidelberg (2010)

# Bigger Buffer $k$-d Trees
# on Multi-Many-Core Systems

Fabian Gieseke[1($\boxtimes$)], Cosmin Eugen Oancea[1], Ashish Mahabal[2],
Christian Igel[1], and Tom Heskes[3]

[1] Department of Computer Science, University of Copenhagen,
Universitetsparken 1, 2100 Copenhagen, Denmark
{fabian.gieseke,cosmin.oancea,igel}@di.ku.dk
[2] Caltech Astronomy, Caltech, 1200 East California Blvd, Pasadena, CA 91125, USA
aam@astro.caltech.edu
[3] Institute for Computing and Information Sciences, Radboud University Nijmegen,
Toernooiveld 212, 6525 EC Nijmegen, The Netherlands
t.heskes@cs.ru.nl

**Abstract.** A buffer $k$-d tree is a $k$-d tree variant for massively-parallel
nearest neighbor search. While providing valuable speed-ups on modern
many-core devices in case both a large number of reference and query
points are given, buffer $k$-d trees are limited by the amount of points that
can fit on a single device. In this work, we show how to modify the original
data structure and the associated workflow to make the overall approach
capable of dealing with massive data sets. We further provide a simple yet
efficient way of using multiple devices given in a single workstation. The
applicability of the modified framework is demonstrated in the context
of astronomy, a field that is faced with huge amounts of data.

## 1 Motivation

Nearest neighbor search is a fundamental problem and an ingredient of many
state-of-the-art data analysis techniques. While being a conceptually very simple
task, the induced computations can quickly become a major bottleneck in the
overall workflow when both a large reference and a large query set are given.
In the literature, many techniques have been proposed that aim at accelerating
the search. Typical ones are the use of spatial search structures, approximation
schemes, and parallel implementations [1,7,11]. A recent trend in the field of
big data analytics is the application of massively-parallel devices such as *graphics processing units* (GPUs) to speed up the involved computations. While such
modern many-core devices can significantly reduce the practical runtime, obtaining speed-ups over standard CPU-based execution is often not straightforward
and usually requires a careful adaptation of the sequential implementations.

Spatial search structures such as $k$-d trees are an established way to reduce
the computational requirements induced by nearest neighbor search for spaces
of moderate dimensionality (e.g., up to $d = 30$). A typical parallel $k$-d tree

© Springer Nature Switzerland AG 2019
H. Senger et al. (Eds.): VECPAR 2018, LNCS 11333, pp. 202–214, 2019.
https://doi.org/10.1007/978-3-030-15996-2_15

based search assigns one thread to each query and all threads process the same tree *simultaneously*. Such an approach, however, is not suited for GPUs since each thread might induce a completely different tree traversal, which results in massive branch divergence and irregular accesses to the device's memory.

Recently, we have proposed a modification of the classical $k$-d tree data structure, called *buffer $k$-d tree*, which aims at combining the benefits of both spatial search structures and massively-parallel devices [8]. The key idea is to assign an additional buffer to each leaf of the tree and to *delay* the processing of the queries reaching a leaf until enough work has been gathered. In that case, all queries stored in all buffers are processed together in a brute-force manner via the many-core device. While the framework achieves significant speed-ups on modern many-core devices over both a massively-parallel brute-force execution on GPUs as well as over a multi-threaded $k$-d tree based search running on multi-core systems, it is limited by the amount of reference and query points that fit on a GPU. In this work, we show how to remove this limitation by modifying the induced workflow to efficiently support huge reference and query point sets that are too large to be completely stored on the devices. This crucial modification renders buffer $k$-d trees capable of dealing with huge data sets.

## 2 Background

Modern many-core devices such as GPUs offer massive parallelism and can nowadays also be used for so-called *general-purpose computations* such as matrix-matrix multiplication. In contrast to standard CPU-based systems, GPUs rely on simplified control units and on a memory subsystem that does not attempt to provide the illusion of a uniform access cost to memory.

The main ingredients for an efficient many-core implementation are (1) exposing sufficient parallelism to fully utilize the device and (2) accessing the memory in an efficient way. The latter one includes techniques that

(a) hide the latency of the memory transfer between host and GPU, for example by overlapping the kernel execution with the memory transfer, and
(b) restructure the program in order to improve both spatial and temporal locality of reference to the global memory of the GPU.

Our implementation makes effective use of both ingredients.

### 2.1 Massively-Parallel Nearest Neighbor Computations

We address the problem of computing the $k \geq 1$ nearest neighbors of all points given in a query set $Q = \{\mathbf{q}_1, \ldots, \mathbf{q}_m\} \subset \mathbb{R}^d$ w.r.t. all points provided in a reference set $P = \{\mathbf{x}_1, \ldots, \mathbf{x}_n\} \subset \mathbb{R}^d$. Usually, the "closeness" between two points is defined via the Euclidean distance (which we will use), but other distance measures can be applied as well. Such nearest neighbor computations form the basis for a variety of methods both in data mining and machine learning including proximity-based outlier detection, classification, regression, density estimation, and dimensionality reduction. The task of computing the induced distances (and keeping track of the list of neighbors per object) can be addressed naively in a brute-force manner spending $\mathcal{O}(nm \cdot (d + \log k))$ time, which quickly becomes computationally very demanding. Massively-parallel computing can significantly reduce the runtime in this case as shown by Garcia *et al.* [7]. Still, for large query and reference sets, the computational requirements can become very large.

Various other approaches have been proposed in the literature that aim at taking advantage of the computational resources provided by GPUs in combination with other techniques [11,14]. The focus of this work is on massively-parallel processing of $k$-d trees. While several implementations have been proposed that address such traversals from a more general perspective (e.g., in the context of *ray tracing*) [10], these approaches are not suited for nearest neighbor search in moderate-sized feature spaces (i.e., $d > 3$), except for the recently proposed buffer $k$-d tree extension [8].

## 2.2   Nearest Neighbor Search via $k$-d Trees

Spatial search structures such as $k$-d trees can be used to speed up nearest neighbor search. $K$-d trees can be constructed as follows [1,6]: For a given point set $P$, a $k$-d tree is a binary tree with the root corresponding to $P$. The children of the root are obtained by splitting the point set into two (almost) equal-sized subsets, which are processed recursively. In their original form, $k$-d trees are obtained by resorting to the median values in dimension $i \bmod d$ to split a point set corresponding to a node $v$ at level $i$ (starting with the root at level 0).[1] The recursive process stops as soon as a predefined number of points are left in a subset. The $k$-d tree stores the splitting values in its internal nodes; the points corresponding to the remaining sets are stored in the leaves.

The tree structure can be used to accelerate nearest neighbor search: Let $\mathbf{q} \in \mathbb{R}^d$ be a query point. For the sake of exposition, we focus on $k = 1$ (the case of $k > 1$ neighbors works similarly). The overall search takes place in two phases. In the first one, the tree is traversed from top to bottom to find the $d$-dimensional cell (induced by the tree/splitting process) that contains the query point $\mathbf{q}$. Going down the tree can be conducted efficiently using the median values stored in the internal nodes of the $k$-d tree. In the second phase, the tree is traversed bottom-up, and on the way back to the root, subtrees are checked in case the query point is close to the corresponding splitting hyperplane. If the distance of the query point $\mathbf{q}$ to the hyperplane is less than the distance to the current nearest neighbor candidate, then the subtree is checked for better candidates (recursively). Otherwise, the whole subtree can be safely pruned (no recursion). Once the root is reached twice, the overall process stops and the final nearest neighbor candidate is returned.

Given a low-dimensional search space, it is usually sufficient to process a relatively small number of leaves, which results in a logarithmic runtime behavior (i.e., $\mathcal{O}(\log n)$ time per query in practice).

---

[1] Other splitting rules might be applied (e.g., according to the "longest" side).

## Algorithm 1. LAZYSEARCH [8]

**Require:** A chunk $Q = \{\mathbf{q}_1, \ldots, \mathbf{q}_m\} \subset \mathbb{R}^d$ of query points.
**Ensure:** The $k \geq 1$ nearest neighbors for each query point.
1: Construct buffer $k$-d tree $\mathcal{T}$ for $P = \{\mathbf{x}_1, \ldots, \mathbf{x}_n\} \subset \mathbb{R}^d$.
2: Initialize queue **input** with all $m$ query indices.
3: **while** either **input** or **reinsert** is non-empty **do**
4:     Fetch $M$ indices $i_1, \ldots, i_M$ from **reinsert** and **input**.
5:     $r_1, \ldots, r_M = \text{FINDLEAFBATCH}(i_1, \ldots, i_M)$
6:     **for** $j = 1, \ldots, M$ **do**
7:         **if** $r_j \neq -1$ **then**
8:             Insert index $i_j$ in buffer associated with leaf $r_j$.
9:         **end if**
10:    **end for**
11:    **if** at least one buffer is half-full (or queues empty) **then**
12:        $l_1, \ldots, l_N = \text{PROCESSALLBUFFERS}()$
13:        Insert $l_1, \ldots, l_N$ into **reinsert**.
14:    **end if**
15: **end while**
16: **return** list of $k$ nearest neighbors for each query point.

### 2.3 Revisited: Buffer $k$-d Trees

A standard multi-threaded kd-tree based traversal assigns one thread to each query. For GPUs, such an approach is not suited since each thread might induce a completely different path, which significantly shortens their computational benefits. The main idea of the buffer $k$-d tree extension is to delay the processing of the queries by buffering similar patterns prior to their common processing [8]. The reorganized workflow is based on buffer $k$-d trees, which are sketched next, followed by a description of the buffered nearest neighbor search.

A buffer $k$-d tree consists of (1) a top tree, (2) a leaf structure, (3) a set of buffers, and (4) two input queues that store the queries, see Fig. 1. The top tree corresponds to a classical $k$-d tree with its splitting values (e.g., medians) laid out in memory in a pointer-less manner. The leaf structure stores the point sets that stem from the splitting process in a

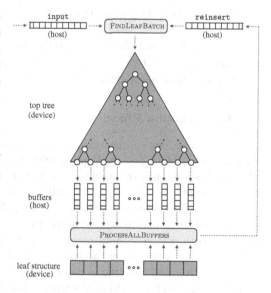

**Fig. 1.** A buffer $k$-d tree [8]: The gray elements are stored on the GPU.

consecutive manner. In addition, a buffer is attached to each leaf of the top tree that can store $B$ query indices (e.g., $B = 1024$). The input queues are used to store the input query indices and the query indices that need further processing after a `ProcessAllBuffers` call.

A buffer $k$-d tree can be used to delay the processing of the queries by performing several iterations, see Algorithm 1: In each iteration, the procedure FindLeafBatch retrieves indices from both the `input` and `reinsert` queue and propagates them through the top tree. The indices, which are stored in the corresponding buffers, are processed in chunks via the procedure `ProcessAllBuffers` once the buffers get full. All indices that need further processing (i.e., their implicit tree traversal has not reached the root twice) are inserted into `reinsert` again. Thus, in each iteration, one (1) finds the leaves that need to be processed next and (2) updates the queries' nearest neighbors.

While the first phase is not well-suited for massively-parallel processing, the second one is and, since it constitutes the most significant part of the runtime, yields valuable overall speed-ups. The main advantage of the reorganized workflow is that all queries are processed in the same block-wide SIMD instruction and exhibit either good spatial or temporal locality of reference, i.e., coalesced or cached global memory accesses. For details of the many-core implementation of the procedure PROCESSALLBUFFERS, we refer to Gieseke *et al.* [8].

## 3   Processing Bigger Trees

Both the top tree and the leaf structure need to be stored on the GPU—this limits the amount of reference patterns that can be processed. We now describe modifications that allow buffer $k$-d trees to scale to massive data sets.

### 3.1   Construction Phase

As shown below, one can basically process arbitrarily large query sets by considering chunks of data points. Dealing with huge reference sets, however, is more difficult: Since the top tree and the full leaf structure (that stores the rearranged reference points) have to be made available to all threads during the execution of PROCESSALLBUFFERS, one cannot directly split up the leaf structure. However, as explained next, one can avoid storing the leaf structure in its full entirety on the many-core device without significantly increasing the overall runtime.

We start by focusing on the space needed for the top tree: From a practical perspective, a small top tree is usually advantageous compared to the full tree used by a classical $k$-d tree-based search, since the efficiency gain on GPUs stems from processing "big" leaves. For instance, given a reference set $P \subset \mathbb{R}^{10}$ with two million points, top trees of height $h = 8$ or $h = 9$ are usually optimal [8]. Further, since only median values are stored in the top tree, the space consumption is negligible even given much bigger top trees. In addition, the top tree can be built efficiently via linear-time median finding [2], which results in $\mathcal{O}(h \log n)$ time for the whole construction phase.[2] Hence, one can (1) build the top tree efficiently on the host system and (2) store it in its full entirety on the GPU.

The main space bottleneck stems from the leaf structure. For instance, one billion points in $\mathbb{R}^{15}$ occupy about 60 GB of space—too much for a modern many-core device. For this reason, we do *not* copy the leaf structure from the host to the device after the construction of the top tree. Instead, we allocate space for two chunk buffers of fixed size on the many-core device. These chunk buffers will be used to overlap the execution of the PROCESSALL-BUFFERS procedure with the host-to-device memory transfer for the next chunk.[3] Note that we also allocate two associated memory buffers on the host (*pinned memory* [13]) to achieve efficient concurrent compute and copy operations. The overall memory layout is shown in Fig. 2, where the memory that is actually allocated on the device is sketched via gray rectangles.

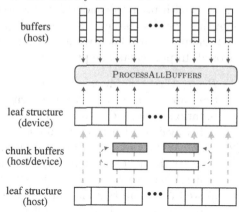

**Fig. 2.** Adapted memory layout

## 3.2 Query Phase

We now describe the details of the modified querying process.

**Processing the Leaf Structure:** In each iteration of Algorithm 1, the procedure PROCESSALLBUFFERS is invoked to retrieve all query indices from the leaf buffers. The queries are processed in a massively-parallel fashion, where each thread compares a particular query with all reference points stored in the associated leaf. Given the modified memory layout, one can now process the leaves in chunks in the following way: The leaf structure containing all $n$ rearranged reference points is split into $1 < N \ll n$ chunks $C_1, \ldots, C_N$ (e.g., $N = 10$). Each chunk $C_j$ contains the points of the leaf structure at positions $k = C_j^L, \ldots, C_j^R$, where $C_j^L = \lceil \frac{(j-1) \cdot n}{N} \rceil$ and $C_j^R = \lceil \frac{j \cdot n}{N} \rceil$. A buffer attached to the top tree corresponds to a leaf in the leaf structure with leaf bounds $0 \leq l_i < r_i \leq n - 1$. All queries removed from the buffers are then processed in $N$ iterations and a query $i$ with leaf bounds $l_i$ and $r_i$ is processed in iteration $j \in \{1, \ldots, N\}$ if $[l_i, r_i] \cap [C_j^L, C_j^R] \neq \emptyset$, i.e., if the leaf bounds overlap with chunk $C_j$.

---

[2] For a tree of height $h = 20$, suitable for more than one billion points, less than ten megabytes are needed. Note that the space for the buffers (e.g., of size 128 each) stored on the host does usually not cause any problems (e.g., less then a gigabyte).

[3] Note that we allocate space for two chunk *buffers* per device; the actual number $N$ of chunks being considered is usually larger (e.g., $N = 10$).

The chunks are processed sequentially $C_1, C_2, \ldots, C_N$. The data needed for each chunk is copied from the host to one of the two chunk buffers allocated on the device prior to conducting the brute-force computations, see Fig. 2. To hide the overhead induced for these copy operations, the copy process for the next chunk is started as soon as the computations for its predecessor have been invoked. In particular, the processing of a chunk $C_j$ takes place in three phases:

(1) *Brute:* First, the massively-parallel brute-force nearest neighbor computations are invoked (non-blocking kernel call). The data needed for these computations (chunk $C_j$) have been copied in round $j - 1$ (for $C_0$, the data is either available from an initial copy operation or from the previous round).

(2) *Copy:* While the brute-force computations are conducted by the GPU, the data for the next chunk are copied from host to the currently unused device buffer.[4] Note that copy operations on the host system have to be conducted as well to ensure that the correct part of the leaf structure is moved to the appropriate pinned memory buffer (which is then copied to the device).

(3) *Wait:* In the final phase, one simply waits for the kernel invoked in the first phase to finish its computations (blocking call).

The iterative compute-and-copy processing of the chunks can be implemented via two (OpenCL) command queues [13]: For the first chunk, phase (1) and (3) are instantiated via command queue A, whereas the copy process (2) is instantiated via command queue B (non-blocking for both (1) and (2)). For the second chunk, phases (1) and (3) are instantiated via command queue B and (2) via command queue A. This process continues until all chunks have been processed. In essence, the use of two command queues allows the copy phase (2) to run in parallel with the brute-force computation phases (1) and (3).

**Multi-Many-Core Querying:** Assuming that a fixed amount of memory is available on the many-core device to store the query patterns and the results at all times (e.g., one gigabyte), one can process an arbitrarily large query set by removing fully processed indices and by adding new indices on-the-fly, see Algorithm 1. An even simpler approach is to split up the queries into chunks and to handle these chunks independently. One drawback of the latter approach could be the overhead induced by applying the procedure ProcessAllBuffers in case the buffers are not sufficiently filled (which usually takes place as soon as no queries are available anymore). However, given relatively large chunks, the induced overhead is very small as shown in our experimental evaluation.

In a similar fashion, one can make use of multiple many-core devices by splitting all queries into "big" chunks according to the devices that are available. These chunks, which might have to be split into smaller chunks as described above, can be processed independently from each other.

---

[4] For $j = N$, the data for chunk 0 are copied from host to the corresponding buffer on the device for next round (i.e., next call of PROCESSALLBUFFERS).

# 4    Experiments

The purpose of the experiments provided below is to analyze the efficiency of the modified workflow and to sketch the potential of the overall approach in the context of large-scale scenarios. For a detailed experimental comparison including an analysis of the different processing phases and the influence of parameters related to the buffer $k$-d tree framework, we refer to our previous work [8].

## 4.1    Experimental Setup

All runtime experiments were conducted on a standard desktop computer with an `Intel(R) Core(TM) i7-4790K` CPU running at 4.00 GHz (4 cores; 8 hardware threads), 32 GB RAM, and two `Nvidia GeForce Titan Z` GPUs (each consisting of two devices with 2880 shader units and 6 GB main memory) using single precision. The operating system was `Ubuntu 14.4.3 LTS` (64 Bit) with kernel `3.13.0-52`, `CUDA 7.0.65` (graphics driver 340.76), and `OpenCL 1.2`. All algorithms were implemented in `C` and `OpenCL`, where `Swig` was used to obtain appropriate `Python` interfaces.[5] The code was compiled using `gcc-4.8.4` at optimization level `-O3`.

For the experimental evaluation, we report runtimes for both the construction and the query phase (referred to as "train" and "test" phases), where the focus is on the latter one (that makes use of the GPUs). We consider the following three implementations:

(1)  `bufferkdtree(i)`: The adapted buffer $k$-d tree implementation with both `FindLeafBatch` and `ProcessAllBuffers` being conducted on $i$ GPUs.
(2)  `kdtree(i)`: A multi-core implementation of a $k$-d tree-based search, which runs $i$ threads in parallel on the CPU (each handling a single query).
(3)  `brute(i)`: A brute-force implementation that makes use of $i$ GPUs to process the queries in a massively-parallel manner.

The parameters for the buffer $k$-d tree implementation were fixed to appropriate values.[6] Note that both competitors of `bufferkdtree` have been evaluated extensively in the literature; the reported runtimes and speed-ups can thus be put in a broad context. For simplicity, we fix the number $k$ of nearest neighbors to $k = 10$ for all experiments.

We focus on several data-intensive tasks from the field of astronomy. Note that a similar runtime behavior can be observed on data sets from other domains as well as long as the dimensionality of the search space is moderate (e.g., from $d = 5$ to $d = 30$). We follow our previous work and consider the `psf_mag`, `psf_model_mag`, and `all_mag` data sets of dimensionality $d = 5$, $d = 10$, and $d = 15$, respectively; for a description, we refer to Gieseke et al. [8]. In addition, we consider a new dataset derived from the *Catalina Realtime Transient Survey*

---

[5] The code is publicly available under https://github.com/gieseke/bufferkdtree.
[6] For a tree of height $h$, we fixed $B = 2^{24-h}$ and the number $M$ of indices fetched from `input` and `reinsert` in each iteration of Algorithm 1 to $M = 10 \cdot B$.

(crts) [4,9]. This survey contains tens to hundreds of observations for more than 500 million sources over a large part of the sky. The resulting light-curves (time-series of light received as a function of time) are used to derive several statistical features.[7] We use ten such features on a set of 30 million light-curves for the experiments described here.

## 4.2  Modified Workflow

While the modified workflow permits the use of buffer $k$-d trees for massive data sets that do not fit in the memories of the many-core devices, it might also induce a certain overhead compared to its original version due to the induced copy operations and reduced workload per kernel call.

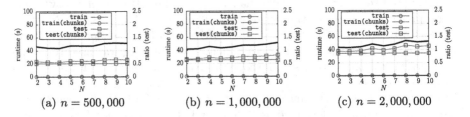

(a) $n = 500,000$    (b) $n = 1,000,000$    (c) $n = 2,000,000$

**Fig. 3.** Comparison of the training and testing times between the original workflow (train and test) and the modified workflow that processes the leaves in chunks (train(chunks) and test(chunks)). A varying number $N$ of chunks and training points $n$ are considered using the psf_model_mag data set. The number $m$ of test patterns and the tree height $h$ are fixed to $m = 10,000,000$ and $h = 9$, respectively. The ratio between test and test(chunks) is shown as black, thick line (a value close to 1 indicates a small overhead caused by the chunked processing).

**Processing Leaves in Chunks:** The main modification is the different processing of the leaf structure in case it does not fit in the device's memory. To evaluate the potential overhead caused by the additional copy operations (between host and device) during the execution of PROCESSALLBUFFERS, we consider data set instances that still fit in memory and compare the runtimes of (1) the original workflow with (2) the workflow that is based on multiple chunks.

In Fig. 3, the outcome of this comparison is shown for a varying number $N$ of chunks and a varying number $n$ of training points. In all three cases, the number of test patterns is fixed to $m = 10,000,000$. Further, the tree height is set to $h = 9$ and a single GPU is used (i.e., bufferkdtree(1)). Two observations can be made: First, the training time is very small compared to the test time for all cases (even though the tree is constructed sequentially on the host). Second, the performance loss induced by the chunked processing is very small for almost any number $N$ of chunks (i.e., the ratio shown as black, thick line is close to 1). In

---

[7] In particular, we make use of the *amplitude*, $Stetson_j$, $Stetson_k$, $Skew$, $fpr_{mid35}$, $fpr_{mid50}$, $fpr_{mid65}$, $fpr_{mid80}$, *shov*, *maxdiff* [5].

particular, this is the case for smaller values of $N$; using more chunks naturally yields more overhead due to, e.g., smaller leaf blocks being processed per kernel call. This overhead, however, decreases again if one increases the number of training and test patterns.

Thus, the runtimes of the new, chunked workflow are close to the one of the original approach—indicating that the overlapping compute-and-copy process successfully hides the additional overhead for the copy operations.

**Multi-Many-Core Processing:** As outlined above, one can simply distribute the test queries to multiple devices to take advantage of the additional computational resources. Again, this can lead to a certain overhead, since invoking the procedure PROCESSALLBUFFERS becomes less efficient at the end of the overall processing (and this happens earlier in case the test queries are split into chunks). Similarly to the experiment provided above, we compare the efficiency of bufferkdtree(4) with the one of bufferkdtree(1), a standard single-device processing with all test patterns fitting on the GPU. For this sake, we consider $N = 1$ leaf chunks (i.e., no modified processing of the leaves), $n = 2 \cdot 10^6$ training patterns, and vary the number $m$ of test patterns.

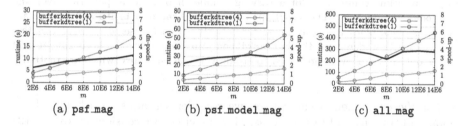

(a) psf_mag          (b) psf_model_mag          (c) all_mag

**Fig. 4.** Runtime comparison for the test phase between bufferkdtree(1) and bufferkdtree(4), where the test queries are distributed uniformly among the devices for the latter one. The speed-up is shown as black, thick line (maximum 4).

The outcome of this experiment for three different data sets is shown in Fig. 4: It can be seen that a suboptimal speed-up of about 2 is achieved in case a relatively small amount of test patterns is processed. However, as soon as the number of test patterns increases, the speed-up gets closer to 4, which depicts the maximum that can be achieved. Hence, the naive way of using all devices in a given workstation does not yield significant drawbacks as soon as large-scale scenarios are considered, which is the scope of this work.

### 4.3   Large-Scale Applications

To demonstrate the potential of the modified framework, we consider two large-scale tasks: (1) the application of nearest neighbor models that are based on very large training sets and (2) large-scale density-based outlier detection.

**Huge Nearest Neighbor Models:** The first scenario addresses nearest neighbor models that are based on very large training sets. Such models have been successfully been applied for various tasks in astronomy including the detection of distant galaxies or the estimation of physical parameters [12].

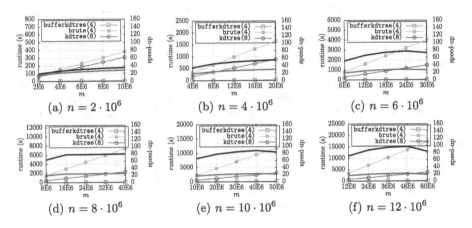

**Fig. 5.** Runtime comparison for a varying number $n$ of training patterns given the `psf_model_mag` data set. The speed-ups of `bufferkdtree` over `brute` and `kdtree` are shown as thick black and gray lines, respectively. In each case, $m = n, \ldots, 5n$ test patterns are considered for the `bufferkdtree` implementation; for both `kdtree` and `brute`, only $m = 10^6$ were processed to obtain runtime estimates (which are plotted).

For the experimental comparison we consider scenarios with both a large amount of training and test patterns. More precisely, we consider up to $n = 12 \cdot 10^6$ training points and up to $m = 5 \cdot n$ test points given the `psf_model_mag` data set. For both tree-based methods, appropriate tree depths are set beforehand (i.e., optimal ones w.r.t. the runtime needed in the test phase). The outcome of this comparison is shown in Fig. 5: It can be seen that valuable speed-ups can be achieved over both competitors. Further, the speed-ups generally become more significant the more patterns are processed. Note that for Fig. (e) and (f), the number $N$ of chunks is (automatically) set to $N = 3$ for the `bufferkdtree` implementation due to the training patterns exceeding the space reserved for them on the device. This results in a slightly worse performance for $m > 30 \cdot 10^6$.

**Large-Scale Proximity-Based Outlier Detection:** As final use case, we consider large-scale proximity-based outlier detection. Various outlier scores have been proposed that are based on the computation of nearest neighbors. A typical one is to rank the points according to their average distance according to their $k$ nearest neighbors, see, e.g., Tan *et al.* [15]. Such techniques depict very promising tools in case many reference points are given in a moderate-sized feature space, which is precisely the case for many tasks in astronomy. Typically, these scores require the computation of the nearest neighbors for each of the reference points, which can quickly become very time-consuming.

To show the potential of our many-core implementation, we consider the `crts` data set described above (with $d = 10$ features) and vary the number $n$ of reference points (here, we have $n = m$ for the full data set). We again compare the performances of all three competitors, where we consider both the runtime for the construction and the one for the query phase. The outcome is shown in Fig. 6. Note

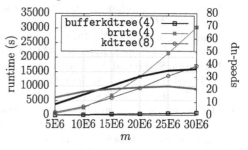

**Fig. 6.** Large-scale outlier detection

that the runtimes for both `kdtree(8)` and `brute(4)` depict estimates based on a reduced query due to the computational complexity (i.e., up to $n = 30 \cdot 10^6$ reference points and a fixed query set of size $\hat{m} = 1,000,000$ are considered; the runtime estimates w.r.t. the full data set instances are plotted). For the `bufferkdtree(4)` implementation, we fix $N = 3$. It can be seen that the buffer *k*-d tree implementation yields valuable speed-ups and can successfully process the whole data set in a reasonable amount of time.

# 5   Conclusions and Outlook

We showed how to modify and extend buffer *k*-d trees such that the overall workflow is capable of dealing with both massive training and massive testing tests. In addition, we provided a simple way of making use of multiple many-core devices that are often given in modern workstations. We further demonstrated the applicability of our modifications in the context of astronomy.

In future, it would be interesting to extend our results to other spatial search structures such as random projection trees [3] and distributed computing environments. We also expect our implementation to be applicable and useful for a variety of other application domains as well. We plan to extend our work along these lines of research.

**Acknowledgements.** The authors would like to thank the *Radboud Excellence Initiative* of the Radboud University Nijmegen (FG), *NVIDIA* for generous hardware donations (FG), the *Danish Industry Foundation* through the *Industrial Data Analysis Service* (FG, CI, CO), the *The Danish Council for Independent Research | Natural Sciences* through the project *Surveying the sky using machine learning* (CI), and ACP, IUCAA, IUSSTF, and NSF (AM).

# References

1. Bentley, J.: Multidimensional binary search trees used for associative searching. Commun. ACM **18**(9), 509–517 (1975)
2. Blum, M., Floyd, R.W., Pratt, V., Rivest, R.L., Tarjan, R.E.: Time bounds for selection. J. Comput. Syst. Sci. **7**(4), 448–461 (1973)
3. Dasgupta, S., Freund, Y.: Random projection trees and low dimensional manifolds. In: Proceedings of the Fortieth Annual ACM Symposium on Theory of Computing, pp. 537–546. ACM, New York (2008)
4. Djorgovski, S.G., et al.: The catalina real-time transient survey. In: Monitoring Variable X-Ray Sources, The First Year of MAXI (2011)
5. Faraway, J., Mahabal, A., Sun, J., Wang, X., Yi, W., Zhang, L.: Modeling light curves for improved classification. eprint arXiv:1401.3211 (2014)
6. Friedman, J., Bentley, J., Finkel, R.: An algorithm for finding best matches in logarithmic expected time. ACM Trans. Math. Softw. **3**(3), 209–226 (1977)
7. Garcia, V., Debreuve, E., Nielsen, F., Barlaud, M.: K-nearest neighbor search: fast GPU-based implementations and application to high-dimensional feature matching. In: Proceedings of the 17th IEEE International Conference on Image Processing, pp. 3757–3760. IEEE (2010)
8. Gieseke, F., Heinermann, J., Oancea, C., Igel, C.: Buffer k-d trees: processing massive nearest neighbor queries on GPUs. In: Proceedings of the 31st International Conference on Machine Learning. JMLR W&CP, vol. 32, pp. 172–180 (2014)
9. Mahabal, A.A., et al.: Discovery, classification, and scientific exploration of transient events from the catalina real-time transient survey. Bull. Astronmical Soc. India **39**(3), 387–408 (2011)
10. Nakasato, N.: Implementation of a parallel tree method on a GPU. J. Comput. Sci. **3**(3), 132–141 (2012)
11. Pan, J., Manocha, D.: Fast GPU-based locality sensitive hashing for k-nearest neighbor computation. In: Proceedings of the 19th ACM SIGSPATIAL International Conference on Advances in Geographic Information Systems, pp. 211–220. ACM (2011)
12. Polsterer, K., Zinn, P., Gieseke, F.: Finding new high-redshift quasars by asking the neighbours. Monthly Not. R. Astron. Soc. **428**(1), 226–235 (2013)
13. Scarpino, M.: OpenCL in Action: How to Accelerate Graphics and Computation. Manning, New York (2012)
14. Sismanis, N., Pitsianis, N., Sun, X.: Parallel search of k-nearest neighbors with synchronous operations. In: IEEE Conference on High Performance Extreme Computing, pp. 1–6. IEEE (2012)
15. Tan, P.N., Steinbach, M., Kumar, V.: Introduction to Data Mining. Addison-Wesley, Boston (2005)

# A Parallel Generator of Non-Hermitian Matrices Computed from Given Spectra

Xinzhe Wu[1,2(✉)], Serge G. Petiton[1,2], and Yutong Lu[3]

[1] Maison de la Simulation, CNRS, 91191 Gif-sur-Yvette Cedex, France
[2] CRIStAL, UMR CNRS 9189, University of Lille, Villeneuve d'Ascq, France
{xinzhe.wu.etu,serge.petiton}@univ-lille.fr
[3] National Supercomputing Center in Guangzhou,
Sun Yat-sen University, Guangzhou, China
yutong.lu@nscc-gz.cn

**Abstract.** Iterative linear algebra methods are the important parts of the overall computing time of applications in various fields since decades. Recent research related to social networking, big data, machine learning and artificial intelligence has increased the necessity for non-hermitian solvers associated with much larger sparse matrices and graphs. The analysis of the iterative method behaviors for such problems is complex, and it is necessary to evaluate their convergence to solve extremely large non-Hermitian eigenvalue and linear problems on parallel and/or distributed machines. This convergence depends on the properties of spectra. Then, it is necessary to generate large matrices with known spectra to benchmark the methods. These matrices should be non-Hermitian and non-trivial, with very high dimension. This paper highlights a scalable matrix generator that uses the user-defined spectrum to construct large-scale sparse matrices and to ensure their eigenvalues as the given ones with high accuracy. This generator is implemented on CPUs and multi-GPU platforms. Good strong and weak scaling performance is obtained on several supercomputers. We also propose a method to verify its ability to guarantee the given spectra.

**Keywords:** Parallel · Non-Hermitian Matrix · Matrix generation · Spectrum

## 1 Introduction

The eigenvalue problem can be defined as finding some pairs $(\lambda, u)$ with $\lambda \in \mathbb{C}$ and $u \in \mathbb{C}^m$ of matrix $A \in \mathbb{C}^{m \times m}$, that satisfy the relation $Au = \lambda u$. Many applications from various fields can be expressed as eigenvalue problems or linear system problems. In numerical simulations, Schrödinger equations, wave mode

This work was partially supported by the HPC Center of Champagne-Ardenne *Romeo*. It is funded by the project *MYX* of *French National Research Agency (ANR)* (Grant No. ANR-15-SPPE-003) under the SPPEXA framework.

© Springer Nature Switzerland AG 2019
H. Senger et al. (Eds.): VECPAR 2018, LNCS 11333, pp. 215–229, 2019.
https://doi.org/10.1007/978-3-030-15996-2_16

analysis [8], etc. are usually analyzed by solving eigenvalue problems and linear systems. In machine learning and pattern recognition, both supervised and unsupervised learning algorithms, such as principal component analysis (PCA), Fisher discriminant analysis (FDA), and clustering, often require solving eigenvalue problems. An insufficient accuracy and a failure of the solvers usually result in, respectively, a poor approximation to original problems and a failure of entire algorithms. A good selection of eigenvalue and linear system solvers becomes especially essential. Researchers urgently require test matrices to benchmark the numerical performance and parallel efficiency of these methods.

Nowadays, the size of eigenvalue/linear system problems and the supercomputer systems continues to scale up. The whole ecosystem of High Performance Computing (HPC), especially the linear algebra applications, should be adjusted to larger computing platforms. Under this background, there are four special requirements for the test matrices to evaluate the numerical algorithms: (1) the spectra must be known and can be customized; (2) sparse, non-Hermitian and non-trivial; (3) a very high dimension, including the non-zero element numbers and/or the matrix dimension to evaluate the algorithms on large-scale systems; (4) the controllable sparsity patterns. The matrix generator should be implemented in parallel to profit from the distributed memory clusters.

Since the eigenvalue/linear system solvers and some of their preconditioners are sensitive to a specific part of the spectra, the test matrices with customized spectra can help to analyze and provide numerically robust solvers. In practice, the spectrum is one of the important factors which influence the convergence of different solvers. Although the impact of spectral distribution of linear system on the Krylov solvers is complicated and cannot be ignored even for the normal matrix [7], the existence of test matrix generator with customized eigenvalues can still guide the study of numerical method. Moreover, the purpose of most preconditioners such as ILU, Jacobi, and SOR is to convert the distribution of related spectrum to another by right or left-multiplying a preconditioning matrix. The spectral distribution of the preconditioned matrix might speed up the convergence. As an example, Wu and Petiton [14] et al. implemented a Unite and Conquer hybrid method for solving linear systems with the combination of a Krylov linear system solver, an eigenvalue solver, and a Least Square polynomial method proposed by Saad [11] in 1987. In the preconditioning part of this method, the dominant eigenvalues are used to accelerate the convergence. It is extremely necessary to evaluate the influence of the distribution of dominant eigenvalues on the acceleration. In addition, some scientific communities may be interested in matrices with clustered, conjugated eigenvalues or other special spectral distributions. It is important to develop a very large set of non-Hermitian test matrices whose eigenvalues can be customized.

The properties of being sparse, non-Hermitian and non-trivial together can add many mathematical features for the test matrices. Additionally, they should have very high dimensions for experiments on large scale platforms, which means that the proposed generation method should be easy to parallelize. Furthermore, since the enormous matrices are generated in parallel, their different slices are already distributed over separate computing units. These data can be used directly to evaluate the solvers, without having to load the large matrix from the file system. It can save time and increase the efficiency of the applications.

In this paper, we present a Scalable Matrix Generator from Given Spectra (SMG2S) to benchmark the linear/eigenvalue solvers on large-scale platforms. Firstly, it has been implemented in parallel based on PETSc (Portable, Extensible Toolkit for Scientific Computation) for homogenous platforms and PETSc+CUDA (Compute Unified Device Architecture) for multi-GPU heterogeneous machines. Then an open source package[1] is available, with specific communication optimization based on MPI and C++ [13]. Its scalability and ability to maintain the given spectra have been evaluated on different supercomputers.

This paper is organized as follows: Sect. 2 talks about the related work on the test matrix collections. Section 3 gives an overview of the proposed algorithm for matrix generation. The parallel implementation of SMG2S is discussed in Sect. 4. In Sect. 5, we evaluate its strong and weak scalability on two supercomputers. The eigenvalue accuracy of SMG2S is tested with different spectral distributions in Sect. 6. Finally, we conclude in Sect. 7.

## 2    Related Work

It's rare but there are already several efforts to supply test matrix collections. SPARSEKIT [10] implemented by Y. Saad contains various simple matrix generation subroutines. The Galeri package of Trilinos provides to generate simple well-known finite element matrices in parallel. Bai [1] presented a collection of test matrices for developing numerical algorithms for solving nonsymmetric eigenvalue problems. There are also two widely spread matrix providers, the Tim Davis [4] and Matrix Market collections [2]. They both contain many matrices from scientific fields with various mathematical characteristics. But the spectra of matrices in these collections are fixed, and cannot be customized. Chu [3] provides an overview of the inverse eigenvalues problems concerning the reconstruction of a structured matrix from prescribed spectrum without parallel implementation. A test matrix generation suite with given spectra was introduced by Demmel [5] in 1989 to benchmark the routines of dense matrices in LAPACK[2]. Their method uses an orthogonal matrix to transfer a diagonal matrix with given spectrum into dense with the same spectrum, and then transform the dense matrix into an unsymmetric one by Householder transform. This method is not suitable and efficient to test the solvers for the sparse matrix, because it requires $\mathcal{O}(n^3)$ time and $\mathcal{O}(n^2)$ storage even for generating a small bandwidth matrix. Furthermore, it was implemented for the shared memory systems rather than larger distributed memory systems, thus it is difficult to generate large-scale test matrices targetting for extreme-scale clusters. That is the motivation for us to propose SMG2S which can generate large-scale non-Hermitian matrices

---

[1] Released package download: https://smg2s.github.io/download.html.
[2] Linear Algebra PACKage.

with given spectra in parallel. This method requires much less time and storage, and can be easily parallelized on modern distributed memory systems.

## 3   Matrix Generation Algorithm

In this section, we introduce the proposed matrix generation algorithm. First of all, in Sect. 3.1, we present a summary of its mathematical framework based on the preliminary theorem proposed by Gachlier et al. [6].

### 3.1   Matrix Generation Method

**Theorem 1.** *Let's consider a collection of matrices $M(t) \in \mathbb{C}^{n \times n}$, $n \in \mathbb{N}^*$. If $M(t)$ verifies:*

$$\begin{cases} \dfrac{dM(t)}{dt} = AM(t) - M(t)A, \\ M(t = 0) = M_0. \end{cases}$$

*Then $M(t)$ and $M_0$ are similar. $M(t)$ has the same eigenvalues as $M_0$.*

Based on this theorem proposed by Gachlier [6], a matrix $M_0$ with given spectra can be transferred to another one $M(t)$ that satisfies *Theorem* 1 and keeps the spectra of $M_0$. Due to page limitation, we do not give the definitive proof of this theorem. We propose a matrix generation method by selecting many parameters such as the matrices $A$ and $M_0$.

Denote a linear operator of matrix $M$ determined by matrix $A$ as $\widetilde{A_A} = AM - MA$, $\forall A \in \mathbb{C}^{n \times n}$, $M \in \mathbb{C}^{n \times n}$, $n \in \mathbb{N}^*$. Here $AM$ and $MA$ are the matrix-matrix multiplication operation of matrices $A$ and $M$. By solving the differential equation in *Theorem* 1, we can firstly get the formule of $M(t)$ with the exponential operator and then extend it by the *Taylor series formula*:

$$\begin{cases} M(t) = e^{\widetilde{A_A}(M_0)t}, \\ M(t) = \displaystyle\sum_{k=0}^{\infty} \dfrac{t^k}{k!} (\widetilde{A_A})^k (M_0). \end{cases} \tag{1}$$

Through the loop $M_{i+1} = M_i + \frac{1}{i!}(\widetilde{A_A})^i(M_0), i \in (0, +\infty)$, a initial matrix $M_0 \in \mathbb{C}^{n \times n}$ can be transfered into a new non-trivial and non-Hermitian matrix $M_{+\infty} \in \mathbb{C}^{n \times n}$, which has the same spectra but different eigenvectors with $M_0$.

It is not reasonable to generate a matrix by infinity times of iterations, thus a good selection of matrix $A$ which can make $\widetilde{(A_A)}^i$ tends to $\mathbf{0}$ in limited steps is very necessary. In this paper, we define $A$ as a nilpotent matrix, which means that there exists an integer $k$ such that: $A^i = 0$ for all $i \geq k$. Such $k$ is called the nilpotency of $A$. In fact, the selection of nilpotent matrix will influence the sparsity pattern of the upper band of the generated matrix.

The exact shape of $A$ is given in Fig. 1a. Inside a $n \times n$ matrix $A$, its entries are default 0, except on the upper diagonal of the distance $p$ from the diagonal.

In this diagonal, its entries start with $d$ consecutive 1 and then a 0, this term repeats until the end. Matrix $A$ can be nilpotent by well choosing the parameters $p$, $d$ and $n$. The determination of $A$ to be nilpotent or not is complicated. Firstly, $d$ should be divisible by $p$, secondly, it should exist the integers $e$ and $f \in \mathbb{N}^*$ that makes $(d+1)e$ be divisible by $i + pf$, for all $i \in 1, 2, \cdots, \frac{d}{p}$. But the cases that $p = 1$ or $p = 2$ are very simple, which can completely fulfil our demands.

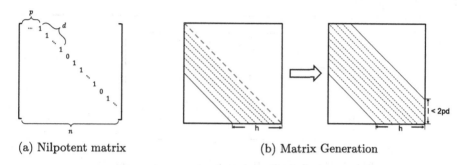

(a) Nilpotent matrix                    (b) Matrix Generation

**Fig. 1.** (a) Gives the nilpotent Matrix, with $p$ off-diagonal offset, $d$ number of continuous 1, and $n$ matrix dimension; (b) shows the matrix generation example.

If $p = 1$, with $d \in \mathbb{N}^*$, or $p = 2$ with $d \in \mathbb{N}^*$ to be even, the nilpotency of $A$ and the upper band's bandwidth of generated matrix are respectively $d + 1$ and $2pd$. Obviously, there is another constraint that the matrix size $n$ should be greater or equal to the upper band's width $2pd$. For $p = 2$, if $d$ is odd, the matrix $A$ will not be nilpotent, thus we do not take it into account.

### 3.2    Algorithm

As shown in Algorithm 1, the procedure of SMG2S is simple. Firstly, it reads an array $Spec_{in} \in \mathbb{C}^n$, as the given eigenvalues. Then it inserts entries in $h$ lower diagonals of the initial matrix $M_0$ randomly or with selected strategies, and sets its diagonal to be $Spec_{in}$, and scales it with $(2d)!$. Meanwhile, it generates a nilpotent matrix $A$ with the parameters $d$ and $p$. The final matrix $M_t$ can be generated as $M_t = \frac{1}{(2d)!} M_{2d}$, where $M_{2d}$ is the result after $2d$ times of loop $M_{i+1} = M_i + (\prod_{k=i+1}^{2d} k)(\widetilde{A_A})^i(M_0)$. The slight modification of the loop formula is to reduce the potential rounding errors coming from numerous division operations on modern computer systems.

For $M_t$, if $M_0$ is a lower triangular matrix having $h$ non zero diagonals, it will be a band diagonal matrix, whose number of new diagonals in the upper triangular zone will be at most $2pd - 1$. Thus the maximal number of the bandwidth of matrix $M_t$ is: $width = h + 2pd - 1$, as in Fig. 1b. In general, researchers use these matrices to test the iterative methods for sparse linear systems. The $h$ lower diagonals of the initial matrix can be set to be sparse, which ensures the

---

**Algorithm 1.** Matrix Generation Method

---

1: **function** MATGEN($input$:$Spec_{in} \in \mathbb{C}^n$, $p$, $d$, $h$, $output$: $M_t \in \mathbb{C}^{n \times n}$)
2:     Insert the entries in $h$ lower diagonals of $M_o \in \mathbb{C}^{n \times n}$
3:     Insert $Spec_{in}$ on the diagonal of $M_0$ and $M_0 = (2d)!M_0$
4:     Generate nilpotent matrix $A \in \mathbb{C}^{n \times n}$ with selected parameters $d$ and $p$
5:     **for** $i = 0, \cdots, 2d - 1$ **do**
6:         $M_{i+1} = M_i + (\prod_{k=i+1}^{2d} k)(\widetilde{A}A)^i(M_0)$
7:     $M_t = \frac{1}{(2d)!}M_{2d}$

---

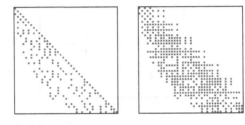

**Fig. 2.** Matrix generation sparsity pattern example.

sparsity of the final generated matrix, as shown in Fig. 2. Moreover, the permutation matrix can also be applied to further change the sparsity of the generated matrix.

The operation complexity of SMG2S is $max(\mathcal{O}(hdn), \mathcal{O}(d^2n))$. The worst case would require $\mathcal{O}(n^3)$ operations and $\mathcal{O}(n^2)$ memory storage with large $d$ and $h$. However, if we want to generate a band matrix with a small bandwidth, or if the lower band of $M_0$ is sparse, it becomes a $\mathcal{O}(n)$ problem with good potential scalability and consuming $\mathcal{O}(n)$ memory storage.

# 4     Parallel Implementation

In this section, we will introduce parallel implementations of SMG2S on homogeneous and heterogeneous clusters. Firstly, we implemented SMG2S based on PETSc on the CPUs, and based on MPI, CUDA, and PETSc on multi-GPU. We chose PETSc because it provides several ways to verify the generated matrices and the basic operations optimized for different computer architectures. After the PETSc-based SMG2S validation, an open source parallel software with specific optimized communication is also implemented based on MPI and C++.

## 4.1     Basic Implementation on CPUs

For the initial implementation, we chose PETSc instead of ScaLAPACK because we want to evaluate the solvers for sparse linear systems. The kernels of SMG2S are the sparse matrix-matrix multiplication (SpGEMM) $AM$ and $MA$, and the matrix-matrix addition (AYPX operation) as $AM - MA$. All the sparse matrices during the generation procedure are stored by the block diagonal Compressed Sparse Row (CSR) format which is supported in default by PETSc. This matrix format keeps separately the block diagonal and off-diagonal parts of a matrix on each process into two sequence CSR format matrices. We use the matrix operations SpGEMM and AYPX provided by PETSc to facilitate the implementation.

## 4.2   Implementation on Mutil-CPU

PETSc does not support SpGEMM and AXPY operations on multiple GPUs, so we implement them based on PETSc data structures, MPI, CUDA and, cuSPARSE. The implementation is given in Fig. 3, by an example of $A \times B$. Firstly, same as in PETSc, $A$ and $B$ are stored by the block CSR format, noted as $A_{dia}^i$, $A_{off}^i$, $B_{dia}^i$ and $B_{off}^i$ the sequence matrices on process $i$. Then $B_{dia}^i$ and $B_{off}^i$ are combined together as a novel sequence matrix as $B_{loc}^i$ on each process $i$. With MPI functionalities, each CPU gather all the remote data of matrix $B$ from the other processes, and construct them to a new sequence matrix $B_{oth}^i$. These matrices from each process are copied to one attached GPU, and calculate $C^i = A_{dia}^i B_{loc}^i + A_{off}^i B_{oth}^i$. The matrix operations on each GPU device is supported by the cuSPARSE. The final result $C$ can be obtained by gathering all slices $C_i$ from all the devices.

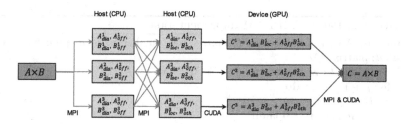

**Fig. 3.** The structure of a CPU-GPU implementation of SpGEMM, where each GPU is attached to a CPU. The GPU is in charge of the computation, while the CPU handles the MPI communication among processes.

## 4.3   Specific Optimized Communication Implementation on CPUs

In fact, the parallel SpGEMM kernel's communication can be specifically optimized based on the particular property of nilpotent matrix $A$. Since $A$ is determined by three parameters $p$, $d$ and $n$ as we mentioned in Sect. 3.1, it is not necessary to explicitly implement this parallel matrix. We note this nilpotent matrix as $A(p, d, n)$. Denote $J(i, j)$ the entry in row $i$ and column $j$ of matrix $J$; $J(i, :)$ all the entries of row $i$; and $J(:, j)$ all the entries of column $j$. As shown in Fig. 4, the right-multiplication $A(p, d, n)$ will cause all the entries of the first $n-p$ columns of $M$ to shift right by an offset $p$. Denote $MA$ the result gotten by the right-multiplying $A$ on $M$. We have $MA(:, j) = M(:, j - p), \forall j \in p, \cdots, n - 1$, and $MA(:, j) = 0, \forall j \in 0, \cdots, p - 1$. Similarly, the left-multiplying $A(p, d, n)$

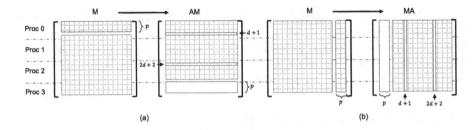

**Fig. 4.** (a) AM operation; (b) MA operation.

on $M$ will shift up the whole entries of last $n - p$ rows by an offset $p$. Denote $AM$ the matrix gotten by the left-multiplying $A$ on $M$. We have $AM(i,:) = M(i+p,:), \forall i \in 0, \cdots, n-p-1$, and $AM(i:,) = 0, \forall i \in p, \cdots, n-1$. Moreover, the parameter $d$ decides that $MA(:, r(d+1)) = 0$ and $AM(r(d+1),:) = 0$ with $r \in 1, \cdots, \lfloor \frac{n}{d+1} \rfloor$.

For the parallel implementation on distributed memory systems, the three parameters $p$, $d$ and $n$ can be shared by all MPI processes, then operations $AM$ and $MA$ are different from a general parallel SpGEMM. Firstly, the matrix $M$ is one-dimensional distributed by row across $m$ MPI process. As shown in Fig. 4b,

---

**Algorithm 2.** Parallel MPI AM Implementation

1: **function** AM(*input*: matrix $M$, matrix row number $n$, $p$, $d$, proc number $m$;
   *output*: matrix $AM$)
2:    Distribute $t$ row blocks $M_k$ of $M$ to MPI process $k$
3:    **for** $p + 1 \leq i < t$ **do**
4:       **for** $0 \leq j < n$ **do**
5:          **if** $M(i,j) \neq 0$ **then**
6:             $AM_k(i - p, j) = M_k(i, j)$
7:    **for** $0 \leq i < p$ **do**
8:       **if** $k \neq 0$ **then**
9:          *isend ith row* $M_k(i)$ *to* $k - 1$
10:      **if** $k \neq m - 1$ **then**
11:         *irecv ith row* $M_k(i)$ *from* $k + 1$
12:         $AM_k(t - p + i) = M_k(i)$

---

**Algorithm 3.** Parallel MPI MA Implementation

1: **function** MA(*input*: matrix $M$, matrix row number $n$, $p$, $d$, proc number $m$;
   *output*: matrix $MA$)
2:    Distribute $t$ row blocks $M_k$ of $M$ to process $k$
3:    **for** $0 \leq i < t$ **do**
4:       **for** $p + 1 \leq j < n$ **do**
5:          **if** $M_k(i, j) \neq 0$ **then**
6:             $MA_k(i, j + p) = M_k(i, j)$

---

for $MA$, there is no communication inter different MPI processes since the data are moved inside each row. Ensure that $\lfloor \frac{n}{m} \rfloor \geq p$, for $AM$, the intercommunication of MPI takes place when the MPI process $k$ ($k \in 1, \cdots, m-1$) should send the first $p$ rows of their sub-matrix to the closest previous MPI process numbering $k-1$. The communication complexity for each process is $\mathcal{O}(np)$. When generating the band matrix with low bandwidth $b$, it tends to be a $\mathcal{O}(bp)$ with $p = 1$ or 2. The MPI-based optimization implementations of $AM$ and $MA$ are respectively given by Algorithms 2 and 3. The communication inter MPI process is implemented by the asynchronous sending and receiving functions. In this algorithm, $M_k$, $MA_k$ and $AM_k$ imply the sub-matrices on process $k$ with $t$ rows. The rows and columns of these sub-matrices in Algorithms 2 and 3 are all indexed by the local indices.

The communication-optimized SMG2S is implemented based on MPI and C++. The submatrix on each process is stored in ELLPACK format, using the key-value map containers provided by C++. The key-value map implementation facilitates the indexing and moving of the rows and columns. We did not implement a GPU version of SMG2S with this kind of communication optimization since its core is the data movement among different computing units, which is not well suitable for the multi-GPU architecture.

## 5    Performance Evaluation

### 5.1    Hardware Environment

In experiments, we install SMG2S on the supercomputers *Tianhe-2* and *Romeo*. *Tianhe-2* is installed at National Super Computer Center in Guangzhou, China, with 16000 compute nodes. Each node composes 2 Intel Ivy Bridge 12 cores @ 2.2 GHz. *Romeo* is located at University of Reims Champagne-Ardenne, France, which is a heterogeneous system with 130 BullX R421 nodes. Each node composes 2 Intel Ivy Bridge 8 cores @ 2.6 GHz and 2 NVIDIA Tesla K20x GPUs.

### 5.2    Strong and Weak Scalability Results and Analysis

In this section, we will use double-precision real and complex values to evaluate the strong and weak scalability of SMG2S's different implementations on CPU and multiple GPUs. All the test matrices in this paper are generated with the $h$ set to be 10 and $d$ to be 7. The details of the weak scaling experiments are given in Table 1. The matrix size of the strong scaling experiments on $Tianhe-2$ with CPUs, $ROMEO$ with CPUs and $ROMEO$ with GPUs are respectively $1.6 \times 10^7$, $3.2 \times 10^6$ and $8.0 \times 10^5$. The results are given in Fig. 5. The weak scaling for the PETSc implementation of SMG2S on *Tianhe-2* trends to be bad when MPI processes number is larger than 768, where the communication overhead becomes dominant for computation. But for the communication optimized SMG2S, both the strong and weak scaling perform well when the MPI process number is larger than 768. The experiments show that SMG2S implemented with

**Table 1.** Details for weak scaling and speedup evaluation.

(a) Matrix size for the CPU weak scaling tests on *Tianhe*-2.

| CPU number | 48 | 96 | 192 | 384 | 768 | 1536 |
|---|---|---|---|---|---|---|
| matrix size | $1 \times 10^6$ | $2 \times 10^6$ | $4 \times 10^6$ | $8 \times 10^6$ | $1.6 \times 10^7$ | $3.2 \times 10^7$ |

(b) Matrix size for the CPU weak scaling on *ROMEO*.

| CPU number | 16 | 32 | 64 | 128 | 256 |
|---|---|---|---|---|---|
| matrix size | $4 \times 10^5$ | $8 \times 10^5$ | $1.6 \times 10^6$ | $3.2 \times 10^6$ | $6.4 \times 10^6$ |

(c) Matrix size for the GPU weak scaling and speedup evaluation on *ROMEO*.

| CPU or GPU number | 16 | 32 | 64 | 128 | 256 |
|---|---|---|---|---|---|
| matrix size | $2 \times 10^5$ | $4 \times 10^5$ | $8 \times 10^5$ | $1.6 \times 10^6$ | $3.2 \times 10^6$ |

GPUs can still have good strong and weak scalability. In conclusion, SMG2S has always good strong scaling performance when $d$ and $h$ are much smaller than the dimension of the matrix $n$, because it turns to be a $\mathcal{O}(n)$ problem. The weak scalability is good enough for most cases. The reason is that the nilpotent matrix $A$ in SpGEMM is simple with not many non-zero elements, therefore there is not enormous communication among different computing units. The weak scalability has its drawback in case that the computing unit number come to be huge for the SMG2S implementation based on PETSc, where the communication overhead become dominant. The special implementation of communication-optimized SMG2S makes his strong and weak scalability better. It is also shown that the double precision complex type matrix generation takes almost two times time over the double precision real type for the basic SMG2S implementation, but the time consumption of complex and real type matrix generation of optimized SMG2S seems similar. The reason is that there is no numerical values multiplication anymore in the optimized implementation of SMG2S.

## 5.3   Speedup Results and Analysis

The speedup of both SMG2S on multi-GPU and communication-optimized SMG2S on the CPUs compared with the PETSc-based implementation on CPU are also tested on *Romeo*. According to the previous evaluation that complex and real value types have always good scalability, we select the double precision complex values for the speedup evaluation. The details of experiments are also given in Table 1c. The results are shown in Fig. 6. We can find that the GPU version of SMG2S has almost 1.9× speedup over the PETSc CPU version. The communication-optimized SMG2S on CPUs has about 8× speedup over the basic PETSc CPU version.

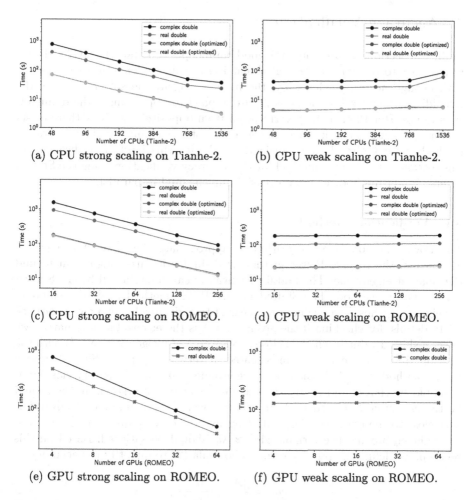

(a) CPU strong scaling on Tianhe-2.  (b) CPU weak scaling on Tianhe-2.

(c) CPU strong scaling on ROMEO.  (d) CPU weak scaling on ROMEO.

(e) GPU strong scaling on ROMEO.  (f) GPU weak scaling on ROMEO.

**Fig. 5.** Strong and weak scaling results of SMG2S on different platforms. A base 2 logarithmic scale is used for X-axis, and a base 10 logarithmic scale for Y-axis.

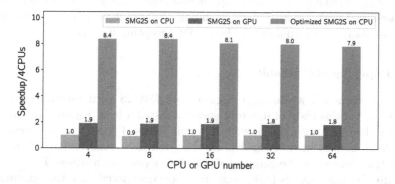

**Fig. 6.** Weak scaling speedup comparison of GPUs on ROMEO.

# 6 Accuracy Verification

In the last section, we presented the good parallel performance of SMG2S, then it is necessary to verify if the generated matrices are able to keep the given spectra with enough accuracy. Generally, the iterative eigenvalue solvers such as the Arnoldi or other Krylov methods [9] are applied to approximate the dominant eigenvalues. But the accuracy verification is an opposite case. Now there exists a value, we want to check if it is an eigenvalue of a given matrix. These iterative methods cannot directly and efficiently deal with this kind of verification. In this section, we present a method for the accuracy verification using the Shifted Inverse Power method, which was easily implemented in parallel.

## 6.1 Verification Method

The Power method is an algorithm to approximate the greatest eigenvalue. Meanwhile, the Inverse Power method is a similar iterative algorithm to find the smallest eigenvalue. The middle eigenvalues can be obtained by the Shifted Inverse Power method. The Shifted Inverse Power method is able to compute the eigenpair whose eigenvalue is the nearest to a given value in a few iterations.

In details, for checking if the given value $\lambda$ is the eigenvalue of a matrix, we select a shifted value $\sigma$ which is close enough to $\lambda$. An eigenpair $(\lambda', v')$ with the relation $Av' = \lambda'v'$ can be approximated in very few steps by Shifted Inverse Power method, with $\lambda'$ is the closest eigenvalue to $\sigma$. Since $\sigma$ is very close to $\lambda$, it should be that $\lambda$ and $\lambda'$ are the same eigenvalue of a system, and $v'$ should be the eigenvector related to $\lambda$. In reality, even if the computed eigenvalue is very close to the true one, the related eigenvector may be quite inaccurate. For the right eigenpairs, the formula $Av' \approx \lambda v'$ should be satisfied. Based on this relation, we define the relative error as Formula (2) to quantify the accuracy.

$$error = \frac{||Av' - \lambda v'||_2}{||Av'||_2} \tag{2}$$

If $\lambda' = \lambda$, this $error$ should be 0, if not, this generated matrix will not have an exact eigenvalue as $\lambda$. In real experiments, the exact solution cannot always be guaranteed with the arithmetic rounding errors of floating operations during the generation. A threshold could be set for accepting it or not.

## 6.2 Experimental Results

In the experiments, we test the accuracy of SMG2S with four selected cases among the various tests of different spectral distributions. Figures 7a and b are cases of clustered eigenvalues with different scales. Figure 7c is a special case with the dominant part of eigenvalues clustered in a small region. Figure 7d is a case that composes the conjugate and closest pair eigenvalues. These figures compare the difference between the given spectra (noted as initial eigenvalues in the figures) and the approximated ones (noted as computed eigenvalues) by

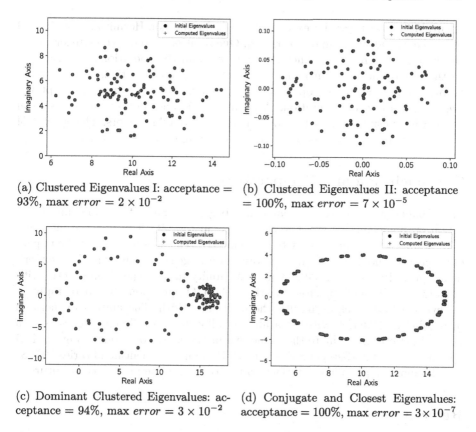

(a) Clustered Eigenvalues I: acceptance = 93%, max $error = 2 \times 10^{-2}$

(b) Clustered Eigenvalues II: acceptance = 100%, max $error = 7 \times 10^{-5}$

(c) Dominant Clustered Eigenvalues: acceptance = 94%, max $error = 3 \times 10^{-2}$

(d) Conjugate and Closest Eigenvalues: acceptance = 100%, max $error = 3 \times 10^{-7}$

**Fig. 7.** Verification using different types of spectra.

the Shifted Inverse Power Method. Clearly, the matrices generated by SMG2S can keep almost all the given eigenvalues in the four cases even they are very clustered and close. The acceptance threshold is set to be $1.0 \times 10^{-3}$.

This acceptance for cases of Figs. 7a, b, c and d are respectively 93%, 100%, 94% and 100%. The maximum $error$ for them are respectively $3 \times 10^{-2}$, $7 \times 10^{-5}$, $3 \times 10^{-2}$ and $3 \times 10^{-7}$. After the tests, we conclude that SMG2S is able to keep accurately the given spectra even for the very clustered and closest eigenvalues. In some cases, a very little number of too clustered eigenvalues may result in the inaccuracy of given ones, but in general, the generated matrix can fulfil the need to evaluate the linear system and eigenvalue solvers.

### 6.3 Arithmetic Precision Analysis

Any floating operations will introduce rounding errors, which is not negligible for the generation of large matrices. Regarding the non-Hermitian matrix, its eigenvalues may be extremely sensitive to perturbation. This sensibility is bounded by $bound(\lambda) \leq ||E||_2 Cond(\lambda)$, with $Cond(\lambda)$ the condition number of related eigenvalue $\lambda$ which can be excessively high for the non-Hermitian matrix and $||E||_2$ the Euclidean norm of errors [12]. One solution is to use the integer values for the matrix generation, since only integers and the operations $+$, $-$, and $\times$ on the microprocessor can make absolutely exact computations. As shown in Algorithm 1, most of the operations in SMG2S are $+$, $-$ and $\times$, except the step 7 with a division operation. Without step 7, we could introduce a special SMG2S fully using integers to avoid the risks of rounding errors. The spectra of the generated matrix will be $(2d)!$ times scaled up over the given one.

# 7   Conclusion and Perspectives

In this paper, we presented a scalable matrix generator and its parallel implementation on homogeneous and heterogeneous clusters. It allows generating large-scale non-Hermitian matrices with customized eigenvalues to evaluate the impact of spectra on the linear/eigenvalue solvers on large-scale platforms. The experiments proved its good scalability and the ability to keep the given spectra with acceptable accuracy. For large matrices, the I/O operation on supercomputers is always a bottleneck even with the high bandwidth. The matrices generated in parallel by SMG2S, with data already allocated on different processes, can be used directly to evaluate the numerical methods without concerning the I/O operation. The interfaces of SMG2S to C, Python and scientific libraries PETSc and Trilinos are provided. Interface to Fortran will be implemented in future.

# References

1. Bai, Z., Day, D., Demmel, J., Dongarra, J.: A test matrix collection for non-hermitian eigenvalue problems. Dept. Math. **751**, 40506–0027 (1996)
2. Boisvert, R.F., Pozo, R., Remington, K., Barrett, R.F., Dongarra, J.J.: Matrix market: a web resource for test matrix collections. In: Boisvert, R.F. (ed.) Quality of Numerical Software, pp. 125–137. IFIP Advances in Information and Communication Technology. Springer, Boston (1997). https://doi.org/10.1007/978-1-5041-2940-4_9
3. Chu, M.T., Golub, G.H.: Structured inverse eigenvalue problems. Acta Numerica **11**, 1–71 (2002)
4. Davis, T.A., Hu, Y.: The university of Florida sparse matrix collection. ACM Trans. Math. Softw. (TOMS) **38**(1), 1 (2011)
5. Demmel, J., McKenney, A.: A test matrix generation suite. In: Courant Institute of Mathematical Sciences. Citeseer (1989)
6. Galicher, H., Boillod-Cerneux, F., Petiton, S., Calvin, C.: Generate very large sparse matrices starting from a given spectrum. In: Lecture Notes in Computer Science, vol. 8969. Springer, Heidelberg (2014)
7. Liesen, J., Strakos, Z.: Krylov Subspace Methods: Principles and Analysis. Oxford University Press, Oxford (2013)
8. Liu, Y., Talbi, A., Pernod, P., Bou Matar, O.: Highly confined love waves modes by defect states in a holey sio 2/quartz phononic crystal. J. Appl. Phys. **124**(14), 145102 (2018)

9. Petiton, S.G.: Parallel subspace method for non-hermitian eigenproblems on the connection machine (cm2). Appl. Numer. Math. **10**(1), 19–35 (1992)
10. Saad, Y.: SPARSEKIT: a basic tool kit for sparse matrix computation (version2), University of Illinois (1994)
11. Saad, Y.: Least squares polynomials in the complex plane and their use for solving nonsymmetric linear systems. SIAM J. Numer. Anal. **24**(1), 155–169 (1987)
12. Saad, Y.: Numerical Methods for Large Eigenvalue Problems, Revised edn. SIAM, Philadelphia (2011)
13. Wu, X.: SMG2S Manual v1.0. Maison de la Simuation, France (2018)
14. Wu, X., Petiton, S.G.: A distributed and parallel asynchronous unite and conquer method to solve large scale non-hermitian linear systems. In: Proceedings of the International Conference on High Performance Computing in Asia-Pacific Region, HPC Asia 2018, pp. 36–46. ACM, New York (2018)

# LRMalloc: A Modern and Competitive Lock-Free Dynamic Memory Allocator

Ricardo Leite[(✉)] and Ricardo Rocha

CRACS and INESC TEC and Faculty of Sciences, University of Porto,
Rua do Campo Alegre, 1021/1055, 4169-007 Porto, Portugal
{rleite,ricroc}@dcc.fc.up.pt

**Abstract.** This paper presents LRMalloc, a lock-free memory allocator that leverages lessons of modern memory allocators and combines them with a lock-free scheme. Current state-of-the-art memory allocators possess good performance but lack desirable lock-free properties, such as, priority inversion tolerance, kill-tolerance availability, and/or deadlock and livelock immunity. LRMalloc's purpose is to show the feasibility of lock-free memory management algorithms, without sacrificing competitiveness in comparison to commonly used state-of-the-art memory allocators, especially for concurrent multithreaded applications.

**Keywords:** Memory allocator · Lock-freedom · Implementation

## 1 Introduction

Dynamic memory allocation is an important component of most applications. Nowadays, due to the use of thread-level parallelism by applications, an important requirement in a memory allocator implementation is the ability to be thread safe. To guarantee thread safety, state-of-the-art memory allocators use *lock-based data structures*. The use of locks has implications in terms of program performance, availability, robustness and flexibility. As such, current memory allocators attempt to minimize the effects of locking by using fine-grained locks, by reducing the frequency of lock operations and by providing synchronization-free allocations as much as possible through the use of thread-specific caches.

However, even with only infrequent and fine-grained locking, lock-based memory allocators are still subject to a number of disadvantages. They are vulnerable to deadlocks and livelocks, prune to priority inversion and delays due to preemption during locking, and incapable of dealing with unexpected thread termination. A more challenging but desirable alternative to ensure thread safety is to use *lock-free synchronization*. Lock-freedom guarantees system-wide progress whenever a thread executes some finite amount of steps, whether by the thread itself or by some other thread in the process. By definition, lock-free synchronization uses no locks and does not obtain mutual exclusive access to a resource at any point. It is therefore immune to deadlocks and livelocks. Without locks,

© Springer Nature Switzerland AG 2019
H. Senger et al. (Eds.): VECPAR 2018, LNCS 11333, pp. 230–243, 2019.
https://doi.org/10.1007/978-3-030-15996-2_17

priority inversion and delays due to preemption during locking cannot occur, and unexpected thread termination is also not problematic.

More importantly, a truly lock-free data structure or algorithm that needs to dynamically allocate memory cannot be built on top of a lock-based memory allocator without compromising the lock-freedom property. This is particularly relevant for lock-free data structures or algorithms that use memory reclamation techniques such as *epochs* or *hazard pointers* [7].

In this work, we present the design and implementation of LRMalloc, a lock-free dynamic memory allocator that leverages lessons of modern allocators to show the feasibility of lock-free memory management, without sacrificing performance in comparison to commonly used state-of-the-art allocators. We can identify three main components in LRMalloc's design: (i) the *thread caches*, which provide synchronization-free blocks and are used in the common allocation/deallocation case; (ii) the *heap*, a lock-free component that manages superblocks of memory pages; and (iii) the *pagemap*, a book-keeping component used to store metadata at the page-level.

Experimental results show that, unlike prior lock-free alternatives, LRMalloc is competitive with commonly used state-of-the-art memory allocators. This has been achieved by reproducing similar strategies to the ones used by lock-based memory allocators to avoid performance degradation due to usage of locks. LRMalloc uses thread caches to reduce the common allocation/deallocation case to a synchronization-free operation, thus avoiding synchronization between threads for most allocation and deallocation requests. When synchronization is necessary, to add/remove blocks to/from a thread cache, LRMalloc attempts to transfer as many blocks with as little synchronization (i.e., atomic operations) as possible, in an effort to amortize the cost of those atomic operations through the subsequent allocation and deallocation requests.

The remainder of the paper is organized as follows. First, we introduce some background and related work. Next, we describe the key data structures and algorithms that support the implementation of LRMalloc. Then, we show experimental results comparing LRMalloc against other modern and relevant memory allocators. We end by outlining conclusions and discussing further work.

## 2    Background and Related Work

Memory allocation as a research topic has a rich history. Starting with the 1960s, and motivated by the exorbitant cost of main memory, researchers poured effort into the design of allocator strategies and algorithms that minimized *memory fragmentation* – a fundamental problem in memory management that implies needing more memory to satisfy a sequence of memory requests than the sum of the memory required for those memory requests. In this regard, numerous strategies and algorithms were proposed and developed to reduce memory fragmentation. Other fundamental concepts, such as *size classes* (e.g., segregated storage), also appeared in this time period, and are still used in state-of-the-art memory allocators. For an excellent survey, that summarizes most memory allocation research prior to 1995, please see Wilson *et al.* [13].

More recently, with the decrease in cost of main memory and the appearance of computer systems with higher and higher core counts, memory allocation research has taken a different path. Focus has shifted into memory allocator performance and scalability, often in detriment of fragmentation. Problems specific to concurrent memory allocation, such as *false sharing* and *blowup*, have also received attention, being first noted and solved by Berger *et al.* in the Hoard memory allocator [1].

Instead of mutual exclusion, lock-free algorithms use atomic instructions provided by the underlying architecture to guarantee consistency in multithreaded execution. The most relevant atomic instruction is CAS (*Compare-and-Swap*), which is widely supported in just about every modern architecture either directly or by efficient emulation by using *Linked Load* and *Store Conditional* instructions. Listing 1.1 shows the pseudo-code for the CAS instruction. Lock-free data structures and algorithms that aim to be widely portable should be CAS-based. However CAS-based designs are vulnerable to the ABA problem – a fundamental and challenging problem which complicates the implementation and design of lock-free data structures and algorithms [2].

**Listing 1.1.** Compare-and-Swap instruction

```
1   bool CAS(int* address, int expected, int desired) {
2     if (*address == expected) {
3       *address = desired;
4       return true;
5     }
6     return false;
7   }
```

The first lock-free segregated storage mechanism was introduced by Michael [12]. Michael's allocator is particularly relevant because it only makes use of the widely available and portable CAS operation for lock-free synchronization. NBMalloc [5] is another lock-free memory allocator, which uses an architecture inspired by Hoard [1]. However, as our experimental results will show (in Sect. 4), compared to modern alternatives, both these lock-free allocators are slow as they uses several atomic operations per allocation and deallocation, operations which are expensive in today's computer architectures. In order to succeed, lock-free memory allocators must amortize the cost of an atomic operation through several allocation and deallocation requests.

Despite the relatively large number of memory allocators developed over the years, there are only a few that are widely used. The most commonly used memory allocator is by far Ptmalloc2 [6], the standard memory allocator distributed with glibc. It is a modified version of Doug Lea's memory allocator [9], a fragmentation-focused memory allocator that uses a *deferred coalescing scheme*. Ptmalloc2 has been updated over time with features to improve its multithreaded performance, such as the use of *arenas* (several independent allocators that can be used simultaneously thus reducing thread contention) and *thread caches* for small block sizes. Applications that are focused on multithreaded performance usually take note of the performance degradation of the standard C lib allocator and change to a different allocator, such as Jemalloc [3] or TCMalloc [4].

Jemalloc is a state-of-the-art memory allocator that focuses on fragmentation avoidance and scalable concurrency support. It is the default memory allocator on the FreeBSD operating system, and is widely used in numerous multithreaded applications. At process start, it creates a number of *arenas* equal to 4 times the number of CPUs in the system in an effort to minimize lock contention. Threads are assigned to the arena with the lowest number of assigned threads. Like other memory allocators, Jemalloc uses thread caches and defines size classes for allocations, but also uses coalescing strategies in an effort to decrease fragmentation.

TCMalloc is a memory allocator which focuses on thread-caching. Unlike other allocators, it does not use arenas to decrease contention on shared data structures. It instead uses fine-grained locks and implements a number of novel cache management algorithms [10] to improve average-case latency, scalability and decrease cache-provoked fragmentation.

## 3 LRMalloc

This section describes LRMalloc in more detail. We assume implementation on a 64-bit system architecture (e.g., x86-64) and, for the sake of brevity, we only show C-like code for the key implementation routines.

### 3.1 High-Level Overview

From a high-level perspective, LRMalloc is divided into three main components: (i) the *thread caches*, one per thread; (ii) the *heap*; and (iii) the *pagemap*. Figure 1 shows the relationship between these three components, the user's application and the operating system.

Similarly to other memory allocators, the thread caches are a synchronization-free component which uses a stack implemented as a singly-linked list to store (a finite number of) blocks that are available for use. A separate stack is kept for each size class. Each thread cache is meant to handle the common allocation case, where a **malloc()** becomes a single stack pop and a **free()** is a stack push using the appropriate size class. When the cache is empty, a new list of blocks is fetched from the heap. When the cache is full, blocks are flushed back to the heap. This simple and speed-efficient common case is essential for a competitive memory allocator.

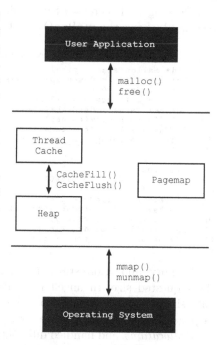

**Fig. 1.** LRMalloc's overview

In LRMalloc, size classes are generated according to the following series (series also adopted by Jemalloc [3]):

1. $2^X$
2. $2^X + 2^{(X-2)}$
3. $2^X + 2^{(X-1)}$
4. $2^X + 2^{(X-1)} + 2^{(X-2)}$
5. $2^{(X+1)}$ (repeat, same as first case)

Note that not all values generated by the series are valid due to alignment requirements on the C standard, and thus those are removed. Without those cases, the above series limits internal fragmentation (unused space inside a block given to the application) to a maximum of 25% of the allocated memory.

The heap and the pagemap are lock-free components. The heap manages *superblocks* from which it carves blocks to be used by thread caches. Superblocks are continuous set of pages, which may either be used to carve up blocks of the same size class or for a *single large allocation*. Similarly to other allocators, in LRMalloc, large allocations are allocations larger than the largest size class. The pagemap stores metadata for pages used by superblocks. Its raison d'être is to find out metadata of a given block, such as the size class and superblock the block belongs to. Therefore, the pagemap is merely a bookkeeping component, kept up to date by the heap. The pagemap stores metadata on a per-page basis instead of a per-block basis, which reduces the amount of memory used for bookkeeping and increases the locality of blocks provided to the application. Listing 1.2 shows the **malloc()** and **free()** high-level routines.

**Listing 1.2.** High-level allocation and deallocation routines

```
1    void* malloc(size_t size) {
2      size_t scIdx = ComputeSizeClass(size);
3      if (scIdx == 0)                                   // large allocation
4        return AllocateLargeBlock();
5      Cache* cache = GetCache(scIdx);
6      if (CacheIsEmpty(cache))
7        CacheFill(scIdx, cache);
8      return CachePopBlock(cache);
9    }
10
11   void free(void* ptr) {
12     size_t scIdx = GetSizeClassFromPageMap(ptr);      // get metadata
13     if (scIdx == 0)                                   // large allocation
14       return DeallocateLargeBlock();
15     Cache* cache = GetCache(scIdx);
16     if (CacheIsFull(cache))
17       CacheFlush(scIdx, cache);
18     CachePushBlock(cache, ptr);
19   }
```

Memory allocation starts by computing the size class corresponding to the requested size. In an effort to decrease internal fragmentation, there are only size classes for *small allocations*. LRMalloc's size classes go up to 16KB (4 pages). Allocations that are larger than the largest size class are treated as *large allocations*, and handled differently. For large allocations, LRMalloc creates a superblock with the appropriate size in number of pages through **mmap()**. When a large allocation is **free()**'d, the corresponding superblock is **munmap()**

and thus returned to the operating system. Large allocations are identified with a size class equal to 0. If the allocation is not large, the cache corresponding to the size class is accessed and checked. In the common case, the cache will not be empty and thus a block will be fetched from the cache with a pop operation. In the uncommon case, the cache is empty and thus it must be filled with **CacheFill()**.

Memory deallocation also starts by finding out the size class of the provided allocation. This is the step where the pagemap component becomes relevant, as it keeps metadata about all allocated pages. As before, large allocations are handled differently, and for small allocations the corresponding cache is accessed. In the common case, the cache will not be full and thus the allocation will just be added to the cache. In the uncommon case, the cache is full and thus **CacheFlush()** must be called to reduce the number of blocks in the cache.

Caches are thread-specific objects, and thus all operations using the cache are synchronization-free. In the allocation and deallocation algorithms, only the **CacheFill()** and **CacheFlush()** routines require synchronization. Both routines are described in more detail next. For the sake of brevity, we will omit the **GetCache()**, **CacheIsEmpty()**, **CacheIsFull()**, **CachePopBlock()** and **CachePushBlock()** subroutines, which are trivially implemented.

## 3.2 Heap

Due to its lock-free nature, the heap is by far the most complex component of the allocator. It is based on Michael's lock-free memory allocation algorithm [12] but adapted with a number of improvements to work with the presence of thread caches. The heap manages superblocks through *descriptors*. Descriptors are unreclaimable but reusable objects used by the heap to track superblocks. Descriptors contain the superblock's metadata, such as, where the superblock begins, the size class of its blocks, and the number of blocks it contains. It also includes an *anchor*, an inner structure that describes the superblock's state and is small enough to fit inside a single word to be atomically updated with CAS instructions. Listing 1.3 presents the anchor and descriptor struct definitions.

**Listing 1.3.** Anchor and descriptor structures

```
1   struct Anchor {
2       size_t state : 2;    // may be EMPTY = 0, PARTIAL = 1 or FULL = 2
3       size_t avail : 31;            // index of first free block
4       size_t count : 31;            // number of free blocks
5   };
6
7   struct Descriptor {
8       Anchor anchor;
9       char* superblock;             // pointer to superblock
10      size_t blocksize;     // size of each block in superblock
11      size_t maxcount;              // number of blocks
12      size_t scIdx;         // size class of blocks in superblock
13  };
```

The **Anchor.avail** field refers to the first available block in the superblock. A free block then points to the next free block on the chain. The exact number of bits used by the **Anchor.avail** and **Anchor.count** fields (31 in the current implementation) are implementation independent and can be adjusted to how large superblocks can be and to how many blocks at most they can have. Unlike Michael's original algorithm, the anchor does not include an ABA prevention tag.

**Listing 1.4.** CacheFill routines

```
1   void CacheFill(size_t scIdx, Cache* cache) {
2       // try to fill cache from a single partial superblock ...
3       bool res = CacheFillFromPartialSB(scIdx, cache);
4       // ... and if that fails, create a new superblock
5       if (!res)
6           CacheFillFromNewSB(scIdx, cache);
7   }
8
9   bool CacheFillFromPartialSB(size_t scIdx, Cache* cache) {
10      Descriptor* desc = HeapGetPartialSB(scIdx);
11      if (!desc)                      // no partial superblock available
12          return false;
13      Anchor newAnc, oldAnc;
14      do {
15          oldAnc = desc->anchor;
16          if (oldAnc.state == EMPTY) {
17              DescriptorRetire(desc);
18              return CacheFillFromPartialSB(scIdx, cache);    // retry
19          }
20          newAnc.state = FULL;
21          newAnc.avail = desc->maxcount;
22          newAnc.count = 0;
23      } while (!CAS(&desc->anchor, oldAnc, newAnc));
24      char* block = desc->superblock + oldAnc.avail * desc->blockSize;
25      size_t blockCount = oldAnc.count;
26      while (blockCount-- > 0) {
27          CachePushBlock(cache, block);
28          block = *(char**)block;
29      }
30      return true;
31  }
32
33  void CacheFillFromNewSB(size_t scIdx, Cache* cache) {
34      Descriptor* desc = DescriptorAlloc();
35      DescriptorInit(desc, scIdx);    // initialize with size class info
36      Anchor anc;
37      anc.state = FULL;
38      anc.avail = desc->maxcount;
39      anc.count = 0;
40      desc->anchor = anc;
41      desc->superblock = mmap(...);
42      for (size_t idx = 0; idx < desc->maxcount; ++idx) {
43          char* block = desc->superblock + idx * desc->blockSize;
44          CachePushBlock(cache, block);
45      }
46      PageMapRegisterDescriptor(desc);            // update pagemap
47  }
```

Listing 1.4 describes the **CacheFill()** algorithm. By default, the algorithm tries to reuse a partially free superblock by calling **CacheFillFromPartialSB()**, which corresponds to start by trying to get a descriptor from a lockfree stack (**HeapGetPartialSB()** in line 10). If there is such a descriptor, it may point to a superblock where all blocks have been freed, in which case the superblock has been returned to the operating system and is no longer usable. In this case, the descriptor is put into a global recycle list (**DescriptorRetire()** in line 17) and the algorithm is repeated. Otherwise, all available blocks in the superblock are reserved, with a CAS that updates the anchor (line 23), and then added to the thread's cache (lines 24–29). No ABA-prevention tag is needed on this CAS, because the only change that can happen to the underlying superblock is that more blocks become available, thus updating **Anchor.avail**, which would fail the CAS. This is opposed to Michael's original algorithm, where blocks could concurrently become available and unavailable due to *active* superblocks.

If there are no available partial superblocks for the size class at hand, a new superblock must be allocated and initialized. This is done in **CacheFill-FromNewSB()**, which allocates a new superblock from the operating system and assigns a descriptor to it. The assigned descriptor is provided by **Descriptor Alloc()**, which accesses a global lock-free list of recycled descriptors. All blocks in the newly allocated superblock are then added to the thread's cache (lines 42–45 in Listing 1.4). Note that in low-concurrency scenarios, only a few CAS instructions are required to transfer a potentially large number of blocks to the cache. The exact number of CAS depends on which lock-free data structures are being used to track partial superblocks.

Flushing a cache is a less straightforward procedure. When a cache is full, several blocks must be returned to their respective superblocks, which requires updating the superblocks' associated descriptors. If each block was to be returned individually, a number of CAS instructions equal to the number of blocks to be removed would be required, which could be too inefficient and a source of contention. Instead, it is best to group up blocks according to descriptor as best as possible, in order to be able to return several blocks back to the same superblock in a single CAS. Listing 1.5 shows LRMalloc's cache flushing algorithm.

**CacheFlush()** starts by popping a block from the cache and by forming an ad-hoc singly-linked list with all next blocks in cache that belong to the same superblock (lines 4–16). Recall that blocks that belong to the same superblock share the same descriptor. We use **CachePeekBlock()** to inspect the first block in the cache without popping it. The ad-hoc list is then added to the corresponding superblock's available block list and the anchor updated accordingly (lines 19–30). At this stage, the CAS only fails if other blocks are being simultaneously flushed from other caches. At the end, if these are the first blocks to be freed, the superblock is added to the lock-free stack of partial superblocks (line 33). Otherwise, if all blocks are made free, the pagemap is updated to reflect the change and the superblock returned to the operating system (lines 35–38).

While our cache flush algorithm is simple and has an obvious worst-case scenario (interleaved blocks from different superblocks will lead to a CAS operation being needed per each block), we find out that in practice the algorithm works well and succeeds in transferring a large number of blocks from the thread cache to the heap with a reduced number of CAS operations. Following prior classical work, where it was pointed out that real program behavior exhibit regularities exploitable by memory allocators [13], one observation is that blocks that are allocated close in the request stream tend to have similar lifetimes, and thus also tend to be deallocated close in the deallocation request stream. This is especially true when those allocations are close (or equal) in size. In our case, as we provide blocks from the same superblock for requests close in the request stream, we can expect those blocks to have similar expected lifetimes and thus be returned (grouped together) to the thread cache. As such, interleaved blocks from different superblocks becomes an unlikely and uncommon occurrence.

**Listing 1.5.** CacheFlush routine

```
1   void CacheFlush(size_t scIdx, Cache* cache) {
2     while (!CacheIsEmpty(cache)) {
3       // form a list of blocks to return to a common superblock
4       char* head, tail;
5       head = tail = CachePopBlock(cache);
6       Descriptor* desc = PageMapGetDescriptor(head);
7       size_t blockCount = 1;
8       while (!CacheIsEmpty(cache)) {
9         char* block = CachePeekBlock(cache);
10        if (PageMapGetDescriptor(block) != desc)
11          break;
12        CachePopBlock(cache);
13        ++blockCount;
14        *(char**)tail = block;
15        tail = block;
16      }
17
18      // add list to descriptor and update anchor
19      char* superblock = desc->superblock;
20      size_t idx = ComputeIdx(superblock, head);
21      Anchor oldAnc, newAnc;
22      do {
23        newAnc = oldAnc = desc->anchor;
24        *(char**)tail = superblock + oldAnc.avail * desc->blockSize;
25        newAnc.state = PARTIAL;
26        newAnc.avail = idx;
27        newAnc.count += blockCount;
28        if (newAnc.count == desc->maxcount)   // can free superblock
29          newAnc.state = EMPTY;
30      } while (!CAS(&desc, oldAnc, newAnc));
31
32      if (oldAnc.state == FULL)
33        HeapPutPartialSB(desc);
34      else if (newAnc.state == EMPTY) {
35        // unregister metadata from pagemap ...
36        PageMapUnregisterDescriptor(superblock, scIdx);
37        // ... and release superblock back to OS
38        munmap(superblock, ...);
39      }
40    }
41  }
```

When a cache flush completely empties a superblock (line 34), note that the corresponding descriptor cannot be returned to the operating system since other threads can be potentially holding a reference to it. Moreover, it cannot be recycled also as there may still be a reference to it in the list of partial superblocks, and guaranteeing its correct removal is a non-trivial task. In our approach, a descriptor is only recycled when a thread removes it from the list of partial superblocks (line 17 in algorithm **CacheFillFromPartialSB()**).

### 3.3 Pagemap

The pagemap component stores *allocation metadata per page* based on the observation that most allocations are much smaller than a page, and that blocks in the same page share the same size class and descriptor. Storing metadata per page instead of per allocation has several advantages. First, it is more memory efficient. Second, it helps separating allocation metadata from user memory, which improves locality, as allocator and user memory are no longer interleaved.

The pagemap can be implemented in a number of different ways. With an operating system that allows memory overcommitting, it can be a simple array, where the size depends on the size of the valid address space and how much memory is needed for each page's metadata. For example, assuming that a single word of memory is enough for metadata, and that the address space can only have $2^{48}$ bytes (common for 64 bit architectures) then this array requires $2^{48-12}$ words, or about 512 GB. Of course, the actual physical memory is bounded by the number of pages required for user applications. LRMalloc uses this type of implementation. A cheaper solution in terms of virtual memory would be to use a lock-free radix tree, at the cost of some performance and additional complexity.

## 4    Experimental Results

The environment for our experiments was a dedicated x86-64 multiprocessor system with four AMD SixCore Opteron TM 8425 HE @ 2.1 GHz (24 cores in total) and 128 GBytes of main memory, running Ubuntu 16.04 with kernel 4.4.0-104 64 bits. We used standard benchmarks commonly used in the literature [1,12], namely the *Linux scalability* [11], *Threadtest* and *Larson* [8] benchmarks.

*Linux scalability* is a benchmark used to measure memory allocator latency and scalability. It launches a given number of independent threads, each of which runs a batch of 10 million **malloc()** requests allocating 16-byte blocks followed by a batch of identical **free()** requests.

*Threadtest* is similar to *Linux scalability* with a slightly different allocation profile. It also launches a given number of independent threads, each of which runs batchs of 100 thousand **malloc()** requests followed by 100 thousand **free()** requests. Each thread runs 100 batches in total.

*Larson* simulates the behavior of a long-running server process. It repeatedly creates threads that work on a slice of a shared array. Each thread runs a batch of 10 million **malloc()** requests between 16 and 128 bytes and the resulting allocations are stored in random slots in the corresponding slice of the shared array (each thread's slice includes 1000 slots). When a slot is occupied, a **free()** request is first done to release it. At any given time, there is a maximum limit of threads running simultaneously, i.e., only one thread has access to a given slice of the shared array, and slices are recycled as threads are destroyed and created.

To put our proposal in perspective, we compared LRMalloc against previous lock-free memory allocators, namely Michael's allocator [12] and NBMalloc [5], and against lock-based state-of-the-art memory allocators, such as Hoard memory allocator [1], Ptmalloc2 [6], Jemalloc-5.0 [3] and TCMalloc [4]. Figures 2 and 3 present experimental results for the benchmarks described above when using the different memory allocators with configurations from 1 to 32 threads. The results presented are the average of 5 runs.

Figure 2(a) shows the execution time, in seconds (log scale), for running the *Linux scalability* benchmark. In general, the results show that LRMalloc is very competitive, being only overtaken by Jemalloc as the number of threads increases. Jemalloc's behavior can be explained by the fact that it creates a number of arenas equal to four times the number of cores in the system. Multiple

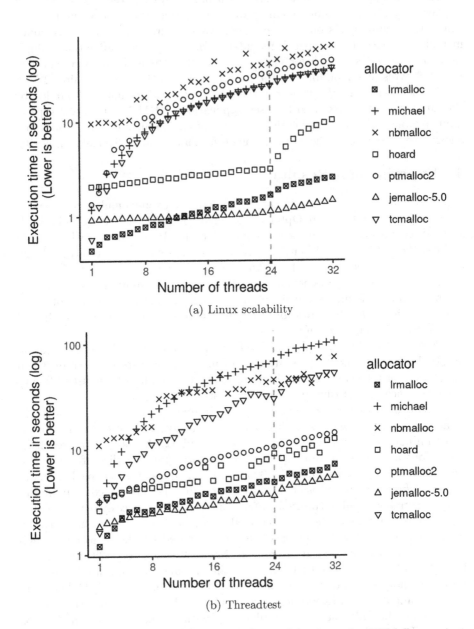

(a) Linux scalability

(b) Threadtest

**Fig. 2.** Execution time results, in seconds (log scale), comparing LRMalloc against Michael's allocator, NBMalloc, Hoard, Ptmalloc2, Jemalloc-5.0 and TCMalloc for the *Linux scalability* and *Threadtest* benchmarks with configurations from 1 to 32 threads

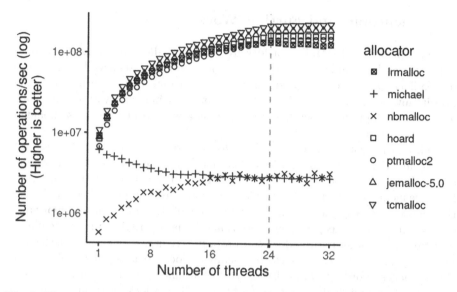

**Fig. 3.** Throughput results (log scale) comparing LRMalloc against Michael's allocator, NBMalloc, Hoard, Ptmalloc2, Jemalloc-5.0 and TCMalloc for the *Larson* benchmark with configurations from 1 to 32 threads

threads may be mapped to the same arena but, with so many arenas, collisions are unlikely and thus little contention happens on shared data structures. On the other hand, LRMalloc's heap has no arena-like multiplexing, and thus there is a greater potential for contention as the number of threads increases.

Figure 2(b) shows the execution time, in seconds (log scale), for running the *Threadtest* benchmark. Again, the results show that LRMalloc is very competitive and only surpassed by Jemalloc by a small margin. In particular, for a small number of threads, LRMalloc is slightly faster than Jemalloc and, as the number of threads increases, LRMalloc keeps an identical tendency as Jemalloc.

Figure 3 shows the number of operations per second (log scale), for running the *Larson* benchmark. Unlike the other two lock-free memory allocators, Michael's allocator and NBMalloc, LRMalloc consistently achieves increased throughput as the number of threads approaches the number of cores available, while carrying out over a order of magnitude more throughput. LRMalloc also performs similarly to all other state-of-the-art allocators, with a small performance degradation as the number of threads increases. This happens due to the cache flushing mechanism triggered every-time a thread exits. This lowers memory fragmentation but, for the kind of programs which create a huge number of threads during its lifetime, it can incur in some extra overhead. This could be improved by recycling cache structures when a thread exits, in order to allow them to be reused by new spawning threads.

# 5   Conclusions and Further Work

We have presented LRMalloc, a lock-free memory allocator designed to fulfill important and desirable properties in a memory allocator, such as, being immune to deadlocks and livelocks, and tolerant to arbitrary thread termination and priority inversion. It is our belief that future progress in memory allocators would involve the adoption of lock-free strategies as a way to provide these behavior properties to user applications.

Our experiments showed that LRMalloc's current implementation is already quite competitive and comparable to other modern state-of-the-art memory allocators. In particular, it has much better performance characteristics than prior lock-free memory allocators, such as Michael's allocator or NBMalloc. We believe that our work clearly shows that a next iteration of state-of-the-art memory allocators can not only keep current performance characteristics but also embrace lock-freedom in order to provide better properties to user applications. To achieve such, we propose that future lock-free memory allocators must effectively employ thread caches in order to amortize the cost of atomic operations throughout several allocation and deallocation requests, as well as a lock-free component that can effectively transfer lists of blocks to and from threads caches.

Nevertheless, there are a number of possible extensions that we plan to study which could further improve LRMalloc's performance. A first example is the support for multiple arenas as a way to reduce allocation contention as the number of threads increases, thus improving scalability. Another good example is the usage of improved cache management algorithms, as the ones implemented by TCMalloc [10], as a way to reduce the average memory allocator latency.

LRMalloc's current implementation uses a lock-free segregated storage scheme which relies on the operating system to provide continuous pages of memory, which we use to represent the superblocks. Another improvement we plan to study is to have an additional lock-free component which handles these memory requests and is capable of general coalescing and splitting memory blocks representing the superblocks. To the best of our knowledge, no lock-free scheme exists that supports general coalescing and splitting. We believe that the results of such research could lead to relevant contributions able to be incorporated also into the operating system memory allocation system calls as a way to extend its lock-free properties.

The current implementation of LRMalloc fully implements the C11 and POSIX malloc interface. LRMalloc is licensed under the MIT license and available from https://github.com/ricleite/lrmalloc.

**Acknowledgements.** We would like to thank the anonymous reviewers for their feedback and suggestions. Special thanks to Pedro Moreno for helpful technical discussion and ideas provided during the development of this research. This work is financed by the ERDF (European Regional Development Fund) through the Operational Programme for Competitiveness and Internationalisation - COMPETE 2020 Programme and by National Funds through the Portuguese funding agency, FCT (Portuguese Foundation for Science and Technology) within project POCI-01-0145-FEDER-016844.

# References

1. Berger, E.D., McKinley, K.S., Blumofe, R.D., Wilson, P.R.: Hoard: a scalable memory allocator for multithreaded applications. In: ACM SIGARCH Computer Architecture News, vol. 28, pp. 117–128. ACM (2000)
2. Dechev, D., Pirkelbauer, P., Stroustrup, B.: Understanding and effectively preventing the ABA problem in descriptor-based lock-free designs. In: 13th IEEE International Symposium on Object/Component/Service-Oriented Real-Time Distributed Computing, pp. 185–192. IEEE (2010)
3. Evans, J.: A scalable concurrent malloc (3) implementation for FreeBSD. In: BSD-Can Conference, Ottawa, Canada (2006)
4. Ghemawat, S., Menage, P.: TCMalloc: thread-caching malloc (2009). http://googperftools.sourceforge.net/doc/tcmalloc.html. (read on 14 June 2018)
5. Gidenstam, A., Papatriantafilou, M., Tsigas, P.: NBmalloc: allocating memory in a lock-free manner. Algorithmica **58**(2), 304–338 (2010)
6. Gloger, W.: Ptmalloc (2006). http://www.malloc.de/en. (read on 14 June 2018)
7. Hart, T.E., McKenney, P.E., Brown, A.D., Walpole, J.: Performance of memory reclamation for lockless synchronization. J. Parallel Distrib. Comput. **67**(12), 1270–1285 (2007)
8. Larson, P.Å., Krishnan, M.: Memory allocation for long-running server applications. In: ACM SIGPLAN Notices, vol. 34, no. 3, pp. 176–185 (1998)
9. Lea, D.: A memory allocator called Doug Lea's Malloc or dlmalloc for short (1996). http://g.oswego.edu/dl/html/malloc.html. (read on 14 June 2018)
10. Lee, S., Johnson, T., Raman, E.: Feedback directed optimization of TCMalloc. In: Workshop on Memory Systems Performance and Correctness, p. 3. ACM (2014)
11. Lever, C., Boreham, D.: malloc() performance in a multithreaded Linux environment. In: USENIX Annual Technical Conference, pp. 301–311. USENIX (2000)
12. Michael, M.M.: Scalable lock-free dynamic memory allocation. ACM Sigplan Not. **39**(6), 35–46 (2004)
13. Wilson, P.R., Johnstone, M.S., Neely, M., Boles, D.: Dynamic storage allocation: a survey and critical review. In: Baler, H.G. (ed.) IWMM 1995. LNCS, vol. 986, pp. 1–116. Springer, Heidelberg (1995). https://doi.org/10.1007/3-540-60368-9_19

# Short Paper

# Towards a Strategy for Performance Prediction on Heterogeneous Architectures

Silvio Stanzani[(⊠)], Raphael Cóbe, Jefferson Fialho, Rogério Iope,
Marco Gomes, Artur Baruchi, and Júlio Amaral

Núcleo de Computação Científica (NCC),
Universidade Estadual Paulista, São Paulo, Brazil
{silvio, rmcobe, jfialho, rogerio, mgomes, abaruchi,
julioamaral}@ncc.unesp.br

**Abstract.** Performance prediction of applications has always been a great challenge, even for homogeneous architectures. However, today's trend is the design of cluster running in a heterogeneous architecture, which increases the complexity of new strategies to predict the behavior and time spent by an application to run. In this paper we present a strategy that predicts the performance of an application on different architectures and rank then according to the performance that the application can achieve on each architecture. The proposed strategy was able to correctly rank three of four applications tested without overhead implications. Our next step is to extend the metrics in order to increase the accuracy.

**Keywords:** Performance prediction · Heterogeneous systems ·
Parallel processing

## 1 Introduction

One trend that has become popular in designing computer clusters is the use of heterogeneous architectures that are composed by different models of multicore and manycore architectures [1], which leads to computer infrastructures that are becoming more complex in scale, as well as in the variety of cores and memory systems. Such a trend can be observed in the configuration of several supercomputers, such as, Stampede2[1], JURECA[2] and Santos Dumont[3].

Characterize the performance of applications on different architectures is essential to efficiently use heterogeneous infrastructures. Such characterization can be carried out by the users by profiling the performance of their applications on each architecture and analyzing the results. Some initiatives have been working on the development of performance prediction techniques, to automatically generate such characterization and support runtime decisions [2, 3].

---

[1] https://www.tacc.utexas.edu/systems/stampede2.

[2] http://www.fz-juelich.de/ias/jsc/EN/Home/home_node.html.

[3] http://sdumont.lncc.br/.

© Springer Nature Switzerland AG 2019
H. Senger et al. (Eds.): VECPAR 2018, LNCS 11333, pp. 247–253, 2019.
https://doi.org/10.1007/978-3-030-15996-2_18

One of the challenges related to performance prediction on heterogeneous infrastructures is identify the architecture that presents the best performance for a given application. In order to overcome this challenge, the contribution of this work is a strategy based on profiling data to do performance prediction of parallel applications on single machines, without overhead implications, capable of rank available architectures according to the performance level that can be obtained executing the application.

The remainder of this paper is organized as follows: Sect. 2 presents the problem definition and concepts, Sect. 3 presents related work, Sect. 4 presents the strategy proposed, Sect. 5 presents the evaluation of the strategy and Sect. 6 presents the conclusions and future work.

## 2   Concepts and Problem Definition

In this section; we present the problem definition and the main concepts related to the strategy proposed.

### 2.1   Concepts

One technique capable of characterizing the performance of an application, abstracting the characteristics of applications and architectures, is called machine balance. Such technique defines the performance of an application using the ratio of the amount of data transfered to the number of floating-point operations for a particular processor [4].

The information to characterize the performance of an application according to this model can be obtained from code profilers, which perform several measurements during the execution of a small part of the applications [8] and can be based on two approaches:

- Source code profiling which is the measurement of source code or assembly code behavior
- Hardware profiling which is the collection of the data provided by PMUs (Performance Monitoring Units) in order to identify the hardware usage efficiency during the execution of an application.

### 2.2   Problem Definition

The problem we are tackling is the performance prediction of an application across different computational architectures to support runtime decisions. In this sense, we impose the following restrictions:

- The user application is provided without the source code.
- The prediction has to be executed within a time limit. This is important to avoid significant overhead in a production environment.
- The user can provide different versions of the same applications optimized for different architectures. Normally, compilers automatically tune the application to different architectures. Also, developers can use instructions that are available on a specific architecture for example.

# 3   Related Work

In [5], the authors present a method for profiling C code with OpenACC directives. From that, they create a computation model that will run on an HPC architecture simulator in order to measure some performance metrics. In our case, we use data collected from the real execution. This is very important since we are dealing with heterogeneous architectures that have different microarchitecture implementations.

In [7], the authors propose an approach that uses small input cases for performing the full execution of the program, in order to collect data of all the code regions. Their concern is the execution time of the program and to predict it, they use a regression model, based on small kernels – a similar approach is adopted by [6] - to estimate the execution estimate. Using such statistical models require training, to learn the correct parameters; That could be a hard task depending on the model used to perform the regression. In our proposal, we plan to identify the architectures that provides lower execution time, and not to predict the execution time; Also, we want to perform such analysis within a time limit.

In [3], the authors propose a tool for making performance prediction named COMPASS. That generates an execution model – a translation of the source code to the Aspen Language, that should be analyzed by a performance evaluation tool, named Aspen Performance Prediction Tools that should also be fed with an architecture descriptor file, containing the information regarding the architecture on which the performance prediction should be done. Also, the code can be instrumented to help the tool to better generate the program execution model. In our case, no manual instrumentation is needed. The metrics are obtained using standard tools and also no source code translation is required.

# 4   A Strategy for Performance Prediction

In this session, we present a strategy to rank a set of different architectures according to the performance that an application can achieve on each architecture.

The strategy proposed receives the following inputs:

- Application: can be one version to be executed in all architectures or can be composed of a compiled version of the same source code optimized for each computational architecture.
- Set of architectures: the architectures we are considering in this work are the following Intel generations:
  - Intel Xeon: SandyBridge, Haswell and Skylake;
  - Intel Xeon Phi: Knights Landing.

We will describe the profiling collection performed by our strategy on Sect. 4.1 and the data analysis and output on Sect. 4.2.

### 4.1 Profiling Collection

Our strategy characterizes the performance of an application on different architectures according to the machine balance model [4], measuring two characteristics of the execution of an application on each architecture: the amount of operations that an application is capable of executing and the amount of work that is wasted due to overhead.

We use Intel VTune[4] to perform hardware profiling and Intel Advisor[5] to perform source code profiling. We fixed period of time of 30 s to execute each profiling tools. A script manages the execution of profiling tools to collect the following metrics to define the measurements:

- Intel Advisor:
  - Ratio of giga floating-point operations per second (GFLOPS);
  - Arithmetic Intensity (AI) which is the ratio of giga floating-point operations to the amount of data transfered;
- Intel Vtune:
  - Clockticks per Instructions Retired (CPI). That is calculated by dividing the number of unhalted processor cycles (Clockticks) by the number of instructions retired, that is the instructions that effectively finished their execution.

The GFLOPS measures the amount of operations that an application is capable of executing considering the useful work and any other overhead that can be present in the application, such as, cache miss, data transfer latency from main memory to processor, vectorization overhead, and so on.

Our strategy identifies the overhead present in the application by the means of AI and CPI:

- The CPI is a measure that helps to estimate the overhead present in the application, because one of the consequences of high overhead is a decrease on retired instructions.
- The AI measures the throughput of instructions execution. In this sense, higher level of AI indicates that the execution of application demands less data transfers from memory to CPU, which means lower latency in executing instructions.

### 4.2 Data Analysis and Output

Our strategy returns the performance prediction by the means of a numbered list that ranks architectures from lowest to highest performance level, based on a metric that we call estimated processing capacity (EPC) which is defined in the formula on Eq. (1).

$$EPC(Application, Resource) = \frac{GFLOPS * AI}{CPI} \tag{1}$$

---

[4] https://software.intel.com/en-us/intel-vtune-amplifier-xe.

[5] https://software.intel.com/en-us/advisor.

The GFLOPS represents the amount of operations that an application is capable of perform on an architecture and AI represents the throughput of instructions execution, so to define the comparison metric we multiply these two variables in order to obtain a quality estimate about how the application is using the architecture. We divide by CPI, because it represents the applications overhead on an architecture, CPI level is proportional to overhead level. In this sense, lower CPI level will have lower impact on EPC.

Our strategy calculates the EPC for an application on each architecture. The values obtained are ranked and the user receives only the rank position. This is important because the absolute value returned from EPC can not be used to characterize a proportional performance level across different architectures.

## 5   Evaluation

In this section, we present an evaluation of our strategy in Sect. 5.1 we present the workload and hardware infrastructure used to evaluate our strategy and in Sect. 5.2 we present the results obtained.

### 5.1   Workload and Hardware Description

The workload chosen to evaluate our strategy is composed by the following sample of applications defined in [9]:

- A matrix multiplication code developed using Intel Intrinsics;
- A numeric model in finance optimized using AVX-512 ER (Exponentials and Reciprocals);
- A N-Body simulation with most of its code vectorized;
- A Diffusion simulation with most of its code developed with scalar instructions.

The hardware infrastructure we used to evaluate our strategy is described in the Table 1.

**Table 1.** Hardware infrastructure used for evaluation.

| Architecture | Processor | Cores | Threads | Dram |
|---|---|---|---|---|
| SandyBridge | 2 × 2.6 GHz | 8 | 32 | 64 GB |
| Haswell | 2 × 2.3 GHz | 36 | 72 | 128 GB |
| Skylake | 2 × 2.1 GHz | 48 | 96 | 192 GB |
| Knights Landing (cache mode) | 1 × 1.4 GHz | 68 | 272 | 192 GB |
| Knights Landing (flat mode) | 1 × 1.4 GHz | 68 | 272 | 192 GB |

## 5.2    Results and Discussion

We executed our strategy with the workload on the infrastructure presented in Sect. 5.1 and the results obtained are shown in Table 2.

**Table 2.** Comparing strategy output: rank of architecture against execution time.

| Architecture | Skylake | Haswell | SandyBridge | KNL (flat mode) | KNL (cache mode) |
|---|---|---|---|---|---|
| Numeric model in finance | | | | | |
| Execution time (seconds) | 458 | 1036 | 3443 | 235 | 224 |
| Rank | 3 | 2 | 1 | 4 | 5 |
| Diffusion | | | | | |
| Execution time (seconds) | 511 | 309 | 220 | 425 | 1557 |
| Rank | 3 | 4 | 5 | 2 | 1 |
| N-Body | | | | | |
| Execution time (seconds) | 306 | 467 | 1253 | 343 | 347 |
| Rank | 5 | 4 | 3 | 1 | 2 |
| Matrix multiplication (intrinsics) | | | | | |
| Execution time (seconds) | 172 | 159 | 344 | 132 | 227 |
| Rank | 4 | 5 | 1 | 3 | 2 |

The results show that our strategy correctly ranked the architectures for three applications, and incorrectly ranked the architectures for Matrix Multiplication application.

All the metrics collected by the profilers (GFLOPS, CPI and AI) corresponds to an average of all loops present in the application. In the three applications that our strategy ranked the architectures correctly one loop dominates the execution of all application.

In the case of Matrix Multiplication, our strategy ranked SandyBridge as presenting the best performance, but the execution time shows that Skylake presents the best performance. This happens because two or more loops dominates the execution time, and currently our strategy does not associate weights to each loop according to its impact on execution time. In this sense, some loops in the critical path that presents great impact on execution time and higher performance on Skylake was not expressed in the average result.

# 6   Conclusions and Future Work

This work presented a strategy to rank architectures according to the performance achieved executing a given application. It can be helpful when buying new compute nodes for a running cluster, decide in which nodes of a cluster an application is preferable to run (schedule decisions for example) and so on. Three of four applications used in our experiments were correctly ranked using our strategy. The low overhead of our strategy is another feature that differs from existing predictions strategies.

As future work, we intend to extend the metrics used to rank architectures to improve accuracy, such as weight of loops in execution time and others events (i.e. cache hit rate).

**Acknowledgements.**  The authors would like to thank the Center for Scientific Computing at the São Paulo State University (NCC/UNESP) for the use of the manycore computing resources, partially funded by Intel in the context of the following projects: "Intel Parallel Computing Center", "Intel Modern Code Partner", and "Intel/Unesp Center of Excellence in Machine Learning".

# References

1. Yang, X.J., et al.: The TianHe-1A supercomputer: its hardware and software. J. Comput. Sci. Technol. **26**, 344–351 (2011)
2. Rosales, C., et al.: Performance prediction of HPC applications on intel processors. In: Parallel and Distributed Processing Symposium Workshops (IPDPSW). IEEE (2017)
3. Lee, S., Meredith, J.S., Vetter, J.S.: Compass: a framework for automated performance modeling and prediction. In: Proceedings of the 29th ACM on International Conference on Supercomputing. ACM (2015)
4. McCalpin, J.D.: Memory bandwidth and machine balance in current high performance computers. IEEE Comput. Soc. Tech. Comm. Comput. Archit. (TCCA) Newsl. **2**, 19–25 (1995)
5. Obaida, M.A., et al.: Parallel application performance prediction using analysis based models and HPC simulations. In: Proceedings of the 2018 ACM SIGSIM Conference on Principles of Advanced Discrete Simulation. ACM (2018)
6. Benoit, N., Louise, S.: A first step to performance prediction for heterogeneous processing on manycores. Procedia Comput. Sci. **51**, 2952–2956 (2015)
7. Escobar, R., Boppana, R.V.: Performance prediction of parallel applications based on small-scale executions. In: 2016 IEEE 23rd International Conference High Performance Computing (HiPC). IEEE (2016)
8. Browne, S., Dongarra, J., Garner, N., London, K., Mucci, P.: A scalable cross-platform infrastructure for application performance tuning using hardware counters. In: Proceedings of the 2000 ACM/IEEE conference on Supercomputing (SC 2000). IEEE Computer Society, Washington, DC (2000). Article 42
9. Reinders, J., Jeffers, J.: High Performance Parallelism Pearls: Multicore and Many-core Programming Approaches. Morgan Kaufmann, United States (2015)

# Posters*

# HPC for Predictive Models in Healthcare

Luiz Fernando Capretz[(✉)]

Western University, London, ON N6G5B9, Canada
lcapretz@uwo.ca

**Abstract.** Increasingly we are faced with complex health data, thus researchers are limited in their capacity to mine data in a way that accounts for the complex inter-relationships between health variables of interest. This research tackles the challenge of producing accurate health prediction models in order to overcome the limitations of simple multivariate regression techniques and the assumption of linear association, also known as algorithmic models, by combining it with a soft computing approach. Predictive models develop methods to enable healthcare researchers and professionals to predict the likelihood of an individual's proclivity to a disease and the likely effectiveness of possible treatments. Personalized approaches focus on the individual - relying on the individual's existing health data across the healthcare system with treatment targeted at the individual.

**Keywords:** HPC for healthcare · HPC application · Large-scale simulation

## 1 Motivation

Predictive analytics can improve healthcare in many ways [1]: increase the accuracy of diagnoses, help preventive medicine and public health, provide physicians with answers they are seeking for individual patients, offer employers and hospitals with predictions concerning insurance costs, allow researchers to develop models that require thousands of cases and that can become more accurate over time, and patients have the potential benefit of better outcomes due to more accurate predictive models [2–5].

There are two main advantages of using high performance computation and machine learning for medical estimation. First, it incorporates learning from previous situations and outcomes. This learning ability is very important for effort-estimation models because there are substantial amounts of available historical data that can assist in predicting similar diagnoses. Secondly, soft computing can model a complex set of relationships between the dependent and independent variables, which can be adapted for clinical use. Overall, prediction and personalization models have the potential to: (a) facilitate diagnosis by reducing the "guesstimation" often used by health professionals; (b) improve the accuracy and performance of the estimations; (c) develop learning and adaptation ability; (d) improve imperviousness to imprecise and uncertain inputs. One paramount feature of this framework is that the architecture is inherently independent of the choice of algorithmic models or the nature of the prediction problems.

© Springer Nature Switzerland AG 2019
H. Senger et al. (Eds.): VECPAR 2018, LNCS 11333, pp. 257–258, 2019.
https://doi.org/10.1007/978-3-030-15996-2

## 2  Research Objectives and Outcomes

Advancing research in prediction and personalization in chronic disease and acute conditions is one key to supporting the increasing demand for healthcare services. Our proposed research meets three objectives:

(1) The creation of robust tools to mine medical databases as well as the necessary interfaces to deliver information in an accessible format to the end user.
(2) An immediate objective entails validating the accuracy and improvement of a soft computing framework against current algorithmic models in order to solve the health-related estimation problems.
(3) A longer-term objective is to apply this generic framework to other aspects of medical estimation, such as the prediction of health conditions and the risk assessment of disease outcomes.

Overall, this work will help physicians in diagnosing and predicting the medical condition of patients with higher accuracy and speed. This innovative project, which utilizes the skills of clinical researchers, software engineers, and mathematicians, moves us closer to translating knowledge into practice by harnessing medical data and facilitating the optimal allocation of treatment in a cost-effective manner The successful implementation of this research, will assist physicians and patient make crucial decisions in a timely fashion, leading to the creation of new healthcare.

The evaluation of new neuro-fuzzy models to predict the medical condition of patients will be carried out in collaboration with physicians and will help them make crucial decisions on-the-fly. At first, we will focus on cardiovascular disease, which is increasing in incidence and prevalence all over the world. There are evidence-based conceptual models of the risks and outcomes of coronary artery disease and hypertension that use statistical techniques, such as hierarchical regression modeling and multilevel modeling. We will incorporate a neuro-fuzzy approach into these algorithms in order to improve their accuracy. The knowledge gained through this project can extend to various diseases and conditions, including Alzheimer, cancer growth, and sepsis.

## References

1. Winters-Miner, L.A., Bolding, P.S., Hilbe, J., Goldstein, M., Hill, T., Nisbet, T., Walton, N., Miner, G.D.: Practical Predictive Analytics and Decisioning Systems for Medicine. Academic Press, London (2015)
2. Huang, X., Capretz, L.F., Ho, D., Ren, J.: A neuro-fuzzy model for software cost estimation. In: 3rd IEEE International Conference on Quality Software (QSIC), pp. 126–133 (2003)
3. Nassif, A.B., Ho, D., Capretz, L.F.: Regression model for software effort estimation based on the use case point method. In: International Conference on Computer and Software Modeling, pp. 117–121 (2011)
4. Nassif, A.B., Capretz, L.F., Ho D.: Estimating software effort using an ANN model based on use case points. In: 11th IEEE International Conference on Machine Learning and Applications (ICMLA), pp. 42–47 (2012)
5. Nassif, A.B., Azzeh, M., Capretz, L.F., Ho, D.: Neural networks for software development effort estimation: a comparative study. Neural Comput. Appl. 27(8), 2369–2381 (2016)

# A Methodology for Batching Matrix Kernels in HPC Applications

Hans Johansen and Osni Marques[✉]

Lawrence Berkeley National Laboratory, Berkeley, USA
{hjohansen,oamarques}@lbl.gov

**Abstract.** We present three optimization case studies for small matrix kernels commonly found in 3D multi-physics applications. First, we improve the algorithmic approach of each kernel by leveraging the matrix structure while simultaneously porting to the target architecture. This requires a combination of skills spanning software engineering, algorithm development, and application- and architecture-specific optimizations. A combination of these disciplines is critical for refactoring scientific applications in an ever-changing high performance computing (HPC) landscape, with threading, SIMD instructions, and memory hierarchies constantly changing between architectures. We summarize performance results and provide a simple methodology to follow to identify trade-offs and improve performance.

**Keywords:** Performance analysis · Evaluation and tuning ·
Numerical algorithms on multicore architectures ·
Small matrix kernels · SIMD vectorization · Performance engineering ·
Software methodology

## 1 Introduction

*HPC Hardware Challenges.* On most multicore systems, the path to performance improvement requires node-level parallelism, including vector instructions for fine grain SIMD (multiple operations per cycle), in addition to optimized memory bandwidth and latency. For on-node parallelism, OpenMP directives are a straight-forward choice, but reorganizing code to thread operations while still providing vector-friendly data layouts can be a challenge. In the example kernels we provide, we show how threading and SIMD-friendly layouts can be introduced to improve architecture-specific performance.

*Performance Engineering Methodology.* Refactoring an application for performance should be seen as the identification of spots where performance has been lost. Performance improvement efforts should be accompanied by versioning (record of compiler flags used, libraries linked to, parameter sweeps etc.) together with performance benchmarks and comparisons. Typically, one should follow three steps: (1) Measure performance, i.e. identify code segments that can be

This is a U.S. government work and not under copyright protection in the United States;
foreign copyright protection may apply 2019
H. Senger et al. (Eds.): VECPAR 2018, LNCS 11333, pp. 259–261, 2019.
https://doi.org/10.1007/978-3-030-15996-2

potentially restructured for a more efficient utilization of the computing resources (more efficient use of processing units or a better access to data); (2) Identify limitations, i.e. code changes that may or may not lead to desired improvements in wall clock times or percent-of-peak (models that combine data locality, bandwidth and alternative parallelization strategies can be used to determine a bound for the performance of the code segment of interest). (3) Collect data, i.e. perform runs with different launching configurations to determine whether the performance is limited by the rate of arithmetic operations or the memory available and the speed of access to data. Tools such as roofline analysis [1] can help guide both the algorithm development and code optimizations.

## 2   Small Matrix Kernels

Our 3D model applications use small matrix solvers that we have turned into kernels: 1D tridiagonal solve, and pointwise ("0D") LU and QR factorization and solve steps. These applications that have 1D or 0D solves embedded in 2D or 3D domains usually include nonlinear, implicit time integrators and interpolation problems. In all three cases, the matrices are small with $O(10 - 100)$ non-zeros, and with the same structure but different entries for every location in the 3D domain. This contrasts with simpler kernels where the same matrix solver is applied everywhere (multiple RHS), or more complex problems where there is a different matrix everywhere (multiple systems) that may have different structure (size and number of nonzeros, for example). More generally, the application programmer's trade-off is between a straight-forward call to libraries such as *Lapack*, or even architecture-specific implementations, or to write custom code that performs better on the target architecture.

*Tridiagonal Solve.* The first kernel is a tridiagonal solver that in only the $k$ direction of a 3D ($ijk$-layout) domain. Figure 1 demonstrates the challenges on of taking advantage of Intel's KNL architecture with a naive approach. A simple implementation simply uses a call to Intel's *MKL* library [2] with a $kij$-layout, which vectorizes poorly across $k$-indexed columns, due to loop dependencies and copy overheads. But because the algorithm is memory bandwidth-bound, a faster approach is to reimplement the algorithm for better vectorization (which we call *simultaneous streaming Thomas algorithm*, or SSTA). This can be more than 5x faster than the naive approach; after reordering memory to a $ikj$-layout and optimizing the loop tile size to improve cache coherency, the speedup is almost 10x and approaches the theoretical roofline model (see Fig. 1).

*Batched LU and QR Solves.* In the 0D kernels for LU and QR solves, by knowing that the matrix structure does not change from point to point in 3D, we can improve on naive implementations. For the LU solver, we a use code generation to provide fast, SIMD-friendly kernels that can be inlined and SIMD-ized by the compiler, instead of relying on separate small matrix optimization in Intel *MKL*. For the QR solver, Intel *MKL* provides a special implementation of mkl_*geqrf_compact, which does not form the Q factors explicitly but instead represents as elementary reflectors. We show that by using OpenMP loops for

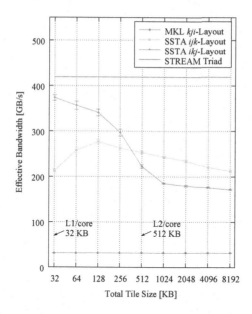

**Fig. 1.** Effective bandwidth vs. tiling size for variants of the tridiagonal solve algorithm, with comparison to theoretical STREAM peak performance from the roofline model for Intel KNL.

computing a least squares solution in this way is more memory- and vector-friendly than the original calls to only *Lapack*-style interfaces.

# References

1. Williams, S., Waterman, A., Patterson, D.: Roofline: an insightful visual performance model for multicore architectures. Commun. ACM **52**(4), 65–76 (2009)
2. Intel Math Kernel Library (MKL). https://software.intel.com/en-us/mkl

# Author Index

Amaral, Júlio 247
Aydoğmuş, Mehmet Akif 45

Baruchi, Artur 247
Bentes, Cristiana 62
Bientinesi, Paolo 160
Bodony, Daniel J. 174
Brandão, Diego N. 132

Cabral, Frederico 132
Camata, José J. 3
Capretz, Luiz Fernando 257
Carneiro, Tiago 16
Charão, Andrea Schwerner 92
Cieza, Elliod 62
Cóbe, Raphael 247
Costa, Gabriel P. 132
Coutinho, Alvaro L. G. A. 3

da Silva, Sherlon Almeida 188
de Carvalho Junior, Francisco Heron 16
de Oliveira, Sanderson L. Gonzaga 132
de Souza, Paulo Sergio Lopes 77
Delbem, Alexandre C. B. 77
Diener, Matthias 174
do Nascimento, Tiago Marques 119
dos Santos, Rodrigo Weber 119
Drummond, Lúcia M. A. 62

Elias, Renato N. 3

Fialho, Jefferson 247
Freytag, Gabriel 105
Frota, Yuri 62

Garcia, Adriano Marques 188
Gieseke, Fabian 202
Girardi, Alessandro Gonçalves 188
Gmys, Jan 16
Gomes, Marco 247

González-Linares, Jose María 146
Guil, Nicolás 146

Heskes, Tom 202

Igel, Christian 202
Iope, Rogério 247

Johansen, Hans 259

Kale, Laxmikant 174
Kischinhevsky, Mauricio 132
Külekci, M. Oğuzhan 45

Lázaro-Muñoz, Antonio-Jose 146
Leite, Ricardo 230
Lima, Benaia S. J. 3
Lima, João Vicente Ferreira 92, 105
Lobosco, Marcelo 119
Lopes, Gesiel Rios 77
López-Albelda, Bernabé 146
Lu, Yutong 215

Mahabal, Ashish 202
Marques, Osni 259
McDoniel, William 160
Melab, Nouredine 16

Navaux, Philippe Olivier Alexandre 31, 105
Nesi, Lucas Leandro 31

Oancea, Cosmin Eugen 202
Osthoff, Carla 132

Petiton, Serge G. 215

Rebouças Filho, Pedro Pedrosa 16
Rech, Paolo 105
Rocha, Ricardo 230

Schepke, Claudio    188
Schnorr, Lucas Mello    31, 105
Silva, Rômulo M.    3
Souto, Roberto Pinto    132
Stanzani, Silvio    247

Teylo, Luan    62
Trindade, Rafael Gauna    92
Tuyttens, Daniel    16

Wu, Xinzhe    215

Printed in the United States
By Bookmasters